# THE LOYALTY TRAP

# THE LOYALTY TRAP

## CONFLICTING LOYALTIES
## OF CIVIL SERVANTS UNDER
## INCREASING AUTOCRACY

### JAIME LEE KUCINSKAS

Columbia University Press   *New York*

Columbia University Press
*Publishers Since 1893*
New York    Chichester, West Sussex

Library of Congress Cataloging-in-Publication Data
Names: Kucinskas, Jaime, author.
Title: The loyalty trap : conflicting loyalties of civil servants under
increasing autocracy / Jaime Lee Kucinskas.
Description: New York : Columbia University Press, 2025. |
Includes bibliographical references and index.
Identifiers: LCCN 2024043274 | ISBN 9780231208147 (hardback) |
ISBN 9780231208154 (trade paperback) | ISBN 9780231557283 (ebook)
Subjects: LCSH: Civil service ethics—United States. |
Public administration—Moral and ethical aspects—United States. |
Executive power—Moral and ethical aspects—United States. |
Abuse of administrative power—United States. | Public interest—
United States. | Allegiance—United States. | Trump, Donald, 1946– |
United States—Politics and government—2017–2021.
Classification: LCC JK468.E7 K84 2025 |
DDC 353.4/60973—dc23/eng/20250208

Cover design: Milenda Nan Ok Lee
Cover photo: Restuccia Giancarlo / Shutterstock

GPSR Authorized Representative: Easy Access System Europe,
Mustamäe tee 50, 10621 Tallinn, Estonia,
gpsr.requests@easproject.com

*The truth is that it's impossible to always get it right . . . We have to deal with imperfect knowledge and flawed—and sometimes criminal—leaders as well as our own domestic limitations. We operate in realms of immense complexity, and yet we Americans are often uncomfortable with nuance.*

—Marie Yovanovitch, 2022, xxi

# CONTENTS

*Acknowledgments* ix

## I AN INTRODUCTION

1 Walking the Moral Tightrope 3

2 A Lurch Toward Autocracy 30

## II KEEP CALM AND CARRY ON: THE BEGINNING OF THE ADMINISTRATION

3 The Spirit and Inherent Challenges of
Public Administration 37

4 "Too Early to Tell": Rationalizing Forbearance 64

5 Split Lives and External Engagement 92

## III ORGANIZATIONAL DAMAGE FROM LEADERSHIP VACUUMS

6 Appointees' Mistrust 111

7 Loyalty Traps 137

8  Signs of Organizational Decline   149

9  To Stay or Go?   194

## IV CIVIL SERVANT RESISTANCE

10  Covert Resistance   233

11  Moral Courage   281

## V CONCLUSION

12  American Democracy at a Crossroads   323

*Appendix A. Tables*   *341*

*Appendix B. Methodological Background Information*   *345*

*Notes*   *349*

*References*   *395*

*Index*   *419*

# ACKNOWLEDGMENTS

A s many authors before me have noted, a book is a collective project.

First and foremost, I am grateful to the many people who trusted and helped me throughout this process, including the many people who vouched for me and those who trusted me with their stories. Like you, I believe in the potential of the American democratic experiment, and think it is imperative to inscribe your experiences during the Trump administration in the historical record for those who come after us, not only in the United States, but around the world.

To Yvonne Zylan, who gave me the courage to start this project, who taught me about the government, and who took the first few steps of this journey with me. I admire your brilliance and skill with words and miss you!

I am indebted to Matt Dull for seeing the value of this project early on and for his consistent support and his generous, important advice at various stages of the research. Matt introduced me to the world of public administration, and I am forever grateful to him for his gracious, knowledgeable, and helpful introduction.

To Rashawn Ray, who invited me to join the outstanding sociology department at the University of Maryland, College Park, during my sabbatical, where I was based while I conducted research for this book, and to Dana Fisher for helping make it a home. Dana, thank you for reading the entire manuscript and supporting this project the whole way through, and for also inspiring me to do research on climate change along the way.

I am fortunate to have had Eric Schwartz take on editorship of this book. I am thankful for his gentle guidance and support: he is truly the author whisperer, knowing how to fan the flames of inspiration and put out fears. I am also continually inspired by his commitment to inclusion and preserving the field of academic publishing so that all may have access to a range of thoughtful and academically vetted ideas.

I owe thanks to others who showed interest and encouraged this project, such as Diane Vaughan, Maurice Isserman, Gbemende Johnson, Bill Resh, Jill Lindsay Harrison, Caroline Lee, Shekhar Chandra, Frank Anechiarico, and Elisabeth Clemens during her editorship at the *American Journal of Sociology*.

I am incredibly thankful of all those who were willing to read and help me develop the ugly first drafts, such as my wonderful writing group—Yagmur Karakaya, Chenyu Wang, and Heidi Ravven—and the Sociology Colloquium and other Hamilton faculty and staff—Alfred Kelly, Dan Chambliss, Kerem Morgul, Matt Grace, Tim Sacco, Alex Manning, and Chris Willemsen. I am grateful to Rhys Williams for reading chapters and helping me write this book for a broader audience. Mahala Stewart and Zack Schuman helped me see where I could split drafts of chapters that were just too long. Janina Selzer astounded me when she generously read the entire manuscript her first year at Hamilton and provided helpful feedback, which helped me sharpen the manuscript and make it much more readable. Thank you, Nat

Reboredo and Izzy Rutkey, for helping format my early drafts. Izzy your editorial guidance is also so very appreciated and valuable over so many drafts!

I am also thankful to the anonymous reviewer of the full manuscript who helped me see more clearly and convey more accurately the key overarching theoretical argument of the book, and then pare back the rest.

It is important to acknowledge as well the wonderful PSG VII on Ethics and Integrity of the European Group for Public Administration. I met you late in the process of this book but very much appreciated your generosity in connecting me more with the literature on democratic backsliding internationally. In particular, thank you Toon Kerhoff, Ciaran O'Kelly, Leonie Heres, Leo Huburts, Ina Middelkamp, and Fabrice Larat for your interest in and support of this book. What I cannot fit in last edits to this book, I hope to put in new work inspired by our conversations.

I am especially grateful to Jim Perry, who read and generously provided feedback on the entirety of this manuscript in progress and helped get some of my insights out into the public. I also appreciate our conversations, his humor, and his encyclopedic knowledge on public servants and the canon of scholarship on public administration.

While in Washington, DC, Kim, Brian, Cian, and Regan, as well as Garrett and Rebecca, helped make the city our home. We are grateful for all the time we had together, and also to extended adopted family, such as Neil, Tory, Melissa, David, Kim, and Frankie. I am also grateful to Aunt Liz and my uncle Paul, whose love of books and learning continues to inspire me.

I am grateful to all the amazing and loving women who cared for our kids so I could work on this book, such as Nelly, Ms. Maria, Mrs. Landry, Cynthia, and Mary Ellen.

To my kids Rylee and Adela: thank you for bringing joy, meaning, purpose, and fullness into my life. You are rays of sunshine when the world appears dark and daunting. I write this in part for you, in the hope that it will help others create a better country and world.

Writing a book is hard: I couldn't have gotten through the most challenging parts of writing and analysis without the unwavering support and astute insights from my beloved husband, Zack. Zack is my partner in everything, including as trusted adviser on this manuscript. You make everything in our life better. Without you, none of this would be possible. I am so fortunate you are in my life every day. Thank you for accepting me as I am and enabling the writing of this book, even in the midst of all our shared responsibilities. I see your sacrifices, and I appreciate your love and support more than you can ever know.

# I

# AN INTRODUCTION

# 1

## WALKING THE MORAL TIGHTROPE

**B**en Lopez seemed friendly, even jovial, as he burst through the door of the coffee shop on a sweltering afternoon in Washington, DC, during the summer of 2018. He apologized for being late and for being so difficult to get in touch with. He had a Clark Kent/Superman quality: the air of an athlete turned into a bespectacled government lawyer wearing a sharp button-down shirt and slacks. As he settled down to speak, his demeanor quickly shifted to a more thoughtful, serious expression. Although he patiently and directly answered my initial questions about his background and work history, his eyes intermittently flashed a sense of impatience revealing an urgency to tell his story.

When we finally got to his more recent work history though, he suddenly began to skirt around his story, peppering it with vague language and euphemisms. He paused repeatedly and glanced around the coffee shop. His eyes lingered on a middle-aged man with long brown hair sitting beside us for a moment.

"Are you comfortable here?" I asked, noting how close we sat to the front window of the café and its entryway. "We can move."

Subtly pointing to the man next to us, he noted quietly that the man had not turned a page in quite a while. I was aware of the many risks Lopez faced as a federal employee willing to speak with me during Donald Trump's first administration, from 2017 to 2021. Lopez was one of dozens of career civil servants I spoke to during that tumultuous term. Career civil servants are typically hired based on a meritocratic basis to work for the administrative state for long periods across presidential administrations. In contrast to career civil servants, "politicals" are appointed by presidents to serve in leadership roles during their terms.

Trump appointees entered various agencies with evident distrust and disdain for career employees. Rather than build bridges with career staff, in places like the Environmental Protection Agency (EPA) under Scott Pruitt and the State Department under former Exxon executive Rex Tillerson, agency heads cordoned themselves off into protected circles of appointed staff. Blacklists of career civil servants supposedly against the administration circulated among Trump's political appointees. Reports of political retribution against civil servants working on pet projects from Barack Obama's administration proliferated across agencies.[1]

Washington, DC, can be a small town, especially in the coffee shops around the Mall. In light of this, and the sensitive nature of his work under the Trump administration, Lopez opted to move to a secluded patio outside. Resettled, he leaned forward. Having witnessed the transition to the Trump administration up close, from the beginning and from several vantage points, he believed Trump's administration was distinct from most executive branch transitions of power. He spoke quietly, with regret in his voice, "I keep telling people I work with, 'We have to stop using gerunds. We have to use past participle—we aren't destroying the agency. We have destroyed the agency.' There are so many opportunities missed. The events that have transpired fundamentally shape the way the world proceeds."

Sitting in on high-level meetings in the White House with a small group of other career bureaucrats, "we started seeing the way things were going askew earlier than most," Lopez said.

"What were the signs that things were going awry and particularly troubling?" I asked.

"The bald lies," he said slowly for emphasis, turning the words over like marbles in his mouth, "about things that we knew not to be true."[2]

Lopez's poignant description of the Trump administration haunted me throughout the years of the administration and beyond. "It's almost like driving down the highway really, really fast in the rain, without your hands on the wheel," he said. "But you know that doesn't mean you're necessarily going to run off the road, but it's super dangerous and you could. And the consequences could be catastrophic and maybe there isn't a curve up ahead. Maybe it will be straight for a while, and we'll be alright—and there won't be a gust of wind . . . but that's what it feels like."

Most civil servants I spoke with did not see it this way. Then again, Lopez was among those closest to the top.

In response to times like these, "collective action matters," Lopez said simply. When I asked him what kinds of collective action he could engage in as a civil servant when he witnessed appointed leaders' legal and ethical transgressions, he said there was not much that civil servants could do. At most, "you try to be mutually supportive and encourage people to exercise their rights. That's pretty much the extent of it. But I think if people do that, then that helps to change behavior, particularly when it involves malfeasance."

Lopez was one of the exceptional federal bureaucrats I spoke with who even mentioned the prospect of collective action among government employees in response to the many ethical and legal breaches of conduct by members of the Trump administration. Yet the way Lopez described collective action was a far cry from the kind of collective action undertaken by seasoned activists. For him, being part of a group of supportive civil servants was a means of sharing information, solidarity, and support for each to take the individual actions necessary to stand up for legal statutes and to maintain the integrity of the state and their own rights; it was not a foundation for more coordinated activism. This would have been too far afield from loyal civil servants' professional culture, which had taught them to serve leadership and the country by being a team player; working with other stakeholders; and often, in the end, bowing to institutional and executive power.

In contrast to Lopez, the vast majority of federal civil servants I spoke to entered the first Trump administration largely unaware of what was happening in the shift in their agencies' senior leadership. They learned about developments secondhand either from the media or through colleagues' accounts. Most of the civil servants I spoke with during the first year of the administration, and some well through the middle or even the end of the administration, expressed how limited communication had been from the appointed leaders of their agencies. They waited for political appointees to be confirmed and for coherent guidance on appointed leadership's intended direction for their agency, all while hoping for the best and trying to give new leadership the benefit of the doubt.

## CAREER CIVIL SERVANTS IN A LIBERAL DEMOCRATIC STATE

To understand the experiences of career civil servants, it is essential to recognize the importance of the structure of the federal government. As the largest employer of Americans, the U.S. federal government is quite complex.[3] The career civil servants included in this book work for the administrative state, a key piece of the American political order since the New Deal in the 1930s. The administrative state is marked by expert agencies that empower unelected officials to make regulations and run the American "welfare/warfare" state, which includes the military; diplomacy; and programs managing public assistance, housing, education, disability benefits, transportation infrastructure, public lands, and so forth.[4] Federal agencies are organizations situated within other organizations, which are themselves multilayered and variegated. Some agencies are located entirely in Washington, DC. Others have satellite offices around the country, or—in the case of agencies involved in international affairs—they have employees working in offices around the world.

Federal career civil servants are distinct from employees in other fields in certain respects, which likely affects how they respond to times of rapid change. They occupy a unique space in the landscape of state/society relations. They are semiautonomous from the political branches of government at the same time as they are semiautonomous from societal interest groups and constituencies. Since the Pendleton Act of 1883, the majority of federal civil servants who are covered by the statute have been hired based on merit.[5] In the years since then, civil servants have been granted additional protections from being fired or demoted for political reasons, most notably through the Civil Service Reform Act (CSRA) of 1978.[6] By necessity, career civil servants are delegated some authority and autonomy because elected leaders cannot make the untold number of decisions required to keep the government functioning every day. Scholars suggest that a meritocratic bureaucracy staffed with trained professionals functions better than alternatives, even when considering the risks and mistakes that may accompany delegation.[7]

Most of the civil servants I spoke with fundamentally believed in the resilience and durability of the American state and strove to protect it. While Americans may have romanticized notions of a democratic state, civil servants have a long history of trying to reconcile democratic ideals with both efficiency and citizen participation.[8] The civil servants I spoke with deeply believed in a liberal democratic state, in which citizens had the right to (1) free, fair elections; (2) protected civil and human rights; (3) active civic participation and "liberty of discussion;" and (4) a rule of law applicable to all.[9] Accordingly, the ideal liberal democratic state is characterized both by pluralism, with protections for minority citizens' rights, and a competition for power.[10] This competition between political parties has typically occurred within legal and normative bounds, in which competing parties exercise *mutual toleration*, treating each other as legitimate rivals, and *forbearance*—restraint in how they seek to achieve their political goals to allow the government to keep functioning.[11]

Career civil servants play an important role in providing continuity for the state in the short and long term while also aiding presidential administrations in advancing their agendas. Career civil servants are supposed to help new presidential administrations and provide them with the technocratic knowledge necessary for governing across a range of complex issues that affect the public while serving as a ballast of sorts, providing some constancy and stability across administrations.

To do this work, career bureaucrats are supposed to uphold various ethical obligations: they are supposed to execute their work in a *serially partisan* way, serving across presidential administrations, as well as in an *overtly nonpartisan* way in accordance with their prescribed roles, their agency missions, and sworn oath to uphold the Constitution.[12] U.S. Code §3331, the Oath of Office, states:

> An individual, except the President, elected or appointed to an office of honor or profit in the civil service or uniformed services, shall take the following oath: "I, AB, do solemnly swear (or affirm) that I will support and defend the Constitution of the United States against all enemies, foreign and domestic; that I will bear true faith and allegiance to the same; that I take this obligation freely, without any mental reservation or purpose of evasion; and that I will well and faithfully discharge the duties of the office on which I am about to enter. So help me God.

Career civil servants take this oath as a sacred moral anchor of their calling to public service. As former director of the Federal Bureau of Investigation (FBI) James Comey described in his 2018 autobiography, *A Higher Loyalty*, when he served as U.S. attorney, he conveyed to new prosecutors that, in taking the oath, they were entering a long-standing community of trust and integrity, marked by a "reservoir of trust and credibility built for you and filled by people you never knew, by those long gone . . . that makes possible so much of the good that is done by the institution you serve."[13] He then explained to these incoming lawyers that "like all great gifts, this one comes with a responsibility, a solemn obligation to guard and protect the reservoir and pass it on to those who follow as full as you received it, or even fuller . . . the problem with reservoirs is that they take a very long time to fill but they can be drained by one hole in the dam. *The actions of one person can destroy what it took hundreds of people years to build*" (emphasis added).[14]

For many respondents, the nonpartisan norms of public service and responsiveness to the agenda of the elected president necessitate a cautious and deferential approach to their roles. Yasin Abadi, a prototypical bureaucrat, explained this to me over coffee sitting among the grand buildings of Federal Triangle. He was a middle-aged, mid-level manager in international affairs, who had simply cut, short dark hair, and wore a standard government uniform of a basic button-down shirt and slacks. Obedience to the new administration was endemic to civil service and to the balance of power, he said. He shared what he had recently explained to a family friend: "People have voted and this is where we're at. And we're not going to change things. We don't do that here." If appointees, he continued, "want to do what you consider bad decisions on their behalf or for themselves, we do our best to give more information . . . to those decisions. And if they still decide to do something damaging to themselves, then we say okay, that's what we're going to do and we have to suck it up." He was steadfast in this loyal and deferential position to the elected president and his administration in 2018 and in 2020 when we spoke again. "If you want to be an advocate, you can leave and work in a different sector. As a civil servant, you work for a government and your job is to serve to the best of your ability," he reiterated.

Even so, many political scientists acknowledge that it is not easy for career civil servants to navigate the various obligations of their roles, which expect them to serve as a source of stability in the government, serve presidents and their specific agendas, uphold the law, and adhere to their professional normative and ethical obligations in their agencies—all at once. Political scientists Joel Aberbach and Bert Rockman, for example, establish that there has been a baseline of continual friction between presidential administrations and career civil servants over the last fifty years, which can be more heightened during presidential transitions. They argue that some of the conflict between appointed administrators and career civil servants is undoubtably "eminently political" in nature.[15] Presidential administrations want to make sweeping changes, and career civil servants have to figure out how to execute such changes pragmatically given extant structures, programs and resources. Administrations may be tempted to blame career civil servants if their programs do not work as hoped. Conflicts may arise about how much discretion administrators should have and, amid fractured leadership and multiple professional obligations and loyalties, who bureaucrats should listen to.

## DEMOCRATIC BACKSLIDING: TRUMP'S AUTOCRATIC AND AUTHORITARIAN SHIFT

When I started interviewing bureaucrats in March 2017, shortly after Trump's election, I had no idea how, with the support of some members of his administration and Congress, Trump would test the foundational norms and tenets of American democracy. As an American, I no doubt unintentionally carried a lingering positivity bias, which meant that I in part hoped and in part presumed that such precipitous democratic decline was unlikely to occur here.[16] I was hesitant to use the words "autocratic" and "authoritarian" to describe Trump's leadership; they seemed hyperbolic in the American context.[17] Now, as I write, it is more evident that the Trump administration was a quintessential case of democratic backsliding.[18] As scholars of governance define, democratic backsliding is characterized by state-led weakening or elimination of "political institutions that sustain democracy," which can make the administrative state an early target of autocratic and/or populist leaders.[19] Although such leaders may depict themselves as standing up for the people, they threaten the government by seeking to radically expand executive power, claiming a mandate beyond constitutional law or other institutional checks.[20]

Autocracy generally refers to a political system in which power and authority are concentrated in a leader who expects unquestioning obedience.[21] Autocratic leaders tend to be domineering, unagreeable, neurotic, power seeking, psychopathic, and task oriented.[22] People also may avoid using the term "authoritarianism" because it tends to refer to entire regimes that demand obedience to authority at the cost of individual rights (e.g., voting or free speech).[23] With the weakening of democracies around the world, however, more recent scholarship on authoritarianism has shifted to focusing on the followers of an autocratic leader,[24] and the shift to authoritarian illiberal practices (rather than regimes) and the weakening of democratic norms.[25]

Rather than being merely a careless driver speeding down the highway, as Lopez suggested, Trump's behavior in 2016 and beyond clearly indicates that he was trying to dismantle the highway of democracy and rebuild it to empower himself and those close to him. In short, as president, Trump was a bad faith actor.

Alarm bells began ringing among American political scientists and historians of authoritarian regimes early in the Trump administration. As Harvard political scientists Steven Levitsky and Daniel Ziblatt explain in their 2018 book, *How Democracies Die*, like other autocrats since the second half of the twentieth century, and in contrast to the blatant dictatorships that characterized autocratic leaders in earlier periods, Trump's first administration "maintained a veneer of democracy while eviscerating its substance."[26]

Trump consistently signaled a disregard for democratic norms, procedures, and the rule of law in U.S. governance and a turn toward autocracy and authoritarianism.[27] He railed against many of the core functions and attributes of the administrative state, including regulatory power, expertise, and evidence-based analysis,[28] and repeatedly accused career civil servants of being members of a "deep state." In evoking this term, he inaccurately appropriated it from countries like Egypt and Turkey, where military and security agencies surreptitiously manipulate state functioning. By contrast, the United States has a very transparent state compared not only to states with weak democracies but to other liberal democracies.[29]

Trump has also mobilized an energized base of followers through an emergent White Christian Nationalist movement, which has come to be embraced by the majority of the Republican Party.[30] Their conservative agenda is explained in the Heritage Foundation's Project 2025 report published in the summer of 2023; they intend to vastly increase presidential power in support of a "unitary executive theory," thus radically altering the system of checks and balances in the U.S. government and giving Trump unprecedented power.[31]

Alongside this structural reform of the state, the Project 2025 agenda hopes to remove or curtail efforts at racial, gendered, and LGBTQ+ equity and rights (including gay marriage), as well as programs in support of addressing climate change, multilateral diplomacy and foreign aid. The plan also continues Trump's scapegoating and criminalization of immigrants and asylum seekers, expands militarization of the U.S.-Mexico border, and intends to deport noncitizens or detain them in mass tent camps.[32]

## HOW MIGHT PUBLIC SERVANTS IN A LIBERAL DEMOCRATIC STATE RESPOND TO AN AUTOCRATIC PRESIDENCY?

This question arises in the wake of notable studies on obedience under conditions of tyranny. Building on a body of research ranging from Hannah Arendt's to Stanley Milgram's simulated electric shock experiments and Philip Zimbardo's insights on obedience from the Stanford Prison Experiment,[33] many scholars tend to agree that powerful authorities, strong role expectations, group pressure, and deteriorating organizational situations can lead ordinary people to act in unethical ways that cause harm to others.[34]

Debates proliferate, however, on professionals' moral psychology and behavior.[35] Arendt suggested that "respectable" members of society, such as professionals, will be the most likely to bow to power, regardless of their education.[36] A common defense among Nazi bureaucrats during the Nuremberg trials, she reported, was that they were "just doing one's duty" in operating the daily, systematic machinery of the regime.[37] Other accounts emphasize the efficiency of the Nazi party and how many Germans came to support the regime via rational choice.[38]

What was most shocking and damning about Arendt's portrayal of Adolf Eichmann, the man who deported Holocaust victims to their ultimate fates, was his diligent mediocrity and moral shallowness.[39] He was absorbed into the Nazi regime, which made what appears to outsiders to be obvious wrongdoing—shipping millions of people to their death—a central part of a moral order in which "the command of the Fuhrer" was the "absolute center of the legal order."[40] In this legal and political system, obedience was part of a new "righteousness," arguably for the public good.[41] Judith Butler has argued one of the most striking aspects of Arendt's analysis of Eichmann is that "what had become banal—and astonishingly so—was the failure to think" among bureaucrats such as Eichmann.[42]

Additional research since on moral psychology, such as Milgram's infamous shock experiments, further underscore how people in institutional settings can default to obedience.[43] Milgram argued in 1967 that this obedience was a "fundamental mode of thinking for a great many people once they are locked into a subordinate position in a structure of authority."[44]

Others suggest such explanations are oversimplistic because they fail to acknowledge multicausal situational processes, bureaucrats' varying relationships with authority figures and ability to influence them, and conditions that enable resistance.[45] The accounts I share of career civil servants build on and affirm these contemporary explanations, even as they reveal the ultimate limitations of career civil servants' power in a hierarchical state.

The civil servants' accounts of the first Trump administration's weakening of the democratic state were different than prior portrayals of bureaucratic order, rationality, and obedience. It may well be that I could capture such differences because I witnessed career civil servants' interpretations of the Trump administration change from 2017 to 2020 *in real time*. The civil servants I spoke with were aware of the ever-present stakes of their work, yet they were constrained by the federal government hierarchy.[46] Their perspectives were also deeply embedded in the strong professional culture of nonpartisan civil service in the United States at the beginning of the twenty-first century, and its attendant commitment and legal oath to uphold the Constitution.

In contrast to other accounts, I saw how deeply many career civil servants *were* thinking: they were trying to make sense of the rapidly changing landscape under the Trump administration and continuing to try to do the right thing. Many read the news with concern: Trump's political developments were the cause of great anxiety among many centrist and Democrat-leaning civil servants with whom I spoke. At work, they continued to fall back on what they had learned from years of experience and trusted mentors on how the government was supposed to work: they were supposed to serve in a nonpartisan fashion, which was rooted in a hallowed culture of liberal democratic thought and predicated on an implicit trust that an elected American president is not only legitimate, but will, in good faith, try to rise to the occasion and serve with the best interests of the country at heart.

Instead, what they were dealing with was President Trump.

Despite—or perhaps because of—their years of education and professional experience, they simply did not have the cultural tools to make sense of what his administration was doing and to respond effectively through their limited roles at work, whose bounds they largely respected.

## THE TRUMP ADMINISTRATION'S SUSPICION OF THE ADMINISTRATIVE STATE AND ITS CONSEQUENCES

My research over the course of the first Trump administration reveals dual structural and cultural changes. First, the Trump administration's suspicion and disregard of career civil servants created what sociologist and network scholar Ronald Burt calls *structural holes* between some members of the administration and career civil servants. As Burt explains, structural holes are not marked by the complete absence of ties between groups or that such groups are "unaware of one another" but rather by "weaker connections between groups." Different groups focus on their own activities "such that they do not attend to the activities of the other group. Holes are buffers," he argued, "like an insulator in an electrical circuit," with different information circulating on each side of the structural hole.[47]

The Trump administration introduced structural holes across different levels of government (figure 1.1). Such holes were inserted in some locations between politicals chosen by the presidential administration and some of the most senior career civil servants, the Senior Executive Service (SES). The SES typically serve as brokers, or conduits, between the politicals and the career civil servants below them. Partly because of the administration's mistrust and emphasis on secrecy, appointees in parts of the government then introduced additional structural holes between SES and the civil servants they managed.

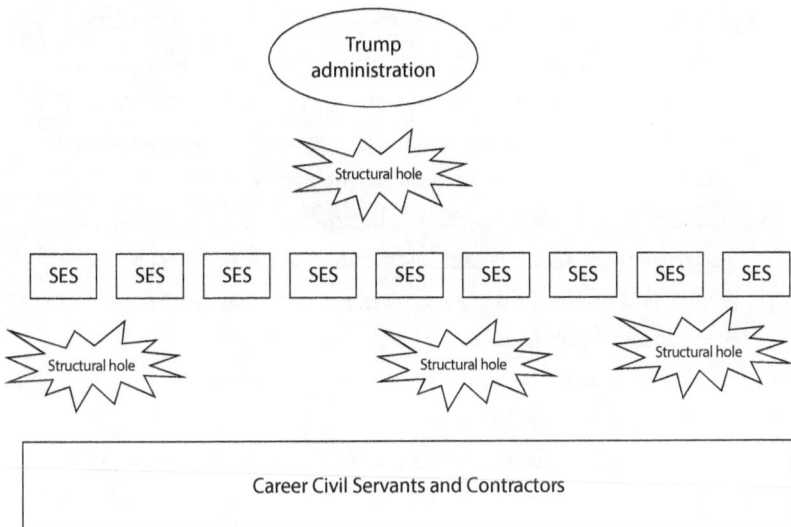

**FIGURE 1.1** The Trump administration's structural holes.

From a leadership perspective, such holes were a missed opportunity for appointees. Instead of developing relationships with senior career bureaucrats, who took their role as brokers between the president's appointed leaders and career public servants very seriously and would have likely helped them more, they chose to forgo such opportunities. They thereby bypassed the opportunity to gain social capital via such relationships, from which they could have gained much valuable advice, instrumental help, access to different perspectives, and more extensive networks that would have carried additional benefits.[48]

The second process I document in this book is how civil servants' local workplace cultures and subsequent perceptions of the first Trump administration evolved over the course of the term. As mistrust, secrecy, and threats of political reprisal pervaded certain parts of the government under Trump appointees' leadership, career civil servants noted how their work cultures changed and trust dropped, as did the possibility of certain actions to hold politicals accountable for ethical, procedural, and legal transgressions.

At first, the career civil servants I spoke with who noticed appointee-induced structural holes between the presidential administration and the career civil servants were perplexed. They wondered how they could best do their jobs running the government if they did not know what the president's and agency leaders' official agendas and instructions were, and which senior leaders had official power to implement such changes. Steeped in the culture of public service, they largely sought to give the new administration the benefit of the doubt and carry on with their jobs as best they could, even as warning signs began to appear that the administration was far more chaotic than normal.

With the insertion of structural holes and the confusion they brought with them, I came to realize that many career civil servants were disempowered to such an extent that there were simply no apparent good options at their disposal in their roles to protect the state, even as they came to realize the potential harm the administration could cause to the federal state they were so devoted to. This gave rise to extremely high levels of psychological uncertainty and anxiety among many career civil servants. They were caught in a series of intractable structural and cultural binds. As I will explain in the book, these range from loyalty traps among senior employees caught between appointee orders and their obligations to uphold the law and democratic norms to impossible situations in which midlevel employees were asked to implement ill-conceived projects.

## AT A LOSS FOR WORDS

As mentioned, many of the federal civil servants seemed to lack the cultural tools to diagnose and respond effectively to the political maelstrom of the Trump administration. This was especially the case in workgroups where trust broke down and employee isolation increased. Invoking critical words to describe Trump's approach to governance—such as autocracy and authoritarianism—was taboo for many civil servants. After an SES member compared the current political situation to Nazi Germany, I asked whether he thought the Trump administration was turning toward authoritarianism. In response, he described the comparison between the Trump administration and the German Third Reich as not only "hysterical," but "a really extreme analogy." Making such overt comparisons put one at risk of being perceived as emotional rather than grounded in reason, neutrality, and forbearance.

Yet this SES member also acknowledged that he was not the only person he knew making that comparison among senior leaders in his agency. In 2018, when much public attention was paid to the Trump administration's migrant family separation policy, five other respondents compared the government's practices to that of Nazi Germany. Of these respondents, about half were particularly knowledgeable about the history of the Nazi regime: two were Jewish, one with a parent who survived the Holocaust, and another had a graduate degree in German European history.

Across my interviews, only eight career civil servants overtly mentioned a turn toward authoritarianism. Of the eight, five were in the Department of State and had a more sophisticated understanding of different political regimes internationally and historically. Three career civil servants used the term of their own accord, and five used it voluntarily only after I asked about it directly (most in my last round of interviews in 2020). Only one person, a Department of State employee, in 2020 voluntarily mentioned the term "autocrat," and no respondents described the government as an autocracy. One person who worked at the Department of Homeland Security used the word "fascism" in 2020 to describe the larger political context.

These words were not widely used during my interviews during the Trump administration, even as many people expressed concern about Trump's erratic enactment of personal whims, unusually high standards of loyalty, damage to the democracy, disregard of the rule of law, attacks on the media and political opponents, degradation of democratic norms, and support—or silence—from Republican members of Congress, in spite of the Trump administration's ethical breaches.

This avoidance of disturbing, uncomfortable, and negative language to describe the American state was one of the most concerning findings of my study. It was my sense that this avoidance occurred more unconsciously than consciously. Civil servant culture and the language of loyalty to the state left civil servants unprepared for a president like Trump. They simply did not appear to have language to describe what the Trump administration was doing at a systemic level to dismantle the democratic checks in the administrative state.

This blind spot and their limited individual power in many cases gradually led career civil servants into unwitting compliance—which enabled the Trump administration to cause considerable damage to the democratic functioning of the American state, and made it ever more challenging to hold it accountable.[49]

Bearing witness to civil servants' experiences and struggles over the course of the Trump administration left me concerned about the fragility and vulnerability of our democracy and reaffirmed how important it is to identify and name the various mechanisms contributing to democratic decline when leadership takes an autocratic and authoritarian turn. It also left me wondering how to foster more spaces of collective reflection and reinforce extant checks and balances of power to preserve accountability to democratic values, the law, the Constitution, and the public in the American administrative state.

## THE STUDY

To examine how career bureaucrats experienced and responded to the Trump administration, I interviewed sixty-six career civil servants and contractors who worked in executive or independent agencies and eleven former employees who worked in contested areas of the federal government prior to the Trump administration (and had since retired or moved to work in other parts of the government); I spoke to seventy-seven people in all.

The latter group had worked in locations with a history of contention at the Department of Justice (DOJ) and the EPA. I spoke with them in an effort to establish a historical baseline of political-career employee contention under prior presidential administrations.[50]

I deliberately oversampled on high-ranking civil servants and those working in contentious locations because they would be the most likely to witness the Trump administration firsthand and discern changes by the administration. At the start of the study, I also oversampled those I thought would be likely to resist the administration.

I completed three waves of semistructured, in-depth interviews to track career civil servants' experiences over the course of the presidential term. I spoke with civil servants during the beginning (March–August, 2017 [$n = 45$]), middle (June–November 2018 [$n = 60$]), and end of the Trump administration (December 2019–March 2020 [$n = 21$]). My data collection ended both before the killing of George Floyd on May 25, 2020, which sparked a wave of racial injustice protests across the country, and before the insurrection led by Trump's supporters on Capitol Hill on January 6, 2021. In total, I conducted 127 interviews. Thirty-two people participated in two sets of interviews, and eight people participated in all three sets. This was in part because new people joined in my second set of interviews, and others left federal service or declined participating in subsequent interviews.

The civil servants with whom I spoke worked in nearly all federal executive branch agencies and in several independent agencies subject to considerable proposed budget cuts, such as the EPA and the United States Agency for International Development (USAID). I spoke to the most civil servants in the EPA, the Department of Health and Human Services (HHS), the DOJ, and the Department of State (see table A.1 in the appendix).

I interviewed employees working in offices in Washington, DC, as well as six regional offices located across the country.

At the end of each first interview, I asked how the public servant identified politically. The interviewees ranged from centrists to Democrats (some reluctantly). It is important to recognize that federal civil servants span the political spectrum.[51] Although I tried to reach Republicans, during the Trump administration, they were not interested in participating in the study, which delimits my results.

Through the course of this research, my perspective on civil servant resistance during democratic decline began to shift away from that of an outsider seeking to examine bureaucrats' choices to comply or resist, their narratives, and their behavior as grounded in their personal characteristics and attitudes to the presidential administration. My focus turned to how the constitutive professional and hierarchical organizational contexts in which they were embedded shaped how they understood the Trump administration and their subsequent actions.

The centrist and Democratic mid- and high-ranking career civil servants I interviewed gave cautiously calibrated responses to a dynamic and increasingly threatening environment, largely seeking to do their jobs, although they recognized that doing so might be viewed by others as either resistance or complicity. Rather than telling a simplistic story of either resistance or compliance, I show how career bureaucrats working between Trump appointees and mid- and lower-level civil servants attempted to walk a moral tightrope in navigating competing loyalties, duties, the constraints of their roles (real and perceived), doubts of their own power and efficacy in their responses to perceived threats, and local work cultures.[52] They sometimes succeeded in this delicate high-wire act. Other times they teetered, or even fell, into one of many stigmatized realms of ill repute, which included failing to protect the basic functioning of democracy, perceived disloyalty to the presidential administration, working against their own professional or personal commitments, or working counter to their agency's missions. For some career civil servants in the most politicized locations, rapidly changing and uncertain workplaces under Trump's appointed leadership added considerable pressure and confusion to their assessments of their situations, affecting their ability to navigate them lucidly and skillfully. They found themselves constrained, hesitant on the best course of action amid contested loyalties.

## THE BOOK'S FRAMEWORK

I first set the stage in chapter 1, then share career civil servants' experiences from the beginning to the end of the three sets of interviews in my study. In chapter 2, I share what is now known about the first Trump administration: Trump dangerously steered the American state toward autocracy and authoritarianism.

In the second part of the book, I shift to how those I spoke with began the presidential administration. In chapter 3, I discuss the baseline professional culture of public service—including the spirit of democracy and legal statutes, such as the Hatch Act and the Oath of Office, which jointly circumscribe and guide the behavior of career federal civil servants. Based on career civil servants' reported trajectories, I explain how many were selected for their positions in part because of their commitments to serve the state in a nonpartisan manner. These norms and structures promote risk aversion, constancy, and stability, inclining most federal civil servants to compliance. But adhering to the ethical expectations and obligations of public service is no simple, straightforward task: Building on Dwight Waldo's explanation,

I describe how a standard part of the job of a public servant is to navigate multiple and at times competing ethical obligations of public service skillfully.

During the beginning of the Trump administration, many experienced career civil servants tried to preserve their professional front and their norms of serial partisanship and political neutrality at work, and to keep calm and carry on in an effort to give the administration a chance, as I discuss in chapter 4. They reiterated many common rationalizations about how they continued to serve the administration and state as they would under any president. For many public servants I interviewed, however, personal concern lurked beneath their seemingly calm exteriors, concern that was rooted in media reports of the new administration and political gossip within and across agencies. These tensions between competing loyalties gave rise to heightened moral and professional role conflict.

In chapter 5, I discuss how many of the civil servants I spoke with coped with such moral dissonance through compartmentalizing their personal and professional lives. Because of the various professional standards and even the law, some—especially upper-level officials—avoided any form of public critique or resistance to the administration, even as warning signs appeared, and instead focused on meaningful personal pursuits or kinds of self-care—or even escapism—outside work. In riding the wave of popular protest in the wake of Trump's inauguration in 2017, others began engaging in what they viewed as appropriate and acceptable forms of resistance to problematic political changes, such as attending protest marches and rallies, engaging in nonpartisan political activity, or devoting themselves to local community work. A large majority of these attendees took care to distinguish their civic and political engagement as acts of personal expression that was disconnected from their work.

As time wore on, the notable discrepancies between career civil servants' experiences in contested and in more stable parts of the government were increasingly apparent; this was especially evident in the second and third sets of interviews that I conducted in 2018 and the end of 2019–2020, respectively. In the third part of the book (chapters 6–9), I focus on how career civil servants in these increasingly chaotic locations perceived the structural and cultural changes occurring around them in real time and tried to respond to them in alignment with the ethical obligations of their positions.

In chapter 6, I describe the leadership shifts that senior career civil servants reported to me from the most tumultuous politicized parts of the government: suspicious appointees prizing expressions of loyalty to the Trump administration cordoned themselves off from career civil servants, fostering structural holes, and in some cases expected SES members to do the same with those they supervised. Appointees' mindsets and behaviors gave rise to loyalty traps for some mid- and senior-level career civil servants interfacing with appointees, as I discuss in chapter 7.

Poor leadership and some notable bad-faith appointees gave rise to organizational decline in the most politicized parts of the administrative state. I discuss the evidence of decline that career civil servants reported across levels in chapter 8. They suggested that leadership infighting, the lack of internal communication, misinformation, visible corruption, and an unclear chain of command created chaos and confusion. This all diminished productivity and morale, weakened intrinsic motivation to serve, and reduced innovation.

In chapter 9, I report career public servants' responses to the tumult and chaos in the most affected parts of the government. Some tried to muddle through all their obligatory ethical expectations, including respecting the president's agenda—even if it entailed weakening their own programs. Because of Trump's leadership, others found themselves stifled, unable to express even their professional opinions. Quite a few career employees headed for the exits.

In part IV, I identify and discuss how some career employees engaged in resistance during the Trump administration. In chapter 10, I describe some limited evidence of civil servants engaging in what they believed to be covert resistance. While these actions may have undermined politically appointed leadership in small degrees, others might view them as insufficient or ineffective. Covert resistance seemed like a low-risk means through which career civil servants could negotiate their conflicting ethical obligations and moral commitments and thus avoid straying too far from their ordinary work. They could diverge just enough to ease their troubled consciences. It seemed, however, that these tactics may have had little impact, especially where political appointees exercised their powers to set political agendas and control decision-making processes. Perhaps as a result, reported use of covert tactics seemed to decline over the course of the administration.

Chapter 11 explains the situational contexts and personal characteristics of the rare civil servants who engaged in visible acts of moral courage at work under conditions of democratic decline. The experiences of the civil servants I profile reveal how crucial a civil servant's position and immediate work environment is on whether, when, and how they take a stand in the face of autocratic political leadership.

In chapter 12, I share some career civil servants' reflections at the end of the term and then step back to discuss my own altered understandings. In contrast to most career civil servants' evident relief that government functioning largely persisted through the Trump administration, I was struck by the fragility of the American state and the perilous crossroads we face in this seemingly enduring moment. I then discuss the significance and implications of these career federal employees' experiences and responses during a period of rising autocracy in the U.S. government and heightened political polarization among the public.

Civil servants' efforts to stay largely within the bounds of institutional and professional norms is ultimately not a simple story of resistance or compliance (or its less savory cousin, complicity). The very nature of resistance and compliance must be reconceived in the context of the federal government under an autocratic turn in leadership. Career civil servants translated and transmuted potential seeds of resistance to cohere with the professional norms and structural limitations of their roles. The civil servants with whom I spoke repeatedly evoked their allegiance to the government and their professions, striving to characterize their actions as keeping with their professional and institutional roles. As the Trump administration adopted increasingly repressive political tactics, however, it contravened long-standing bureaucratic norms and challenged civil servants' pragmatic, moral, and ethical assessments. I observed many civil servants struggling to make sense of these changes in real time during our interviews.

There are both long-term merits and concerning implications of civil servants' inclination to stay within their roles. Under typical conditions, civil servants' responsiveness to elected leaders is incredibly important to maintaining a functioning democracy, as is their responsibility to serve as knowledgeable experts, especially in a massive government facing increasingly complex problems. However, under conditions of an emergent autocratic leader and authoritarian shifts enabled by powerful congressional leaders, typical civil servant compliance in certain, particularly contested areas of the government can lead to a weakened democracy or even, in some particularly dire cases, to losing parts of a functioning democracy.

The first Trump presidency serves as a natural experiment in which it is possible for social scientists to see how bureaucrats experience the reverberations of a bad-faith president through the lens of their everyday work across the government. To what extent are they aware of these changes, and how do they choose to respond to them? What lessons can we learn from them about resistance to poor leadership and organizational decline, or about the limitations of such efforts from mid- and high-level career bureaucrats? And what does it mean for these processes to have happened in one of the most powerful economic and military powers on the planet?

Although civil servants generally tend to abide by a strong professional moral code of loyalty to serving the public, performing their roles, and serving elected and appointed leadership, they are not a monolith. Their position in the government and the specific situations that unfold around them dramatically shape what they see and how they believe they can respond to problematic political developments. Only a select group had close enough access to leadership to see harmful behavior up close. And it was an even rarer group that had the perceived efficacy and wherewithal to attempt to push back directly. In this book, I share the stories of civil servants' experiences across the government during the first Trump administration in the hope that we may all learn from their lessons to be better prepared for future autocratic leaders elected to the highest office in the land.

# 2

# A LURCH TOWARD AUTOCRACY

D onald Trump's campaign and presidency, from 2016 to 2021, felt like a frenetic barrage of information. Even for me, during my sabbatical year in 2018 devoted to trying to understand the administration's changes, it was daunting to track and make sense of all that was happening. It would be nearly impossible for others working full-time jobs and managing kids, aiding other loved ones in need of care, and/or upholding other community responsibilities to make sense of what transpired.

As this book goes to press, in the wake of many more published insider accounts, and hundreds of pages of reporting—and planning—from conservative groups, the damage that Trump and his administration has done to the American democratic republic is far clearer now. The threats that he and others in his image will bring in the future are also more evident.[1]

President Trump risked inflicting lasting damage on the U.S. democracy by reshaping the political playing field to his own advantage. He praised government repression in other countries and publicly admired authoritarian strongmen, like Vladimir Putin of Russia, Xi Jinping of China, Kim Jong Un of North Korea, Recep Tayyip Erdogan of Turkey, and Rodrigo Duterte of the Philippines.[2] Like other autocratic leaders, he sought to consolidate power by capturing the referees—such as those in law enforcement, the intelligence community, ethical accountability offices, and the courts—by insisting that their leaders express their loyalty to him personally rather than to the Constitution, democracy, and the American public.

As president, Trump sought to punish and cut down the civil servants and federal agencies that acted independently.[3] Near the end of his first term, in the spring of 2020, he went so far as to fire the inspector generals of the State Department and the intelligence community, along with the acting inspector generals of the Department of Defense, Health and Human Services, and Transportation.[4] This egregious encroachment alone, which received little public acknowledgment, should give pundits and the public alike pause. But by the time this occurred, people seemed accustomed to such flagrant abuses of power from the president.

President Trump repeatedly exhibited a readiness to curtail the civil liberties of opponents and the media, which he called "an enemy of the American people."[5] He set about sidelining key political and civic players, such as major media outlets like the *New York Times* and *CNN*, which he repeatedly claimed were releasing "fake news."[6] He sought to restrict protest and criticism of the government and expand libel laws, and he threatened legal and other punitive actions against critical politicians, journalists, and members of the public.[7] Early in his administration, in May 2017, his administration also created a presidential advisory commission on election integrity, which aimed to suppress voting among Americans likely to vote for Democrats, such as people of color.[8]

Trump breached other hallowed democratic norms as well, such as respecting the legitimacy of political opponents and elections. For a democratic government to continue functioning, it is necessary that politicians treat other parties as legitimate rivals, exercise restraint in executing their goals, and abide by legal constraints.[9] Trump instead vilified political opponents. During and after his campaign, Trump's denigration of his Democratic opponent Hillary Clinton as a criminal rather than as a legitimate opponent was a common battle cry. His dismissal of Joseph Biden's allegedly fraudulent election win through his claims of the "Big Lie" had similar themes, suggesting that Biden was not a legitimately elected president.

As veteran reporters Bob Woodward and Carl Bernstein reported, Trump and his team of lawyers, aides, and loyalists were historic in their false claims of voter fraud; "unprecedented public intimidation of state election officials;" and attempt "to prevent the peaceful transfer of power to his duly elected successor, for the first time in American history." They argue Trump was the first "seditious president in our history."[10]

To make matters worse, the Trump presidency engaged in a "norm-shattering expansion of private interests in government," suggest other *Washington Post* reporters.[11] Corruption was publicly visible in his circles and across his administration.[12] Trump has been criticized for using considerable amounts of government money to pay for his family's and the Secret Service's stays at his own hotels around the world, for bypassing laws and norms intended to prevent nepotism in hiring his son-in-law Jared Kushner as a senior adviser, and for awarding large government contracts to allies professing their loyalty to the president.[13] This dismissal of long-standing ethical norms intended to prevent appearances of a presidential kleptocracy appeared to many civil servants and reporters alike as evidence of political corruption.

With regard to the administrative state, Trump's administration is a textbook case of democratic backsliding. Claiming to try to fix "an excessively 'liberal' and 'establishment-elitist' civil service" and it's inherent "pockets of resistance," Trump tried to expand and centralize executive power and control. He sought to expedite decision-making and policy formation by cutting out scientific and expert feedback mechanisms, to reduce some departmental budgets, to curtail administrative regulations, and to sanction those ideologically different from him and his agenda. Instead he rewarded those loyal to himself, who were willing to undermine democratic norms and checks, and reduce transparency and accountability.[14]

As became especially apparent near the end of his first term, President Trump went so far as to tacitly and explicitly endorse political violence by his supporters and by other authoritarian leaders in the past and around the world.[15] Under his leadership, on June 1, 2020, police and officers from Customs and Border Protection (CBP) used rubber bullets, tear gas, and stun grenades to clear peaceful Black Lives Matter (BLM) demonstrators against police brutality from Lafayette Square in Washington, DC. Trump followed the incident with a photo op.[16] When military leaders stood up for just treatment of Black Americans and for the Constitution, Trump and Attorney General William Barr activated others forces, including 132,000 security and law enforcement officers from the Bureau of Alcohol, Tobacco, Firearms and Explosives; the CBP, the Federal Bureau of Investigation (FBI), the Secret Service, and the Drug Enforcement Administration (DEA) as well as approximately 3,800 National Guard members, mainly from red states.[17]

Trump's support for violence culminated in the breach of the U.S. Capitol and the ensuing violence on January 6, 2021, as explained by the Congressional House committee's public hearings.[18] The hearings depicted the president and members of his administration as initiating and orchestrating an attempted coup.[19]

President Trump's seeming disregard for the law was another striking aspect of his presidency. With his America First campaign, he rejected international law by leaving global treaties on migration and asylum; multiple international treaties intended to impede war and maintain peace, such as a nuclear nonproliferation treaty with Iran; and the Paris Climate Agreement. The Trump administration left multilateral decision-making bodies such as the UN Human Rights Council, the UN Relief and Works Agency, and other international commitments such as the World Health Organization (WHO) and the UN Scientific and Educational Cultural Organization (UNESCO) as well. As Yale legal scholar Oona Hathaway argues, this approach fundamentally misunderstands international law, which actually tends to promote state sovereignty. Trump's approach also weakened the U.S. geopolitical position, degrading it to that of a "voluntary outcast."[20]

On May 30, 2024, the former president was the first U.S. president convicted as a felon. He was found guilty of thirty-four felony counts of falsifying business records.[21] As this book goes to press, he continues to face another seventeen felony counts in remaining state and federal criminal cases.[22] For all these reasons, a multitude of prominent scholars and journalists of political history agree: people should be concerned about Trump, his supporters, and other future politicians building political careers in his image and thus harming the foundations of American democracy.[23]

As Steven Levitsky and Daniel Ziblatt write: "No other major presidential candidate in modern U.S. history, including [Richard M.] Nixon, has demonstrated such a weak public commitment to constitutional rights and democratic norms."[24] Historian Heather Cox Richardson and others point to how Trump gained the power he did with the support and complicity of many members of the Republican Party: "at no point in America's history," she writes, "has one of the two main parties literally rejected the rules of the game."[25]

# II

# KEEP CALM AND CARRY ON

## The Beginning of the Administration

# 3

# THE SPIRIT AND INHERENT
# CHALLENGES OF PUBLIC
# ADMINISTRATION

I n 2017, when I began speaking with U.S. federal civil servants, much of what I reported in chapter 2 was not widely known or had not yet happened. To wind back time, in this chapter, I explain what I encountered at the start of my research: the everyday running of the state seemed largely business as usual. Most civil servants reported, midway through 2017, that changes at the top levels of the government, for the most part, had yet to affect them. "You're too early," I was told. As such, their reports provide what now seems like a nostalgic baseline of how government workers perceived their work before Donald Trump's administration had made much of an impact.

## SETTING THE SCENE

The Capitol in the heart of Washington, DC, is not a typical workplace. The center of the government, marked by the Mall, the White House, Federal Triangle, and other federal buildings, is both a museum and memorial, attesting to the endurance, strength, and glory of the American democratic state. The federal buildings' formidable Indiana limestone façades, massive colonnades, and lofty domed roofs were carefully crafted to inspire awe and a sense of the sacred history of the country.[1] Inside these grand edifices, paintings and sculptures of storied leaders that shepherded the democratic republic through wars, recessions, and other challenges permeate the buildings, as do bright red, white, and blue American flags in building interiors and exteriors.

Some of the civil servants I spoke with referenced the at times inspiring and at times imposing elements of these settings in passing. One public servant, for example, mentioned with excitement where he had worked the previous week, flashing a photo of an ornate room with an oval wood conference table and an American flag off to the side. To the left of the flag, a large window overlooked the White House. Working in such esteemed places was both a formative influence and a perk of the job.

Several civil servants mentioned seeing the images of the president and vice president every day upon entering work. Such images had a palpable emotional impact on how they felt entering work, which could either boost or harm morale, depending on one's political fit with the president at the time. As one senior Department of Defense (DOD) employee put it in 2018: "the president and the White House is never far from your mind." He continued, "If you personally . . . have admiration for the president, it helps your morale when you work with them. And if you don't, you have to fall back on the fact that you're a public servant and you serve neutrally." He also mentioned regularly seeing the president and his staff on the news being streamed through CNN or Fox News in breakrooms in his building. A number of federal civil servants living and working in Washington, DC, discussed how inescapable Trump's presence felt, especially with his heightened media and social media presence.

As the DOD employee noted, presidential influence could lead to a sense of professional alignment between personal and professional commitments, which could boost intrinsic motivation and morale. Career civil servants could also experience *moral dissonance*, either from disjunction between their personal moral and/or political beliefs and their professional duties to serve the presidential administration, or from competing professional obligations and loyalties. In the case of moral dissonance between personal beliefs and professional responsibilities to serve leadership, many career civil servants explained that it was their professional duty to fall back on their professional ethical code to reduce dissonance and execute their job—or they could quit. This expectation and norm prioritized professional ethics and morality over personal moral codes.

It is far less clear, however, how career bureaucrats should navigate competing professional values, especially during periods of democratic decline and organizational tumult. As economist Albert O. Hirschman theorized and some public servants suggested, under poor organizational conditions, members may try to exercise *voice* and speak up in an effort to correct course, motivated by their *loyalty* to the spirit of public administration and their prescribed roles, or head for the *exits*. Alternatively, if exits seem a poor option or impossible, they may align themselves with the organization and thereby express a different form of *loyalty*, in this case to leadership or the organization in its present state.[2] From my early interviews, it was evident that federal career civil servants had loyalty in spades because of the strong professional culture of service in which they were immersed. How they would use it, however, remained another question.

## THE SPIRIT OF PUBLIC ADMINISTRATION

Public administration scholar Hugh Heclo describes how critical the "spirit of public administration" is in the administrative state. In evoking a "spirit," he refers to that "inspiring and animating principle" that touches on the deepest meaning or essential truth of something's existence and that can both infuse and temper a doctrine.[3] In the case of public administration, Heclo and others characterize its ideal spirit as the "simultaneous striking of many notes such as impartiality, efficiency, non-partisanship, rationality, public service, and fiduciary responsibility" in "stewardship . . . of the wellbeing of the public household."[4]

Although various lineages of organizational and rational choice theory, as well as sociology and public administration scholarship, may discount value-based motivations and considerations, Heclo warns academics not to dismiss summarily the power of normative systems that "encompass the realization of values" and can serve as "a master ideal addressed to behavior as well as to many specific norms."[5] As the public service motivation literature suggests, public sector employees tend to be particularly motivated by intrinsic rather than extrinsic rewards compared to private sector counterparts.[6]

According to Heclo, career civil servants both serve as a stabilizing force in the federal government—providing continuity in knowledge, relationships, coordination, standard operating procedures, and democratic norms across presidential administrations—and must adapt to regular shifts in partisan leadership.[7] Public administration "is expected to exhibit the peculiar neutrality of being serially and equally partisan by working in good faith during successive exchanges of partisan leaders. Loyalty to the office, not to the person or party, commands this."[8]

Career civil servants described their serial partisanship with pride and as a central part of their collective identity as public servants tied to their patriotism to serving the country. As a Senior Executive Service (SES) member at the Environmental Protection Agency (EPA) told me in 2018:

one of the great things about the country was there was a very strong cadre of civil servants who prided themselves on the ability to serve any new administration. It was actually a real point of pride within the bureaucracy to prepare for any new administration, regardless of party, regardless of ideology. The orderly transition of power was something, is something that is a dearly-held tenet of the senior service, the high-level bureaucracy.

Nearly everyone I spoke with expressed what Heclo called the "spirit of public administration"—noting their multiple professional commitments to serving the democratic bureaucracy, which included executing their work in a rational, technocratic, and nonpartisan manner; adhering to serial partisanship and serving to the best of their ability across presidential administrations; striving for fiscal prudence and efficiency; and abiding by the limits of their roles.

Many also expressed an additional tenet of the spirit of public administration, rooted in Thomas Jefferson's moral philosophy, that is key to public service: benevolence.[9] This was at times expressed through a generalized sense of loyalty to working for the government, inspired by a sense of patriotism, duty, and dedication to serving the American public and reinforced through their years of work on the job.

## THE PROFESSIONAL FRONT STAGE

Regardless of their political views or private concerns, the civil servants I spoke with almost always presented as cautious and exceedingly professional in describing their work, especially at the outset of the first Trump administration. Many espoused a practiced self-control and an ability to hide or set aside their emotions and thus appear rational, politically neutral, and in support of serial partisanship.

Civil servants take their roles, or "sets of behavioral expectations (or 'scripts') which are attached to positions in the social structure," very seriously.[10] They often referred to their work identities, based on their professional roles, as guiding them based on a profound sense of who they were "(in an existential sense) and how they ought to behave" in their particular positions.[11] Roles give people a sense of meaning and purpose and provide normative behavioral guidance; this is particularly true for those who value serving the public.[12]

Sociologist Erving Goffman describes curated self-presentations, in which actors strive to present themselves successfully as fulfilling expected roles to external audiences, as *front stage* performances.[13] Particular settings, such as federal buildings and the Capitol itself, can serve as stages and props, cueing actors to play certain roles. Compared to normal everyday interactions, career civil servants had particularly formidable front stage rhetoric. Lewis Waters was a case in point.[14] During our initial meeting, Waters hit all the appropriate notes of a conscientious and loyal public servant. When I began asking about his work history, Waters noted the importance of understanding his position in a broader institutional context from the start. He began explaining the structure of the federal government as staffed by a majority of career civil servants and his role in it as an objective technocratic career civil servant. "Most people don't realize this," he said, "most jobs don't change . . . regardless of the President." At his agency, the Office of Management and Budget (OMB), he said, "success is giving the decision makers the best possible information, not evaluating whether their decisions are good or bad. It's a different question to ask: did they make the best policy choices? That's not our job."

Noting his commitment to working for leaders of both major parties, he stated that his agency "has a long history of working well under different leadership. And it's not just partisan. There are different leadership styles." Under the administrations of George W. Bush and Barack Obama, he said, "I had leaders I respected and admired in both administrations. Organizational leaders in both administrations respected the value of the work we did—we do." Waters's presentation of self and deep embedding of himself in the institution in which he worked were not exceptions; they were normal among federal civil servants with whom I spoke.

## LEARNING THE ROLE OVER A LIFETIME

How do career civil servants' deeply held professional values and standards develop and how are they reinforced? For many, it starts when they are young and is reinforced at every stage of their education and professional development. To frame this process of professionalization, I present a composite view with real examples gleaned from my interviews (figure 3.1).[15]

Rarely did civil servants arrive in their position by accident. For many, the inspiration to serve started early—through a parent, major national or international event, or popular media. Interest in and academic knowledge of government grew in high school, college, and graduate school. Commitment grew through internships and early forays into service through the military or Peace Corps. Socialization in the profession began long before day one as a bureaucrat and would be reinforced every day thereafter.[16]

Department of Homeland Security midlevel manager, Annette Foster, described it this way, "As a kid, I loved civics

| Early Education | | | | | |
|---|---|---|---|---|---|
| Public school civics and history courses<br>Parental role models<br>Participation in youth civic extracurricular organizations<br>Inspirational leaders and national events<br>Positive representations of federal civil service in popular culture | **College and Graduate School** | | | | |
| | Courses on history, democracy, political science, and public administration<br><br>Professional training on particular area of expertise | **Initial Forays into Government Service** | | | |
| | | Military service<br>Peace Corps<br>Presidential Management Fellows Program<br>Internships<br>Selection by commitment to serially partisan service in the government | **Legal Obligations** | | |
| | | | Civil Servant Oath<br>Hatch Act | **On-the-Job Training** | |
| | | | | Reinforcement of civic values<br>Mentorship and normative influence of serial partisanship, political neutrality, and responsiveness to excecutives<br>Ethical trainings and reminders<br>Shaped by specific offices and agency locations | |

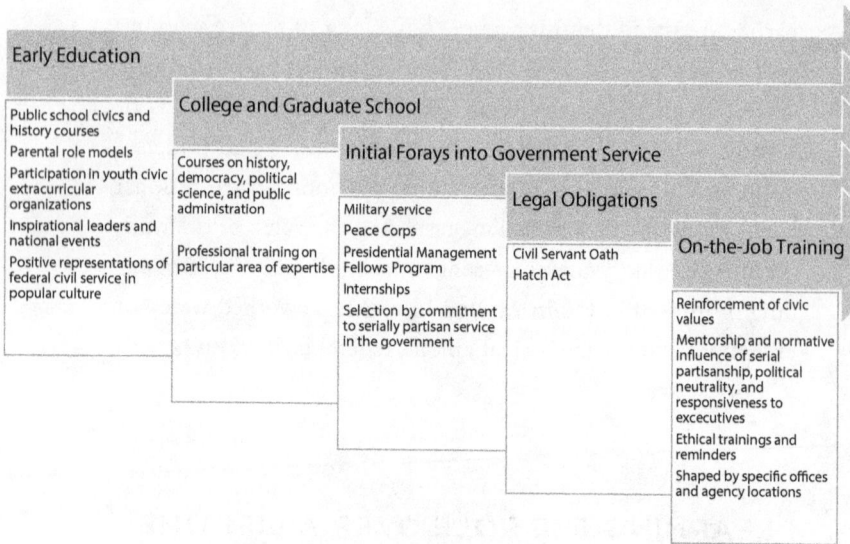

**FIGURE 3.1** Civil servants are a select group of people who are committed and socialized into civic duties and loyalty to government and nation.

and history." In 2018, she explained how her knowledge of history inspired her commitment to do her best every day in her work in immigration. She referenced how American forefathers fought in the Revolutionary War and that having "a sense of our country and why it was founded . . . is important to me" and was an anchor in her "moral compass" and "decision-making when it comes to work."

A Department of Justice (DOJ) lawyer hired under a Republican administration attributed some of his interest in public service, his commitment to upholding political neutrality in his role, and his acceptance of the sacrifice it required to his father's influence: "My father, as a civil servant, was Independent. I am a registered Independent . . . My father always told me it was a privilege to work in government and it was important to take an apolitical position. It is a sacrifice. I don't post on Facebook and can't write op-eds. I wouldn't want to be filmed or recorded at a march."[17] As a lawyer, he viewed his job as "not political. I believe in the judicial process," he said. "I believe in public service." Others, such as a midlevel manager at a regional EPA office, expressed similar familial influences, for example, "growing up in a pretty politically motivated family" and wanting to work for the government "to do the right thing."

Various civil servants also referred to participation in civic extracurricular activities in their childhood and youth, such as Boy Scouts, debate teams, or 4-H clubs, as precursors of their careers in federal service. A long-time EPA employee recounted, "I was interested in government from a pretty young age, like in high school." He participated in debate teams and organizations like 4-H clubs and Future Farmers of America. These early experiences, he said, stoked his idealism; honed his leadership skills; and taught him about farming, which seeded his interest in agricultural policy. They also helped develop his "interest in government, strangely, because I kind of felt like government could do good things, like public service," he said.

Others similarly recounted joining the government because they wanted to do positive influential work to help others. A former Civil Rights Division lawyer recounted opting to pursue law school rather than mathematics "because I wanted to practice civil rights law and to have a real-world impact in solving social justice problems." As a result, he then interned in the Civil Rights Division at the Justice Department because "it was really the highest form of public service I could have imagined doing."

Some older civil servants were drawn to work for the government because of inspirational leaders or historic national events. As a former DOJ lawyer in the Civil Rights Division told me, he was inspired to work for the government by John F. Kennedy's election and the passing of the Civil Rights Act of 1965. He had seen Kennedy speak in Union Square in New York. "He was so inspiring for people in my generation," he told me. And then as the Civil Rights Act came into effect, he recounted feeling like he was in the right place at the right time: "This is it, man. This is the golden age of civil rights . . . Working for the government was a great thing. And Lyndon Johnson—the Great Society and all that." He was buoyed by a sense of efficacy and the belief that "you can do really good things" working for the government.

Some of the youngest civil servants I met suggested that positive depictions of working for the government in popular media led them into careers in government service. An EPA employee at a satellite office, for example, "wanted to work for the EPA ever since I was little" because of a movie "called *Civil Action* . . . they really make the EPA look like the good guys and I was really wowed by that." A Department of Health and Human Services (HHS) employee recounted watching "*West Wing* when I was in high school and college." She thought it was "the most amazing show" and "part of the reason, probably, that I have a degree in political science and a Master's in public policy." Although as a civil servant she realized the show is not "real," and does not accurately depict "how it works," she said that it has left a lasting impression: "I still absolutely believe in public service."

It is important to acknowledge that the mostly mid- and high-level civil servants I spoke with are a select group of people in many respects: they are not a random cross-section of Americans. Many described how they were drawn to work for the federal government out of intrinsic commitments to serve their country through government service. This aligns with decades of literature on the public service motivations of civil servants, in which they commonly depict themselves as altruistic, dedicated to advancing the public good, and committed to the goals of their agencies.[18]

They not only seemed particularly intrinsically motivated, but many had attained impressive credentials. All but one person I spoke with had at least a four-year college degree, and nearly half (46 percent) had a master's degree. Nearly two-fifths (39 percent) had a PhD or JD. Most had graduated from prestigious universities around Washington, DC, or other top universities across the country. Many had completed degrees in public administration, law, or international affairs, which taught them about the structures of government; key political, legal, and diplomatic processes; and honed their reasoning skills. These privileged educations not only helped inspire them to public service but also made them feel part of a specially chosen group. As one long-time DOD employee described during his early years of federal service, "We all felt like we were super-smart and super-capable. We all had very, very similar backgrounds . . . from the really good small liberal arts colleges or the Ivy Leagues or other good universities. We all went to the top Master's programs in international affairs and so we probably had big heads and thought we knew a lot. But we were bullish and excited and we got some great opportunities to do really super-interesting stuff and to learn a lot."

The impressive credentials of the federal civil servants I spoke with not only put them well above average educational attainment among the American public but also among the full population of federal civil servants. In 2020, about 38 percent of the population in the United States over the age of twenty-five had a bachelor's degree or higher. Only 10.5 percent of those over twenty-five had a master's degree, and a mere 3.6 percent had another professional degree or doctoral degree.[19] Within the federal government, 27 percent had attained a master's degree, and 10 percent had another professional or doctoral degree in 2020.[20]

Many civil servants started government service with stints in the military or Peace Corps, as Presidential Management Fellows, or as interns. Through these pathways, many career civil servants came to understand working for the government as a sort of calling in which they were serving a higher purpose.[21] In these entry-level roles, some described further developing a sense of patriotism, a commitment to service, and discipline. A senior official at the State Department said how he was drawn to "serve through Peace Corps and to be a volunteer and to be helpful in some way." From there, he said he "kind of got bitten by the bug of continuing to work internationally, continuing to work across cultures, and continuing to do something that was of service to others." Even though nongovernmental organization (NGO) and government work "are not the highest paying careers in the world," he said, "that became less important to me than having a sense of purpose, having a sense of contributing and having a sense of helping." This sense of meaningfulness and intrinsic motivation for their work aligns with the culture of elites fostered in prestigious colleges and universities, as well as in many esteemed professional careers.[22]

The career civil servants I spoke with suggested that their professional education left a lasting impact beyond their credentials on paper. They were particularly likely to exercise caution and social skill in how they presented themselves and justified their actions.[23] It was not uncommon for me, as a professor at a selective liberal arts college, to have the sense while speaking to my study participants that my interlocutor had been at the head of the class in school. Generally, they articulated well-reasoned, thoughtful accounts that conscientiously grappled with different perspectives and took into account how I might be interpreting what they said. Many exuded confidence, earned and honed through stories of advancement and past successes, which bolstered their credibility. This was a very privileged, polished, and capable group of people.

Lawyer Annette Foster described how her sense of patriotism and service had grown over her decades of service to the federal government and through her graduate education in public administration. She not only felt she was "making a difference" and expressed "care about the government," but she also, as part and parcel of this spirit, accepted the structure of the government as an article of faith:

> With my background in management and MPA and all of that, I think it's just the way the government is. The head of the government of the executive branch is the president and we all know that they set the policy and our job is to work the policy and that's what I know. Studying government history, . . . I was kind of schooled in that—so I understand how the government was set up and I understand that when administrations come in and if it's a Democrat, then it's going to swing one way and if it's a Republican, it's going to swing another way. That's just the way it works.

Some civil servants described being selected for their ability to serve in a responsive manner, which is appropriate in a government ruled through serial partisanship where the president changes every four or eight years. A civil servant at HHS shared in a follow-up email:

> In my interview for my job, it was made very clear that as federal employees we may not always agree with the administration, and they asked me to provide an example of when I've had to work on something that didn't fit with my personal beliefs. My understanding is everyone in my office is asked a similar question, though theirs were more neutral along the lines of "can you work

on something you don't agree with?" I'm guessing mine was not as neutral because my résumé made my political views pretty clear.

Another employee working in the White House reported:

> One of the first things that I was told when I was interviewing for this position and ultimately decided to take this position was that when you enter this building you are serving the president, period. And if you choose not to, then don't work here, period. And whatever his different policies are and the way that they are, if that aligns to your personal beliefs, great. And if it doesn't, then you don't bring in your personal thoughts to the analysis and the data and the recommendations that you make here. And so, I can't say my personal thoughts. I really do take that seriously and understand that we're working with the office of the president and really will respect that and so I honestly don't think of that at all.

These reports suggest that mid- and upper-level federal career civil servants are not a random group of people. Through various steps of the process, they are selected not only for their rational and technical abilities associated with having trained at some of the best colleges and universities in the country but also because they are capable of serial partisanship and responsiveness to changes in administrations.

## Career Civil Servants' Legal and Institutional Ethical Obligations to Serve

Upon getting their job, civil servants take an oath of office, swearing allegiance to the Constitution and to defend it against enemies.[24] Civil servants across agencies remembered their oath and their civil servant values through the turbulence of the first Trump presidency.[25] As a longtime EPA employee Jeffrey Thompson told me in 2017, his "testament to his commitment to public service" was his four decades of employment. He laughed, saying, "There's not going to be a lot of money. You're not going to be close to the 1 or 10 percenters. I came in with an eye focused on what I can do to affect goodwill and the well-being of people's lives and a commitment to the Constitution." DOD lawyer Ralph McCafferty also mentioned his commitment to his sworn oath as a civil servant. To him, it seemed as an anchor through the storm, as he told me in 2018:

I don't want to sound like so laudatory, but I serve the Constitution not the president. So when you come into the government, you make an oath to the Constitution, just like the president and this situation is really, I've heard employees talk about that, that we're serving the Constitution. A lot of rank-and-file employees that I've talked to, have talked about being neutral, that you have to, no matter who's in office or who it is, you're serving the public and the Constitution. And that sounds really overblown but it's like that's how you maintain sanity in these days.

A second legal structure delimiting career civil servants' behavior is the Hatch Act. The Hatch Act prohibits career civil servants from running for a partisan political office, fundraising for a partisan political campaign, or engaging in political activity while at work, wearing a uniform or official emblem, or using a federally owned vehicle. The Hatch Act applies to all federal civil servants working for the executive branch and the postal service but not to the president or vice president.[26]

When I asked about career civil servants' political and civic engagement, many mentioned how the Hatch Act restricted their political behavior. EPA SES member Sean Butler told me, as senior leadership, "we're forbidden to engage in any political activities, so we don't . . . So I can take on an issue, but I can't take on a party and I can't support any partisan political candidate for office—the Hatch Act prohibits that activity. I have to stop short of that and don't say things that cross the line." In discussing the Hatch Act, several federal civil servants, like Butler, invoked their official positions, and spoke from a "we" perspective, situating themselves firmly in their official identities and roles.

A considerable number of career civil servants interpreted the Hatch Act even more broadly than its official stipulations in practice. When I asked about his civic and political involvement, an information technology specialist at the General Services Administration (GSA) responded simply, "Well, we can't." Then he clarified, with respect to the Hatch Act, "We can do civic engagement, but we can't engage politically outside of work at all. That would be a violation even though it's our own personal time; we're still federal employees. So I believe we're not supposed to do that at all." This was quite a broad interpretation of the Hatch Act, well beyond its specific stipulations.

A career civil servant at the Census Bureau explained in more detail about her concerns about the Hatch Act under the Trump administration because Trump "declared his candidacy for president on inauguration day so," she said, "that's a really gray area." As a result, she "had anxiety," and was "concerned about what I can say, what I can participate in . . . as a federal employee," and, she said, "even I have a little concern about—with this call about how this could actually come back to me." She then went on to list quite accurately the official stipulations of the Hatch Act, but she expressed a fear of breaching the act that seemed to extend beyond its official stipulations. Similar to others, she said if it were not for the Hatch Act, "I would be more vocal."[27]

Career civil servants' adherence to the rules and norms of public service were evident not only through their explicit claims of loyalty that they repeatedly expressed but also in more subtle elements of how they presented themselves. As I recorded while sitting in a public outdoor eating area near several agency buildings waiting for an interviewee to arrive, "I noticed in the midst of so many government agencies, most people were wearing badges. In contrast, not a single person I have spoken with has arrived wearing a badge," despite a number of them meeting me on their way to or from work. In speaking with me, they expressed in many subtle and explicit ways they were not speaking with me on the clock. When my study participant arrived ten minutes late, he apologized, saying, "It's not like I was going to say I had to leave to do a non-work activity."

Another HHS employee described how she interpreted federal civil servant restrictions broadly in her posting on social media. "I'll post news," she said, "but I don't ever talk about [the policy area she worked in]. Which is kind of just a rule I've always had. Like if people ask me, I'll share my thoughts. But I don't like to post about stuff just 'cause it gets weird." Civil servants' norms of professionalism seemed to extend beyond the official prohibitions of the Hatch Act, and for many of them, reinforced their adherence to notably firm boundaries between work and personal life.

Civil servants across agencies reported that they had annual ethical trainings detailing Hatch Act prohibitions and other restrictions around gift giving or family members bidding on government contracts, which are designed to prevent corruption. They also mentioned that their agencies raised awareness of the Hatch Act restrictions during elections through emails or posted fliers. Others went out of their way to attend Hatch Act and whistleblower trainings outside work in 2017 to ensure they fully understood their political restrictions.

## THE FEDERAL GOVERNMENT'S MULTIPLE REQUIRED LOYALTIES

While career employees' careful professional self-presentations and overt expressions of patriotism and loyalty may seem unconvincing to some or even a bit pat—their job is anything but that. Former federal civil servant and public administration scholar Dwight Waldo mapped the many, potentially contradictory moral and ethical commitments public servants seek to uphold in the course of their work (see figure 3.2).[28] First, he made a distinction between public and private morality and noted the "possibility of a conflict between them."[29] The public commitments he distinguished comprise the ethical bedrock of public administration: these include a duty to uphold the Constitution and the law, and a commitment to serving one's nation or country, democracy, organizational/bureaucratic norms, middle-range collectives, one's profession and professionalism, and the public interest. Beyond their ethical professional obligations or loyalties specific to public service such as their commitments to their agency missions, their professions, and their colleagues, civil servants hold other personal moral commitments and values rooted in their families, religion, and/or a commitment to humanity writ large.

Waldo depicted public servants' work not only as an inspired calling but also as a perpetual and honorable challenge to navigate competing ethical obligations with integrity in service of the democracy.[30] He acknowledged that governments engage in actions deemed immoral at an individual level in service of public interest. Thus, he concluded that those in public service, from time to time, may "of necessity," have to engage in acts like lying, cheating, or even killing. "What must be faced is that all decision and action in the public interest is inevitably morally

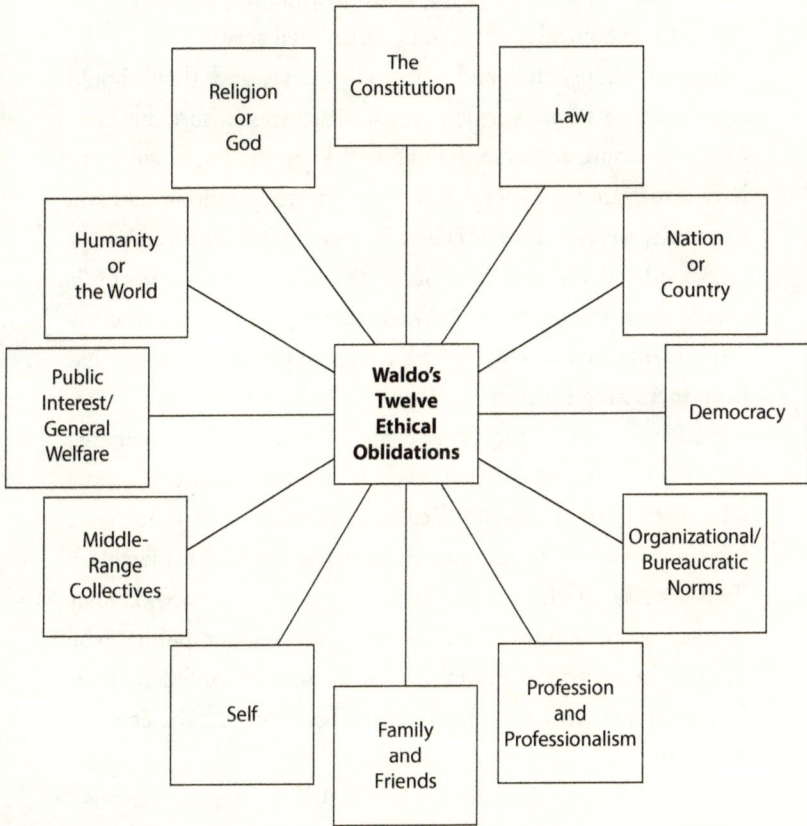

**FIGURE 3.2** Dwight Waldo's ethical obligations of public servants.

*Source*: Dwight Waldo, as cited in Rosemary O'Leary, *The Ethics of Dissent: Managing Guerilla Government*, (Washington, DC: CQ Press, 2020).

complex, and that the price of any good characteristically entails some bad," he wrote.[31]

In light of these competing ethical and moral commitments and based on his experience working in public administration and his political scholarly expertise, Waldo (2006 [1948]) argued that, rather than err on being value-neutral, dispassionate, and "almost mechanical" bureaucrats, career civil servants should be informed, thoughtful, and politically savvy, and they should actively strive to protect democratic structures, ensure due process, and ensure access to the public.[32] They should, he suggests, have a tolerance for moral ambiguity in organizational life and the ability to discern what is best in particular circumstances.[33]

An ethical obligation to serve the president specifically is absent from Waldo's model. Much research documents and my respondents have noted, however, that the president's power has been increasing for decades,[34] which likely gives rise to increasing ethical conflicts for career civil servants.[35] Political scientist Marissa Golden found that, even under the anti-bureaucratic administration of Ronald Reagan, career civil servants were largely responsive to the directives of the political leadership.[36] This loyalty to the elected president and their agenda may be seen as an outgrowth of loyalty to serving the public, who elected the president, and to serving the dictates of federal public servants' specific roles within the larger bureaucratic chain of command.

In relation to executive power, civil servants are simultaneously constrained and protected by bureaucratic rules and structures. They enjoy a measure of independence as rational technocrats.[37] In a functioning democracy, and by nature of their position, career civil servants should not only be responsive to elected leadership and society but also independent and protected enough to resist clientelist or patrimonial practices that characterize corrupt government agencies.[38] Such resistance may express loyalty to democratic governance, its laws, and the Constitution. In exercising voice and providing expert advice, career civil servants enjoy some protections from political retaliation by virtue of civil service laws while they remain subordinate to the politicals.

Federal civil servants' perceived rights have varied, however, under different presidential administrations and legislative congresses. Some elected government leaders suppress the exercise of voice and ethical dissent, while others may seek to foster open constructive dialogue across the government. During the Red Scare of the early 1950s, for example, Senator Joe McCarthy of Wisconsin stoked fear with his probes of communism and associated threats to civil servants at the Department of State, the Treasury, the White House, and the Army. Hundreds of federal civil servants were fired or marginalized.[39] President Kennedy then responded to the "stifling air of suspicion and conformity in which the loyalty oaths, security investigations and anticommunist hysteria of the previous decade had smothered the federal workforce" in his first State of the Union address to Congress on January 30, 1961, saying famously: "Let every public servant know . . . that this administration recognizes the value of dissent and daring—that we greet healthy controversy as the hallmark of healthy change. Let the public service be a proud and lively career."[40] Again, however, during the Vietnam War, amid mass antiwar protests across the country, civil servant reporting in the State Department was stifled.[41]

In the 1980s, the Reagan administration was also known for its "concentrated assault on the bureaucracy" through an administrative presidency strategy.[42] The Reagan administration sought to bring federal civil servants more firmly under the control of the executive branch through ideologically motivated political appointments, budget and personnel cuts, and increasingly centralized regulatory control in the OMB.[43] Political scientists argue that this use of executive management has become common by modern presidents.[44]

The election and administration of President Trump was distinct in its expectation of unusually high loyalty to the president.

The administration heralded another period of executive suspicion of civil servants, which raised the stakes surrounding civil servants' expressions of overt loyalty to the president and the challenges of maintaining the multiple loyalties their professional positions commanded. As the executive-led agenda sought to cut back or even eliminate their work, which they were personally and professionally devoted to, moral consonance was all but impossible for some.

Trump's antipathy for the bureaucratic state and its democratic norms and procedures forced some career civil servants began to wonder privately: what would they do if faced with competing loyalties between, say, serving the Constitution, serving the presidential administration, adhering to democratic professional norms and procedures, serving the public, and doing their job as they saw fit based on their professional expertise and work experience?

## THE POWER OF PUBLIC ADMINISTRATION CULTURE

Most career civil servants tried not to overreact to critical media reports of the Trump administration in the course of their work. Once on the job, as one former EPA employee described, employees undergo so-called cultural climatization, where they learn from supervisors and colleagues that to be a public servant means upholding the duties and norms of nonpartisanship and collaborative dialogue with supervisors and other stakeholders across the government. Decision making is grounded in collective deliberation, reason, and expert knowledge.[45] They also learn emotional forbearance and discretion. This employee described "a lot of groupthink," at the EPA. "That's part of what makes it work," she said. "You go to a lot of meetings and you're gradually, slowly trying to coalesce opinion to move in a particular . . . direction . . . And I came to realize that these interminable meetings—and there were meetings like literally all day—that was a process for sort of gradually getting everybody on the same page."

Annette Foster at the Department of Homeland Security (DHS) said that she had learned, over decades of working for the federal government, "being an executive employee in the executive branch, we kind of learn how to bend and to sway whatever happens. That's our job." She described this as a fundamental and often taken-for-granted part of being a federal civil servant. In describing this duty, she spoke as a member of the collective rather than as an individual.

Many longtime career civil servants accepted that there would be challenging times and that serving as a stable workforce through these challenges was a key part of their job. Yasin Abadi, a civil servant at the United States Agency for International Development (USAID), made the case for emotional forbearance, levelheadedness, and a long-term perspective. He said that he had been hearing "that it's the end of the world" since he joined the government more than a decade earlier. But the world does not end, he said,

> because you have enough professionals who look out for the best interests of essentially what the agency's mission is—because your client at the end of the day is not the administration, it is not Congress—these are all things that you need to deal with to provide the public service to the population, to the American public—that is your client. At the end of the day, you're just part of a big jigsaw puzzle that you have to navigate. And it's going to suck. There's years where if you were a rational—like you're getting funded to do crap that you ought not be doing, not because

it's in the best interest for the American people, but because it's excessive and it's ridiculous. But some Congressmen worked out some deals or because . . . they know it's going to provide jobs in their district.

His perspective at the outset of the Trump administration reveals how civil servants come to accept a degree of moral dissonance as part and parcel of their job and have a host of rationalizations under typical administrations to justify the importance of their continued work through it. This long-term perspective of the government contextualizes and can minimize counterproductive or even harmful short-term political developments. On one hand, such an explanation accurately portrays civil servants as an important source of stability and continuity in the federal government. On the other hand, such a perspective can serve as a dispassionate rationalizing cognitive framework. While this is fitting given his role as a rational technocrat, a number of psychologists and historians warn that under conditions of democratic decline, "euphemistic language," can be a means of rationalizing immoral actions.[46] Abadi's example was centered on fiscal responsibility rather than an example with clear human costs, which would raise even more questions about this rationalizing long-term view of government functioning.

When facing the early chaos of the Trump administration, some of the most experienced and senior civil servants affirmed core values and norms of public service for newer hires and those around them, modeling caution and forbearance in their assessments and reactions. As EPA SES member Sean Butler said at the beginning of the administration, "The most important thing we can do is show them [the new administration] our values. If we pack it in now and say we're insulted, we're hurt, we're worried and we don't do our jobs, then it's just a self-fulfilling prophecy, so let's get on it. And we did." Expressing their values and loyalties to service was a practical strategy intended to help build relationships with appointees and ensure the continued functioning of the government.

A seasoned public servant who had worked in various agencies that underwent challenging presidential transitions similarly grounded civil servants' work during presidential transitions in their values and duty to build relationships with appointees. As an example, she cited a former political administrator of an agency who many career civil servants had at first been skeptical of but then who went on to become one of the best leaders the agency had ever had. She said:

> During those times too, the civil service people are very committed and very passionate and really quite resilient about getting through these things. Our jobs are really important to us and in the case of EPA, some of these folks worked . . . their whole careers in one particular area, so it's their life work. And so, a new administration comes in and it looks jeopardized, or like a ton of change and civil service people are pretty resilient in finding common ground. And that's where we are today too. The senior civil service leaders, in times of chaos—their job is to try to find some clarity and identify common ground and then to help their employees. And in this case, there are a lot of people who have not been through a transition before, and to help mentor them and to model resilience and leadership in these chaotic times and to keep those young people from being panicked when they hear things like: "it's a skinny budget;" "we're gonna cut EPA by a third." And it's really important that leadership models resilience and patience and calm for the other folks who are probably a little more vulnerable and very nervous about what does this mean.

She, like others, remembered "coming in and watching administrations come and go. You know," she said, "it was from those senior leaders that I learned what my role was in the executive branch as far as doing the right thing and doing my job and helping to make sense out of things and learning to manage up and helping to educate others and helping to—and I think also, assuming that people have good intentions."

Other long-time senior leaders echoed the importance of mentors' calming influence. Another senior official at EPA remembered during the Reagan administration how his supervisors "provided the support and we fed off their reactions, which weren't in panic." Career civil servants took care not to appear too emotional or reactionary.

## CONCLUSION

To understand career civil servants' experiences during the Trump administration, it is crucial to understand their lengthy process of socialization into becoming federal public servants. Infusing this process is the spirit of public administration, which inspires and guides many civil servants' work, making it a deeply meaningful and purposeful calling.

Career civil servants are both selected and trained to subsume their personal and political views to the work of the agency and observe institutional norms of continuity and obedience to political leadership.[47] Federal civil service comes with varied professional ethical obligations, however, and civil servants vary in which obligations they view as most important.

Woven throughout the fabric of mid- and high-level career civil servants' sensemaking of the first Trump administration, from start to finish, were the elements of civil servant professional culture outlined in this chapter. These formed familiar touchpoints that civil servants regularly referred to for inspiration and rational grounding when facing both familiar and unusual circumstances during the Trump administration.

As I show in the chapters that follow, however, these foundational cultural and legal sources of stability would be challenged during the Trump administration. This was true particularly for career civil servants in the most politicized areas of the government.

# 4

## "TOO EARLY TO TELL"

### Rationalizing Forbearance

In response to Donald Trump's inauguration as the forty-fifth president of the United States on January 20, 2017, over 3 million people participated in the Women's March on the Capitol and across the country the following day. Some political scientists suggested at the time it was the largest march in the history of the nation.[1]

Trump's election sparked protest from people one might not expect. While social movement scholars document a long history of marginalized people challenging inequality through public protest,[2] institutional insiders may instead opt to influence institutions from within.[3] Yet Trump's disregard for propriety and women's rights, as evident in a 2005 Access Hollywood video, in which he proclaims his ability to grab women by their genitals, provoked righteous anger from a wide array of women and others in the United States. In response, millions showed their discontent at the Women's March, where many wore emblematic pink knitted "pussy hats" with their distinctive cat ears.[4]

I was similarly struck by the unusual protesters at the Science March on April 22, 2017. In my field notes of the event, I wrote:

As we walked in, it seemed to me like nerd heaven. There were all sorts of people with signs with scientific symbols on them. It had

a very different feel than other protests I've been to. It seemed like
a lot of geeky people of all ages had come. For example, we saw a
sign with a Star Wars theme, as well as a lot of signs from professional associations of all stripes. It seemed like a good number of
people had come with their kids, which ranged in age from babies
through teenagers.

The widening of public interest in protest in response to the
president had, for me and others, evoked the question of whether
government bureaucrats would join this wave of progressive
popular and professional resistance.

During the Women's March and in the weeks that followed,
teams of bureaucrats across agencies stood ready to receive the
incoming president's transition teams. Many transition teams,
however, did not show up when expected.[5] Despite changes in
protocol, which senior staff noted had made them especially
prepared for the transition in leadership, the transition was
uncharacteristically chaotic in many agencies.[6] Senior Executive
Service (SES) members across agencies were unclear about who
they should be communicating with, and they were alarmed by
the lack of interest shown by the president-elect's representatives in even the most basic information prepared for them on
what their agencies did, how they functioned, and key issues of
importance.[7]

Based largely on news reports and rumors they heard circling through their networks, many public servants told me they
thought Trump seemed like a particularly obvious sign of democratic decay that had actually begun years earlier. Some mentioned the partisan strife and deadlock in Congress dating back
to Newt Gingrich.[8] Others mentioned a heightening popular
mistrust and animus toward the federal government and its public servants or the corrosive influence of moneyed interests on
Congress and the executive branch. Still others were concerned

about the chaos, lack of clear guidance, and Trump's unusual public use of social media to communicate important messages.

In contrast to the explosion of national marches during the first year of Trump's presidency and media reports of chaos at the top levels of government, and of resistance by the so-called deep state, federal civil servants were notably measured in the early days of the first Trump administration. In the absence of clear guidance from senior leadership, they sought to maintain the norms and spirit of public administration.[9] The federal bureaucracy was a massive sea, and the Trump administration was so ill prepared and disinterested in the day-to-day workings of the bureaucracy in many parts of the government that most career civil servants simply were not (yet) affected. Given their risk-averse culture and the bureaucracy's complex structure, for most mid- and high-level career public servants I spoke to, the sensible response to the change in administration was to look around, take stock of their immediate environment and the seemingly minor changes that had occurred, and continue their typical work largely as they had always done. A common refrain among the centrist and Democrat-leaning federal bureaucrats I talked to during the first year of the presidency was that "it was too soon" to tell. Employees wanted to "wait and see" and give the new administration a chance, suggesting they were not yet ready to define their agencies as in decline, even as most agreed that the Trump administration was qualitatively different from previous administrations. As a midlevel manager at the State Department said:

> I think there was a huge paralysis at the beginning of like, oh my god, up is down and down is up now, and do we have to completely overhaul all of our foreign policy and how do we do that? Do we wait for guidance from the White House? Do we read

Twitter and see how the president is talking about the kind of foreign policy issue of the day? Do we take his campaign pledges as policy? And then the ultimate conclusion was we await directive from the White House formally and then we follow whatever that guidance is, and absent guidance, you just continue to do what you've been doing. So that had been happening and I think there was less immediate oversight in the shift than I think many people were expecting.

Like this midlevel manager, many career civil servants sought to continue patiently doing their work, maintaining political neutrality, and awaiting further guidance. Given the slow pace of Trump's political appointments, the Trump administration at first seemed like a distant influence on the work of many mid- and even some high-level career civil servants I spoke to in 2017 and through part of 2018. Many career public servants reiterated to me their steadfast faith in the resilience of the federal government and did their best to adhere to their varied professional standards at work. In response to the divisive 2016 election and the chaotic first six months of the new administration, most careerists exercised restraint in their responses as a way of demonstrating that they were adhering to their official roles and ethical obligations.

## THE LEAST AFFECTED AND MOST CAUTIOUS

About a fifth of the mid- and high-level centrist and Democrat-leaning civil servants I spoke with reported that they were not adversely affected by the administration either in or outside work during the first half of Trump's first term. Among the

seemingly unaffected by the transition to the Trump administration and the most risk-averse, some viewed the presidential transition as normal and carried on as though nothing had
really changed. Others described their work as still operating as
normal, even as they witnessed "friction" between the president,
Congress, and the judicial system. A few civil servants simply
did not seem to be interested in politics at all.

Agency location and position influenced both exposure to
changes wrought by the administration from its inception as
well as career civil servants' responses to those changes. Many
of the least affected careerists noted that they were (1) located
in less politicized agencies (such as at the National Science
Foundation [NSF], General Services Administration [GSA], or
Department of Labor [DOL]); (2) worked in niche areas of the
federal bureaucracy, which they perceived as insulated because
of the nature of their work (e.g., doing scientific or data analysis
largely on their own or working on technology); or (3) worked
in lower levels sufficiently removed from political leadership. As
one GSA employee put it in 2017, for example, working in "technology, it doesn't really matter the policy or the politics or any
of that stuff. Me writing a Python script to look at data and do
an analysis across the government is not political at all." I heard
similar perspectives from others in less affected parts of the government. A midlevel manager at NSF, for example, suggested
that "the Trump administration isn't paying that much attention
to what's happening at statistical agencies and the data."

Others at lower levels conveyed that much of appointed senior
leadership's operations and decision making were not visible to
them. A longtime employee at the National Institutes of Health
(NIH), for example, said to me: "Keep in mind I'm a foot soldier,"
she said, "so I'm not in high-level meetings." Even almost halfway
through the administration, in mid-2018, she told me, "There's

nothing atypical about it. It is another presidential transition. They are *all* different."

It is important to note that, even though I in part sampled from agencies where conflict would be likely, I still found a sizable number of employees there acting as if they were operating as "business as usual," entirely untroubled by the change in administration. Although I did encounter a few senior officials in this camp, my findings generally aligned with my expectations that lower-level civil servants in operational roles would be more insulated and thus less affected by political changes.

## COPING WITH MORAL DISSONANCE

In the face of inflammatory media coverage of Trump's unusual approach to the presidency, many career employees I spoke with emphasized their competing ethical obligations in serving the government and their requisite political neutrality in their workplaces. Senior Department of Defense (DOD) official Ralph McCafferty reflected on the Trump administration in early 2020: "I believe in my agency's mission, I believe in the government's mission, and I'm a loyal American. I can do that, and I'm educated enough and I think mature enough to realize the two paths. So I serve the president and whoever the president is, good or bad. I serve them, so I can be neutral in my role. But it does cause dissonance."

Over time, however, such cognitive dissonance can take a psychological toll. Renowned psychologist Leon Festinger argues that cognitive dissonance results from inconsistencies between one's knowledge, beliefs, and/or behavior. The mental discomfort from facing conflicting goals or goals with uncomfortably high costs can motivate a person "to reduce dissonance and achieve consonance"[10] through rationalizing "justifications."[11] Moral psychologist Philip Zimbardo warns, "People will go to remarkable lengths to bring discrepant beliefs and behavior into some kind of functional coherence."[12]

More specifically, I witnessed a large majority (approximately 80 percent) of the career civil servants I spoke with grappling with notable and sustained moral dissonance because of the Trump administration's visible autocratic and unorthodox leadership instead of demonstrable commitments to the democratic ethical bedrock of the state.[13] In particular, some faced professional moral conflict based on conflicts between their varying ethical obligations. Others faced personal moral conflict between their personal values—the "desirable, trans-situational goals which act as guiding principles in people's lives"—and contrary pressures emanating from senior leadership.[14]

A considerable number of career civil servants I spoke to privately abhorred Trump but stated that, because of Hatch Act restrictions and professional codes of political neutrality, they should not speak about their beliefs at work. Those concerned about the early Trump administration's leadership who were averse to resistance because of their jobs were particularly likely to face moral dissonance and unease regarding their own complicity in an administration weakening democratic governance.

As social scientists of cognitive dissonance suggest, people facing their own potential complicity or immoral behavior can reduce cognitive dissonance and negative portrayals of themselves through rationalizations "to convince themselves that their behavior does not violate their personal moral standards."[15] People can justify "unexpected" or "untoward" behavior deviant from moral and/or social expectations through a number of neutralization techniques that reduce dissonance. They may diminish "personal blame by attenuating its pejorative quality," distract themselves away from dissonance so it can be forgotten, deny responsibility by blaming others or denying injury, appeal to higher loyalties or self-fulfillment and thereby trivialize dissonant behaviors, or cite the necessity of "normal" behavior.[16]

On balance, in speaking with career civil servants in 2017 at the outset of the Trump administration, their mindsets in such a moment of rapid political change could instead be viewed as sensible and steadfast rather than reactionary. After all, they ethically anchored themselves by reverting to their core duties, professional values, and faith in the long-term stability of the government, in keeping with what their experienced peers and mentors suggested was appropriate.

Most federal civil servants at first minimized the risks and moral dissonance they faced with the Trump administration's new leadership style and policy agenda through a number of common rationalizations (see table 4.1), even as media coverage and political scientists emphasized the dramatic changes wrought by the administration threatening democratic decline.[17] These exceedingly cautious career civil servants fell back on professional norms of serial partisanship, political neutrality, the importance of maintaining continuity and stability, their belief in the long-term resilience of the government, and their seeming relative stability and comfort—especially compared to those in other parts of the government—to justify keeping calm and carrying on. In short, they tried to portray the government as functioning normally. They said it was too early in the administration to say otherwise. These tempered reactions aligned with their prescribed duty to be steady, nonreactionary stewards of government across presidential transitions and justified their response of treating work as business as usual.

Such rationalizations may feel more authentic and earnest under stable times, but they struck a different tenor for some

## TABLE 4.1 CIVIL SERVANTS' RATIONALIZATIONS OF THE PRESIDENTIAL ADMINISTRATION

| | |
|---|---|
| Obligation of Political Neutrality | • Affirmed their ability to support elected and appointed leadership regardless of political affiliation, as required by civil servant professionalism.<br>• Means of prioritizing professional role and avoiding partisan conflict at work. |
| All Administrations Have Transitions | • Cited "good" leaders in agency (appointed and career).<br>• Noted what had not changed or what was within the bounds of a typical transition.<br>• Means of normalizing changes and reiterating long-term stability of the government. |
| Respect for and Loyalty to the State | • Displacement of responsibility: deference to elected and appointed leaders, who have the legitimate right to make policy and budget decisions.<br>• Emphasized that duty to role and serving its higher loyalties overrode personal moral commitments in their position.<br>• Affirmed maintaining intrinsic commitments to their role.<br>• Underscored importance of stability of the state.<br>• Means of subsuming personal concerns into professional role and duties. |
| Downward Evaluations | • Identified their position as fortunate compared to others.<br>• Means of self-comfort, as well as providing hope and motivation. |

during the Trump administration, leaving telltale emotional signs that something was awry. For those who had experienced the transitions of prior administrations, these rationalizations sounded like practiced refrains. Yet I witnessed cracks in their refined professional exteriors during our interviews as the political conditions rapidly changed around them. For some, rationalizations came to seem more like an all-too-thin veneer of an excuse than an authentic and inspired professional principle. The career civil servants were largely self-aware of this dissonance, and it provoked more candid and thoughtful reflections. A good number of others I spoke with, I believe, earnestly tried to make sense of what they were experiencing during our interviews. I show throughout the book the dissonance, loss of words, inarticulate narratives, self-awareness of bounded rationality, and confusion some expressed in muddling through their answers as evidence of such inchoate and emergent cognitive processing.[18]

## Invoking Political Neutrality

Throughout the first Trump administration, career civil servants emphasized the importance of political neutrality and of not bringing their personal politics into work. Many career civil servants reported largely avoiding the topic of Trump's contentious leadership and the early changes from his administration. As an employee at the Census Bureau said in 2017, "I try not to say what my leanings are [at work]. I think most people that I work with have a similar mindset as I do and even if there are different political leanings, I think most people have similar values, so there's not really been any issues."

Especially in agencies where career civil servants reported more Republicans, such as the DOD and Department of Homeland Security (DHS), progressive and independent career civil servants reported a continued emphasis on political neutrality to maintain professionalism at work and avoid conflict during times of heightened partisan cleavages. One midlevel manager at DOD described her workplace during the presidential election as "really upsetting" because "it really seems like the majority is very right leaning" and "like we're getting our news from completely different sources." She remembered:

> I would be upset about something I couldn't even repeat that I heard on the news that Trump has said. And it was really frustrating to see people still supporting his politics and just kind of turning a blind eye or not even having heard some of the stuff, like in particular with what he said about women. . . . It was really heated and you just tried not to talk about it at work . . . because you're supposed to be apolitical and not really bring that in. You support the commander-in-chief and not bring in your party affiliation. We're not supposed to anyway. And so, it was refreshing a little bit that you didn't have to talk about it and you kind of had a good out, like when it comes up you say, "Listen we're not supposed to bring up politics at work." And I think there's even a prohibition against campaigning and using our public office that way, which was also a bit of a relief.

Not speaking about politics at work not only prevented interpersonal conflict but tamped down this civil servant's personal emotional disturbance at the president's disrespect toward women. Highlighting the importance of political neutrality also evoked her related duty to serve the president. Together, these habits and appeals to higher loyalty shifted her attention away from her discontent with the president, which came, as she said, as a cognitive and emotional "relief."

Career civil servants working in technical areas and more bipartisan or conservative agencies reported at times using sarcastic humor to deflect the political tension of the administration and, more often than not, avoiding talking about politics at work. A Democrat working at DHS described using a combination of humor and reminders that "we have to stay neutral" as ways to deal with her far-right-leaning colleague. This, she said, was not too hard for her because she described herself as politically neutral and seeing "positives on both sides," even as she acknowledged "some negatives about it personally."

## "ALL ADMINISTRATIONS HAVE TRANSITIONS"

Some career civil servants highlighted aspects of the early Trump administration that signaled a normal presidential transition. Under this perspective, a remarkably wide swath of politicals' behavior can be characterized under the umbrella of a normal partisan shift in administrations. Career civil servants tried to highlight continuity and potentially positive aspects of the Trump administration in their workplaces.

Annette Foster at DHS, for example, welcomed the Trump administration's support for enforcement in immigration and at first viewed the change in administration as "a stock transition." In contrast to news reports, she reported that in her agency, "stock Republicans" who were "long time staffers" "chosen from the Hill at the working and bottom levels" of the government were "the ones running the place." "They are doing the same thing that any administration would do for a Republican administration," she said. She assessed the Trump administration as a normal partisan shift that strengthened her ability to do her work at the beginning of the administration, although she acknowledged that "the higher you go up, you might see something different" several times.

Citing a loyalty to the law, and continuity in her work, she explained, "If you really read the immigration act, it's very strict and so I've always enforced that law . . . A lot of people who work with me are happy about that aspect, and so I spent a lot of energy and a lot of training to do the right thing and that means enforcing the immigration law, and a lot of times you can write around those policies. But I don't think anything with morality or morals and I'm the wrong person to ask because I don't care who's in an important position."

Here Foster falls back on her prescribed ethical obligation and duty to enforce the stated law in her role. This was self-affirming and served to trivialize concerns of unusual senior leadership behavior. She also grounded her account as akin to those working around her, who seemed largely content with the shift in the presidential administration. She hearkened back to a personal experience in an office she had formerly worked in, in which weaker enforcement had failed to stop an immigrant to the United States from harming many people. Just remembering this case demonstrably upset her, even years later. These rationalizations enabled her to dismiss any concerns of chaos at the top of her agency or the government as a whole during the first half of the Trump administration. Her concern would increase, however, during the second half of the administration.

Foster was not alone in acknowledging areas of continuity in the government under Trump. In an effort to give accurate and measured accounts, a number of civil servants noted some "experienced" political appointees whom they felt fortunate to work under. Even some career civil servants who raised concern about the administration's leadership at the start, such as DOD lawyer Ralph McCafferty, noted elements of normalcy around him when we spoke in 2017 and 2018. In 2018, he pointed to "fairly good" appointed leaders in his agency. He approved of Secretary of Defense James Mattis's "clear" and "good" messaging to the department. He was pleasantly surprised that, despite not getting pay raises or sufficient explanations why, around him, "morale remains high. And so when you reflect on that," he said, "you know there really is an ethos of public service, that people work for public service reasons. And that's what keeps morale high." Here again, McCafferty hearkens back to the spirit and ethic of public service as a buffer that provided meaning, which enabled some devoted public servants to continue to offer reasoned, seemingly politically neutral assessments of the new administration. It also gave them a chance to view some of the turmoil of the early Trump administration as within the bounds of "normal" and the functioning dissonance as typical of the massive state bureaucracy.

Others, such as Lewis Waters at the Office of Management and Budget (OMB), kept reiterating in 2017 the "caveat of how early we are." He said, for example, "it's easy to sprout some anecdotes to support the private narrative, [but] it's not something I could say," given his role. He cautioned, "I strongly feel it's too early to tell. But if I suggest . . . to step back, there's not a major dislocation. *All administrations have transitions* [emphasis added]. It's a messy process in general. All administrations must make the transition from campaign visions to governing. It's a turning from blue sky thinking into the realities of governing. It's easy in the first months to point out different disconnects."

Thus, Waters, like McCafferty, tries to rationalize that any "disconnects" or elements of the "messy process" of leadership transitions he witnessed in his work as being part of a normal presidential transition shifting from campaigning to governing. Waters continued rationalizing that much of his job was the same at the beginning of the Trump administration and that the administration was within the bounds of a normal transition of power: "The vast majority of what I'm doing is the same based on my job," he said. Yet even to his own ears, such rationalizations left out notable personal turmoil, which I discuss more in the pages to come.

## RATIONALIZATIONS JUSTIFYING LITTLE RESISTANCE

Some of the most risk-averse career civil servants I spoke with suggested that resistance to Trump was not an option despite concerns about the administration. In the face of critical media reports and the chaos that marked the Trump administration, career civil servants sought simultaneously to exercise forbearance and to wait on condemning new leadership in an effort to be serially partisan. They did so while not fully knowing what was actually transpiring, although they were aware that they would be open to external criticism from either colleagues or external audiences should they misstep. For civil servants working in some areas affected earlier in the administration than others, such as immigration, international affairs, or environmental protection, more rationalizations were needed to neutralize moral dissonance and choices not to speak up or resist concerning changes.

I spoke with midlevel manager at DHS Elaine DiFranco in the summer of 2017. At the time, she was working on what would shortly become a particularly politicized portfolio. She said that the administration's "radical change in the rhetoric [on immigration] . . . was super discouraging. So that's from me." This was "hard for people" she worked with "because, for the most part, those who work with the organization believe in the organization and the mission of the organization," she said.

In the face of such moral dissonance, she doubled down on the importance of executing her prescribed professional role in the government and clearly separating that from her personal beliefs and accountability. Her work faced uncertainty and cuts, but in communicating with people outside the agency, she said that "basically all of our efforts have been remaining in touch and indicating that it's also not my personal thing. We represent the government and at the end of the day we need to proceed

based on the policies and the regulations that are given or authorized. And it's tough." She thereby denies responsibility for her
actions, which is a common means of reducing dissonance.[19] It's
not her fault: she's doing her job.

Later during our interview, she reverted to a long-term perspective on serving the government with a spirit of serial partisanship and resilience as a grounding mechanism when facing
challenges at work:

> At the end of the day, we are public servants and that's something
> that I love and that I have a passion for. Regardless whether it's
> the pretty or the ugly work, someone has to do it. And I believe
> at the end of the day we need to be there to ensure that the insti-
> tutions function as they should, but you know, always thinking
> that there is a light at the end of the tunnel. And I believe in
> delivering results so you need to work, and you don't know how
> long things are going to last, and also while working with differ-
> ent administrations, you adjust.[20]

Here, as the political storm started to swirl around her, she
reverted to her intrinsic motivations that inspired her work, her
commitment to her designated role in the government and a
long-term perspective of the government. She is, as psychologists would note, appealing to higher loyalties and a positive
appraisal of her position despite the looming threat she faced in
her specific area of work, and the internal moral dissonance she
was already starting to feel.

Her example allows a double-edged analysis. In mid-2017,
it is unclear whether her sense of her situation was indeed her
being appropriately loyal to the government or an exhibit of
her complicity to a punitive regime that would incur, as some
would argue, human rights violations, for example, in separating

children from their families at the U.S. southern border. Situated in her position in the government, however, her perspective makes sense. More cynical and psychologically savvy analysts might argue that this civil servant's perspective sets the precedent for using these moral justifications later to rationalize and portray in a positive light potentially immoral behavior that further deviates from her personal and professional commitments to supporting immigrants through DHS.[21]

In 2017, another analyst at the DOL whose work was not directly affected by the presidential transition similarly rationalized his role as a positive stabilizing force in the government through an appeal to higher ideals of public servants:

> I still feel that it's important to have good people in government. I still feel it's important to have a knowledgeable bureaucracy that can push against an administration for whatever reason. And I don't mean referring to what I do specifically, but just like, you know—we're the experts—we push against any political desire, regardless of party. I mean, it could be somebody whom I'm more inclined to agree with politically that may advance an idea that I think is unviable. That's what our *duty* is and I still feel that's an important goal, even if it just happens to be Donald Trump now.

Underlying these civil servants' early responses was a view of a largely stable and resilient government in which change was a normal and constitutive part of democratic governance.

This narrative came up again and again. During the first year of the Trump administration, in response to my question on what he had learned over his years working in federal government about being an efficacious civil servant, Ralph McCafferty said:

One thing is the administrations change, but the mission of the agencies and the nature of public service actually does not change. And so we've just had a dramatic change in the presidential administrations, right? And policies that are coming down from the new administration are dramatically different than ones that were in the last administration. And yet the mission of my agency and the department itself has really not changed. And so you really have to keep an eye on that, and the simplistic notion that President Trump was elected and surely he will leave one day. And the Department of Defense and public service is larger than any particular administration. But you sort of have to have that perspective as you're working on these day-to-day issues.

A midlevel manager from HHS reiterated a related analogy he had heard from a previous secretary of his agency, which I heard from several civil servants: "The government is not a speed boat, it's a shipping liner . . . and you can't just turn around on a dime. Cargo boxes are falling off and, in the end, that's going to hurt the administration. And as an American, regardless of my political views, I would like our administration to be successful because I want my country to be successful."

Even as many career civil servants noted early problematic behavior on the part of the Trump administration, most hearkened back to and took some small comfort in this general narrative of a behemoth government that, by its very nature, was slow to change and was resilient, in no small part because of the crucial work of career public servants. Federal civil servants trusted that the government was resilient based on their previous work experience and their professional ideology extolling public service and American democracy. Such trusting perspectives in the stability of American democratic governance fail to illuminate and analyze in a sophisticated way when leaders' policy shifts breach the bounds of typical partisan swings in either their means of change or their content, which may undermine democratic functioning. Such steadfast loyalties neutralize their concerns, even as some witnessed unusually rapid and deviant leadership choices, akin to "cargo boxes falling off" the shipping liner of American government early in the first Trump administration.

Some senior leaders in more contested agencies, such as the Environmental Protection Agency (EPA), Department of Justice (DOJ), and Department of State, evinced caution because of a heightened desire to be seen as politically neutral. Those occupying public-facing and especially high-level positions, such as the SES, were particularly likely to fall in this camp. They emphasized their duty to build working relationships with elected and appointed leadership. As several mentioned, they were aware of the Trump administration's accusations that they operated as an obstructive and unresponsive deep state and actively sought to disprove such beliefs. As an EPA SES member described, "the vast majority" of EPA civil servants are "very professional, and they do understand we work for the president. We work for the administration and we are career employees and so you have to follow that direction, provided it's not illegal."

Years later, in 2023, when I shared a draft of my results with a discerning senior official at the State Department, he was more forthcoming about this dance to be seen as politically neutral, while implying his own personal loyalties were more complex and lay elsewhere. In the draft, I had written that career civil servants sought to "support" Trump appointed officials. Over email, he corrected me, saying instead that they sought to "work with" the politicals; "Using the word 'support' infers a like-minded direction, which was not the case."

Even so, various senior career officials indicated they took care during the Trump administration not to exhibit their personal or political beliefs or values. As a senior EPA official (and others) told me, "As an EPA employee," he said, he "couldn't go" to climate protests. EPA SES member Sean Butler reiterated this idea: "Protests are fine, but not by government employees. I'm not sure that that gets us anywhere. And you have to be really judicious on when to protest." He had told his employees, with respect to protest:

> You have the right to do it. It's still America. You have free speech rights, as long as it's not doing something that is contrary to law. You can have a press conference outside work time. You can't take work time to do it. You can't use work space to do it, but besides that, it's completely lawful to do.
>
> The question is, should you do it? And strategically if you did it and angered the administration, what is it that they're likely to do to our region or whatever is it that pulls their hand up like that? It's probably not the best policy to antagonize people and it's making it a self-fulfilling prophecy eventually. They kept talking about the deep state and resistance and all of that and if you're out on the streets with placards and you're protesting and doing it in the name of the environment and the EPA, then you're making the case for them.

He continued: "No matter how political, how amped-up the rhetoric that tried to vilify the bureaucracy," we, as civil servants, should "do our jobs to the absolute best of our ability, discharge it as we would under any administration, to be as good to work with as possible. Win over trust even when the other side— I don't mean to call them the other side, but that's how it turned out to be. Take the higher ground. Just because they're ignoring you doesn't mean you can ignore them." Butler is here both pragmatically strategizing based on his role as he understands it based on his years of experience and appealing to higher loyalties in justifying not resisting the looming threat of the Trump administration to his agency.

In terms of when would be an appropriate circumstance to engage in ethical dissent, he cited the example in the news at the time of Immigration and Customs Enforcement (ICE) employees separating families. "You don't have to follow an unjust instruction," he said. Having ancestors who were separated from their families during war, he told me that:

> If I were an ICE agent and I was ordered to separate families, to rip a child away from her mother, I would refuse that instruction. At whatever cost, I would not do it. And it might mean that . . . I get fired or whatever, but I wouldn't do it. Same thing in environmental. If there's some instruction that is going to lead to harm, so in other words, immediate direct, not a policy issue long-term, but you know—don't add chlorine to this disinfection tank—and there was something along those lines and I really believed that it was an unjust instruction, then I wouldn't follow it. But that's extremely rare, extremely judicious.

Here, Butler drew a personal moral line for himself in another area of governance far away from his area of work that was tied to a personal issue that had affected his family in the past.

In contrast, Butler shifted back to a more seemingly objective policy perspective: elected and appointed leaders have the right to make policy and budget decisions. He provided an example of a coal-fired power plant: "Statistics show that there are about three thousand premature deaths per year due to coal-fired power plants." Rather than take a position against coal-fired power plants, "I saw that as an election issue . . . [and] a congressional issue and to the extent that they had made those choices, I'm not free to fail to execute. It was a reasonable policy choice to say, you know what, we'll control those power plants in a different way and something that way depends on free market forces. I don't necessarily agree with it, but it's a legitimate policy choice and I respect it." Butler thus rationalized complex bureaucratic policy decisions as within the purview of leaders' decision-making power. He similarly categorized "pay cuts or FTEs [full-time employees] or budget choices" as within elected and appointed leaders' legitimate powers to decide. Protesting such decisions, he thought, would not "move the needle any. In fact, those people that are predisposed not to like government will say, 'Good, I hope it hurts them more. I'm glad to see the policies or this guy are having an actual effect. And people are protesting the FTE cuts. Great. Fantastic. I can see that I voted to reduce the size of government and it's having that effect, good for me.' . . . And the protest doesn't do any good."

Then Butler tried to explain civil servants' professional moral code:

> So my own take on it is—*civil servants remain loyal to the institution* [emphasis added]. We have a different set of obligations, and I don't think it's wise, especially the higher up you go, to protest. The other thing is it looks like we're captives of perhaps one party and that's not true either. I hate to even make it a partisan issue because it really shouldn't be. As much as possible, we *execute the law* [emphasis added], and it's not a partisan issue at all. And to the extent we don't like the policy, it's unfortunate, but elections have consequences and even if we don't like dismantling the clean power plant, if Congress tells us to do it, we do it. That's how we function as a democracy. We can't overrule another branch, and

we can't overrule the political choices that are being made. I carve out that one exception, which is, if you're asked to do something that is immoral and unethical, you have to stop it and consider it very carefully.

According to Butler's professional ethical code, if an elected leader's administration set a particular policy agenda at the institutional or organizational level, he had to comply in order to respect the democratic structure of governance and the confines of his role as a bureaucrat, even if it contrasted with his personal partisan beliefs. Should a moral conflict arise on an issue in which he had direct power over harming an individual, rooted in his family's past experience of religious persecution, he thought he had the right to intervene and contest carrying out the decision. By nature of his high-level position in the EPA, however, he was likely never to be in such a situation. When I asked if he had encountered such a situation, he confirmed that he had not faced such an immediate pressing moral quandary in his career.[22] As the Trump administration wore on, however, his perspective would change.

Some senior civil servants described their commitments to upholding the ethical requirements of their position as simply displacing personal ethics and politics. Such perspectives align with psychological rationalizations that justify bureaucrats' compliance as acting out of necessity based on their specific roles, which demand responsiveness to appointed leaders, even if they privately worry such actions may be inappropriate or detrimental. They also view such responsiveness as aligning with their desire to serve loyally in their designated role as appropriate and necessary in a democratic republic to maintain it as such.

SES members frequently discussed their obligations to be responsive to appointed leaders, even though they were aware there were costs of such expressed loyalty. DOD lawyer Ralph McCafferty said, "When it's in law, appointees or the deep state people, the people like me . . . would be charged with implementing that and I would be charged with advising them [political appointees] on how to do it, and it would come down, *and we would just have to do it. Just like many other things that come down which are unpalatable but we have to do it. Morale will suffer* [emphasis added]."

McCafferty believed that federal employees sacrificed their autonomous values and political rights and had to endure resulting dips in morale while working to support intolerable appointed leadership's guidance. Like many respondents, he described the Hatch Act as having "fairly broad prohibitions . . . which discourages any type of political act from federal employees. So I can't run for office and federal employees tend to be quite restricted in what they can do politically, which is why you don't see a lot of them working on political campaigns. I don't do anything except drink beer." McCafferty's perspective reveals that some career civil servants view it as part and parcel of the job to execute political appointees' agendas, even if they find it abhorrent.

While this is an important component of serial partisanship during normal transitions of presidential administrations in a functioning democracy, this can set the stage for further degradation of the government under an autocratic president. Psychologists describe the rationalization of blaming abhorrent orders from above rather than taking responsibility for them as a displacement of responsibility.[23] Stanley Milgram's famous 1974 shock experiments showed how this can occur and how easy it is for people to displace responsibility for their actions, blaming decisions made by those in authority. One might presume that in the federal bureaucracy, where professional norms and duties command obedience to elected and appointed leaders, there is even more of a predilection to obey than in isolated experiments.[24]

As career civil servants watched the arrival of the Trump administration with concern, McCafferty voiced a common rationalization I heard from many people in relatively unaffected and affected positions in the government alike: that it was worse elsewhere. During our first interview, he reflected:

> The Trump administration has said that they're going to cut federal employee retirement benefits and there's been talk of reducing furloughing and getting rid of people. So it could impact me personally, but in a larger sense it also impacts me and my federal employee colleagues because they've talked about vastly reshaping some federal agencies. Cutting some, building some others up and I think at a scale that we haven't seen in modern history, and so although sitting here doing this interview I haven't really felt much impact, probably because I work for the Department of Defense which is not under much fire, I think there is going to be dramatic changes in the next year or two.

McCafferty acknowledged that, despite the differences the media described and that he perceived between the administrations of Barack Obama and Trump, "all of them are interested in a strong defense. All of them are interested in the military being protected. All of them are interested in providing strong defense to citizens and beyond the rhetoric of the news media, all of them are interested in the country doing well." The notable presidential support of DOD, he believed, made his agency more stable and able to execute its core mission with continuity under the Trump administration compared to other more politicized agencies.

Various federal employees at agencies such as the Department of Energy (DOE), the Department of the Treasury (USDT), the

DOL, and the Department of Commerce (DOC) noted that their everyday work had not changed. Many of these people watched developments in other areas of the government with concern, but they felt their agencies were less at risk of disruption than others. They urged me instead to speak with people in other agencies reported in the media as having problems, such as in the EPA, DOJ, and the State Department.

Psychologists Shelley Taylor and Marci Lorbel suggest that, in groups under threat, it is common for people to compare themselves with less fortunate others via "downward evaluations," while seeking information from and affiliating themselves with "more fortunate others (upward contacts)."[25] They explain these processes as serving different needs: downward comparison contributes to one's self-esteem, while information and affiliation with those in better positions can provide hope and motivation. However, such rationalizations can ameliorate underlying concerns only to a limited extent. As many civil servants pondered their work deeply in interviews, they shifted from their steely exteriors to more private ruminations and selves. At this point, they expressed lingering concerns and dormant political passions as particularly knowledgeable private citizens. McCafferty advised me to ask others what they would do if they could be more politically involved. Had the law allowed, he said that he "would write letters. I would do an op-ed piece in the *Washington Post*. I might volunteer for a political campaign . . . I might go to a rally. I might be more politically active instead of just sitting at home and drinking beer."[26] Even though McCafferty expressed concerns about the Trump administration and desired to be more politically engaged, he did not consider quitting, in part because of the high costs of exit. As someone nearing retirement, he wanted to stay to get promised benefits.

For risk-averse career civil servants such as McCafferty and Butler, legal strictures, professional norms of nonpartisanship, and their duties to build relationships with political appointees provided them with effective tools that rationalized compliance and little civic and political engagement. It is possible that McCafferty felt more restricted because of the norms at his particular agency, the DOD; some civil servants suggested that certain agencies interpreted ethical constraints more rigidly than others and used DOD as a case in point. But McCafferty's restrictive understanding of the legal and normative strictures operating on federal employees was echoed by many respondents. Their inaction did little, however, to quell what they relegated to personal concerns about Trump administration leadership.

Federal civil servants used a lot of common rationalizations that dampened and justified their limited political engagement. A consequence of the many legal and normative restrictions on federal civil servants' partisan political engagement in and outside work was that some of the most informed political minds in the country were unwilling to raise alarm bells, either internally or externally, when they witnessed troubling and sometimes illegal behavior by appointed leaders.

## CONCLUSION

In the beginning of the first Trump administration, amid critical media reports of its leadership, the centrist and Democrat-leaning career civil servants I spoke with were largely personally disturbed, but they wanted to avoid letting their personal feelings affect their day-to-day work or their ability to build relationships with political appointees. Those with little leadership turnover around them and those working in less politicized areas reported feeling far less affected and being able to continue doing their jobs largely as before.

The civil servants experiencing moral dissonance working under a president disrupting democratic ethical obligations and other professional norms tried to steady themselves by rooting themselves in the ethical bedrock of federal service. They cited their professional ethical obligations and rationalized calm, patient responses rooted in their professional culture, as they had been trained to do and had been reinforced over years of service. Many of these elements neutralized a sense of risk and rationalized responsiveness at work in the face of aberrant and potentially harmful leadership behavior.

While these parts of the professional culture of public servants are crucial to a functioning democracy in normal times, under more autocratic leadership, they may enable or even hasten the weakening of democracy. Common rationalizations could be used to override career civil servants' personal consciences that would ordinarily alert them that conditions were indeed abnormal. Such risk-averse and neutralizing rationalizations and norms failed to prepare the most affected civil servants for an administration with such patent disregard for institutional checks and balances and the law.

Those unable to paper over personal or professional concerns about politicals' ethically aberrant behavior with sufficient rationalizations were left with what some saw as an unattractive, but possibly necessary, last resort: leaving federal service. This too could cede power to the new administration.

# 5

## SPLIT LIVES AND
## EXTERNAL ENGAGEMENT

U nderneath their polished professional exteriors, most of
the mid- and high-level federal civil servants I met were
personally disturbed by the rhetoric of Donald Trump's
first campaign and administration.[1] Not a single person felt personally loyal to Trump and his agenda. Their professional roles,
however, took precedence. Every career civil servant I spoke with
conscientiously limited their civic and political engagement in
and outside work in some way to uphold professional ethical
obligations and duties. Even when federal civil servants cared
deeply about certain political issues, most treaded carefully.

Some compartmentalized their lives, with sharp divisions
splitting their personal and professional lives, and selves, as a
means of avoiding moral dissonance and conflict. Among those
with split lives, some took comfort in their family or other hob-
bies and pursuits on their own time, such as advanced education.
Others turned to acts of self-care or personal indulgence, such as
drinking more wine or beer.

About a third of those I spoke with engaged in substantial
civic activity during the first Trump administration outside
work. Some attended marches, rallies, and protests during the
administration as a means of expressing personal values and

concerns. A subset of these did so with excitement and zeal as a means of channeling pent-up frustration about political developments and sharing such grievances publicly alongside friends. Others attended protests with divided minds and hearts, wanting to attend personally or being compelled to do so by friends, while remaining concerned about possible repercussions at work. Another subgroup preferred aiding schools, raising environmental awareness, and engaging in other nonpartisan political activities as a means of community involvement. Nearly all those who engaged in civic and political activities took care to distinguish such acts as expressions of personal opinion that were separate from their work and within the bounds of the Hatch Act.

## SPLIT LIVES

About a third of the civil servants I spoke with exhibited notable splits between their professional and personal time as a means of coping with their sometimes divergent ethical and personal moral codes. These career civil servants displayed very different parts of themselves based on where they were and whether they were occupying their professional roles or not.

Several people exhibited stark changes when the interview setting changed across or within interviews. Some unleashed how they really felt when our interview had officially ended or during follow-up interviews over the phone. For example, one lawyer I spoke with in a coffee shop, with an audio recorder running, displayed a hardened and careful professional way of speaking, evincing little emotion. When the coffee shop closed in the middle of the interview, we went outside to speak at a table nearby. There he asked to turn off the audio recorder, and his demeanor changed entirely. He burst forth, letting out a stream of coarse language and pent-up feelings.

Some experienced split lives in different ways as the administration wore on. A Department of Labor (DOL) analyst described in 2018, for example, that he was feeling "better as an employee . . . these guys aren't as threatening or destructive as I previously feared they were." Although his experience at work was less affected than he had feared, he said, "I feel bad as a concerned voter because everything—like I just hate—I dislike everything they stand for and everything they do and what's happening to this country and the direction we're going in. But," he clarified, "that's separate. I mean, like the whole point of a bureaucracy is that my political views aren't specific to my work," and they don't affect his work, he said.

In his private time, this analyst attended protests. Such demonstrations could help reduce the sense that he wasn't doing enough in the face of moral dissonance. But he was careful that his protest attendance was within the bounds allowed under the Hatch Act. He would not discuss such events at work and was careful about what he posted on social media. He explained that on social media, "it's hard for that information to come out about me that I'm a government employee. I deliberately make that . . . hard to find . . . I think every government employee should be very careful about how they say things." He then said, "You are hardwired into your brain that you can't say things as a government employee" such as your opinions on appointee choices. Should he comment on the appointed leader of his agency, "I would rightly be fired . . . and I make a point of never saying those things now."

Among those risk-averse civil servants who had little civic or political engagement, many actively cultivated personal interests unrelated to politics or their jobs, which they suggested helped them cope with stress and/or moral dissonance. Some described volunteering at museums, blogging, doing yoga, exercising, participating in their religious community, and spending time with friends and family because they were personally meaningful. Others suggested such activities helped them cope with increased stress at work and national politics. By 2018, one career civil servant had even written a novel, which expressed some frustrations he had experienced at work in a completely different, unrelated outlet. Several people, such as Ralph McCafferty (who was introduced in chapter 3), mentioned an uptick in their drinking in 2017 and 2018 as a personal, albeit unhealthy, means of coping with stress at work.

Psychologists may look to personal fragmentation and the compartmentalization of one's professional and private lives as a social-psychological coping mechanism. It can also be a foundation that can support harmful behavior under authoritarian and autocratic regimes.[2] Executors of the Holocaust consoled themselves with the belief that they submitted to the regime "'only' in their outward behavior" while remaining "masters of their consciences, faithful to themselves in their private lives."[3] Psychologist Jo-Ann Tsang explains this personal fragmentation and compartmentalization with self-affirmation theory: by emphasizing that personal parts of themselves were good, such as that they were loving husbands or parents, Nazi doctors affirmed to themselves that their global selves were indeed good.[4] While these examples are quite different from working under the Trump administration, I witnessed some similar kinds of psychological coping mechanisms at play among some of the career civil servants I spoke with who wrestled with moral dissonance.

There was only so much rationalizing that some civil servants could do, however, to minimize dissonance and assuage their own concerns to themselves. Amid lingering personal moral quandaries, the cracks began to emerge in many civil servants' seemingly polished, professional presentations of self. As we talked, their concerns bubbled to the surface, sometimes in response to my direct questions and sometimes unprompted.

For Office of Management and Budget (OMB) manager Lewis Waters, moral dissonance between his professional role and personal values simmered beneath the surface, despite his best efforts to disregard it. During our first conversation (described in chapter 3), he tried to present himself in an exceedingly professional manner, but the more we spoke, the more apparent it became that his formal narratives were falling short under the leadership of the Trump administration. Peppered throughout our interviews were his apologies for being "cautious," and his self-awareness that his answers might seem scripted or inauthentic. He told me he was not intentionally holding back anything.

Well into our first interview, when I asked Waters directly how he was personally responding to the transition to the Trump administration, his demeanor changed dramatically. "From my personal perspective, it is profoundly different from anything we as a country have experienced. I have concern, but it's early," he said. He reiterated the continuity and normalcy of some of his day-to-day work: "The particular mission and types of analysis we do—for both we are doing the same things we always do. I am overseen by the appointee. He is a very reasonable person." Yet he admitted to struggling with "the meta-question of how it all fits in the bigger picture. I have to be careful with ideas. In thinking about it, imagine serving in the military in a war you don't support, but you have a competent, fair commander of your unit. You carry out your work with pride, and you're trying to carry it out. Yet, overall, there is the balance of the situation. There are the questions about work with ties to the bigger picture."

He then opted to complete our interview in the privacy of his own home by phone. When I picked up the interview where we had left off, this time on the phone, he remarked, "This is going to go into the feelings area." With that shift, he said, he was "personally extremely uncomfortable with the policies of this administration and the people leading this administration. I know these are not uncommon in the area I work in. Those are not informed by my job. That is coloring my thinking." He confided he was being "candid" and was "very out of sync with this administration." He had experienced "a discontinuity or rupture in that I went from being really happy with my work and proud of it to—that is straight up because of my politics, not because of how I'm being treated as an employee. I am struggling to separate my political filter from my job. When it all shakes out, I'm going to have to leave because of this. It's important to me as a person that I am working for something I believe in. There's a ton to be written about this: how federal employees are struggling. And I don't say this without regret."

Despite the fact that his boss, his team, and the content of his job remained largely the same, he remained morally fraught, oscillating between rationalizations of the positive and stable aspects of his job and his underlying concern. "I do believe in the U.S. government and I don't believe everything this administration does will be evil . . . [But] I'm nauseated by what is going on." Acknowledging his frequent communication with the White House, he said, "I need to find something else." He then tried to rationalize: "I'm not building concentration camps." He continued by acknowledging other elements of his job he loved, "like writing and policy analysis . . . It's a skill set I've honed over time and I enjoy that creative/analytic process. Our agency attracts good people and I've had multiyear relationships and friendships with colleagues. After having been there

so long, my work is a rewarding social and professional experience." Although Waters firmly believed in the important "ethos"
and mission of his agency to provide nonpartisan support,
enjoyed his work, and appreciated his colleagues, in the end, he
concluded loyalty to those things was not a "sufficient thing" for
him under the Trump administration, even though it seemed to
be "enough for most of my colleagues." In speaking with him, it
seemed that all the rationalizations and benefits of his job were
insufficient in soothing his conscience. Telltale emotions of discomfort and disgust signaled that something consequential was
awry with the presidential administration and that it breached
his personal values. This moral dissonance pushed him to consider changing his behavior by heading for the exits. (He no longer works in federal service.)

## TEMPERED RESISTANCE OFF THE CLOCK: PROTESTERS AND COMMUNITY VOLUNTEERS

Many career civil servants had rich lives outside work, where
they released the pent-up concerns and frustrations in the public sphere. Those attending protests and involved in local politics interpreted the Hatch Act precisely: they attended protests
during the first Trump administration on their own time and/or
became involved in local politics or nonpartisan political activity,
such as voter registration. During the first several years of the
Trump administration, most of the people I spoke with attended
at least one mass protest, such as the Women's March, the Science
March, and March for Our Lives. They nearly always described
attending such protests as "separate" from their work. A DOL
employee explained his attendance this way: "I'm just going as a

concerned citizen. I'm very aware of the Hatch Act and what's considered an acceptable political activity and what's not . . . For me, it just so happened that I'm just concerned about the climate . . . But I see that as separate [from my job]." When I asked if attending protests would be frowned upon by his colleagues or supervisor, he said, "It's not their business," reasserting a divide between his public and private lives. Others said during the summer of 2017 that they supported women's rights by attending the Women's March, or LGBTQIA+ rights by participating in the Pride March, and that these issues were more related to their personal identities than their jobs.

While many civil servants put some distance between their daily work and their protest attendance in 2017, some sensed that this distinction might collapse in the future. When pressed, some people suggested that, although the marches were not related to their jobs or were "nonpolitical" in that they did not have "a partisan approach," the issues they supported at marches had "become politicized." A U.S. Department of Agriculture (USDA) employee who attended the Science March said that, while science had never seemed political to him in the past, in the current political climate, "if you say you believe in science, you can then associate politics to that." During the summer of 2017, other employees had a sense of foreboding about what was to come. A Veterans Affairs (VA) employee noted, "As of yet," attending marches was "not connected to my job . . . but it's connected to things I feel passionately about," but in the future, Trump's ideological stances might affect his work.

Civil servants' positions and agencies had palpable influence on their activism outside work. Senior Executive Service (SES) members and lawyers who worked with more Republicans and political appointees at the Environmental Protection Agency (EPA), Department of Homeland Security (DHS), Department of Defense (DOD), and some parts of the Department of Justice (DOJ) tended to be more careful and restrictive in their political engagement than many other civil servants. In contrast, some lower-level employees seemed more comfortable attending protests by virtue of their lack of professional visibility, regardless of their agency. One lower-level DOD manager said that she felt comfortable attending protests "because I didn't have a highly visible position." She did not recall being "explicitly educated on specifically what I could or could not do as a federal employee," "still went to protests," and "did a lot of stuff at the local level on a volunteer basis."

Some protesters cited how agency guidance permitted attending such events. For example, an employee at the U.S. Department of Treasury (USDT) said that he attended marches with colleagues and friends in 2017:

> In [Washington,] DC, you still feel like you have a critical mass. We outnumber them in DC. I mean, this is like a 94 percent Democratic town. So I think that's people's outlet . . . something like marches, Facebook, social media . . . people find a lot of relief in things like that. This place really throbs when there are marches occurring; everybody goes to those. All types of federal employees. We did receive instruction earlier on about marches when Trump first came, when people were particularly upset. Our ethics office told us that, 'You can go to marches. Don't worry about it,' and I've not received any pressure not to do something like that. You know, they don't really have the level of organization to really care about those kinds of things.

For this civil servant, attending protests in the early years of the Trump administration was, as he said, a "relief" to those like him who were concerned and experienced moral dissonance working for the administration. At protests, they could be part of a lively and vocal group standing up for their personal and political beliefs during a time of historic mass protests in the United States.

Career civil servants across agencies seemed to get caught up with the enthusiasm for mass gatherings at the time. They reported attending the most protests during the first half of the Trump administration. Some midlevel and senior staff were uncomfortable attending these acts of resistance at first, but they became more comfortable as their sense of urgency grew under the administration and as people they knew attended protests. Despite her initial caution about protests in 2017, by 2018, a Department of Health and Human Services (HHS) employee said: "I've done a ton of protests because I feel it's too important. And I know I'm not violating the Hatch Act because I do it on my personal time. I'm really careful."

Attendance by family and friends contributed to many civil servants' participation in protests, marches, and rallies during the first Trump administration. Some of the more and less risk-averse civil servants alike reported attending protests thanks to the influence of friends. Others cited wanting to set an example or to take a stand for their children. A number of protest attendees living in Washington, DC, noted the ease of doing so during the beginning and middle of the administration because of the proximity of many events. It seemed protest attendance waned during 2019 and the first half of 2020, when I conducted my final interviews, based on the reports of those civil servants with whom I spoke.[5]

Most of the civil servants I spoke with navigated the boundaries between their job and protest participation with caution and noted how attending could, in some cases, give rise to further moral dissonance. As another HHS employee recounted, at the Women's March in 2017, "I ran into one of my staff and took a picture with her and her pink hat and everything. And it was like okay, we took this picture, we know that we were both here, but we can't ever talk about this at work. And just that tension of that has been really difficult." She also encountered a reporter she had worked with at the march. This was especially difficult for her. "For a long time, I felt like your face is the one thing you can't really hide, and so I felt really nervous about going to protests." She was not alone. Others civil servants I spoke with said that they did not attend protests or rallies because they were concerned about seeing colleagues or having their photo taken.

At the EPA, an agency that faced significant budget cuts, had an administrator with seemingly little regard for the agency's mission, and had a risk-averse technocratic scientific culture, civil servants' moral tensions and differences of opinion with respect to attending protests were particularly evident.

In 2017, EPA staffers in regional offices across the country were covered in the *New York Times*, *Washington Post*, *Boston Globe*, *Chicago Tribune*, and other media outlets for their early protests, which were supported by their union. They spoke out against the nomination of appointed administrator Scott Pruitt, the Trump administration's proposed budget cuts, and the proposed shift in policy agenda from environmental and human protection to supporting business interests.[6] Such protests were subject to some consternation from top career civil servants, as expressed by SES member Sean Butler (see chapter 4). With respect to the outburst of protests, Butler acknowledged that, despite his pleas for forbearance and for building relationships with the Trump appointees, "at the end of the day, it's their decision to do—and some people would not be dissuaded. They did have the press conferences. They did go to newspapers and try and get those stories." He said, "That all happened at the staff level, way, way below us. And not one of the high-level career people took part in any of that."

He noted how the fact that the EPA had a union was consequential. He described the union as "very active" and "very antagonistic" in holding "protest rallies and so on." As a manager, the union involvement was difficult he said, because "we were bound by law not to interfere. We could ask them to consider their tactics and ask them if it's calculated for success, or are they gonna give up on somebody that's gonna crack down on us or abolish us. They didn't take that in their calculus."

EPA staff who attended protests described their participation in notably emotionally muted ways, trying to align their actions with their professional loyalties. They reiterated the common refrain that nonpartisan and serial partisan norms were an important part of public service. For example, Gail Hailwood, a former EPA employee working to preserve the EPA from outside it in 2017, said:

> In the past, whether it was Democrat or Republican, you knew the emphasis would shift. That's just part of it and part of what you get used to in the EPA. We were trained and I think we still are to stay in the middle . . . One of the challenges for those who are outside and trying to help mount a resistance to what's going on, [is] it's not in EPA people's DNA to be activists. We get accused of that all the time, but we're not because . . . our charge was to take all opinions into account and administrations come in and they sway back and forth, but there's still a core mission that they wouldn't veer that far from for the most part.

I contacted Rhonda, an EPA employee, after she was referenced in the national media for attending a union-organized EPA protest against Trump's budget cuts in 2017. She insisted that she and her colleagues were not activists. "We have a union . . . [but] I could never remember the number," she said, and "a lot of us aren't real kind of rah-rah people." Even though there were signs that this administration was "an order of magnitude worse" than others, Rhonda wanted to continue her work and try to have a positive impact. Despite the 31 percent cut the Trump administration sought at the EPA, she reasoned, "Often the president's budget will even have a sacrificial element to it because they'll be confident that Congress will negotiate back in. So it's just like a political position . . . So I've tried to keep people calm that this is not a political death wish. Let's just keep showing results. I think it's too early to have a real culture shift."

This metered response was learned through the dominant culture of federal civil servants and deeply intertwined with career bureaucrats' ethical obligations.[7] "I try to make it clear that I'm neutral and just trying to share information in services of the truth," Rhonda said. Upon reflection, she said, "I almost welcome a little bit of a shift to the Republican perspective. I grew up with sensible Republicans. My father was one of them and he said to realize that you have to prune and then you blossom and then you prune again and so it's just natural for human systems to get a little disorganized." Rhonda was not alone in demonstrating her political centrism and openness to working with colleagues and political appointees from both sides of the political aisle.

Unlike the career employees working in Ronald Reagan's administration, who were studied by Marissa M. Golden, I found no evidence of bureaucrats lining up decisively behind the new president or his agenda.[8] Instead, I discerned their unease about complicity amid the deterioration of various agencies across many levels. When directly questioned about the contradictions in her concerns about the Trump administration's impact and her cautious commitment to being nonpartisan at work, Rhonda fretted that she "could be asleep at the wheel" and like the proverbial "frog in boiling water"—that her ability to keep calm might be masking a "disaster" in the making.

I spoke with a number of EPA SES members at length over the years of the first Trump administration, and it was apparent that they also felt compelled to be more civically and politically engaged. These desires seemed to increase among some EPA SES members over the years of the Trump administration in comparison to some lower-level staffers, whose concerns somewhat diminished as the administration wore on and they became more accustomed to it. As one lower-level regional staffer I spoke with in the fall of 2018 noted, at his office, it was "actually not nearly as bad as we were all worried about a year ago. I mean it's definitely not our glory years, but things seemed a lot scarier than they actually turned out to be. I mean there's still plenty of time for that to change and for things to really hit the fan. But in my experience, I found the bark a little worse than the bite."

By contrast, EPA SES member Sean Butler acknowledged near the end of the administration that "it's hard, especially in this environment, not to engage in any sort of political activities." By 2020, he had written some issue-based letters to members of Congress, had attended a March for Science rally, and posted "every now and then about environmental matters" on Facebook. "But on national political things," he said, "it doesn't sit well with me. It's difficult to keep views to yourself in this climate. I'd say we try to do as much as possible, and we do a pretty admirable job of it." Had he not been an SES member and an EPA employee, "then certainly I would be doing a lot more," he said. "I'd want to campaign for candidates." He said that he might "run for office . . . Some folks have resigned from EPA and are running for office and doing pretty well." He would also "consider working on the Hill."

This civic and political inclination was shared by other EPA SES members. In speaking with one recent retiree in 2020, he noted that he "always got frustrated" when his wife attended demonstrations, and he wanted to go, but he "didn't feel it was my role to be in a demonstration. I could, but I didn't want to do that to stain my position." In retirement, he looked forward to the ability to be engage more freely, as he wished.

A number of civil servants at the EPA and other agencies described focusing on local community issues, which they understood as being within the constraints of the Hatch Act. As one former EPA employee told me: "I have always been an activist on some level, on local issues, not so much on EPA issues, and I've never been involved in partisan issues, which is still the case for a lot of EPA people today. We always took the Hatch Act very seriously." Another EPA SES member said in 2020 that his political activity was limited "because of the position" so he was engaged "only really at the local level." He likes engaging in local "nonpartisan municipal elections," in which his involvement was not restricted. He said that he enjoyed meeting the candidates and taking part in the process.

Another lawyer at a regional office who was "offended by" Trump and felt "stifled," as if she was not allowed to discuss or act openly on her private political inclinations because of Hatch Act restrictions, reported volunteering, but "not for political causes," and donating money. Such engagement could in part neutralize some moral dissonance about working for an administration she had concerns about, but it was safely within the purview of what she thought the Hatch Act allowed. Due to the Hatch Act, others reported opting not to participate in political activities at all.

## CONCLUSION

The early years of the first Trump administration were perceived by many federal civil servants as an unmoored time when they lacked clear direction, heard unsettling accounts of the administration from mass media and other public servants, and tried to await further direction at work patiently and calmly. Among these people, however, some remained unsettled by news and social media reports of the Trump administration's behavior. After work, they could release pent-up frustration through discussions about political uncertainties with friends or attending one of the many mass protests that occurred during the first Trump administration.

Others, including some directly affected by a chaotic transition of power, felt the need to continue presenting the markers of civil servants' revered culture of serial partisanship and political neutrality, even as they personally experienced doubts and quite serious concerns about the functioning of the American democratic experiment. Some faced potentially consequential cuts and policy shifts that could undermine their agency missions. Many of these people reported experiencing sustained moral dissonance and moral conflict between their professional obligations and personal values and politics, but they felt uncomfortable with any public displays of resistance. Instead, they turned their focus after work to acts of self-care, creative outlets, their families, and sometimes supporting local communities.

# III

# ORGANIZATIONAL DAMAGE FROM LEADERSHIP VACUUMS

# 6

## APPOINTEES' MISTRUST

Senior Executive Service (SES) members at the Environmental Protection Agency (EPA) noticed unusual behavior among the members of Donald Trump's transition team and appointed senior leadership from the start.[1] Like in other politicized parts of the government, the first Trump administration arrived ready to do battle rather than ready to build relationships with career staff. Sean Butler, an experienced senior official at an EPA regional office reported that, despite their "extensive preparations" for the Trump administration, when it arrived, it was "different" than any other administration: "None of us have ever seen a situation like what we have this time," he told me in 2018. "The first is, in contrast to other transitions . . . For a long time, . . . there was no team appointed. And then when there was a team, it was called the beachhead team and that was like, 'Take the beachhead': It's like a warfare analogy, which was . . . a very strange analogy for a transition of power. And then when they did appoint those people, they didn't seem very much interested in getting briefed. There were a number of false starts," he said.

In EPA headquarters, another senior official reported that it was "remarkable" the transition team and Administrator Scott

Pruitt "didn't really care about the stuff we prepared for them." EPA officials had prepared detailed information on how the agency functions, briefings on important environmental problems and health hazards, press announcements, internal messages, lists of suggested meetings, and other crucial knowledge to help new leadership get started. Instead, the administrator and transition team "had their own ideas . . . This team did not really want to sit down for briefings and they pretty much already had their agenda—which struck us as a little bit off." The new agenda intended to cut the agency to a third of its size and roll back or stop the enforcement of many environmental regulations.

The transition team had already called off multiple meetings when they "finally" arrived at Butler's office. "There was a team of people that were sort of thrown together," and "they were deeply suspicious of how we told them it was in the past." They were led by "a real far right ideologue" who was "very opposed to all the things that were happening with climate change in the last administration."

The transition team leader stayed for "literally five minutes" and said he had to leave for another obligation, Butler reported. When Butler tried to raise some "urgent" environmental health risks, they instead tried to bring the conversation back to "climate change . . . and not the nuts and bolts of what we do every day," despite the fact that "there are fifteen thousand [people] at EPA roughly, [and] maybe three or four that did things related to [the] Paris Accords." Butler said that the appointee "didn't really care about any of the other matters that we were briefing on." Butler tried to pique the transition team leader's interest: "You need to know certain things going forward," the SES member remembered telling the transition team, but their leader just stood up and excused himself.

"So, in our experience, that was completely unique," Butler said. He found this early meeting "disappointing," and "not in accord with what we pride ourselves on, which is the orderly transition of power, which is a hallmark of American democracy."

In a more typical administration, members of the transition team "wind up in the administration and there's continuity." But this time, Butler explained, "They all left or were fired, and the new team didn't read our briefing book. They weren't interested in that." The one person who was hired in the administration was fired shortly after. He suggested to Butler that "the new team wasn't interested in following the rule of law, so he was not interested in working with them." All of this, Butler repeatedly said, "was very different than any other administration change that we've ever had."

The behavior and mindsets of Trump appointees created structural holes, which stood in stark contrast to what most SES members expected: based on their past experiences, they expected good-faith appointees seeking to build bridging ties to run the administrative state effectively by drawing on its vast resources.[2] Instead, Trump appointees seemed to weaken connections and sow distrust across the presidential administration and career staff deliberately. These weakened ties and communications gaps allowed each respective camp to attend to their own priorities and activities and to maintain quite different professional cultures on each side of the hole. In and through the Trump administration, a culture of loyalty to a president seeking unitary authority became paramount, and it began to spread. Ethical obligations to anything else became viewed as suspect, especially if it got in the way of the administration's agendas.

What mindsets and behaviors distinguished Trump leadership from prior administrations? I depict the distinctive leadership mindsets and behaviors of the Trump administration, as reported to me by civil servants, in table 6.1.

### TABLE 6.1 POLITICAL LEADERSHIP'S MINDSETS AND BEHAVIOR IN AN AUTOCRATIC TURN

1. Suspicion and sidelining of career employees.
2. Retaliatory threats and behaviors (firing, demotion, or isolation) against those perceived as against the administration.
3. Expectations of loyalty to the president above all else.
4. Disregard for democratic and institutional values, norms, and laws.

Political scientists may recognize that other modern anti-bureaucratic administrative presidencies in the United States and abroad have used some of these leadership approaches.[3] What distinguished the Trump presidency was the autocratic tendencies of the president and some of his highest-ranking administrators, who held unusually high expectations of loyalty to the president and inclinations to reward allies. During the first Trump presidency, these toxic conditions worked in tandem with a high degree of chaos because of infighting among appointed leadership, poor communication across levels, and incompetence (discussed in more detail in chapter 8), which unmoored and destabilized parts of the government and made it all but impossible for some career civil servants to do their jobs effectively.

## SUSPICION AND SIDELINING OF CAREER EMPLOYEES

One of the defining features of the Trump administration noted by those in the most politicized agencies was its suspicion of career bureaucrats. President Trump signaled to workers and the public his disregard for bureaucrats and continued commitment to his campaign pledge to "drain the swamp" throughout his first presidential term.[4] He enacted several executive orders weakening civil servant protections, including advising managers to fire employees who were underperforming or had committed misconduct; limiting employee grace periods for improvement; and creating a new Schedule F category for high-level career civil servants, such as lawyers and scientists doing policy work, with weaker protections so they would be easier to fire.[5] While it is in the best interest of the government to retain only employees who properly do their job, Trump appointees have alluded repeatedly to their underlying—and I think overstated—fear that these senior career civil servants were widely resisting and obstructing the administration's orders, to justify the implementation of Schedule F.[6] Trump also took executive action to weaken federal unions by reducing the time federal employees were paid for union work, limiting the window for negotiating union contracts to less than a year, and charging unions for their use of space in federal buildings. He repeatedly tried to cut federal civil servants' retirement and health benefits as well.[7]

In some agencies, such as those managing international affairs and the environment, Trump appointees' suspicion of employees created particularly toxic work environments, especially for public servants who viewed themselves as responsive, nonpartisan professionals. An international affairs expert reported that at his agency, "they're treating the staff as hostile."[8] Another civil servant working in international affairs reported working under an appointee with an "enemies list," and a third said that he was criticized on a list published by *Breitbart News*, a far-right outlet. Steve Bannon, a chief strategist and senior counselor to the president during his first year in office, served as executive chair at *Breitbart News* prior to and following his seven-month stint in the White House. A fourth employee at the State Department told me in 2018 about how "some of those people around [Rex] Tillerson were fucking nasty." He angrily remembered a senior adviser saying "things on the record like 'oh, well, of course, they're opposing; they're just these government employees.'" This employee felt like they "don't understand anything we do" and was upset by the "bullshit" they were "rolling out . . . It was just like such condescension from these people and hostility."

An SES member in the EPA Washington, DC, office said it was as if there was "a secret playbook" that explained to appointees "how to run your agency: don't listen to the people that are there." Despite offering a lot of advice at first, Administrator Pruitt brought in his own chief of staff, and the SES member reported that the latter "took over" career civil servants' normal duties. "And slowly," she reported, "we felt like he didn't really want any of our advice."

EPA SES member Butler similarly remembered that, in his regional office at the start of the administration, "they held their cards really close to the vest. Usually at high levels, the new administration works with the bureaucracy, and they tell you, 'Hey, sorry we're not doing this; we're doing that,' and we salute . . . And we would have saluted, but they really didn't trust the bureaucracy and wanted to keep us from knowing everything that was going on . . . I don't think that's too strong, that really was the case."

A deeper divide emerged between senior EPA leadership and civil servants because of Pruitt's obsession with security. He had new locks put on his office door and broke a long-standing tradition of administrators sharing their calendars by blocking his calendar from career staff. When Pruitt finally came to visit one regional office (much later than is typically the case), he arrived "with a huge army of guards, and had to be driven in . . . the building in a car with cars all around," a senior official told me. This struck the official as "really weird." Pruitt "had to be very carefully protected as he walked through the office, and he would only go to certain areas" of the building. His visit was designed to avoid most staff members, who were not even aware he was in the building, which was also unusual.

In another annual meeting with senior career officials, Pruitt displayed his distrust among the three hundred or so career SES members by mandating "extremely tight security," in which "everyone had to have a clean check-in." An attendee reflected, "I don't know why he was so concerned with being with us . . . these were the career SESes. I don't know what he had to fear from them." Pruitt seemed "incredibly paranoid" to senior career officials.

An EPA SES member in the Capitol reported another notable difference in Trump politicals' management: some leadership seemed to be unusually focused outside their agencies rather than inside them. At the end of summer 2017, he said, for example:

> The administrator of EPA who's really the only official leadership person at the agency, he is almost never at EPA. He has *never* [emphasis by the speaker] visited the regional office. He has *never* visited other EPA field offices. He does not spend time in EPA in Washington meeting with people there. He's entirely focused on the outside world and going around and making speeches and things, and that's really new for us . . . They're not at all focused on the workforce at their agencies, and it really seems like they're almost acting as a *separate government* [emphasis by the speaker], so that the EPA administrator and his group of political advisors are just trying to function as a separate EPA without making connections to the fifteen thousand people who work at EPA, and it's a really weird experience.

As an administrator, Pruitt did not meet with EPA SES members as much as was typical. And when he did, it seemed to them that he put little effort into such meetings. A third SES member at headquarters in Washington, DC, described their building as having "a powerful palace guard . . . the doors were locked," and "you had to make an appointment because really very few career people were even invited to meetings with the administrator." Even though they previously "had a weekly meeting which the administrator used to preside [over] just to see everybody at least once a week and have some interaction," Pruitt "just skipped them almost all the time. He'd go to the White House and have lunch at the White House mess. His style isolated himself from the agency. It was almost like it was a place for him to have an office to run a political campaign, not a place where he integrated with the agency. It's like there was no desire to develop relationships."

I heard similar reports from career civil servants in other parts of the government. One career civil servant at the General Services Administration (GSA), which various employees described as being a more politically neutral agency, said in 2018 the following about the appointee above him: she kept "her circles very small" and controlled and closed off "the communication that's going to her and . . . that's going upwards."

Another career civil servant at the Department of the Treasury (USDT) repeated similar ideas in 2018: "The secretary does not meet with any career staff, and that's unusual. So the secretary only meets with his politicals. So that really cuts the secretary off from institutional knowledge and analysis by career staff," which, he said, was "mirroring many of the problems in the White House. There are no in-depth, balanced, informed viewpoints being presented to the top leadership." This style of leadership, he said, "feels very different . . . certainly we're less integrated in the policy-making decisions."

At the State Department, a midlevel manager reported similar observations:

> Secretary Tillerson . . . was very disengaged . . . I mean the press basically got it right: he did not really convene meetings; he did not engage with the building; he would leave memos unanswered for like months and months and months and so we hadn't been able to get any real guidance out of him on the topics. There's a process where we send up a memo and ask for his sort of decision—it's called an Action Memo—and then the process is the Secretary would have it for a couple days and would return it and say like, "yes, I agree with this approach," or "no, I don't," or "get me more information," and . . . with him that we didn't hear back on so that meant we just kind of continued to implement the existing policy.

Another senior official at the State Department, who took much more care to express his obligation to serve the administration's agenda, affirmed this report on the state of their agency under Tillerson's leadership. "Tillerson," he said, "was a very weak secretary" who "basically did very little." Underlying the lack of communication across levels, he explained how Tillerson and his administrative team "forced" out a group of "senior career, mostly Foreign Service" officers, most of whom worked in the Washington, DC, office. He continued:

> And so they lost a whole upper echelon of very smart and very committed diplomats and very seasoned [people] who could have been excellent advisoes and really contributed to helping the political appointees navigate foreign affairs and diplomacy. But they were all dismissed and not seen as important, and I think that really sent a very clear signal to people like myself, that in fact career people were not valued, and, you know, we'll put up with you, we'll allow you to do your jobs, but . . . we know what to do, we don't really need you.

Such distance and intent contributed to a detrimental lack of trust between appointees and career civil servants. This State Department official described his colleagues as "guarded" against such leadership. There was a lack of trust in the integrity of the administration's aims as well. As one USDT analyst told me in 2017, although he had worried that the newly appointed administrator of his agency would ask his office to lie about the statistics underlying a policy they championed, he instead found they "were not consulted," even though his office's "full purpose is to advise the White House" on the associated policy. And rather than get statistics they did not like, "the response" of appointed administrators was "to just not ask us," he said.

News reports confirmed the perception among civil servants that the Trump administration was actively sidelining them. Another career employee from USDT reported the following in 2017:

> Just a lack of understanding or a contempt for the normal political process of interagency vetting, which I think they just probably don't understand or they don't care about. Things like executive orders that come out and involve multiple agencies like DOJ [Department of Justice], Immigration [Immigration and Customs Enforcement (ICE)], Commerce [Department of Commerce (DOC)], et cetera, that have not been run through the attorneys at those agencies, that they learn about them on the news—while you can't really execute on those proposals if you don't have, if they're unconstitutional, for instance. So that's the type of thing that would take months under . . . [Barack] Obama's administration for an agency-wide or a government-wide interagency vetting process for something like an executive order just gets—goes on in the middle of the night with like four people drafting it. And I think it's just intended to—it's a political document. It's intended to appease political supporters, but it has no legal validity.

A shift to a state within a state of loyalists, sidelining the technocratic experts, and disregarding typical political decision-making
processes are all hallmarks of autocratic governance, as political
scientists of democratic backsliding note.[9]

It seemed like Trump appointees' weak relationships with
career civil servants were not the result of a lack of effort on the
part of the latter. Most civil servants I spoke with extolled building relationships with appointed leaders, emphasizing that serial
partisanship and giving the administration a chance were part of
the core of what they did as civil servants. One high-level EPA
SES member said:

> I mean we weren't secretive at all. Not career people. We always
> invited—we never met without the political—well we did, but
> not by choice, we had already invited them. I think we were also
> very sensitive to the charge that we might be subverting or doing
> something contrary to their wishes, so we were always above
> board. My own personal take on things was I probably over-
> communicated because I never wanted to be open to the charge
> that, even in the absence of policy direction, . . . I decided to do
> something for myself on my own. So I would send emails fre-
> quently that said, "Hey, FYI [for your information], I'm intend-
> ing to do this unless I hear otherwise from you, this is my plan
> of action." . . . I always wanted to give them the opportunity to
> weigh in even if they didn't . . . And I know the others [in his
> position] did the same thing.

Leaving career civil servants out of decision making may have
seemed expeditious to some members of the Trump administration. Reports from career civil servants in some particularly
politicized agencies suggest that, under leaders who were more
interested in building relationships with the White House
and external stakeholders, some of their agencies were at best

neglected and at worst sidelined deliberately. Although some appointees did not seem to care if career civil servants did not like or trust them, it led to other negative consequences.[10]

Career civil servants reluctant to disparage their workplaces instead showed their unease working under escalating suspicion from appointed leaders in other ways. Two employees working at the Office of Management and Budget (OMB) and Department of Homeland Security (DHS), for example, called me in a panic after I contacted them on their personal emails, through which we had previously corresponded. A mutual acquaintance of the OMB employee later told me that, in their efforts to find leakers, leadership at the White House had collected employees' phones, searching for apps that encrypted messages.

A high-level Department of Health and Human Services (HHS) employee, who was heading to the exits in 2017, explained: "It's not that I'm saying anything I'm not allowed to say, it's that the culture has turned into saying anything is punishable." To the Trump administration, even the definition of "leaking" had changed. A leak is typically described as a government insider's anonymous disclosure of confidential information to the media, which, according to law, policy, or convention, should not be divulged outside a formal process.[11] Instead, the HHS employee reported, "they call things leaks that are not leaks." She described how people in her office were suspected of "leaking," even when advocates were aware of "a fact that changed on a public website . . . I think advocates are looking at all the sites to see what's changing on a regular basis, so the fact that something has changed doesn't mean there's a leak. And even if I called all these advocacy groups and said. 'Look, there's all these changes—that's still not a leak because it's public.'" Suspicion about leaking led some legal experts to suggest that the president and his administration were using the specter of leaks, which pundits and some civil servants I spoke with suggested were actually coming from some members of the administration, as a "pretense . . . to engage in political retaliation."[12]

## RETALIATORY THREATS AND BEHAVIORS

Suspicion of civil servants sometimes escalated into threats or even full-blown retaliation against those who the administration believed were getting in the way of the presidential agenda or who worked in policy areas championed by the Obama administration.[13] In other cases, the reasons were seemingly arbitrary. Media reports, rumors, and direct knowledge of such punishments further quieted already cautious civil servants, limiting options for them to express discontent or dissent.

When we first spoke in the summer of 2017, international affairs manager Yasin Abadi appeared unconcerned by the change in administration. One year later, his tune had changed. Recent news reports about the sudden departure of a respected senior-level administrator at the United States Agency for International Development (USAID) had rocked him. "Not only have they failed to build trusting relationships, they've actively undermined those by the punitive action they've taken against us, that would be considered arbitrary," he said.

Given the secretive nature of the political appointees in his agency, Abadi was relying heavily on media and reports from colleagues at the time. He pointed me to a BuzzFeed news article: "Here's What Happened to a USAID Official Who Ran Afoul of Mike Pence,"[14] the headline read. This article reported that respected USAID acting assistant administrator of the Middle East Bureau Maria Longi had "quietly . . . resigned from her position" and taken a job as an adjunct professor at the National

War College. Why? Republican Representative Chris Smith of New Jersey and Ronald Reagan's controversial national security adviser Robert McFarlane had criticized USAID civil servants in a *Wall Street Journal* column for ignoring Pence's promise to provide direct aid to Iraqi Christians.[15] The article said that they were thereby thwarting the "intent of the Trump administration," and someone had to be held accountable.[16] Even though the former administrator had not opposed Pence's office nor been the primary person managing the contentious issue at hand, she had been "removed from her position," and "reassigned" to an inferior position while remaining on USAID's payroll.[17] Along with other career bureaucrats in his agency, Abadi saw this administrator's "reassignment" as part of a "shocking" recent trend that contrasted with career civil servants' views of themselves as nonpartisan and protected from such political retribution:

> Removing somebody from their position because the vice president's office or anybody at that level didn't like a decision that was made is almost unheard of, especially about something that's *so* [emphasis by the speaker] gray . . . Honestly it looks like an acquisition decision that wasn't liked by certain interest groups that essentially petitioned the president's office for a reaction. And so they found someone to punish. And that obviously had a very chilling effect on everyone. And if they're going to go after people and they're going to remove people from their positions because of using their best discretion, their best judgment about how to do their jobs, that's terrifying . . . There has [*sic*] been other instances of things like that happening: people being asked to go onto detail comes to mind as something that has happened recently, which is just unheard of. You don't shift people around that way because you don't like the way that they're doing their job.

For employees working under some Trump appointees, the risks of a misstep were real. Several career employees I spoke with were moved to jobs far afield from their area of expertise, considerably below their demonstrated skillsets and abilities, or to locations far from Washington, DC. Director of policy analysis at the Department of Interior (DOI) Joel Clement, who worked on climate adaption in public lands in the Arctic, for example, was reassigned to an office specializing in auditing and dispensing revenue from fossil fuel royalties. Those who were reassigned suspected political retribution because they worked on projects favored under the Obama administration.

Such tactics were not necessarily new in federal service: previous administrations, such as Ronald Reagan's and George W. Bush's, had also reassigned civil servants who worked on policies or projects believed to counter their political agenda. These comparisons suggest that, while many career civil servants saw Trump as an outlier due to his autocratic bent, he was also part of a much longer trajectory of presidents exercising growing executive power.

The high degree of suspicion of career employees, the high expectations of loyalty to the president and his appointees, and the threat of political retribution combined, however, to foster particularly fearful work environments in some parts of the government. Civil servants' fear of retribution in these parts of the government was palpable. Several civil servants warned me that their participation in my study could lead to their dismissal. Others repeatedly asked questions about confidentiality and nondisclosure of certain parts of their identity, and a few began to avoid me as the temperature turned up in their employment locations.[18]

As the administration progressed, I increasingly heard reports of seeming political retribution from career civil servants as well as from popular media reports. For example, the media extensively covered the intimidation campaign and political retribution that key witness Army Lieutenant Colonel Alexander Vindman faced prior to and following his testimony during President Trump's impeachment inquiry.[19] President Trump fired Vindman from his role as senior Ukraine expert on the National Security Council (NSC).[20] As Vindman's attorney David Pressman put it: "The President of the United States attempted to force LTC Vindman to choose: Between adhering to the law or pleasing a President. Between honoring his oath or protecting his career. Between protecting his promotion or the promotion of his fellow soldiers." He suggested that Vindman "did what the law compelled him to do; and for that he was bullied by the President and his proxies."[21]

## EXPECTATIONS OF LOYALTY TO THE PRESIDENT ABOVE ALL ELSE

Under these conditions, loyalty came to have a new meaning in some offices and agencies. Career civil servants across federal agencies described unusually high standards of loyalty expected by some political appointees in their agencies. All signs pointed to the culture set at the top. The Trump administration received a lot of attention in the press and among some political pundits and civil servants for hiring and firing based on political loyalty to the president rather than professional experience or competence.[22] Federal Bureau of Investigation (FBI) Director James Comey's experiences with Trump in the first half of 2017, for example, were a harbinger of what was to come. As he told friends, who reported to the *New York Times*, Trump directly questioned whether Comey would pledge his loyalty to him over a private dinner only a week after his election.

Comey declined, telling Trump that he would always be honest with him, but he was not "reliable" in the conventional political sense. Later in the dinner, Trump again told Comey that he needed his loyalty. In keeping with the cultural and ethics of public service, Comey said he would give "honesty" and did not pledge his loyalty. Trump pressed him on whether it would be "honest loyalty." "You will have that," Comey reported responding.[23] Although the term likely meant different things to each party, it served as a short-lived compromise. Comey was unceremoniously fired by Trump via a tweet months later. In his autobiography, Comey compared Trump's leadership to that of mob bosses, exacting loyalty oaths, as part of "a warped code of loyalty" in groups marked by allegiance to the boss, lies, secrecy, a "silent circle of assent," and an "us-versus-them" worldview.[24]

In alignment with Comey's report, others I spoke with, such as an employee at USDT, noted that the Trump administration was unusual in hiring based on "loyalty tests." During the administration, the Treasury employee said that "everyone needs to be vetted either through our secretary or through Trump's White House and have their social media brought to light, their past *WSJ* [*Wall Street Journal*] opinion pieces, any other publications they have to their name, looking for potentially negative or even not positive discussion of Trump," which he suggested "has really limited the pool."

Experts in international affairs were particularly likely to identify President Trump's emphasis on personal loyalty above all else—a key feature of an autocrat—as problematic, especially given their considerable knowledge about different kinds of political regimes globally. No one, however, used the term "autocrat." Instead, they pinpointed leadership patterns common under autocratic leaders. One person, for example, described Trump's administration as very "transactional" and "narrow in terms of the approach that it's taking. It seems to be very much driven by the whim of the president, not by any coherent policy-making process." Other civil servants working in international affairs connected developments in their areas of work to, as one noted, "the embrace of a dictator impulse." Another expert in international affairs said:

> There's a real fear that foreign policy has become a political weapon of the president and that of a small circle of advisers around him . . . And so there's like this lack of faith that the institutions are making clear-headed decisions that are in the national interest and instead are becoming tools and weapons of the president, and that decision making is being concentrated and that laws are being tested, if not outright broken. So yeah, that's I think the fear, as these are all authoritarian tendencies and impulses and they continue. They're not being curbed effectively.

Through media and firsthand accounts, career civil servants saw Trump and his appointees advocating for their private economic and political interests above public and national interests. One particularly egregious example referenced by several international affairs experts I spoke with was how the Trump administration withheld crucial State Department–approved funding of military support that Ukraine needed to protect itself from Russia in 2019 based on its own domestic political motives. As House impeachment documents and other reports publicly revealed, representatives of the Trump administration informally and improperly pressured the newly elected Ukrainian president Volodymyr Zelenskyy to investigate into Ukraine's alleged support of Hillary Clinton during the 2016 election and into profitable business ties beginning in 2014 between Joe Biden's son, Hunter, and a company in Ukraine.[25] Trump himself personally asked for such favors on his call with President Zelenskyy on July 25, 2019. The incident resulted in the first impeachment of President Trump, which ultimately failed to remove him from office.[26]

Many career civil servants, especially those working in international affairs, worried that Trump's example signaled to other leaders and civil servants throughout the bureaucracy that standard ethical obligations were unimportant. In 2020, Department of State employee Steve Marsh voiced concern about Russian influence on the Republican Party and viewed some Republican senators as "spineless" and "afraid of mean tweets from the administration." He supposed that "the corruption is not limited to Trump and his immediate cronies." He noted in comparison that some longtime public servants, like acting ambassador to Ukraine Bill Taylor, had been "the ones who testified" during the impeachment hearings and were "willing to push back," unlike newer "political appointees or White House offices." Taylor, he said, "argued it was crazy" to withhold "military assistance to Ukraine . . . and he testified to that. And other career Foreign Service people," Marsh said, "stood up and testified under oath, . . . [and they] tried their best to inform the policy process."

"But," Marsh concluded, "if you're dealing with a corrupt administration that is operating with an entirely different agenda than advancing U.S. interests, it's kind of hard then for your arguments aimed at advancing U.S. interest to win the day because those aren't the interests that the administration seems to be interested in advancing, you know, to be quite honest about it." Such public examples of the inefficacy of career civil servants' testimonies of Trump appointees' flagrantly corrupt behavior concerned and demoralized a number of career civil servants following the impeachment hearings in 2019 and 2020.

These public "spectacles," as they were called by DHS lawyer Annette Foster, revealed to some career civil servants that key democratic checks on the president were not operating properly. By 2020, Foster worried that Trump constituted an autocratic threat to the American government that the Founding Fathers had feared: foreign interference. Trump tried to extort the Ukrainian government's leaders to interfere in a U.S. election, and then he did everything in his power to obfuscate and obstruct investigations into his misconduct. To withhold witnesses or documents in the impeachment trial and "not cooperate—was a spectacle," Foster said. The fact that "nothing happened—that opens the door in the future. A president can say, 'I'm not giving you anything.'" She noted, "There has been a shift in the late last century giving power to the president. After the impeachment, I see this as 'power to the president plus.' Congress couldn't even get witnesses in the trial. There were no documents. It was very partisan." She cited the underlying structure as "a problem. Senators want reelection. They said he did something wrong but not impeachable." This is "how we bring foreign countries into our elections," she said.

By prioritizing loyalty to himself above all else—and repeatedly demonstrating that he could get away with it—President Trump set the tone for those working in the executive branch and beyond. Some appointees serving the president adopted the same priorities, which civil servants both observed firsthand and heard about in the media. Senior career civil servants working in international affairs noted how appointed leaders' approaches were in step with those of the president. As one SES member confided in 2020, even though he thought Secretary of State Michael Pompeo at times "says the right things," he believed that Pompeo had a quicksilver leadership style within their agency that fostered mistrust.[27] He said that Pompeo:

talks about honor and integrity and, you know, people being accountable, but then he's clearly not been very transparent about some of the things he's been doing for the president, and he has tried to prevent people from testifying even though some State Department people did testify in the impeachment hearings. And he continues to behave in a way that suggests he tried to help with a cover-up of wrongdoing. And that does not instill a whole lot of confidence among rank-and-file people in the State Department. He is not seen as somebody who is really standing up for the institution. He's really standing up for, you know, trying to aid and abet the president to engage in activities that are, that would appear to be counter to U.S. interests, if not outright criminal activity. How's that to be blunt about it?

The discrepancy in moral codes between Trump, some of his appointees, and some visible allies in Congress, who seemed to be demonstrating loyalty to the president above all else, and career civil servants who were devoted to carefully weighing their varying ethical obligations to the state points to the underlying cultural clash between an administration careening toward authoritarianism and career civil servants seeking to uphold the integrity of the democratic state.

## DISREGARD FOR DEMOCRATIC AND INSTITUTIONAL VALUES, NORMS, AND LAWS

Career civil servants admired leaders who were stewards of the democratic state. In their eyes, such leaders upheld agency missions, modeled professionalism, listened to technocratic subject matter experts, employed properly documented collective decision-making processes, and sought to serve the American public dispassionately. Yet Trump and many in his administration held antagonistic views toward the bureaucracy's size, technocracy, and powers. As a regulatory expert described, the Trump administration was "trying to undermine every agency." Based on his work experiences, he thought the Trump administration was "far more odious" and "malicious" than other administrations. He described their strategy as follows:

> One, you rob the agencies of the ability to actually do anything that it's [*sic*] supposed to be doing. Second, you fill each one with an administrator or a secretary that is known, at least as politely as possible, to be biased against those very agencies . . . You put Rick Perry in charge of the agency he literally said he would dismantle if he [Trump] became president. Or Rex Tillerson, whose company was fined for violating the same sanctions that he and the State Department would have been in charge of . . . enforcing. You have EPA, Scott Pruitt. Everyone, basically Betsy DeVos in [the Department of Education . . . She doesn't even believe in the mission. If they don't believe in the mission, you can forgive that if they're trying, they're not aware—but no, they're actively trying to oppose it.

Across these agencies, and more, including USDT, HHS, the Department of Housing and Urban Development (HUD), DHS, DOJ, and the Federal Emergency Management Agency (FEMA), career civil servants reported dissonance between appointed leaders' agendas and their professional values, norms, and standard operating procedures. For example, employees at the EPA mentioned conflicts around EPA leadership prioritizing private business interests and politicians' supporters over preserving human health and environment, which were codified

APPOINTEES' MISTRUST • 133

in the agency's mission. They also noted the presidential administration's substantial proposed cuts to EPA programs and personnel. Some early interview-based analysis of changes at the EPA in particular forewarned that, under the Trump administration, the EPA faced the greatest risk of regulatory capture—in which regulation is directed "toward the interest of the regulated industry" and away from public interests by the "intent and action" of such industries—in the agency's history.[28]

The list of the aggrieved continues. Civil and human rights lawyers and experts described working under leaders who were not advocating for protection of such rights. International affairs experts described political appointees advocating strategies contrary to expert approaches to diplomacy, the promotion of democracy around the world, and U.S. interests. An employee at HUD described department administrator Ben Carson and his leadership team as seeking to alter the wording of the agency's mission by removing reference to "safe, sanitary," and "fair housing" conditions. While some argued that these were merely policy shifts, which are legitimate alterations by an executive, career civil servants described how some of these changes cut against some of the basic structures (e.g., agency missions) and functions of the government.

As one SES member at the EPA described, one of his most important priorities, which aligned with the mission of his agency, was to protect human health. Under past administrations, he said, "I've never doubted other administrations' commitment," to such ends. "Person to person you can make a connection and they say, 'Oh yeah. There's a Venn diagram and that's well within the Venn diagram of the things we both care about.'" By contrast, under the Trump administration, he said, "There was just no one home. The people that they appointed for the beachhead team were single issue and they just would not tune in."

The regulatory expert referenced above went on to discuss how harmful the president's stand against regulatory power and its expansion was through Executive Order 13771, which was enacted on January 30, 2017, to limit the creation of new regulations. This order, he said, was one of the "surreptitious ways the administration has undermined the public interest," which he thought "most people don't understand." In a state that has faced increasingly complex problems and risks to its citizens,[29] the executive order mandated "for every one new regulation issued, at least two prior regulations be identified for elimination."[30] The order also stipulated for the fiscal year 2017 that "no rules can have costs," he explained, and that for each year thereafter, costs must be more strictly regulated.

This nearly completely stymied those in his position from doing their jobs. Under normal conditions, "you could have costs as long as you have benefits to offset them, right? [But] now, by saying you can't have any costs, you're essentially discounting the benefits to society. So even if I cost anybody a dollar but I save or I have benefits of a billion dollars, that will no longer pass this administration because it has a cost." By his estimation, after Trump's executive order, the government could no longer "regulate or operate in areas where there's any costs, *even if there's a huge societal benefit* [emphasis by the speaker]. To me that is either lazy, irresponsible or is poor public service.". To this expert, this defied the fundamental purpose of "the federal government, which is supposed to be active as serving the public."

Others discussed how the president and some political appointees in his administration seemed to disregard democratic values and norms tied to the underlying professional spirit of public administration. One longtime member of the State Department described the "extraordinary" conditions in his agency under the Trump administration:

I've worked under both Republican and Democratic administrations, but, you know, usually it's clear that a new administration will come in with different priorities, and a different emphasis on things, but for the most part, the thrust of U.S. foreign policy has generally followed a pretty predictable path. We want to promote democracy. We want to promote transparency, rule of law. We want to promote more free and open trading systems and things that will, you know, boost the export of U.S. goods and services. We want to promote sustainability because environmental problems tend to create or contribute to or aggravate underlying social and economic problems. So those are the kinds of things that I think the U.S. government for many years has been working to advance. This administration has come in and has basically disregarded the overall imperative that we have to promote democracy, and to promote transparency.

His account depicts the chasms between the political appointees at the Department of State and the career civil servants with regard to their views on democratic norms.[31]

Although some of these changes could be viewed as legitimate partisan shifts, a considerable number of civil servants described them as outside the ordinary and problematic in terms of forcing them to choose between doing their job properly or serving the agenda of the president. These civil servants felt that their professional assessments, technocratic expertise, prescribed duties, and dedication to serving the public simply no longer mattered.

## CONCLUSION

Was the first Trump administration distinct from other presidencies? When it came to leadership mindsets, many of the mid- and high-level career civil servants I spoke with suggested it was. Appointees' suspicion, sidelining, and threatening of career civil servants—which no doubt was modeled after the president himself—not only instilled mistrust and fear but also created structural holes. These gaps in communication, trust, and relationships formed a precarious foundation for the administration across the administrative state.[32] The divide between the presidential administration and career civil servants was all the worse because of the president's emphasis on loyalty to himself above all else and his administration's seeming disregard for democratic and institutional values and laws; this sharply contrasted with the spirit of public administration and career civil servants' commitments to upholding the Constitution as fellow stewards of the state.

The cultural and structural crevasses between some members of the Trump administration, whose leadership styles seemed to stem from the president himself, and career civil servants' ethical code led to loyalty traps for senior career officials and other perplexing binds for those below them. I will share civil servants' reports of their struggles under such leadership in the chapters to come.

# 7

## LOYALTY TRAPS

With Donald Trump's appointees suspicion of career civil servants and unusually high expectations of loyalty to the president and his administration, workplace culture morphed. The lines between truth and untruth and laws and their transgressions all blurred. Best practices in particularly politicized locations were also undermined. Senior career civil servants working in such locations were the canaries in the coal mine, although they concealed a good deal of what they experienced from those who were working below and alongside them.[1]

Public administration scholars have long acknowledged the moral challenge of working as senior executives. Public administration scholar Stephen Bailey described the moral side of this work as "above the timberline," which Dwight Waldo later explained as signifying "the severe moral climate in which the high executive must operate and the dangers to which he is exposed."[2] American businessman and public administrator Chester Barnard acknowledged the hazards of moral breakdown in such positions and suggested that leaders need "moral creativeness" in the face of the challenges before them.[3]

Under the first Trump administration's most distrustful appointees, even following normal protocols became a harrowing ethical process, ridden with political complexities and second-guessing. For example, Environmental Protection Agency (EPA) Senior Executive Service (SES) member Adele Sullivan received questionable expenditure requests from political appointees, in an agency where the administrator eventually resigned likely in part because of ethical violations.[4] While "mission critical," requests could be approved in an expedited manner, she told me, her agency administrator used this exception to gain approval for requests that did not seem critical, such as "to attend a publicity event with the president." Yet when she raised questions, she said that "we were told, 'Well, the administrator decides what's mission critical, you don't get to decide . . . and he thinks it's mission critical. So sign the authorization.'"

Incidents like these occurred frequently, she reported, while working under the Trump appointees in her agency. With "that kind of thing, you're like, 'Well I could push back more or I could sign it,'" she said. "And it's like every day there's something like that, and you just can't make a career defining decision every day."

"So what did you do?" I asked.

"Mostly we held our nose and signed it," she said. "We kept records. And then on occasion we would ask the general counsel to review something. But we were given a little bit of push-back for frivolously raising ethics questions . . . it wasn't too long before they just . . . took away some of my authorities as a senior official and let somebody else sign the stuff. Remarkable."

"I think whenever you raised a question in this environment you were thought to be leaking as well. It just didn't make any sense. If I wanted to get people in trouble, I'd just leak it. I wouldn't tell them that I have a concern and give them advice and then leak it. But I think if you were raising concerns, it was

LOYALTY TRAPS • 139

seen as leaking." In this environment, she said, "Loyalty is to not question."

This senior official faced an intractable loyalty trap, a situation where what was being asked by appointees to demonstrate loyalty to the president and administration conflicted with her ethical obligations as she understood them. Should she express blind loyalty to a political appointee disregarding the bureaucratic rules, or should she remain loyal to the structure of the government and the duties of her role? At what point should she raise these "inconvenient" questions about EPA administrator Scott Pruitt's breaches in conduct, especially when they were happening so frequently? Those who raised too many questions inevitably found themselves increasingly excluded from decision making and even from participating in the normal functions of the agency. By doing their work as they had always done, they were suddenly viewed by the appointed executives as disloyal, pesky, and obstructionist. As a result, suspicious Trump appointees took their responsibilities away.

Such episodes signaled to other career civil servants that chain of command and ties to the presidential administration superseded professional and democratic ethics, organizational structures and norms, and perhaps even the law under these Trump appointees' leadership. Although Pruitt resigned from the EPA for his excessive spending habits and conflicts of interest, the suspicion and even contempt for members of the professional civil service remained common across many federal agencies. This tone was set at the very top of the administration.[5]

Career civil servants working in such conditions may know the right thing to do in their role based on their professional and/or personal moral code, but they may feel they do not have the power or efficacy to execute it from their position. They may feel especially disempowered when leaders enact political retribution, fail to include them in decision-making processes, or take away their powers if they ask questions. Those just beneath the political fray are also left with intractable professional binds, navigating loyalty to an administration with explicit aims to undercut bureaucratic processes, agency missions, professional norms and values, democratic ideals, and at times the rule of law.

For some career civil servants, the administration's leadership made their work difficult, if not impossible, to carry out appropriately. Prior to the Trump administration, Ines Blackburn had thrived in federal service. She was well educated, with a master's degree from a top university. Upon entering her agency, she had quickly gained the trust of senior career and appointed leadership, and had also worked well with top officials in the White House. She reported having trusting supervisors and the "full support of my work from the full chain of command" during that time.

Under the first Trump administration, her agency started disengaging from international multilateral organizations. Blackburn thought this was "dangerous," believing it was "very easy to break things, but it's a lot harder to build different systems and structures" of the state. She was concerned by the loss of support for "human rights and open societies" as well. However, being loyal and doing her duty was important to her. "I followed the direction of my job," she said. "What I'm hired for is to follow up directives of the president and the Secretary of State. And that was a real official directive, and we followed it."[6]

Yet following orders and the rules became especially difficult for Blackburn in 2018. At the time, she was working "nonstop, every day" under a vindictive, "truly dysfunctional," ideologically driven political appointee. "The things that I've been most concerned and frustrated by are that there is potentially illegal activity going on, and there's been no action taken to date by the senior leadership" of her agency to hold appointed senior leaders accountable, she said.

Another challenge Blackburn faced was that her politically appointed supervisor had "no respect or interest in following a process" in decision making, "so it creates really uninformed outcomes where he's just making the decision, but he doesn't know anything about this topic. So," she concluded, "that's been a big frustration and a big concern of the career people that have been working on [the topic]."

In the face of such leadership incompetence and disregard for standard operating procedures, decision making became all the more difficult because Blackburn never quite knew whether orders were "guidance from the White House" or were merely "his [the political's] own personal preference on policy." She said, "He'll often use this term, 'Oh, the White House, the White House,' but never will tell us who it is. [He] never will be specific about what they're asking for or advising us on, so I think he's manipulating us to say, 'Well, I'm the one that has contacts at the White House: this is what they're saying.'"

The stakes got higher when decisions cut against democratic norms, long-standing values, and American law. "I don't know if taking equality out—or he also stripped out all references to international law in all documents he sees—whether that's something that the White House has advised him to do or if this is just like his own opinion as to what he thinks is the right thing." The chain of decision making was unclear, which made it difficult for Blackburn to take a stance in defense of international law or human rights.

Such conditions were ripe for sustained loyalty traps and the perceived constriction of the use of efficacious voice among career employees.[7] Some career civil servants described having to choose between either supporting an appointed administrator by being complicit in, or even part of, illegal behavior or deciding not to support the appointees and continuing to do their work in accordance with legal statutes. Another midlevel manager said that, although "there are only a few things that would really get you in trouble legally," given the public examples of political retribution he had witnessed in his agency, it appeared that "if it's actually legal or not legal is not even part of the equation anymore." This put him and others in a series of loyalty traps:

> Because everything you should do is absolutely legal and in fact I would say nonattributionally, that the things they were asking you to do *were illegal* [emphasis by the speaker] and so you're screwed. If you do something . . . that they want that's illegal or something that's legal that's not what they want, so you're screwed. And so . . . those are the questions: the legality or the keeping it afloat because, honestly, I don't think anybody really understands what they want. [laughs]

Others witnessed corrupt behavior firsthand, which put them in the difficult position of deciding what to do. A senior EPA official described the Trump administration as being different from other administrations in "the separation between political and career [civil servants]," "the focus on rollbacks," and "just how blatantly political this one [administration] is in terms of the link between what we are doing here and electoral politics and campaign donors and things like that." To provide an example, he described how during a meeting, a political official announced a "major rollback" for "a Republican congressman who this is really important to who's having a difficult reelection, and so we have to do this, and that is why we are doing it." The rollback was for "one small company that happens to be a campaign donor and so we're rolling it back for them . . . I would call it political corruption and the fact that policy now is being driven in some cases by trying to help a specific elected official get reelected or to help a campaign donor." He reflected, "I've just never seen that before in any administration . . . I was sort of in shock."

Across the government under the Trump administration, some political appointees—and even the president himself—seemed to simply disregard typical core ethical obligations requisite of federal civil servants.[8] These sometimes flagrant breaches of conduct came as a shock to career employees and caught them in loyalty traps for which they seemed unprepared and struggled to navigate.

Increasing pressure to extol loyalty to the president trickled down throughout agencies and offices. For example, a midlevel manager in a regional EPA office reported being admonished by his supervisors for failing to show overt support for the president in 2017. "Don't forget you work for Trump," he was told. In response, he retorted, "I don't work for Trump. I work for the people, not for Trump." In reflection, he continued, "And it doesn't matter who's in the executive office. I didn't work for [Barack] Obama either. I supported him, but I never worked for him. I still work for the people. That's what the application says."[9] This manager's primary loyalty lay in his commitment to work for the American people, which aligned with the official mission of the EPA, rather than the president.[10] In insufficiently demonstrating a commitment to the president, he was chastised by his supervisors. This left him feeling angry and isolated. It also struck him as unusual at the time. "People are weird right now," he told me during the first year of the Trump administration.

The real danger, however, is what happens when these civil servants experience these conflicting loyalties as intractable over time and opt to remain silent, neglect their ethical obligations or stated duties under pressure, or quit.[11] Such experiences undermine not just the civil servants' health but also that of the democracy.[12] These conditions open the door to further corruption and democratic decline.[13] Corrupt workplace cultures can "neutralize" the immorality of employees' actions as normal behavior, which is then also enacted by others around them.[14] Employees may instead begin viewing previously ethically transgressive behavior as part of typical conflicts with their superiors, administrators, or other professional groups in their organization. Such potential ethical conflicts also may merely fade into unconscious habitual action that no longer provokes critical reflection.

## APPOINTEES' LOYALTY TRAPS

Although the focus of this book is on career civil servants, it is important to recognize Trump appointees' degrees of loyalty to the president varied and there were known cleavages and infighting between some appointees. A number of political appointees described experiencing loyalty traps under the first Trump administration. Kirstjen Nielsen's experiences as secretary of the Department of Homeland Security (DHS), for example, revealed how the leadership approach modeled from the top down by the president fostered loyalty traps for political appointees. Such modeling was often characterized by his flagrant disregard for law and democratic process, suspicion of civil servants, unusually high standards of loyalty, threats and acts of retribution, and disregard for civil servants' expert opinion. As the *New York Times* reported in a series of articles in 2019, Nielsen endured considerable suspicion from Trump because she had served previously under President George W. Bush and because of her close relationship with Trump's former chief of staff and secretary of homeland security John F. Kelly. While Nielsen was secretary of homeland security, Trump repeatedly pressured her to curtail migrant border crossings from Mexico even more by implementing illegal actions, such as barring migrants from asylum seeking. Nielsen refused, noting the federal laws, settlements in court, and other international obligations that constrained her department. Nielsen described experiencing a loyalty trap, which various reports suggest pushed her to resign. After her resignation and amid public outcry over human rights abuses over the treatment of immigrants, Nielson explained, "There were a lot of things that, there were those in the administration who thought that we should do, and just as I spoke truth to power from the very beginning, it became clear that saying no, and refusing to do it myself was not going to be enough, so it was time for me to offer my resignation."[15]

## CONCLUSION

In trying to understand career civil servants' experiences working in the most ethically challenging locations in the government, I've been asked by other scholars about the specific ethical and moral turning points individuals faced and about trying to discern patterns in their experiences in these heightened moments. Such an analysis presumes that such turning points exist, actors are consciously aware of them, and actors involved feel like they have conscious choices in such moments. It also assumes that such turning points occur in the midst of everyday work (rather than being acknowledged in post hoc reflections) and are part of an articulate enough narrative that the actor experiencing the incident understands the turning points as such and can coherently convey the events to a listener. Such an analysis implicitly assumes that individuals are the key actors in a story that makes sense and in which they have some decision-making power. This was not what I heard in many reports from people working in supporting roles in the most contested areas of the government during the first Trump administration.

Rather than finding such ordered narratives, what many people in the most contested locations in the government conveyed to me was that they had a steady stream of challenging circumstances resulting from some appointed leaders' mindsets and behaviors that prioritized loyalty to the president above all else and that clashed with career civil servants' ethical and, at times, legal obligations that their positions mandated. Civil servants recognized these challenging leadership approaches early, but their understanding of their effects on their workplaces changed as the administration wore on and affected their workgroups in different ways.

In this chapter, I showed some rare examples of more clear ethical turning points, such as Adele Sullivan's. Even Sullivan suggested that she was working under conditions in which she was pressured to engage in unethical behavior "all the time." As a career civil servant in a role subordinate to appointees, she said, you could not make decisions of loyal dissent every day. She reported that, in her workgroup, most of the time "we held our nose(s)" and complied, as I reported above. Through listening to the career civil servants in such locations, I realized that the most comprehensive way to analyze the bulk of the experiences reported to me, including the sometimes cognitively inchoate ones, was to focus on the work conditions fostered by the leadership within the hierarchy rather than just reported events (which I also included in my analysis.)

Although some political scientists may view the Trump administration's mistrustful leadership strategies as tools of an administrative presidency style that has been fairly common since Ronald Reagan's presidency, the Trump administration prized loyalty to the president and administration at the expense of democratic norms and processes.[16] As some career civil servants closest to the top described to me, loyalty under the Trump administration meant not questioning the deviant and suspicious behavior of leadership. This led to an obfuscation of ethical standards and truth, which undermined democracy, suppressed voice among rank-and-file and senior career civil servants alike, and increased the odds of civil servants finding themselves in loyalty traps.

All these factors combined to disempower career civil servants, tamp down and narrow their ability to speak up, and perpetuate an overarching patina of compliance under aberrant administrators. Such developments, which foster suspicion and fear, bring to mind conditions of totalitarianism described by political theorist Hannah Arendt. She wrote in her renowned book *The Origins of Totalitarianism*: "The ideal subject of totalitarian rule is not the convinced Nazi or the convinced Communist, but people for whom the distinction between fact and fiction (i.e., the reality of experience) and the distinction between true and false (i.e., the standards of thought) no longer exist."[17]

Again, the experiences I share in this chapter and in the chapters that follow, where I further discuss organizational changes under such leadership and some career civil servants' responses in such challenging, morally fraught situations, reflect some but not all areas of the massive federal government. Employees' accounts of what transpired in such contested areas are particularly important to document and analyze because they provide clues to much deeper and important questions about the strengths and weaknesses of our American democratic experiment in the face of burgeoning autocracy. Can it withstand such leadership assaults on democratic norms and structures? How do the select career civil servants who see it emerging and escalating from within the government understand such leadership? How do the workplace conditions created by such leaders shape the repertoire of potential responses for career civil servants? I turn to these questions, and career civil servants' responses in the next four chapters.

# 8

# SIGNS OF
# ORGANIZATIONAL DECLINE

Although many civil servants did not directly inter-face with appointed leadership, the latter's mistrustful approach to governance affected some agencies quite deeply. Deficits in communication and coordination within and across agencies notably impeded the first Trump administration's intent to alter the administrative state. As a Senior Executive Service (SES) member with a graduate degree from a top management program described in August 2017, people in his agency:

> know there's this desire to make big policy changes, but there's no communication to people about these changes. And I think about this a lot. If you want to make big changes in a place, the key is just continual communication with the frontline workers about: here is why we need to change; here are the changes we want to make; here's your role in it; here's how it's going; here's the feedback; this happened last week, this was a real good example of the change we want to make, keep it going. And just the continual internal communication to make that change happen. And the fact that these guys want to make bigger changes than what we've seen before with *no* internal communications is a really weird way to handle it. [emphasis by the speaker]

At first, career employees attributed such little information to the first Trump administration's lack of preparedness to take office,[1] their strategy to sideline career bureaucrats, and sheer leadership incompetence.[2] In affected locations, career civil servants attributed leadership vacuums to politicals' infighting and secrecy, an unclear chain of command, lack of internal communication, and sometimes seeming leadership neglect.

For example, well into 2018, Department of Energy (DOE) midlevel manager Sarah Farmer reported that communication from senior leadership in her agency remained "practically nonexistent," even though Rick Perry assumed office as Secretary of Energy early in the administration, on March 2, 2017.[3] She described seeing Secretary Perry only during signing memorandum of understanding ceremonies. "That's literally all we've seen. He's not in the building most of the time," she said. Based on photos with foreign ministers of energy and other counterparts, she gathered that he was "constantly on trips or meeting with his counterparts in other countries," and described him as "very engaged in international affairs."[4]

Midlevel managers and others lower in the hierarchy in the most politicized government agencies also reported being left out of much of the decision making and communications. While some were aware of aberrant appointed leadership, they lacked the power to influence decision making because of their exclusion. Many of these civil servants expressed anxiety and frustration, especially when they had been more involved under past administrations. They had to work with whatever (possibly underdeveloped) initiatives trickled down to them, sometimes with insufficient or contradictory guidance.

While many career civil servants I spoke with at the middle of Trump's term in office continued to assume the leadership vacuums in their agencies would pass, these vacuums remained throughout the administration in certain locations. As I show in

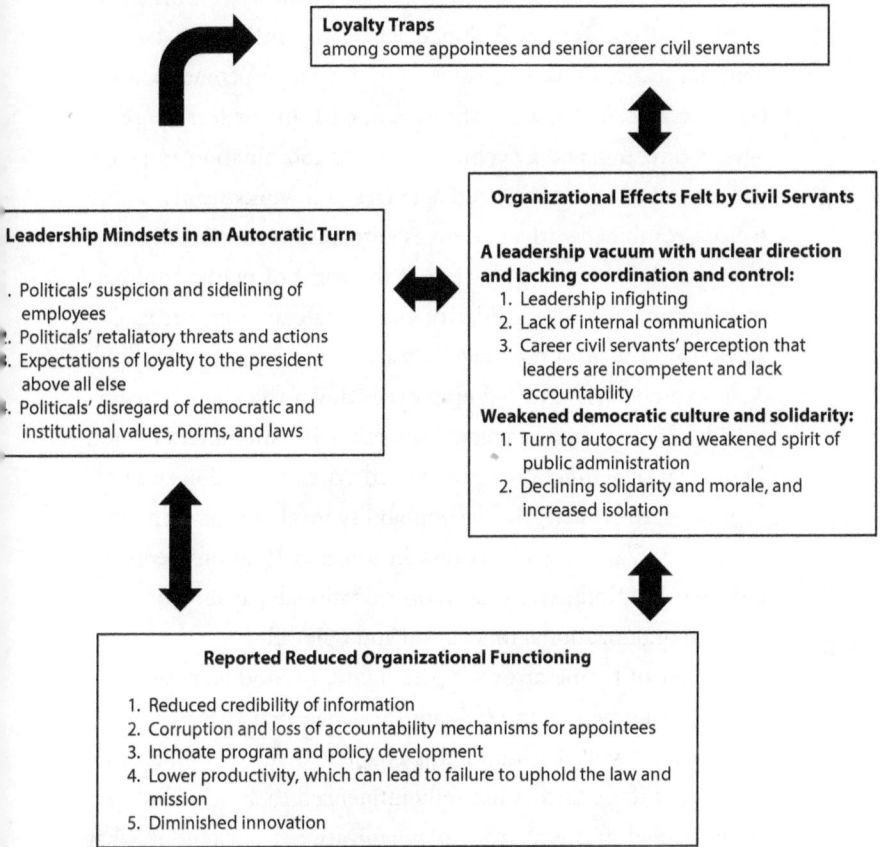

**Loyalty Traps**
among some appointees and senior career civil servants

**Leadership Mindsets in an Autocratic Turn**

1. Politicals' suspicion and sidelining of employees
2. Politicals' retaliatory threats and actions
3. Expectations of loyalty to the president above all else
4. Politicals' disregard of democratic and institutional values, norms, and laws

**Organizational Effects Felt by Civil Servants**

**A leadership vacuum with unclear direction and lacking coordination and control:**
1. Leadership infighting
2. Lack of internal communication
3. Career civil servants' perception that leaders are incompetent and lack accountability

**Weakened democratic culture and solidarity:**
1. Turn to autocracy and weakened spirit of public administration
2. Declining solidarity and morale, and increased isolation

**Reported Reduced Organizational Functioning**

1. Reduced credibility of information
2. Corruption and loss of accountability mechanisms for appointees
3. Inchoate program and policy development
4. Lower productivity, which can lead to failure to uphold the law and mission
5. Diminished innovation

**FIGURE 8.1** Reverberating negative effects of Trump's leadership on politicized locations.

figure 8.1 and below, leadership mistrust, unusually high expectations of loyalty to the president, and the gaps between the administration and career staff created by these leadership styles led to loyalty traps among some appointees and senior career officials as well as to notable organizational decline in politicized agencies. In this chapter, I first focus on the organizational factors that career civil servants reported as contributing to what they described as an increasingly toxic and uncertain work environment; these factors included leadership infighting, lack of communication, and perceived appointee incompetence. Career civil servants in these locations reported an unclear sense of agency direction and a declining sense of coordination and control over the most politicized agencies and workstreams. These factors, combined with appointees' autocratic leadership tendencies, contributed to a withering of the spirit of public administration and declining solidarity and morale among career civil servants in the most politicized areas.

These changes affected employees down the chain of command, whether they interacted directly with appointees or not. Organizational functioning weakened. Misinformation and corruption were evident, and accountability mechanisms seemingly weakened. Career civil servants in affected locations reported declines in productivity and organizational capabilities, and reduced organizational innovation and renewal.

As shown by the arrows in the figure, I found complex causality and numerous interrelationships between these different factors. As I will discuss in this chapter, there was much evidence that these factors not only influenced each other but also compounded and gave rise to organizational pockets of what Environmental Protection Agency (EPA) SES member Adele Sullivan called a "self-reinforcing cycle" of organizational decline.

## A LEADERSHIP VACUUM: UNCLEAR DIRECTION AND LACK OF COORDINATION AND CONTROL

Career civil servants in the most politicized locations reported experiencing leadership vacuums. Under the first Trump administration, they said leadership in their agencies failed to establish a clear direction for where they were trying to go collectively. They reported their agencies lacked coordination and control. They attributed these conditions to leadership infighting, little communication throughout and across some agencies, and some leadership incompetence. Coinciding with an absence of strong leadership, they described experiencing work conditions marked by a sense of uncertainty, chaos, mistrust, an unclear chain of command, other indicators of poor leadership from appointees, and a seeming lack of accountability across levels.[5]

## Leadership Infighting

Within and across agencies, senior officials and midlevel managers alike reported challenges in executing their core work due to infighting, mistrust, and insufficient coordination among the president, his innermost circle, appointed leaders in their agencies, and career civil servants.[6] The apparent lack of trust and coordination among the most senior officials undermined employees' trust in leadership across levels of various agencies. As a senior official at the State Department described, the contentious relationship between Secretary of State Rex Tillerson and the president undermined confidence in the former within the agency: "He wasn't seen as somebody who had a lot of influence positively on the president because, you know, he would say something and the president would undercut him with a tweet. So, it was just not a very positive environment."

Mistrust among appointed leaders also led to leaks. Multiple career civil servants I spoke with from several agencies suspected leaks were coming from appointees rather than career staff. A civil servant at DOE described contention among senior administrators in his agency: "We'll discuss an article about a meeting that leaked, and this meeting probably had twelve people and this paper somehow has eight sources." I heard similar reports from EPA officials. Such visible signs of fractured political leadership undermined career employees' confidence in them, increased mistrust and suspicion at work, and contributed to the confusion described below.

The lack of trust between Scott Pruitt's administration and career bureaucrats grew into a self-reinforcing cycle. As EPA SES member Adele Sullivan explained, "When you lack trust and when information leaks, you lack trust more so. And then something else leaks." Even though Sullivan and other senior EPA careerists suspected the leaks were coming from "other political people, because his team had very toxic relations and were jockeying for position amongst themselves," as leaks occurred, "the career people were all deemed untrustworthy," she said. After leaks occurred, "the administrator and the top people were trying to figure out who it was," and "they'd try to cut more people out of the decision making, and the circle would get smaller. And the trust gets even worse, and it just becomes dysfunctional."

International affairs manager Yasin Abadi's experience provides more insight into how infighting and inadequate coordination among senior White House leaders and agency leadership affected rank-and-file public servants' experiences working in politicized workstreams and agencies. Although Abadi had previously acknowledged a history of organizational dysfunction in his agency, the United States Agency for International Development (USAID), based on its inherent structure, by 2018, he said that chaos, uncertainty, and a climate of fear had noticeably increased and permeated the agency under the Trump administration.

Even though he and his colleagues were surprised by the rapid pace of change under the Trump administration, as a seasoned career bureaucrat, Abadi tried to make sense of it all in an even-keeled way. "I'm in a pretty good agency," compared to others, he said. He recognized the administrator was in a "difficult position," for a number of reasons. He knew senior leadership were "reacting to things they are getting from their leadership that's higher in the administration, and they're trying to do the best they can to maintain relevancy, stay part of the reconstruction, and work with as much freedom as we can to execute missions as we see fit."

In contrast to some others I spoke with at the most politicized agencies, Abadi thought the political appointees in his agency had "enough knowledge . . . to make good decisions," and said that all the political appointees in his agency were "not incompetent." Yet Abadi said that relationships among appointed leadership across USAID were "fractured" and communications between them and civil servants were incoherent. Although he thought the "administrator has a strong sense of what he wants, I don't think that everyone's on the same page from the front office and on its way down." He reported that this continued to be the case throughout the administration:

> The administration itself doesn't seem to be necessarily unified in their approach to things. And that—obviously any organization that's made up of multiple people, their kind of outlooks and kind of perspectives—the diversity is what makes organizations strong. But really, they just don't get along with each other. That's the difference, I guess, where some parts of the administration are kind of like disavowing other parts of the administration, so that's been interesting. So from the civil service side, it almost feels like, well, they're kind of having a fight with themselves, so just stay clear of that and let them sort it out.

It is notable and sensible in the face of such fractious leadership for career civil servants like Abadi to avoid it. I heard similar reports of leadership infighting from others, and like-minded responses to duck and cover, from civil servants across levels in particularly disrupted agencies such as the EPA, Department of State, DOE, Department of the Treasury (USDT), and Department of Health and Human Services (HHS).

Career civil servants reported how challenging it was to navigate their work with discrepant advice from different Trump administration officials, which included some influential members of the Trump family. A midlevel manager at HHS noted how difficult it was to work on a program that his appointee and one Trump family member championed, but which President Trump and Office of Management and Budget (OMB) director Mick Mulvaney wanted to cut. "You don't know what they're arguing or saying," he said. His supervising appointee couldn't "figure out what anybody thinks of it" and offered little helpful advice on how to operate his program in the midst of these contradictory political winds, even though, he noted, it was the appointee's job to do so. He expressed frustration at this lack of guidance. This put him in an uncomfortable situation in which he felt he could not "stand behind the position in support of the program" that he was working on. Such contradictory signals resulting from divisions within the administration not only caused confusion but also basically immobilized this career employee.

Lacking appointee coordination, trust, and reliance on the chain of command also led to some episodes of overt conflict, which some career employees described as signs of a toxic and stressful workplace. For example, in one location where lower-level Trump appointees struggled with a more experienced, rational Republican appointee over them, the lower-level appointees appealed to the White House to overturn decisions. One senior official noted how such conflict between appointees of different levels led to "unprofessional and stressful" behavior, such as "screaming," which contributed to less frequent subsequent meetings and confusion over who had the power to make decisions. These examples reveal the challenges of working with a fractured administration characterized by appointee infighting, unclear guidance, and suspicion. As a result, chaos, confusion, and mistrust reverberated through the most politicized locations and agencies. Work slowed because of confusion and fear and, in a few cases, civil servants reported that open conflict erupted.

## Little Internal Communication

A culture of secrecy stemming from the politicals and their deliberate sidelining of career bureaucrats led to poor communication across levels within and between agencies. Structural holes were evident not only between appointees and SES members; they also formed between SES members and their staff. This all led to further organizational dysfunction, uncertainty, and chaos, which slowed work considerably.

An SES member at an EPA regional office said that management was not only "disorganized and slow," but "we don't ever get messages" from the administrator. "We don't get emails saying, 'Hi, I'm Scott Pruitt. Here are my priorities. Here's something we did last week and I'm really proud of this work.' There's no interest at all in internal communications." He said that, even in 2018, "most" of the information he was getting "is from the media and not internally." He continued:

> There's so much more secrecy now than there ever used to be. Everything's a secret now, and that's kind of a default. And there are some things that because of my position I'm in on the secret, but then I can't tell my management team. And we've never had

that before. If there was something that was okay for me to know, there was no reason I couldn't share it with other people in management. Sometimes you can't go to staff because there is a union issue, and you have to deal with it through the bargaining unit, and sometimes management has to keep things confidential for a while until they go to the whole agency. But we've never had this kind of division where there are *many* layers of hierarchy and there are some things that *only* the political team knows and there are some things that the political team plus the top layer of managers know, but we can't share and then there's—and a lot of things that are secret, and there is just no reason for them to be secret. There's just so much desire to control the flow of information, that's almost a reflex.

The new pressure from leadership to keep secrets created further divides between this SES career official and those underneath him. It also left many staff in his office "pretty much in the dark," as one employee told me in 2018. In terms of appointed leadership in Washington, DC, she said, "We don't really hear from them. There's a lot of things that are happening that I find out pretty much the same time the rest of the country does, like, the gutting of the Clean Power Plan.[7] . . . There's no all-employee memos. Unless you're in that program, you really won't know."[8]

I heard about similar poor communication in other agencies, such as HHS, DOE, USAID, the Department of Commerce, the Department of State, and others. Such lapses in communication led career staff who cared about their jobs to rely on the rumor mill, government publications and websites, and the media for information about changes in the government. In our first interview in 2017, DOE manager Sarah Farmer mentioned that the secretary had not communicated any long-term vision. Instead, she reported, "The only emails we get from the secretary" were about seemingly trivial matters like "early release for holidays." In the absence of more substantive information and direction, she said that communication was "much more word of mouth," via her supervisor, her staff meetings, and "friends on the Hill." In her office, she reported that they "signed up for a lot of newsletters to keep track of laws and bills that might affect our program," and "we basically just share our gossip and that's how we try to keep track of what's going on." In speaking with her boss, who had been with the agency for decades, and who she described as "usually pretty good about keeping his thoughts to himself about political appointees because, you know, you're supposed to be nonpolitical at work," she said, "I can sense his frustration of the unpredictableness of it."

Farmer acknowledged that "departments are [not] always good at communicating, but it's definitely worse than normal now." She described, "Normally I'd work through my chain of command, and go through the 'Schedule Cs'—the adviser-level political appointees—to inquire how to approach and engage an undersecretary or how to prepare for a meeting." The Schedule Cs, she explained, "are picked by the Senate-confirmed appointees, so they've got a good working relationship. And so you know when you go to the Schedule C or adviser that they speak for their boss." But what struck her as "unusual" was that she could see "they're trying to figure it out as well." Although she said that lower-tier appointed leadership were "more engaged" than top leadership, and "whenever they do get information, they're pretty good about sharing it," they "don't get information with a huge lead time, so we find out things like 'this is happening next week' or 'this just happened.'" The chaos that resulted from leaders' lack of agenda setting and communication was apparent.

Farmer also reported not knowing about developments in her agency, such as a reorganization that occurred in 2018. She described finding out about the reorganization "that just happened that hasn't been announced yet in the department . . . because I was preparing a meeting invite and I needed to look up to remind myself of someone's position and saw the org chart had changed." There was "no department announcement," she said. Farmer's experience reveals the challenges of working without clear guidance in a rapidly changing organization of which she did not even know the structure.

Others, such as an employee at the Department of Homeland Security (DHS), similarly reported learning about developments in their agencies through the mass media, or even social media, rather than through internal channels of communication. As one lawyer confided in 2017, "I remain on my toes every day," under the Trump administration. In contrast to previous administrations, which she characterized as more attentive to planning and times when coworkers knew what was transpiring in the agency, under Trump leadership: "We learned through the media; we didn't learn through any memos or anything, which is different from what we've been used to, because previously there was a heads-up planning or 'We're going to publish these [reports] tomorrow.'" Another longtime career civil servant described in 2020 the "constant ups and downs and ever-changing tweets" and how some employees "feel this causes mania and confusion. It causes personal anxiety. The last three years there has been constant tweeting. North Korea. Iran. This way of communication is problematic."

Abadi described getting used to this chaotic form of communication by 2020: "So I think what people just got to essentially was, this was just the new normal . . . we're not gonna get really great definitions." Instead, "we'll kind of be building this as we go, and we're going to help the administration figure out what they're trying to articulate by enacting this thing and kind of putting it into place." Farmer, the midlevel manager at DOE, similarly reported "guessing" that "maybe" the secretary was focused on operational issues because "we did a lot of work preparing all of these new ideas of how we can do things more efficiently," but "you never really hear about whether they're getting implemented." Civil servants in various areas seemed to be grasping at the little bits of information they received from agency leadership and trying to do their jobs based on such limited information.[9]

What is more apparent is that the lack of internal communication from appointed leadership led to information sharing based on more unreliable sources (such as via gossip or social media), an increased sense of uncertainty and unpredictability among career civil servants, and information gaps that hindered their ability to do their jobs.

## Perception That Leaders Are Incompetent and Lack Accountability

Bureaucrats I spoke with across agencies and positions attested to an unusual level of incompetence among appointed leaders in the first Trump administration. This varied considerably, however, by agency and administrative team, which changed over the course of the administration. Career civil servants described structural problems because of the administration's failure to get a sufficient number of appointees in office and their lack of care with establishing and adhering to a clear chain of command. Staff also noted problems stemming from just plain poor leadership—which was evident when leaders lacked agency-specific knowledge and/or did not seem to care about being good stewards of their respective organizations.[10]

## UNFILLED POLITICAL POSITIONS

Incompetence from the top caused structural organizational problems throughout some agencies. One striking indicator of the administration's incompetence in some career civil servants' eyes was the number of unfilled appointee positions over the course of the administration.[11] This added to the chaos, lack of information and communication from above, and perceived inability for some career civil servants to advance their work and do it well. As *Politico* reporter Nancy Cook noted at the beginning of Trump's fourth year in office in 2020, at the time, the presidential administration had filled only 515 of 714 appointed positions requiring Senate confirmation, despite Republican control of the Senate; this, Cook noted, "limited Trump's influence."[12]

Career civil servants across agencies noted the missing appointees and the palpable effects in their workplaces. Someone at the State Department said in 2020:

> Unlike prior administrations, instead of putting in political appointees who can provide leadership, they've got, you know, people [career civil servants] who are acting capacity, who are stretched maybe beyond their prior experience level, and so the number of people in the State Department who have the clout that a political appointee would have, I mean, has been very few. They've left many ambassadorships unfilled. They have left many senior positions in the State Department unfilled. And so when you have a bunch of acting people, there's a reluctance to make hard decisions because people don't have the authority as political appointees to make certain decisions. So sometimes decisions are deferred or they're not made, and things just sort of happen by default. And that's really unfortunate.

A senior State Department official described how the administration's nominee for the political leadership position in his office "got hung up last year in the nomination process. He has dubious credentials, frankly, to do this job, so even the Republicans up on the Hill never forwarded his name," so "nobody expects any action." Their acting leader, he continued, also did not have "a lot of credentials to do this job . . . nor does he really have the authority to do this job because he has not been Senate-confirmed." He also lacked "strong political connections . . . so he doesn't have the ability to reach into the political network of the Trump administration to get things done."

Others reported that that lack of political appointees led to burnout and acting senior leaders being stretched too thin. During the middle of the administration, an employee at DOE said that he has "definitely seen my boss complain about incompetence in the White House more than ever before," such as "seeing the revolving door of people, that they can't keep anyone on." As a result, he said, people in acting positions are "burned out," and "some of my work has suffered just because we can't get time with leadership, because they're doing too many jobs."

At USDT, a career civil servant reported that the lack of appointees contributed to the unclear guidance and poor communication discussed above, as well as other egregious displays of leadership ineptitude:

A feature of this administration . . . [is] there's not a consistent tone setting within the building. They're so thinly staffed that it's whatever random person happens to be the person tasked with overseeing it . . . will have an outsized impact on that aspect of the report that we're looking at. A great example to look at is a lack of messaging cohesion last week when Mulvaney, OMB, and Mnuchin, secretary, were on the Hill testifying about the impact of the tax reform/tax cuts . . . and were asked, I think in separate meetings in separate rooms at the same time . . . "Will your tax cuts be fully paid for by offsets?" Mulvaney said, "Yes, they'll be fully paid for by offsets," and [Steven] Mnuchin, at the same time said, "No, they're going to be paid by explosive economic growth." So that's the kind of messaging incohesion that you would not have under a competent administration.

Although career civil servants saw such egregious mistakes and disorganization, they did not see appointed leadership take accountability for mistakes or being held accountable in other ways. Instead, many chalked up such mistakes to organizational problems and leadership vacuums.

Annette Foster at DHS described in 2020 that what was missing under the Trump administration was "stability. We don't have it. I've discussed [this] with other pretty high up people. They can't help it. It's the acting positions. Kenneth T. Cuccinelli is the senior official performing the duties of the deputy secretary for the Department of Homeland Security. The director is vacant. The secretary is vacant. This is abnormal."

Michael Chertoff, secretary of Homeland Security under President George W. Bush, suggested the considerable vacancies and acting roles made the agency particularly vulnerable to politicization.[13] This seemed to be the case. Foster's comment represented the tip of the iceberg when it came to instability at her agency, which revealed a disregard for the law tracing its way up to the president himself. After Kirstjen Nielsen resigned as Secretary of DHS, rather than adhering to the Federal Vacancies Reform Act, which dictated the director of the Cybersecurity and Infrastructure Security Agency should have succeeded Nielsen, the administration instead improperly placed Commissioner of Customs and Border Protection Kevin McAleenan as acting secretary. When he resigned, McAleenan appointed Chad F. Wolf, a known Trump loyalist, to be acting secretary of homeland security and Cuccinelli to be his deputy.[14] A federal judge and the Government Accountability Office (GAO) concluded in 2020 that both the appointments of acting Secretary Wolf and Deputy Cuccinelli were illegal because they violated the Federal Vacancies Reform Act.[15]

In response, the Trump White House did nothing. A White House spokesperson at the time responded that: "DHS is expressly authorized by Congress in the Homeland Security Act to designate its acting secretaries . . . GAO is not. And GAO's opinion substituting its views for that of the agency's is not only wrong, but laughable." Such a combative stance revealed the administration's disdain for administrative state authority and potential checks and balances of power that might hinder or limit executive power.

In addition to lacking confirmed appointees, the official chain of command within agencies was unclear to some career civil servants across levels. Without an official chain of command, they did not know who to listen to, or which orders were legitimate. A senior EPA official reported in August 2017:

> [It was] very difficult and there was very little communication between the new transition team . . . and the rest of the agency. It was a very confusing time. We didn't know who to talk to. We didn't know who was making decisions about anything. Normally what happens is they [appointee positions] are filling pretty quickly . . . and I think there are fourteen positions that need to be confirmed by the Senate, who basically run the agency. And we don't have any of those confirmed yet except for the head administrator of the agency . . . The EPA administrator . . . has a bunch of political people who work as his aides. And some of them communicate with us, but it's still not clear who has authority in what. And so, from our point of view, we're trying to identify people we can talk to and trying to figure out who has authority and it seems

like nobody has authority for anything. And we'll talk to some-body, and it seems like they have authority. And so we're doing the best we can in a very confusing situation.

Influence also seemed to come at times from external sources rather than from within the administration, which led to further confusion and perceived chaos.[16] A Department of State career civil servant compared his experience working under previous administrations, in which he trusted that if he provided advice to the appointee he worked under, she would analyze it and inform the president, to the Trump administration, when "extraneous uninformed lines of input" were coming "through the national security decision process" from "outside ideological and political interests." This wide range of private and political influences and career employees' uncertainty about who to listen to and what would be in the best interest of the state contributed to confu-sion: "it's unclear what exactly is happening," he said. He con-sequently described the Trump appointees he worked with as "incompetent," and working under them as "incredibly chaotic."

## POOR LEADERS WITH LITTLE KNOWLEDGE

While many career bureaucrats felt like they were waiting for more stable leadership during the first Trump administration, others were troubled by some appointees who made it through the appointment process. In many areas, career bureaucrats reported that Trump appointees did not have the educational credentials, experience, or expertise in the subject areas they worked in that was typical of appointees under other administra-tions.[17] At the Department of Housing and Urban Development (HUD), a longtime employee described "a lot of people from the private sector" hired by senior leaders who had "no constitutional knowledge . . . and they don't come in loyal. . . . It's like they're forcing their world on us." He also raised concerns about corruption, suggesting that "they hired their friends" and then gave them better benefits, such as leave time, which typically took years to accrue.

Career civil servants across the government shared many other examples of appointees' ineptitude and lack of knowledge. At EPA, a senior official similarly reported seeing "mostly political people" appointed who "had roles in the Trump campaign but who didn't really have any environmental experience." A career civil servant at USDT described "a lot of incompetence in the building." He thought the hiring pool under the Trump administration was considerably limited by "whether they have been positive for-Trump people in the past" and had concerns about Trump's transgressions and possible looming impeachment, even as early as 2017. "The qualified candidates" who typically come "from the financial service sector, Wall Street, or the top white-shoe law firms in New York City," he said, care about preserving their reputations. As a result, he supposed, they were "not really on board the Trump train, even though that's ultimately the exclusive constituency that he's serving."

Among those he worked with, this civil servant reported, "We view the people that have come in as political appointees as not very qualified compared to the people in the past . . . either inexperienced, no government service, they don't understand how the bureaucracy works. They're just not of the caliber that we saw previously because the pool is so small, I think." Because they lacked government experience, he said, "You would never in a normal administration rank them among the top two to three thousand people who would be qualified for this job."[18] As a result, he said, "You just see astounding incompetence," in examples ranging from their interagency decision making to seemingly small details "like, executive orders that are numbered

1, 2, 3, 7, 9, 12," rather than in numerical order. Another USDT employee in 2020 similarly described hires by the Trump administration as "not good at what they do" based on "everybody I talk to." They're "amateurs," he said.

Employees described similar forms of appointee ineptitude at the Department of State, where they reported "an incredibly chaotic" work environment. When a midlevel manager at the State Department briefed Trump appointees on his projects, he said, "They tend to not understand the topic I briefed them on, and they tend to repeat the same few talking points . . . they're always recycled ideas." He was not alone in thinking so. He reported, "After one of these briefings, I chatted with my boss, and he's usually a nice person," but he was struck by:

> how blunt he was about his perception of this individual's intelligence and the fact that he wasn't understanding when we tried to explain the same concepts even more clearly, or that his proposals are things we've tried before. And we tried to explain why they haven't worked. That doesn't mean there isn't another way they could make it work, but he wasn't proposing anything that seemed remotely feasible. There's always people that have a solution in search of a problem, and that's the impression I get from these individuals; they think they have the perfect idea, and they're trying to figure out some reason why we need to implement it.

I asked, "Do they have experience in the government?" He replied, "No. These people typically don't have experience. They were probably lower-level campaign aides that got the job that way."

A considerable number of career civil servants attributed problems with the implementation of policy ideas in the most contested agencies to appointee incompetence. Midlevel manager at HHS Nick Pratt described what it was like working under inept leadership. Although the appointee he worked for had previously worked in the Bush administration, he "didn't pay attention for like the ten years he was out of the government." Even though a lot had changed in the interim, "he just hasn't bothered to learn it still," he said, which was evident in how the appointee incorrectly represented their welfare policies, suggesting their agency aided more people with fewer restrictions than they did. Such inaccurate arguments could be construed as intending to appeal to and inflame more conservative audiences.

Under this appointee's leadership, Pratt described unorganized, chaotic meetings and an inefficient haphazard delegation of work. He reported that the appointee fixated on "topics . . . that he's really interested in and he just brings them up every meeting." One of the repeated topics of conversation was what a highlight it had been for the appointee to meet with a member of the Trump family. Another abrupt interruption made in meetings was the appointee sharing photos of his family's cat.

Pratt struggled with when to speak up and with the fact that it seemed this appointee "usually needs to hear something like three times, at least, because he really doesn't read whatever we give him . . . Part of the issue is he just talks. So the only way really to talk in the meeting is to interrupt him . . . It's interesting," he said.

This leadership approach contrasted with how he had previously seen appointees run his unit. He told me:

I met with an old political appointee and she was saying how like she has this management philosophy of that you never—if you're the highest-ranking person at a meeting or you've called the meeting, you don't speak first because it sets a tone. Like you let everyone else talk and then you gather and then you kind of jump in. And so, it's really interesting to hear that versus how meetings with him are run. He's also always late and meetings go long. There's not a lot of respect for anyone's time, I guess.

The appointee he worked for was also "very into busy work," Pratt reported. When I asked what he meant by "busy work," he responded that the appointee would "just ask for random data points that he thinks might be useful or interesting. And he'll have already asked for something similar before, but he'll have forgotten that we gave it to him, and he doesn't really like being reminded that we've done it already." Adding to the challenge, Pratt said, was that "it's a lot more controlled than it was into the [Barack] Obama administration. So, he's our only person speaking for us in any meeting with anyone higher and that's when I get worried."

Such accounts reveal not only the poor leadership of some Trump appointees due to their lack of knowledge, but their seeming lack of care in trying to be good leaders according to best practices in management in public administration or elsewhere. This may have been because such aims were not a priority of the president and his senior staff.

## BAD-FAITH APPOINTEES?

At times, career employees described appointees as incompetent, but it was unclear if they were actually quite competent at a goal hard to digest for devout career employees: dismantling their agencies and deliberately firing senior career officials.[19] A middle-level manager at the Department of State for example, described Secretary of State Tillerson and his administrative team as "really incompetent.":

He just didn't understand how to create policy or to manage the building or to like get anything done. Like in everything he was

completely incompetent. I mean he couldn't manage his relationships with the Hill and he was so arrogant, like I think it in part
came from like this master of the universe syndrome that he'd been
master of the universe for so long at ExxonMobil . . . administer-
ing government is slightly different than that. We have different
missions. We have different purposes. We have different processes
for getting things done . . . The bizarre thing was that he wiped
out all of the leadership levels and so all of a sudden you have like
just [General Schedule (GS) level] 15s and 14s steering the ship.

As a result, this State employee thought, "He did incredible
damage because of the loss of expertise, the exodus of really
seasoned career people, and the way they were treated and the
level of disrespect for experts and civil servants and people who'd
been there decades." Pushing out experienced career bureaucrats
likely aligned with the Trump administration's aims to change
and shrink the federal government dramatically, and so, from the
Trump administration's perspective, eliminating senior career
employees might be viewed as a sign of success. From the perspective of longstanding employees, this occurrence, in conjunc-
tion with the other actions of the administration such as failing
to appoint politicals and its perceived inefficacy at accomplishing policy goals, was viewed as yet another tangible indicator of
their incompetence.

Another USDT employee provided examples of incompetence that might have been viewed as successful actions by
Trump's political appointees. Trump appointees were described
by this civil servant as being engaged in work as "an ideological political exercise" rather than doing so based on technocratic
knowledge and data. The USDT employee discussed sending
off "documents and recommendations into the dark to some
extent" that got passed through the White House. "And then

they get changed and modified out of our control and printed," he said, and they "are often changed in ways that are highly ideological. So, there's also a lack of expertise there as well." To explain further, he said, "We're only looking at sources from the far right for instance . . . we're not doing any kind of research on centrists, empirically driven statisticians, economists, lawyers. That large body of the literature is not represented, and I think anyone reading that report like this will recognize that if you go to the footnotes and see Heritage Foundation again and again."

This process, and what he perceived as incompetent alterations to his group's reports, frustrated him, and his supervisors as well: "I've certainly seen senior career staff express a lot of frustration around how their analysis has been modified by the politicals or by the White House, by other outside actors in a way that is illogical." He concluded in reflection, "It's a much less integrated process. And a much more hierarchical and less open and transparent process then it was before." While this career civil servant described these outcomes as politicals' incompetence, they seemed in accordance with some of the administration's goals; thus, they would possibly be described as successful according to their alternative perspectives.

It sometimes seemed that career civil servants' strong commitments to adhering to their professional ethical obligations gave rise to a blind spot: they struggled to articulate when appointees simply did not care to adhere to typical ethical obligations of public administration. Some appointees may have instead sought to support the president's aim to dismantle the state as career civil servants knew it. Historian Heather Cox Richardson is one of a growing chorus identifying Trump as a quintessential autocratic leader seeking to weaken the state democracy and its balance of powers and shift to an authoritarian system of governance.[20] As a case in point, she suggests that Trump actually preferred filling senior positions with acting administrators rather than Senate-approved appointees because it was a means of circumventing the Senate. She attributes his hiring of unqualified but loyal bureaucrats (because they would not otherwise have had access to such positions) as one of many pieces of evidence pointing to his efforts to destabilize the government and shift toward an autocratic and authoritarian system.

It is also possible that career civil servants knew such harm to the most affected agencies was deliberate, but they did not want to say so directly and accuse appointees of harm to me, as an interviewer. One policy expert at USDT was more candid. He reported some colleagues were directly criticizing appointees, raising questions about their motives and intentions, and said how the term "bad faith" had been used "many times" in his agency to describe political appointees.

## WEAKENED DEMOCRATIC CULTURE AND SOLIDARITY

Amid such leadership and organizational changes, career civil servants in the most politicized locations raised concerns about the weakening of the spirit of public administration, intrinsic work motivation, and morale. They also described a loss of a sense of camaraderie in some work units, which led to increasing feelings of isolation among some staff members in such units.

### Turn Toward Autocracy and Weakened Spirit of Public Administration

Across agencies, senior leaders expressed concerns about the declining spirit of public administration and its associated ethical obligations and democratic norms under an administration prioritizing loyalty to the president and private business interests. One pathway through which career civil servants in politicized agencies reported a weakening of their ethical culture occurred when loyalists were advanced for currying favor. In addition, standard democratic ethical norms, like the importance of factual information, truth seeking, and reason-based assessment, fell by the wayside in everyday work. EPA senior official Adele Sullivan reported the following:

> Even under the most—it's called toxic leadership, no matter what leadership there is—there are gonna be some people that thrive in that environment . . . I think even under this regime there are some career people on my team, in my view not the ones that are the best leaders or most mission-focused, but there are people that move up and so that changes the agency . . . they're a different group of people than would've otherwise moved up . . . Some of the worst people I ever worked with are now moving into jobs like my job . . . Not the head, but all the senior career jobs have been filled by people that were completely fine in this . . . 'don't question them' leadership style. Don't raise questions, just do it, no matter what harm might come.

Sullivan noted the many reverberations on the agency from the promotion of such career civil servants who were willing to switch camps and prioritize some new administrators' autocratic leadership style over other ethical obligations and duties. This expedited the leadership-led shift in workplace culture and likely caused sustained moral dissonance and role conflict for those working under their leadership, which, as some management scholars note, can lead to decreased loyalty to the organization among employees.[21] Sullivan saw this happening. Such changes, she thought, not only damaged the "agency's credibility" but also affected its "ability to attract young people" and "retain some of the senior people."

Career civil servants, as particularly politically knowledgeable citizens, were disturbed by the Trump administration's ethical transgressions, but given their legally and normatively circumscribed abilities to engage in partisan politics, they felt there was little they could do about it. This caused further moral dissonance and strain, dampening their sense of purpose in serving the government and previously idealistic patriotic depictions of government service. DHS lawyer Annette Foster expressed concerns about the president and democratic decline in early 2020. "The bottom line is the president is selling out the government for his own personal gains," she told me. She was concerned about foreign interference, lies circulated by the president and his administration, and evidence of democratic decline across the executive and congressional branches of government.[22] It deeply disturbed her that the president seemed to trust the Russian president more than the government's own intelligence experts. As Foster said, "How would you feel if you worked in intelligence?"

These developments contradicted her varied professional and civic values. "I try to be a good American," Foster said, but "I consider him [the president] 'high maintenance.' I'm just a general citizen. We have to weave around truths and falsehoods. The leader is supposed to tell the truth." She noted the "disturbing" proliferation of claims she knew to be "not true," such as how Republicans were defending the president's argument that Ukraine meddled in the 2016 election. As "Dr. Hill [Fiona Hill, a former National Security Council official and career diplomat] explained," during the House impeachment hearings, these stories "were pushed out by the Russian misinformation campaign to destabilize our democracy," she said. "These are antics. It's *misinformation* [emphasis by the speaker]."[23]

Foster was also concerned about the deterioration of democratic norms and procedures and the loss of a sense of unity and stability. Like many other career civil servants, she was disturbed by increasing divisions in the federal government and in the public. She said that is why then–Speaker of the House Nancy Pelosi ripped up Trump's speech at the 2020 State of the Union: "It's supposed to be a union, not a dividing position." Foster blamed Trump's erratic inflammatory communications through social media and "the amount of acting positions." It felt like "it's always a new problem," she said. "It's a sea of disarray. We need to move to the center and get it back. It's a lot of instability. It's a lot of separation . . . There is a lot of chaos."

Like Foster, other career civil servants raised questions about the seemingly unethical behavior of the president and his administration, the deterioration of democratic norms, and the chaos of it all. Visible ethical breaches among the administration raised concerns and created moral dissonance for some civil servants because of the higher ethical and normative standards expected of them in their daily work. Even some of the most risk-averse civil servants who steered clear of any and all forms of resistance, such as Department of Defense (DOD) lawyer Ralph McCafferty, shared concern about visible evidence of *corruption* as the Trump administration wore on and how it could weaken the democratic bedrock of civil service. "The president and his staff have a variety of ethics issues," McCafferty said. "For example, financial conflicts of interest, benefitting from their positions, those sorts of things. Things that on their face appear contradictory to the ethics regulations, and so employees . . . [of] mine who have similar issues ask me, 'Well why do these rules apply to me and they don't apply to those very top people?'" McCafferty acknowledged:

Certainly all the ethics rules and all the other prescriptive rules that apply to the federal government are in full force at my level, but it is questionable whether some of these rules apply to the president and his staff. I mean courts have thrown out lawsuits related to, for example, the Emoluments Clause recently for significant ethics things, and he is the unitarian head of the executive branch, so from a legal perspective it may be questionable whether some of these rules and regulations that we have to follow apply to him and his staff. But nevertheless, from a leadership perspective, it's difficult for career civil servants like me to reconcile that behavior with the rules and explain it to employees.[24]

In responding to employees, McCafferty referred to civil servants' core duties and loyalties, focusing on the ethical bedrock of the democratic state. "I try to be practical," he said, "and I say, 'Well, our job is to do the mission of the agency and so let's just focus on accomplishing our mission and making sure that we don't do things that are antithetical to the agency's mission.'" While "I can't advise the president," he said, he could advise the people in his agency. McCafferty continued, "Everyone that I advise are career civil servants or military people and I mean they're grown people. They understand they have to follow the rules, but it lends dissonance to working because people question it. They still follow the rules, but then they're like, 'Why do I have to follow this rule and these people apparently don't?'"

Longtime senior officials, such as Adele Sullivan, worried "about the concept of public service a lot." Sullivan said:

My self-image is like a public servant who cares about the government doing the right thing on behalf of the American people—but I worry about whether that's sort of an arcane, an archaic concept and that a lot of people just view the government as a tool for their own ends. It's like a power struggle to control the government, to pursue other agendas. And the idea of public service, I worry if that's getting lost. I feel like the other administrations that I worked for, those people we had, I think I used a term like they viewed themselves as stewards of the organization, but I mean I think they had an idea of public service that was old-fashioned and I think the correct reason to be in government was public service.

To Sullivan and some of the other older, long-standing career civil servants who had joined the government decades earlier, their work was a calling.[25] The spirit of public administration and their loyalties to serving as steadfast stewards of the government in service to the American public were sacred to them, and they worried this spirit was withering under the influence of the Trump administration and private interests. Sullivan worried that federal organizations were getting "more politicized." She explained, "The bigger picture is that policy decisions are just a bargaining chip in the use of government for supporting private interests and interests in industry for politics." Her assessment of the situation aligns with that of economist Robert Reich, who suggests that corporate interest groups' influence in politics have grown tremendously over the last fifty years.[26] While Sullivan acknowledged that this had been occurring before Trump, she saw it up close at the EPA during his administration. She witnessed Pruitt "being attacked by Republicans," she said, who "just used his scandals to help push him out. But really it was because . . . the corn industry was upset by his policy decisions . . . The ethics didn't matter to them—but because of the interests of one industry, they wanted him to go."[27] She reflected, "The idea that just coming to serve the public doesn't seem to be the priority . . . And I don't know if it's like that at all agencies, but to just be involved in this power struggle for control of certain policies that are favorable to your constituency is just terrible. That's not following the science; that's not serving the public—that's like just raw political spoils of war. I don't like it. But I don't know that getting out helps. I think people on the inside need to be trying to continue to fight for the public service." Sullivan ended up leaving public service, however, in the wake of her experiences under Pruitt's leadership.

Others opted to stay but acknowledged the loss of their spirit of public administration and intrinsic motivation to serve the government and the public. Although Andrew Williams at USDT still remembered when "it was very exciting" when he was "doing good things for other fellow citizens in the tail end of the Obama administration," he reported in 2020 that "having that be sort of amputated from your life is very hard." He had taken "an enormous amount of pride" in his work helping others, "and it was just something you can tell the people about and intersected with what you'd see in the newspaper," he said. "I mean, you really felt a sense of civic purpose."

During the years of the Trump administration, I saw him age before my eyes. When we reconnected for our second interview in 2018, I was struck by a change in his demeanor and appearance. Although he was only a year older, deeper creases lined his face than I remembered, and his hair appeared to have thinned. He was as eager to talk and passionate as he had been, but seemed to lack some of the confidence and energy he had exuded the prior year. Williams told me how his agency as a whole had deteriorated. They had released reports on a number of issues that seemed obviously grounded in ideology rather than empirical analysis, and he reported that the agency had been stepping into the "sandbox" of "other agencies' jurisdiction," which struck him as "very political and very strange."

Williams felt powerless in the face of organizational decline and unable to address the biggest problems in his agency. When he assessed the state of his agency at the end of the Trump administration and considered some of the most egregious illegal acts by appointees, he concluded that, as civil servants and given their levels and duties within the bureaucracy, "we have no ability to change that outcome." Top appointed leaders in his agency were only listening to "industry representatives" and "people who have made a ton of money in the private sector," he thought, which made their policy choices cater to such interests, which harmed the interests of the rest of the American public. As he looked to the next election, should Trump be reelected, he said, "I would probably stay at this point, but . . . solely because it works for my family and not because I have any optimism about our future in this country. So it's not out of any sort of patriotic or civil service ideal. I don't really know anybody who has a lot of that anymore, which is concerning. I mean that's not a good outcome. That's very worrisome." He rationalized that this shift made him "focus" on his "family and, and that can be very fulfilling. But it's incomplete at the same time." He also rationalized that "even if I were to leave, I would probably have all those same concerns . . . I'm not sure there's really a refuge for concerned people outside the government either necessarily."

Career civil servants described how, under the Trump administration, the spirit of public administration withered across levels in the most politicized areas of the government. This led to diminishing intrinsic motivation among career civil servants as well as declining morale, solidarity, and mental health.

## Declining Morale and Solidarity

Much research documents, and affected career civil servants expressed in their firsthand accounts, a loss of morale can lead to negativity,[28] emotional exhaustion,[29] and lower job satisfaction.[30] Career civil servants also reported a loss of their own perceived sense of efficacy and diminished overall mental health.

Career civil servants working across politicized areas of the government attributed declining morale in part to how different facets of Trump administration leadership dampened solidarity and a sense of community in their workgroups and across their agencies. A HUD employee, for example, described in 2018 how the Trump administration's leadership wasn't "very warm at all," and this "does affect morale" in palpable ways every day. He said that appointees "don't even go around and say good morning or anything like that. And not even, you know, where you can be in the elevator with somebody and you have an awkward smile . . . They don't even try," which suggests "they don't actually care." These strained relationships were evident in all-hands meetings, where there was a clear lack of collective commitment: "no one really anticipates much, and so it's not like they offer much, and so no one really participates that much," and that "affects the morale," he told me.

I heard reports like this across affected agencies, such as the EPA, USDT, Federal Emergency Management Agency (FEMA), HHS, Department of State, USAID, and others. Along with other senior career EPA officials, Sean Butler disclosed that the mistrust Trump appointees displayed toward career civil servants was "destructive of morale" and exacerbated divides between the administration and career bureaucrats. "It frustrates communication because we don't know what to tell our staffs," he said, who then "take it for the worst."

Department of State lawyer Brian Taylor described in 2020 how the arrival of an appointee to supervise his cohesive and energetic workgroup incited more separation there:

> There's a lot more like hunkered down endure rather than kind of an esprit de corps kind of approach. There's a lot more like well, you're working on that shit sandwich, so that's what you're doing, and there's no point in really commiserating—everybody has their particular burden to carry—and a lot more just frustration that normal processes just aren't working. So yeah, a real decrease in morale, but I still have a good group of colleagues. We're just all super depressed.

It is evident from Taylor's report that morale was down in his workgroup under their Trump appointee, and his sense of efficacy and job satisfaction had also declined. Meanwhile, his sense of isolation, frustration, and depression had increased.

Others across agencies reported an increasing sense of isolation amid decreasing esprit de corps and morale. Because of the number of vacancies in his agency and appointees' failure to include his workgroup in relevant policy decisions, as was typical under other administrations, a midlevel analyst at USDT in 2018 said that he was "not getting out as much as I should, and I'm isolated from the rest of government." He described how his workgroup as a whole had become more disconnected from the larger agency and government as well: their "means of communication just happened to be contained in our group or the group next door; it's now entirely based on informal acquaintances." He seemed even more isolated in 2020. He began our interview noting, "It's good to have a confidant." He later described his work as "increasingly solitary" in his group. A steady stream of colleagues whom he thought were particularly hardworking and previously committed to their work had headed for the exits.

A sense of isolation crept up obliquely throughout some other career civil servants' interviews as well. By the time she left her position under the vindictive appointee at the State Department, for example, Ines Blackburn seemed to feel quite alone in her workgroup. She had not discussed her challenges working under her former appointed supervisor much: "You are probably the first person that I'm talking to in any sort of capacity," beyond her family and friends, "that would long-term memorialize the experience," she told me in 2018.

It was clear that the fear and suspicion fostered by the administration dampened communication within and across affected workgroups. When I asked one senior official at the EPA if he knew of any colleagues who "refused to sign things or refused to support things," as Sullivan had done, he said, "I don't know the answer to that question." Although, "we know what happens in the end, but we don't know exactly who said what. People are very tight-lipped about things, and there is some common paranoia." He reported not seeing anyone do that in his "office, and in other offices," he said, "sometimes we don't ever quite find out how things played out."

Increasing isolation left some mid- and lower-level employees stuck with facing challenging problems on their own. For example, an HHS employee I spoke with in 2017 said that when she had a "tough spot with a work situation a few weeks ago," her "immediate supervisor had kind of left me high and dry and went on vacation . . . It was one of those situations where I didn't have a person to report to." She said that this kind of neglect likely would not have happened "last year at this time," when "there would be somebody who could kind of help me out. But in this situation, I felt like everybody was so involved with their own stuff," and no one was available or willing to help.

Amid anxiety and stress, the HHS employee reported various signs of weakened common purpose and camaraderie in their work, such as "fewer social events and fewer collaborative meetings." She reflected, "I think when people get worried about their own situation here, they're worried about their own program and their own job—you are, I think, much less likely to collaborate or to coordinate or to go out on the ledge a little bit to try and help somebody else make something." She reported that colleagues had become "very protective" and "more skeptical. There's more of a bad vibe. And this is not a dramatic shift; it's just little things here and there," she said. These seemingly subtle changes, however, had consequences for her work. It seemed that people were losing faith and a sense of shared responsibility in their collective work. Cynicism was creeping in. As a result, their quality of work was starting to crumble.

## COMPOUNDING PROBLEMS REDUCE ORGANIZATIONAL FUNCTIONING

The challenges of working under increasingly autocratic forms of leadership in such conditions of chaos and uncertainty compounded over time in varied ways, giving rise to career civil servants' perceptions of workplace dysfunction and inefficacy across agencies. Career employees, for example, described politicals' increased use of misinformation and their seeming lack of accountability to law and democratic norms. They also described experiencing professional binds in trying to execute inchoate projects rooted in insufficient or conflicting guidance, slowed productivity, and insufficient trust and solidarity to be innovative.

Various midlevel managers noted the spread of misinformation across levels of the government, starting at the top and infiltrating the middle of some of the most politicized agencies. As a midlevel manager at HHS described, suspicion led to sidelining experts and less information sharing—which led to the passing of more inaccurate information upward by the appointee under whom he worked. He said that the appointees:

> are really scared of leaks. And so, they don't run a lot of things by us. Or they'll maybe only tell him [his supervising appointee] and . . . he just doesn't realize that no one else is being told, so that's partially like an issue of his management—but they won't share information with us. It used to be in these meetings with the secretary about the budget . . . you know, like one staff person from the office would get to go to provide backup information or something. They don't allow that at all . . . And if he represents it incorrectly . . . (1) we don't even know how he did it, and then (2), we're not able to . . . follow up or correct things. We don't have a counterpart in there either. You know, at the staff level we all have connections with each other and know how to follow up informally.

Even if this HHS manager wanted to correct misinformation passed up the chain, it would have been difficult working under the appointee and given the secrecy and limited vertical communication under the Trump administration in his agency. It seemed some politicals lacked typical accountability mechanisms and fact checking that occurred as part of standard operating procedures and meetings under other administrations—procedures that the appointees were deliberately avoiding. This could empower ideologically driven politicals in the short term, and it could also lead to more organizational inefficacy, poor program and policy development, and confusion over the long term.[31]

Another midlevel manager at HHS discussed similar problems resulting from a combination of appointee incompetence and the failure to learn from career civil servants' expert advice. He characterized leadership in his agency as making "decisions without understanding how to implement decisions," which he thought could have been prevented had they taken "a little more time" to meet with career staff and ascertain "the downstream effect" of their decisions. Such uninformed decisions, he said, caused confusion among career staff, who viewed them askance and did not understand their orders. Orders were further convoluted, he said, "with the hiring freeze . . . where we've gotten conflicting messages and people are doing it different ways and its turning everything into more turmoil." Such descriptions on the ground reveal not only various facets of the poor and inept leadership some career civil servants experienced working under but also the consequences of such ineptitude on their policy work. Chaos ensued as people tried to do their work more on their own without sufficient guidance or oversight and sometimes in response to conflicting messages.

Confusion among bureaucrats on how to best do their jobs abounded in the most contested parts of the government under the Trump administration. As Yasin Abadi described in his work, "Execution is really part of my situation . . . and the ways they work are just idiocy, and so it doesn't make any sense." Without going through the standard "rule-making process," which involves engaging various stakeholders, including expert bureaucrats, foreign countries, and others to "press" and "gauge" a proposed plan to "develop it," Abadi said that you can end up with a poor policy, which lacks sufficient stakeholder buy-in and is difficult to implement. As a result, he said in 2018 that, in his area, "what we have is not at all anything that makes any sense." The "optics" and "the optimization" were "bad," he said, and "a whole list of textbook examples show: you don't know what the hell you're doing."

Because of the confusion in his agency and across the federal government, he faced a paralyzing series of impossible professional binds. "They [political appointees] want things which are in direct contradiction of each other," Abadi told me. When I asked for an example, Abadi explained that some of the professional binds he felt trapped in concerned the Trump administration's approach to providing aid internationally. The Trump administration, as he understood it from his work and media accounts, was pushing diplomats and foreign policy experts to base relationships on partner nations' state of development and "how it is related to the national security process." This, he said, "was rather disturbing" as a seemingly "tit for tat" kind of relationship with other countries in which, "we give you this, if you vote the way we want you to vote." This conflicted with his understanding of how aid operated at his agency.

Yet "they want the USA to be the preferred development agency of available donors," he said, and for other countries not to "select other donors that we think are going to be worse for [their] development journey." At the same time, the United States was putting more restrictions on countries seeking aid, making such processes more difficult, and treating "the recipient nations . . . as incompetent to make their own decisions. And so, if we're trying to court these people, then we don't treat them as incompetent, and we don't give them a scorecard," he said. "Those things are kind of in opposition to each other. And so, then you leave it to us." Facing such binds was incredibly stressful for career civil servants, especially those sensitive to possible retaliatory actions from politically appointed leaders. These situations, which were exacerbated by the weak relationships between senior appointed leadership and career public servants, hindered productivity and progress.

"And so I don't know what's going on. I don't know what all this stuff means," Abadi said. In facing such uncertainty, Abadi said that he also felt like he had to choose between being "a slick salesman and come out of it looking good," but then have to face "unintended consequences down the line," or "you could also be not a slick salesman, have trouble now, but maybe no unintended consequences down the line. So take your pick, and neither of them sound very great."

Given senior leaders' failure to listen to experienced middle managers, career employees found themselves not only falling short in their agency missions and specific role responsibilities but also in upholding the law. For example, when one middle-level manager's office was closed abruptly for political reasons, "a lot of legacy issues" and "legal obligations" were not heeded, which had adverse "important foreign policy and national security implications." Even though "the work didn't stop . . . and needed to be done," he suggested, senior leadership, "were more concerned with their individual professional advancement" and consequently "would not speak truth to power" or "even stand up in the least bit . . . on matters related to personnel . . . and good policy." Although this career manager and his colleagues "put it all on the record," he said that "they didn't care and they disregarded it." In this case, his leadership's failure to listen to careerist expertise led not only to neglecting legally obligated work but, he thought, negative impacts on national security and foreign relations. He concluded, "The way to get things done is to have people who are engaged at senior levels. And they're not. Or they are through a lens that is incomplete or distorted." Even though he tried to speak up, he found he lacked the power to be efficacious or hold the political appointee accountable.

The fearful and suspicious workplace climate fostered by some Trump appointees in the most politicized locations decreased productivity and innovation in several ways. It was too risky to stand out when career civil servants did not have much information and a mistake could cost them their job. Abadi and others noted that the risks of political retribution from speaking up not only dampened motivation and "doesn't make you want to do your job" but also caused productivity to plummet. Abadi admitted that he had dramatically pared back his approach to his job. He said that not only were "Congress and the president not seeing eye to eye on these things," but his agency was "trying to find its place in the administration." He acknowledged that these uncertain conditions were "hard to work with." He did not know how senior elected and appointed government leaders would react to policy and how these different leadership preferences and organizational conditions would then interact. He said that "we're in a situation" rife with "confusion" where "we really don't know what's going to be the right answer. And so you don't want to get too far ahead of anything because you might just get cut off." With all this in mind, he said, in 2018, that "I spend a lot of time just thinking." Abadi's experience reveals how appointed senior leadership's untrusting and punitive treatment of career bureaucrats made work "slow down."

Abadi was not alone in being less productive.[32] Even with basic work, he said, "people just don't want to move [their work] along, and they triple check everything like five times." As others also reported across agencies in the government, Abadi said, "I think we're doing more stuff that means less. So it's still a lot of work, but we just know it's not as meaningful or as important as it was before . . . It seems like we're just doing stuff." Because they were required to spend more time doing busy work, civil servants' intrinsic motivation to work hard decreased further.

This loss of power and control over their work can lead to feelings of helplessness and reduced hope. Psychological research also suggests that this process then tends to reduce the likelihood that one takes further action to reclaim influence.[33]

Operating in a climate of fear, mistrust, and unclear communication, Abadi reported that people were especially reluctant to submit distinctive work on their own. He said that, in the "tense environment" of his agency, among civil servants, "it's just sort of like, 'Don't get out too far ahead of anything . . . and don't be the only person who does that.'" New initiatives either were not started, or their progress was stymied by employees' apprehensions about making a mistake or being blamed. "Substantive things," he said, "don't really happen, and you kind of just get down to the lows. And so new initiatives aren't going to really get started." He said that he was "definitely not coming up with ideas of how to do stuff." By 2020, Abadi acknowledged he had also grown "more reticent" in "taking on projects."

This slowing of work and new projects as a result of insufficient communication and mistrust of political appointees occurred in politicized locations across agencies. As a young, new civil servant at the EPA told me, the atmosphere of suspicion of career civil servants and mistrust at her agency meant that she was slow to move projects she was working on forward. "I don't want to say too much about what I'm doing," she said. While normally her work would require her team to apprise and get approval from more senior leadership and build relationships with external partners, her team instead focused on creating a new program and gathering data.

At the DOE, a midlevel manager reported that work and innovation stalled. Although he said he was not afraid of getting "fired or reprimanded" by new appointed political leaders thanks to well-known civil servant protections, substantial innovations no longer seemed possible in his agency, which had little internal communication and low trust between political and career civil servants. "There's so many things that takes building up good-will among the people that you need to approve things," he said, "so you don't want to start on the wrong foot by the first thing you send up getting rejected." He said people around him worried about being "pushed out of a position and then float[ing] around without much meaning. So you're more worried about that, and getting cut out of potential future promotions, future exciting projects." For example, he had an idea that "will save the government—and [his agency]—a lot of money," but, he said, we "don't even try" to propose it, knowing that they could not get the attention of senior leadership. Instead, his team chose to "stick to the initiatives that are far enough out of the spotlight that someone low enough that could be a career civil servant can approve it." This manager could make only small changes to his program. "You can't propose any radical changes that might have, you know, major efficiencies or major proved benefits to your program," he concluded.

Other public administration research has documented that, under distrusting leadership, career civil servants can also respond through neglect.[34] Some people seemed to take this route, how-ever, not by choice but because of a failure to be included by agency leadership in the work they were supposed to be doing. For example, amid a lot of political vacancies and the admin-istration's disinterest in his unit, one midlevel USDT employee reported that he was "not being pushed too hard to kind of waste time with the administration," and he had "checked out" from his primary role at work. This neglect could be "beneficial," he acknowledged, perhaps as a personal coping mechanism, because he could focus his time on other work he found meaningful. By 2020, however, he seemed both apathetic and frustrated. "The point of administration right now," he said, is to "shut down work" and, "as an anti-intellectual administration," to get people in his role not to do their job . . . I guess it works," he reflected, "because a couple of people have made comments like that and . . . nobody's able to do anything."

## CONCLUSION

Although most government workers I spoke with did not work in frequent contact with appointed members of the first Trump administration, a considerable number of those working in politicized agencies reported feeling the reverberations of poor political leadership in their everyday work in both subtle and obvious ways. In this chapter, I shared how these centrist and Democrat-leaning career civil servants across the middle and top levels of their agencies saw parts of the Trump administration affecting their work units and agencies. The career civil servants I spoke with reported experiencing a sense of chaos and uncertainty amid a leadership vacuum and loss of trust in leadership. They attributed this leadership vacuum to leadership infighting, increased secrecy and inadequate internal communication, and widespread perceived appointee incompetence.

Across levels in the most politicized agencies, career civil servants noted declining intrinsic motivation to do their work. Tied to this was decreased morale, weakened solidarity, increasing feelings of isolation, a weakening obligation to ethical norms, and a faltering faith in the spirit of public administration. Like senior career officials, many midlevel career bureaucrats in these contexts reported experiencing a sustained sense of professional role strain in which they felt that they could not meet the demands of their respective roles as well as they had under prior administrations.

Career civil servants reported that these changes all led to diminished organizational functioning, and they provided numerous examples demonstrating various kinds of organizational decline, including the proliferation of inaccurate information, episodes of corruption, a seeming lack of accountability for appointee ethical and legal transgressions, and inchoate program and policy development. These conditions in the most politicized areas immobilized career employees in loyalty traps and other professional binds and decreased their productivity—which could lead to a failure to uphold the law and/or mission. Career employees also became wary about standing out and/or innovating in their workgroups.

This organizational decline then fostered a sense of escalating chaos, uncertainty, employee frustration, decreasing morale and perceived efficacy, and deterioration in mental health in some locations under the leadership of more autocratic or seemingly incompetent appointees. Especially in these organizational pockets of decline, the employees I spoke with wondered: should I stay or should I go? In the next chapter, I examine how they responded under these conditions.

# 9

# TO STAY OR GO?

I n light of the precarious workplace conditions described throughout this book, how did affected career civil servants in politicized locations respond at work during the height of Donald Trump's first administration? While some journalistic and popular accounts oscillated between stories of deep state resistance versus civil servant compliance and endorsement of the new regime, scholarship on organizational change and public administration suggests that there are several pathways employees can take.[1]

In his canonical book, *Exit, Voice, and Loyalty*, economist Albert O. Hirschman suggests that, when organizations decline, members can opt to *exit* and leave their division or organization, or utilize *voice* to air grievances to those who can make improvements.[2] Research suggests civil servants will generally prefer to find solutions internally through airing grievances to superiors, and should that fail, choose to exit rather than engage in open confrontation.[3] Hirschman describes loyalty as influencing members' decisions to exit, dissent, or take an alternative approach. They may wait to see if conditions improve or try to correct the course of the organization: "[a]s a rule . . . loyalty holds exit at bay and activates voice."[4] A study of public administration employees conducted in 2002 suggests this then held true across levels of the public workforce.[5]

By most accounts and as described in previous chapters, civil servants maintain high degrees of loyalty across multiple dimensions. As one would expect from past research, because of their loyalties and role expectations senior public officials are particularly likely to exercise voice internally. They are also less likely to leave when discontented because of the high costs of leaving and increased risk aversion over time.[6]

Under the Trump administration, however, one might anticipate a different scenario. If civil servants find themselves working under politicals who are deeply suspicious of them, unwilling to meet with or listen to them, and likely to threaten or punish them for dissent, the employees might be more tempted to forgo voice and head to the exits.[7] As other research on public administration suggests, another option when working in dysfunctional conditions is that civil servants may try to resist leadership decisions they disagree with, sometimes with external support.[8]

To what extent did unhappy career civil servants comply with or resist the first Trump administration? I spoke to dozens of such career civil servants, and they reported trying to remain loyal and work within the lines of their particular roles in a professional and appropriate manner nearly all the time. Although many experienced frustration or anger, they still rationalized their limited powers in the chain of command, commiserated with some political leaders, and sought to ground themselves in the ethical bedrock of the state. They sought to uphold their agencies' missions, serve the public interest, and defer to the presidential administration and chain of command as prescribed by their roles. Those interacting with politicals noted the importance of building relationships, trust, and serving the presidential administration. Yet some civil servants felt directly threatened, even for using appropriate dissent.

Although federal civil servants' perceived ability to speak truth to power has varied historically and by agency, some career civil servants emphasized the importance of doing so to maintain the integrity of government functioning, especially at the outset of the Trump administration. As longtime State Department employee Steve Marsh explained at the start of the administration, "I owe it to my bosses, I owe it to the institution, and I owe it to the tax payers to give my best advice unvarnished, truthful, but respectful."

When asked if he thought he "could push back" against an unethical or illegal order, he said, "It's not only okay, it's utterly necessary. No organism, no institution, will long survive if decisions are not based on reality. If it's based on bullshit or if an organization begins to believe its own propaganda, they're headed for a fall."[9] He paused, and said, "Look no farther than the current White House. You have to look at reality, what the numbers are telling you. You can't navigate through the traffic here in Washington, DC, wanting the traffic to clear away; you have to navigate based on reality . . . I feel it's incumbent on any career officer, whether it's foreign or civil service, or frankly in any organization, to make their best case . . . why they think one policy choice is superior to another, supported by facts and data, right?"

Echoing Golden's research, Marsh, and others who used voice, recommended doing so when appointees and managers sought their feedback as experts. After political appointees and supervisors made their decisions, "then it's time to execute," Marsh said. "As career professionals, we have an obligation to carry out lawful instructions, even if we don't fully agree with it." He also believed, however, that "if I am instructed to do something that's unlawful or unethical, I have an obligation not to do it."

Walking this moral tightrope every day, however, was particularly challenging under the exaggerated expectation of loyalty to the president and his administration above all other professional loyalties, including to mission, to the Constitution, and to country in some parts of the government. Civil servants attempted to maintain their sense of balance, leaning on professional norms and standard procedures, and focusing more narrowly on the needs and goals of their agency, workgroup, or themselves. Rather than resist, these civil servants might describe their efforts as "alternative forms of compliance," "appropriate loyal dissent," or perhaps just doing their job.[10] Although this seemed to project a seeming continuity to career civil servants, the many challenges some faced wore on them over time. Even Marsh, who had a history of engaging in vocal loyal dissent in an agency with an official internal Dissent Channel, turned his attention to focus on internal team development and external civic and political affairs by the end of the administration.[11]

In this chapter, I discuss those who tried to remain loyal and support the presidential administration as best they could and muddle through, others who spoke up under a narrowing window of opportunity to use their voice, and those who opted to exit. In chapters 10 and 11, I will turn to the civil servants who approached the Trump administration with a spirit of resistance, albeit tempered by their roles and ethical obligations.

## LOYALLY MUDDLING THROUGH AMID COMPETING ETHICAL OBLIGATIONS

Some bureaucrats in the most politically contentious parts of the government under the first Trump administration adamantly denied that they participated in any form of resistance against the presidential administration. They argued they could loyally do their work within the lines of their job's duties and government ethical structures, even in the face of potential loyalty traps. To orient and sustain themselves amid the chaos and uncertainty, these bureaucrats grounded the narrative of their experiences in the ethical bedrock of public administration.

International affairs expert Yasin Abadi, for example, described the moral tightrope he walked throughout the administration. Across multiple interviews, he affirmed that, despite the "unusual" and "not healthy" changes he had witnessed in his agency and across the national government, he still earnestly wanted to be "a good steward as much as possible" and "serve as a bureaucrat . . . and use my judgment the best that I can to get us through the high degree of uncertainty that we have. And I'm going to try to help." While this could be "awkward," he said, "because you're trying to help your leadership execute its goal and protect them at the same time, that's sort of what the job is at this time. They just need a little more precaution than past leadership has had."

In the middle of the administration, I saw how difficult it was for Abadi to balance his different loyalties and risks while working under Trump-appointed leadership. He acknowledged that, under the first Trump administration, helping sometimes meant "just doing little, quite frankly. And it means just doing what's necessary, and it means waiting to help educate folks about what their options are as we go forward, as opposed to getting too fired up about things. Because it's safer. Because . . . I get back to other cascading problems down the line, and try to anticipate something where they don't even know where they are going." Here, Abadi tries to do his job loyally while also referring to the context of chaos, inadequate planning, and mistrust amid the increased sense of risk of political retribution at his agency. Taking all this into account, he simply slowed to a standstill sometimes and waited.

The changed work climate in his agency under Trump leadership made Abadi shift how he approached his work. Under former presidential administrations, decision making operated according to a collective deliberative process. As part and parcel of the job, Abadi explained, one inevitably makes choices that favor certain stakeholders over others. In government, he said, "If you favor industry, then you're necessarily not favoring individual citizens, and if you favor the safety of individual citizens, then you will be pissing off industry." In the past, he said, agency leaders had valued those who had "a strong opinion about everything all the time . . . Everyone is supposed to be the loudest squeakiest wheel." He described how career civil servants would argue their preferred positions and try to bring "to ground that what we're doing is right." Then, he said, leaders would "take a part in making a decision." But under Trump leadership, "the fact that you say the wrong thing at the wrong time, there's political consequences that are just *political* consequences but not actually in the best interest of anything is quite terrifying" [emphasis added]. This punitive shift narrowed the perceived window of possible and appropriate voice.

Despite the challenges, Abadi tried "to keep things moving along." He shared in 2018 that his daily work entailed quite a bit of muddling through the chaos and uncertainty, and trying to address his different responsibilities and loyalties in his workgroup and across agencies. Politicals were sending down policy work that was "not aligned" with the Department of State. "And so," he said, "it's easier to call my counterparts [there] and say, 'You're trying to survive this,' and, 'How do we keep our political leadership afloat without breaking any of the laws and making this coherent?'" He reflected, "The situation is very tenuous, and we worked through it that way."

Under the shared pressures of working under the Trump administration, Abadi noted that some career civil servant solidarity erupted, even in places where it had previously been absent. In his agency, which he had described in 2017, prior to the Trump administration, as siloed, contentious, and rife with bickering across different experts, Abadi noted some wellsprings of emergent solidarity among career employees under the Trump administration. Because it was such a "difficult time," in his agency, he said:

> You need a lot more solidarity in this situation . . . if something is screwed up, you probably know why it's screwed up, and people are more patient about it. I think because there's less space to maneuver, all of these ideological things are left behind, and it's okay. So we need to get through this budget cycle, and no one knows what's going on . . . and so you have to fight these budget battles and it's so dire and so you just have to get through these things, so there's that solidarity . . . We're all in this together, and we're all pulling in the same direction.

Some of the most senior career officials described the challenging moral and ethical tightrope they walked between their professional ethical obligations where they worked, the limitations of their particular duties and powers, and their duty to serve the elected president and his administration, which sought to cut their programs, offices, and agencies. When I met senior State Department official Rick Anderson in 2020, he had been through a lot. From his neutral tone and emotional register, however, one might incorrectly think that work under the first Trump administration was business as usual. In his experience, however, it was not. Despite a supportive immediate supervisor, Anderson was subject to what appeared to be politically motivated retribution as a result of political appointees' influence: he was transferred to several positions during the middle of the administration, including one unrelated to his work and another position overseas.[12] (He was later reinstated after appointees turned over, with the support of human resources.)

Anderson managed a program that "had very bipartisan support until the beginning of the Trump administration" because of its "apolitical" and "humanitarian" nature. It was "pretty easy to have shared values and shared purpose . . . There wasn't really a change," he said, "in terms of how people, I think perceived the work" under other administrations. Upon Trump's election, "things have flipped," he said. His area of work was one politicized and vilified by Trump at his rallies. As a result, he reported, Republican representatives, who controlled both chambers, were "not as willing to be champions for the program," even though, Anderson thought, "individually if you had talked to them," they "were still supportive" of it. "But I don't think people were willing to stick their neck out and go against the president," he said.

Like these congressional representatives, Anderson expressed his overt loyalty to executing the duties of his position "for the president." He carefully navigated between his competing loyalties to serve the president and to maintain his loyalty to his professional commitment to manage his program. "The president is not a fan of this program, so I don't advocate for this program, so to speak. That's not what I get paid to do," he explained. Instead, he said, "I get paid to operate a program, which has been, you know, directed by the president to be at a certain level. And right now we're at an all-time low." Like others, he said he could voice his opinions and "advocate prior to setting up that target, but once the target is set, my job is really just to carry out the program in a way that meets the conditions that have been prescribed by the president."

After his program was cut considerably, Anderson said it was "demoralizing." His work unit was "extremely busy" and "had a lot of challenges, which is always fine, frankly," he said, "to try to figure out how to operate under new conditions, or whether we can operate at all." Politicals' questioning of the purpose and legitimacy of Anderson's program took a toll on his work group's morale because they were "really committed" to the program.

In the face of such challenging situations during the Trump administration, Anderson was matter of fact. He acknowledged he had been in some "hard" situations, but "frankly," he said, "that's the nature of life." He acknowledged his commitment to being a stabilizing force in the government amid change: "Policies change, I wouldn't say all the time, and one does want to have a kind of consistent direction as much as one can."

He did seem to maintain a continued commitment to his program throughout the first Trump administration, despite how politicized it became. In the wake of a tremendous cut to his program, he said, "If you don't have support from the top, then frankly, you just have to find it in other places." He continued to work with his team, which he said "pulled together" and "was very good about supporting each other" to try to execute their program. He emphasized aspects of his work unit that he had the power to influence positively, such as ensuring his programs had "strong staff" and "leadership" with "the right instructions on how to operate in this changing environment" despite "turnover [for] . . . a variety of reasons."

Anderson described seeking to maintain the "overall footprint of the program." He reported hearkening back to values he and his office stood for, such as how to "serve" and "protect" their most "vulnerable" clients, even if his agency had to be "more discriminating now in terms of how we operate."[13] To justify this, he said, "Even if it's a lower number, we're still helping that number of people. We're still changing people's lives. In some cases, we may be saving their lives—but we're certainly changing them forever . . . So again, even if it's not volume, the quality is still there." His personal and professional commitment to the program was apparent.

It was clear that Anderson had done deep personal work to come to a place where he could earnestly hold together his loyalty to serving the presidential administration, which was hellbent on cutting his beloved program. "It's more than just a talking point," he said. "You actually have to live it for a while and really let it sink in, and then become comfortable with that, which, again, I think I've done pretty successfully." He reiterated his moral anchor to me, and likely to himself: "What were the opportunities or, how did you try to preserve your program and protect it as much as possible and continue doing the great work you were already doing?"[14]

Although Anderson's program was considerably pared down by the first Trump administration, he managed ultimately to maintain its fundamental structure. After being reassigned to his position, he described having support from his work group and from some other parts of his agency, affirming his right to be there and do his job. Anderson also cited the moral and ethical bedrock of the state, emphasizing his responsiveness to the administration and his ethic of service. More critical outsiders might inquire, of course, about the extent to which he helped weaken and cut down his program, which he and his office evidently cared about.

Other senior officials described a similarly delicate dance of exhibiting responsiveness to the president and his administration while maintaining the structures of their offices, which the first Trump administration sought to cut, and relationships with their staff who were loyal to their agency missions and their professional areas of work. At the Environmental Protection Agency (EPA), senior officials noted the continuing challenges of wanting to support the Trump administration despite lacking appointees' trust and also managing concerned staff. During the first half of the administration, one senior official said that he felt he couldn't do his job as an intermediary between the administration and his office staff, even though he wanted to. Amid contention and divisions, he said, it "doesn't have to be that way because we would help out; we definitely would support, as professionals, the new administration." Yet the many divides between the administration and career staff persisted throughout the administration. As a senior EPA official reported in 2020:

> I think we're just treading water. I think if you'd ask almost all the people that are there, they would say we're looking forward to a day when—how do I put it—the leadership values more align with the career staff's values. And right now, we're executing. We're doing the things that we need to do. I think morale is very low. There's a lot of concern about the direction because at very high levels, especially at the administrator and presidential level certainly, there has not been a lot of support for the mission of the EPA.

Even at the end of the administration, he still reported that "people are waiting to see what comes next." He also expressed relief "that we didn't get more damage done to us." Despite "a lot of discussion of things, a lot of things that could've happened," such as abolishing a regional office, the "changes were very minimal." After years of the administration's threats, various senior officials mentioned similar relief that core structures remained in place. Many rationalized that the government had remained resilient amid the administrative onslaught.

Even in the most tumultuous areas and among some of those senior officials who likely experienced political retribution first-hand, through internal conversations with themselves and reaching out to colleagues in other related offices, some career civil servants continued trying to maintain all their expected, and sometimes contradictory, loyalties to the government in their roles. Such processes were incredibly precarious and involved considerable self-work and many rationalizations. They told themselves and me that they indeed were trying to maintain loyalty to their position, the organizational structure, and the long-term stability of the government and that they had sufficient efficacy to help some people where possible.

Even among some younger EPA staffers who were particularly critical of Trump appointees early in the administration, I witnessed some of their relief at the government's perceived resilience. They also tried to muddle through the chaos of Scott Pruitt's leadership term. As a young staffer described in 2018, although Pruitt made "bold statements," he then seemed to "move on to the next thing." He seemed more of a "nonpresence" after a while than a serious threat to this particular staffer. "There was a big sense of these statements are being made, but the staff to actually implement them . . . aren't there, in which case," he said, "we're not going to change anything." Since the election, he reported, they had been particularly "conscious" about "following more by the rule book . . . as a precaution because we actually felt the headquarters, you know, putting their knees on our backs." To some of these lower-level employees in offices around the country, where appointees had less influence and presence, they muddled through this notably volatile term and believed that, in the second half of the administration, that it had not been as destructive as they had feared.

Career civil servants, mostly in the mid- to high-level ranks, reported that another common means of responding to the Trump administration was trying to "stay under the radar" of the administration and continue doing their work to the extent it was possible. Employees of all ages across levels and agencies (including, but not limited to, the EPA, Department of Justice [DOJ], Department of the Interior [DOI], Department of Energy [DOE], National Science Foundation [NSF], Department of the Treasury [USDT] and the United States Patent and Trade Office [USPTO]) told me that they had been trained to avoid the attention of the Trump administration and its politically appointed leadership. As a DOE employee told me in 2017, "You don't want to be the one to rock the boat." A midlevel career civil servant at the Department of Education also said, "I have been trained to keep my head down and stay away from whatever political influence that I can."

Older, more experienced career civil servants who had survived tumultuous leadership transitions in the past, such as one DOI employee nearing retirement, told me that they were adopting a "hunkering down attitude," knowing, after all, that "we've been through this before." An older DOJ lawyer, who had worked in a contested area for decades, told me that, along with some other colleagues, he had taken the same tack. He had "tried to burrow in" to survive "certain administrations that I was not wholly comfortable with," such as the Trump administration. "I had little to no contact with what I call the political people," he said. "That was deliberate. I did not seek to participate, and I went through my intermediary." When I asked him next if there had been any leaking from his office, he responded, "Not to my knowledge, but I would not want to know even if there were that happening. And so you stay insulated." An analyst at USDT similarly described his response to the administration as in keeping with "a long tradition of technocrats avoiding promotions to management."

In some agencies, such as the Department of Defense (DOD) and Department of Homeland Security (DHS), career civil servants reported mostly being able to do their work at their level in part by avoiding the fray at higher levels. Reflecting on his experiences during the administration in 2020, DOD Senior Executive Service (SES) member Ralph McCafferty said:

> There is a duality to it . . . the government is functioning well despite still not having a lot of senior political positions filled throughout the government. The government, to the surprise of some, has continued to function and is funded so government continues. And yet there's also a dissonance that there's so much political turmoil and chaos at the top of the government that career civil servants have just sort of hunkered down, and we're just focusing on doing our jobs and trying to tune out what's going on at the very top tier of government.

Some employees noted a degree of comfort working far below in the political administration. When I spoke with mid-level manager Sarah Farmer at DOE in 2018, she said that, in her work unit, "we tend to just hope that we stay out of the spotlight because then at least we know what the civil servants are going to do as opposed to the political appointee becoming the gauge: we don't always know how that's going to impact a program or situation."

## FORECLOSING OF APPROPRIATE VOICE

Tied to civil servants' wariness was a sense of the narrowing window of opportunity in which they felt comfortable exercising voice and sharing their expert opinions under the suspicion and political retribution of the administration. As Yasin Abadi disclosed, there was a shift in his work unit. Prior to the Trump administration, they maintained a process in which their opinions as subject matter experts were valued and people argued "vociferously" for their positions on policy and their applications. "Now," he said in 2018 (in reference to Maria Longi's job transfer, which was discussed in chapter 4), "basically what they're saying is, if we make the decision, based on what you told us, you might get *fired*." He laughed. "That's what this is signaling to us. So *don't* be that free with what you're thinking [emphasis by the speaker]."

"People are scared to participate," Abadi said. He described a contagion effect, in which people stopped sharing their ideas and opinions. "One thing I've been noticing more lately," he said, "is that no one is going to speak truth to power lately." No one will say, "'This is a stupid idea.' No one wants to hear it, and no one cares whether this is a good idea or bad idea. They just do what they're told." Their fear led to further isolation, distrust, and suspicion: "and they're not really relying on anyone that is there," he said.

Various career civil servants across agencies reported that seeing how the politically appointed supervisor in their department responded poorly to their raising questions or concerns, as well as others' use of voice, they quickly realized such an approach was not welcome or effective. Some career civil servants in the most politicized locations stopped communicating directly and instead went to great lengths to avoid negative attention from political appointees. This occurred for some people whom I would not have expected to bow so easily to power. Ines Blackburn was one such person. While she was careful not to define herself as an activist, Blackburn was civically and politically engaged. She had donated to political campaigns and attended one mass protest shortly after Trump's inauguration. She also attended meetings for civil servants working across government agencies early in the administration, a group that had provided social support. This attendance reminded her "that you're not alone in feeling this way" and that the Trump administration was "not normal."

Despite Blackburn's inherent trust that the government worked and her loyalty to serving leadership, her experiences under the first Trump administration had been so disturbing and disorienting that when I spoke with her in 2018, she seemed bewildered and as if, in the midst of so much political turmoil, she had yet to make sense of her experiences. Blackburn's experience working under the Trump administration had gotten worse over the prior year. Before political appointees arrived, her office was led by different rotating senior career executives, who, she said, were "incredibly talented" and "well versed in the subject matter," which made her work group feel largely "insulated from the broader political trends because we didn't have a political appointee or appointees in our office."

Because of changing leadership in a contested agency, their dampening morale, and their growing sense of inefficacy, however, Blackburn and most of the senior career leadership in her office began looking for other positions. As she was looking for another job, several political appointees arrived. One appointee in particular created a "stressful" and fearful work climate by, among other "unethical and borderline illegal things I have seen him do," breaching civil service protections on political affiliation by creating an "enemies list" of Democrats he believed did "not support the president's policies." As a result, Blackburn seemed to feel as if she had little power. This made her work incredibly "challenging." When I asked her, "Strategically how do you interact with him then?," she said, "I kind of play dumb. My strategy has just been to not get on his enemies list." When her appointed supervisor stripped mentions of human rights protections from documents, which Blackburn thought were very important, "I just kind of ask him, in an attempting-to-be-innocent way, 'Oh, can you help me understand these edits? I want to make sure you're getting what you need, and I need to represent these edits to the other government that's asking for this. What's the story where it's not wanting anything on equality?'"

Blackburn also tried "to limit my interaction with him as much as I can, but also—when I do need something—just to appear helpful and neutral and not talk back to him or give him any fodder to put me on his list of enemies of the president." When it came to implementing his suggestions, Blackburn would pass them to others and try to avoid engagement as much as possible: "I just forward his edits along and say 'Here are his edits. Please go to him with any sort of questions.'" She said, "I don't try to represent them to the people that are receiving the edits, because I want him to speak for himself. I don't want to get in the middle of it. I would've loved to have a full argument back and forth with him on the structural reasons as to why we have goals of equality," given "the historical disadvantages some communities have faced in our country and abroad," Blackburn said, but "he just doesn't get it, doesn't see it, so I've just disengaged on that with him." Blackburn had chosen not to speak up further because "I have kind of determined that it is totally pointless to argue with him because he does not take on any alternative. I've never seen him change his position when he learns the full context. I think anything that doesn't fit his worldview he just rejects . . . I think one choice is to argue the case with him, and I have not seen that win with anybody who's tried to. It's only gotten them put on the bad list. So I've not done that."

From working in close proximity to a vindictive appointee for an extended period of time, Blackburn had learned to fear retaliation, lost her sense of efficacy, learned to avoid ownership over parts of her work tied to the appointee, and taken to avoiding the appointee when possible. Given her work conditions, she felt trapped, as if she lacked any good options.

Like other civil servants who typically deferred to poor leadership in an effort to preserve civil relations, Blackburn admitted that, on a few occasions, "I've had a couple of negative interactions with him, just because I found it to be so morally offensive that I had to say something." It seemed that for some people working under extreme strain, they could control their behavior only so much before they reached a breaking point. On these occasions, such employees, like Blackburn, seemed to view such behavioral transgressions, where they lost self-control and composure, with regret. "In a couple of instances where I feel like he's stepped over such a strong moral line of mine, I've said something, but it also accomplished nothing," Blackburn said, "and it probably hurt me in my relationship with him . . . I'm sure I got on his bad list for a couple weeks after" the incidents, in which she spoke up on behalf of human rights and agency policy.

With the option of exercising voice off the table, Blackburn said that she had instead chosen "self-preservation," or "just escaping," by moving to a different position. Given the rapid changes she experienced at work and the assault of standard democratic norms by appointed leadership in her agency, there were moments when she seemed to have lost the ability to understand what was happening around her. She confided in 2018: "I'm kind of beginning to come to the conclusion, I think a little bit later than most, that this is just not an okay environment to work in." She reflected feeling torn and immobilized in this context, which was notably different from her prior record of professional competence and accomplishment in her agency under the former administration. Blackburn left her position feeling unhappy: "It is incredibly stressful and I also feel like

I haven't done enough to bring to light the situation because I feel personally embattled." She was acutely aware of the appointed supervisor's "campaign to target the leakers, and I am personally concerned about being lumped in with the people that he thinks are leaking stuff. And I don't want his wrath, so my default has just been not to do anything that could even have a perception that would put me in this camp."

Blackburn's experience reveals not only the multiple loyalty traps pitting her political expertise against the appointed supervisor, and allegedly the president's agenda, but also the confusion of working under seemingly unclear, suspicious, and incompetent appointed leadership who were arguing for potentially illegal and ill-informed action. Such conditions exacerbated the stakes of her actions and her moral dissonance, and depressed her ability to speak up. This paralyzed Blackburn. Feeling disempowered, she opted, like many others, to keep her head down and leave her position.

Blackburn's experiences at the midpoint of the administration bring to mind the social psychology of accommodation to repressive leadership. One's reaction to fear has a powerful effect on one's likelihood of standing up to repressive regimes, as Samuel Oliner and Pearl Oliner found in their extensive study comparing those who rescued the Jews to bystanders during World War II. In contrast to the rescuers, the bystanders were markedly more passive, equivocating, and accommodating. "Despite their hostility toward the Nazis," the Oliners wrote, "the majority of bystanders were overcome by fear, hopelessness, and uncertainty. These feelings, which encourage self-centeredness and emotional distancing from others, provide fertile soil for passivity. Survival of the self assumes paramount importance."[15]

In contrast to the Oliners, who compared those who acted morally to those who did not, and assumed that people's personalities drive their moral behavior, Blackburn's experiences suggest something different: they highlight how situations can encourage or repress voice. Even though she had admitted not doing enough while working under her particularly threatening political administrator, after she left this position in the second half of the administration, she opted to speak with the Office of the Inspector General in her agency to report her experiences through formal grievance procedures. In her new position, she said, she "felt more protected" and was also compelled to report to support a colleague. She had chosen not to report to the press because she did not want to be seen as a leaker, she said in 2018, even though she clarified that "everything that's come out in the press so far is not classified information—so it's therefore not a leak." She also rationalized her lack of further reporting by acknowledging that others with similar experiences had already shared information with the press.

After the 2018 midterm elections, when the House of Representatives became majority Democratic, she thought reporting would be more efficacious. She then chose to report to a House oversight committee. She disclosed grievances only through officially sanctioned reporting mechanisms, in part seeking to stay within the bounds of her role by using institutionally sanctioned forms of voice. Speaking to the press was "a line I drew for myself that I didn't want to cross," she said in 2020.

Reflecting on her experiences at the end of the administration in 2020, Blackburn explained how career civil servants' particular situations mattered a great deal in their ability to use voice efficaciously. In making sense of her experiences throughout the administration, she saw her experience differently depending on the position she was in. "You are probably seeing the snapshots in time," she accurately assessed. In her experience, she said, "It's not like a one, constant feeling." The ability to speak up, she said, "often depends on who you happen to be reporting to at the time, what your experience is working in your job."

The amount of power, protection from above, and support from colleagues—as well as her sense of the perceived efficacy of speaking up—all contributed to Blackburn's later decision to speak up rather than keep her head down. Like most civil servants, she was careful to operate within the lines of her official role and the norms of what being a good, loyal civil servant should do: she chose to report only through conventional accountability channels that are part of the structure of the democratic state, and was clear that she did not want to breach professional norms by sharing information with the media.

Blackburn was also cautious about how she made sense of her experiences. Given the turmoil and chaos she had experienced, she seemed to hypothesize what had happened to her in the midst of the administration, more so than explain it in a clearly articulated narrative. Near the end of the administration, she remarked that she felt her story still was not fully written. In 2020, she reflected: "I think I am still in the middle of it so it's hard to have the perspective right now. I know that it's been a very emotionally draining three years." She was not yet out of the Trump administration and her personal narrative could not be determined conclusively until the following election took place. She thought, "Probably if there's Democrat who wins, I'll say like, 'Oh, this is the right decision that I stayed—like I'm here to help rebuild—all that suffering was so worth it.' And then, of course, if Trump wins again, I'll be like, 'What a stupid decision that I stayed; I wasted four years of my life.' So it's gonna be one or the other and we'll know in November."

It is important to evaluate people's moral sensemaking and actions situated in their immediate work groups and larger organizational and institutional contexts. As Blackburn describes above, during times of rapid change and heightened political suspicion and risks, moral decision-making can be quite dynamic, incoherent, and subject to local situational factors and constraints. She shows that people can also use historical events as markers that can sway how they interpret their story, efficacy, and morality. In her case, Blackburn was awaiting a future happening and left very much in an inchoate middle ground, not quite sure where she stood.

When I spoke with those below Blackburn's employment level, it seemed that opportunities for voice were conditional on a supervisor's support. When senior career officials and midlevel managers stopped speaking up to the administration, it signaled to those working below them to do the same. This gave rise to no small amount of frustration among some of the rare mid- and lower-level employees who preferred to air their grievances. Such grievances were palpable across levels. A senior EPA official reported that when career civil servants were shut out from sharing their expert opinion, morale, trust, and faith in the administration could be lost, potentially sowing the seeds of future resistance:

> I've always said, "Look, we live in a democracy. The president gets to make appointments. The president gets to make policy decisions and as long as it's ethical and legal, you need to follow those decisions." And I think most people can. But if they don't feel they got to do their part, they don't feel like their knowledge was used or respected, or they were shut out, or they weren't consulted or really informed, they really need to understand why. They like to hear the thinking. They can handle the truth. It could be look, you know, this is a close call, but politically we're gonna have to decide this way. I think they can accept that. I think the resistance within agencies comes from feeling shut out or disrespected in

the process, not being able to give their briefing, not being able to dispense their knowledge, and not being informed about the basis of the decision, and I think you lose the career people. I think they become disaffected and they feel like the decisions aren't being made honestly and they're not using science. They feel untrusting, and that's where I think the leaders that don't include the career people, they can lose the agency in the sense of losing trust and support from the troops and morale.

Midlevel analysts, lawyers, and policy experts across politicized agencies expressed such frustration from not being able to do their jobs as they saw fit.

Some career civil servants expressed frustration at not being able to communicate upward and share grievances with senior leadership when appointees deviated from their agency mission. This even occurred in offices with prior solidarity and good relationships with senior career officials. For example, even though one longtime EPA midlevel manager worked in an office where, he had said, "everyone's all in" on supporting the EPA mission and where they were fortunate to have "good people" working above them in administration, I watched his anger with his supervisors grow over the course of the first Trump administration. This manager found it incredibly frustrating that senior career officials were not "stepping up to fight" for the mission of the agency. "And so I have all these arguments with managers about being strategic and laying low and all that kind of stuff. I disagree with that . . . I think they're being complicit," he said. When he voiced his concerns about leaders' approach in dealing with EPA rollbacks, he doubted that his complaints were passed along to more senior leadership. He also suggested that should he take his grievances to senior leadership directly, he would be punished.

Christina Whitman, a midlevel manager at NSF, had a similar experience. When "management was strategically trying to not draw attention to us," she said that she felt like "nobody is fighting for us. And I'm really angry that nobody is willing to stand up and say that my employees are good employees, and I have a legal right to approve their work. Nobody wants to put themselves on the line for me." Whitman admitted that she was unusual in continuing to exercise voice and "make a scene" at staff meetings. Although she was aware of the personal risks of being the most vocal person in the room, she said that she was willing to do so because she was "not that invested in my career there" and had the confidence that she "was very talented at what I do" and "if, in the end, I get fired, someone will hire me because I still live in a world of privileges that I have due to being educated and white." As a "young" person, she said, "I'm not going to stay quiet for thirty years." To Whitman, important things are worth "fighting for."

In contrast to her own willingness to speak up, she said that, in her office, everyone else seemed "to awkwardly sit there." Afterward, she said, despite how a few people had thanked her for speaking up, "I've been in an office full of a lot of very passive, timid people. They don't rock the boat when somebody says something inappropriate. They don't really stand up to them. They've recruited people like themselves over the years and so there isn't anybody to stand up and say, 'This is bullshit.' They haven't said it to their management, and they won't say it to the top local leadership, and so local leadership won't argue on our behalf to the White House, and everybody is so afraid." She noted colleagues' concerns that "the Trump administration is vindictive." Their office was told when they got the budget not to talk to the media about it for fear that information in the media was "getting back to the Trump administration," and if they complained, they might get a bigger proposed budget decrease. These managers' experiences reveal that when bureaucrats, and particularly leaders, suppress their own voices and that of others, it can stymie the use of voice from those around and below them. This not only harmed employee morale but also could foster a workplace of complicity.

From Blackburn's and others' experiences, it is also apparent that the ability to use effective voice was perceived as emergent and situational rather than as an enduring condition and feasible possibility. This approach was mainly available to senior officials who interfaced with other senior career officials and appointees. For those at lower levels, they could get angry at their immediate supervisor, keep their head down, leak information, or quit. As shown above, none of these options seemed ideal to some mid-level career servants.

## EXITS

Over the three years of my study, more than a quarter of the people I spoke with left the administration.[16] I witnessed a steady trickle of people leaving throughout the administration for a variety of reasons, but most noted part of their decision to leave was tied to some frustration with the first Trump administration. It is important to recognize that exits during or shortly after presidential transitions are not uncommon. Past research suggests that rates of exits might rise slightly following a transition but typically remain under 10 percent.[17] During the Trump administration, there seemed to be a slightly higher rate of people quitting on average (14 percent higher) than during Barack Obama's last term.[18] Compared to the first year of Joseph Biden's term,[19] it also seems like the turnover during the Trump administration in my sample was notably high, even when taking into account how retirements over both Biden's and Trump's terms have been high due to baby boomer retirements.

Because I spoke only with career civil servants who identified as politically centrist and Democrats and oversampled those in particularly politicized locations, those in my sample were particularly likely to leave under a Republican president like Trump. My results align with patterns of exits documented under other presidential transitions from the late 1980s through the first decade of the twenty-first century, in which SES members and employees in agencies with a political mismatch between agency policy and presidential agendas are more likely to leave than others.[20] Because agencies such as the EPA, Department of Health and Human Services (HHS), and Department of State worked on issues of great political interest to the first Trump administration, the level of exposure to the administration appears to have been an important factor in their departure. Such departures enable the presidential administration to hire more ideologically aligned replacements and thereby increase their power.

I did not see a substantial number of General Schedule 15 (GS-15) employees waiting it out in the hope of gaining promotions as has been documented under past administrations, likely because of the political inclinations of those I spoke with or their self-selection into my study. I also did not see many career civil servants eager to stay because Trump's agenda focused on their work and they were excited by the opportunity to influence it, as has been documented during other presidential transitions.[21]

Exiters took different paths. Some older, long-serving employees retired. Others transferred internally to other agencies or branches of government or left particularly politicized locations and agencies for nonprofit work or higher education. Some went on temporary detail and left after that. A few sought to avoid particularly contentious locations, while others veered into positions where they thought they could hold the Trump administration more accountable, such as positions in an Office of Inspector General or Congress. Nearly all exiters chose to leave quietly rather than opt for a resistant exit.[22] A few mentioned not wanting to cause trouble for those they were leaving behind.

Exiters tended to be among the younger (average age was forty-seven) of the more senior career civil servants (General Schedule level 13 [GS-13]—SES positions) and had relatively fewer years of federal work experience than the others I spoke with. This group was high enough in the bureaucracy to witness the Trump administration's leadership but likely did not hold enough power to influence it. As one person mentioned, "I really just felt like I was banging my head against the wall on a lot of policies . . . that I work on." Another SES member left because he felt sandwiched between the poor communication of Trump administration leadership and those he managed. "You're going to get in trouble no matter what you do," he said. "You don't even have good information to tell your people, so they're looking at you like 'I don't understand.' And sometimes you do know things, but you're told for months and months that you can't share them. So that's horrible. Just it was a really hard place to be a manager." This civil servant's frustration was tied to appointee incompetence, lack of leadership direction, and a particularly threatening work environment in which any form of perceived dissent was considered a demonstration of disloyalty.

In environments like this, characterized by scrutiny and mistrust, various career civil servants evoked a deeply held professional norm in assessing whether it was time to go or not: you "implement or find a new job." As Yasin Abadi told me, "We are a government agency, so especially if this is how the election has gone and this is what people want, then this is what we're doing . . . And it's always like a good check on one's self" to inquire: "Have I become so far gone [chuckles] that I don't connect essentially with what people need anymore? In which case, maybe it is time to go do something else."

For many of those who chose to leave, it became increasingly impossible to reconcile their professional and institutional loyalties to their agencies and the larger government. At the Department of State, an agency that lost a lot of career employees during the first Trump administration, an employee said that some colleagues had "serious reservations and have been taking steps to try to shape outcomes that they think are in the interest of our country, . . . like less damaging . . . And some people just said, 'I can't do this, period, and I'm gonna go.' Which was a lot of people." Facing intractable competing demands and loyalties, these career civil servants opted to leave their agencies or federal service entirely. After speaking with her friends who worked in other agencies across the government, one person said that she realized the work climate did not seem better elsewhere in federal service, so she chose to shift to working in higher education.

Others left because of downstream effects of government malfunctioning under the first Trump administration. One midlevel manager in a stagnant and neglected agency told me, "Because we're constantly in this sort of wait-and-hold position, there aren't new opportunities opening up, and so my only personal frustration is being early to mid-career and looking for the next challenge and growth, and it's frustrating there just aren't apparent opportunities." I heard this from several other devoted younger and midlevel career bureaucrats, some of whom, to my surprise, left their jobs in 2018 for work in the private and non-profit sectors. This steady trickle of talented, experienced, young and middle-aged people leaving federal civil service no doubt will have negative ramifications on the bureaucracy over the longer term.

For those who remained, the steady stream of colleagues heading for the exits was demoralizing. It was particularly troubling when the colleagues they held in the highest esteem were leaving, people who they thought would likely not be replaced by others with equivalent ethical standards and professional abilities. One employee at USDT said that his work group had lost "a good number of people every year," during the administration. Near the end of the administration, he recalled losing "another batch of people . . . And frankly, they were the more dynamic people who are still, like working on their career and pushing forward." He explained that, in his unit, "there's a range from people who are working super-hard and trying to do really well to people who are kind of like there" and when "the five most dynamic people, or in the top ten, are leaving," that "changes the tenor of the place a little bit." When I asked why they left, he said that most provided other professional and politically neutral reasons for leaving their office. Only one used "the word 'anti-intellectual' to describe the administration," he said, while others used "normal reasons why you look for a new job," for example, "better pay, 'I wanted to go back to academia,'" or "'I kind of like the type of work I'll be doing there better.'" He continued, "People are not going to tell me that they are super-frustrated by the administration. I'm very confident that that is part of it, but again, that's not—they're not going to state that reason." Such accounts reveal how challenging it is to parse out, both qualitatively and quantitatively, why people leave their jobs, and particularly why career civil servants, who are strongly socialized to be politically neutral and serially partisan technocrats, opt for the exits during periods of heightened political contention.

Those leaving and those remaining also raised concerns about the administration's disinterest in preserving their institutional knowledge, which they had acquired, in several cases, over decades of service. One retiree noted how he had applied for a position to help transfer knowledge. He had painstakingly kept boxes of historical records during his tenure and shared with me some newspaper clippings and other public records about the work at his office. His application to stay and aid a smooth transition was rejected.

Another person at the Department of Housing and Urban Development (HUD) described how difficult it was to watch "all the foolishness of firing people, detailing people and pursuing them left and right" in his agency under the Trump administration and see the many "high ranking . . . [GS-]14s and [GS-]15s" retiring. As a result, "morale is down, and the attrition is just incredible," he said. Positions were not always refilled, and when they were, it was often by temporary employees. In these transitions, he reported that institutional knowledge was not being passed along, and new hires lacked knowledge of how the government operated.

When I asked another long-term EPA employee who was about to retire about the impacts of his leaving, he painted a bleak picture. "Well, what I have control over, I've had control over for more than two decades," he said. "I'm the only one that does what I do, so when I leave I think . . . the roof will fall in . . . drastic failure will seep in." But, he said, "I also have a perspective on how things change here: something has to fail. And once it fails, it has to fail miserably. And if it fails miserably, then the taskmasters are then taken up, and change will then trickle down from the top. And so, at this point, because things have not failed miserably, people say, 'Well, put a Band-Aid on it, and keep working.' "[23] As other public administration scholars have noted,[24] these losses of human capital atop various government agencies are consequential. When experienced career civil servants leave, they enable new administrations to hire their own loyalists, which can give rise to institutional memory loss, reduction of skill and declining social capital, which further harm organizational performance.

## CONCLUSION

So how did career civil servants in the most politicized parts of the government under the first Trump administration navigate increasingly contradictory ethical obligations at work? Career civil servants reported using Hirschman's three options in organizations perceived to be in decline: exit, voice, and loyalty. Some midlevel and senior career civil servants tried to muddle through and maintain their multiple, at times seemingly contradictory ethical obligations despite chaotic and threatening conditions in their agencies. It seemed that under the most vindictive appointed leaders, the perceived opportunity to use their voices appropriately narrowed. As both Rick Anderson and Adele Sullivan (in chapter 7) experienced in the beginning of the administration, and as Ines Blackburn alluded to, such leaders had the power simply to remove senior officials from their positions or assigned duties. Career officials and midlevel managers could also be excluded from high-level planning meetings and/or relegated to an "enemies list." In undergoing such treatment, career civil servants lost efficacy and trust. Considering Hirschman's explanation of potential responses, with the window of voice considerably narrowed, this made loyalty through compliance more likely or the option of exit more appealing.

Senior career civil servants in the most politicized and contentious agencies, such as the Department of State and the EPA, described how, under Trump's leadership, those career civil servants willing to comply and support some Trump appointees'

more autocratic bent, and willing to let other longstanding loyalties tied to their jobs and their spirit of public administration
wither, were trusted more and promoted. The large majority of
respondents I spoke with who depicted themselves as political centrists or Democrat-leaning did not fall into this camp of
achievers. Only two people could: they were a small minority
of the total number of public servants with whom I spoke. This
pattern could be the result of a selection effect in my sample—
the people who spoke with me and who were interested in my
study of change under the Trump transition were undoubtably
less risk-averse and responsive to the administration, and they
were less ideologically aligned with it than those uninterested in
speaking with me.

To have any efficacy—and to have any perceived choice in
how to conduct their work with ethical and moral integrity—
career officials needed to have some power. They could have
such power in part from their official roles as high-level officials
and supervisors, but this was insufficient in the face of appointees occupying even higher positions with greater power. To gain
more power, career officials needed some support from superiors and likely from colleagues in their work group or elsewhere.
With some power, they had more latitude in making decisions.
This is an unfamiliar and perhaps uncomfortable truth for people steeped in beliefs of moral and ethical action rooted in individual agency and people's personalities.

For those who had some of this power and latitude in making choices, they described some situations in which they could
rely on the ethics of public service and try to muddle through
their conflicting required loyalties at work, with some limited
success. As Anderson described, this could involve taking some
considerable hurtful hits, such as being removed from his job,
and taking part in the shrinking of his program. Like some other

senior career officials at the EPA, he took some comfort in being able to protect the structure of his office and rationalized that he was still able to help some people, although less so than he could in the past. To survive the moral dissonance he experienced during the administration, Anderson had to do deep personal emotional work, molding himself conscientiously into a responsive and loyal public administrator who let go of hurt and potential resentment from mistreatment at the hands of appointed officials. Although some critics may point out that such officials were compliant and in part complicit with the administration, others might counter that such officials provided continuity, contributed deep knowledge of their program and policy areas, and helped to preserve some archipelagos of government functioning amid the larger chaos and contention in the uppermost echelons of their agencies.[25] In such locations, senior officials collaborated with appointees to form a new version of the state together. Of course, even at seniormost levels, it is important to recognize that the politicals held more agenda-setting and decision-making power and, as Anderson mentioned, after providing his advice, he then had to comply with what the politicals wanted.

Across the most politicized and contested parts of the government, career civil servants reported experiencing a sense of uncertainty, a fear of retaliatory actions, and declining morale. Some career civil servants described such conditions as paralyzing and contributing to a decline in their decisiveness, confidence, and sense of efficacy in their work. Others reported an increase in anger and frustration. Comparing such emotional experiences of workplace decline to Hirschman's framework, it seemed that under the Trump administration's autocratic turn, those in the most affected locations experienced a narrower window of opportunity to use their voice when things went awry, as well as concerns about the efficacy of taking such an approach. This led many civil servants to stop speaking up and to avoid attention from political appointees whenever possible.

Even in the face of unusual and, in some cases, unethical or even illegal behavior on the part of political appointees that left civil servants feeling threatened, stressed, and uninformed, the majority of civil servants demonstrated overt loyalty and responsiveness at work most of the time. The more career civil servants' colleagues and supervisors shut their mouths and bowed to power, the more they did the same. This made work increasingly uncomfortable for the few vocal lower and midlevel careerists, whose concern quickly turned to anger.

The one choice always on the table for all career employees was that of leaving if staying on the moral tightrope of federal service became too difficult. More people than I expected from my study availed themselves of this option over the course of the four-year administration. While leaving could reduce the individual role strain that career employees experienced from loyalty traps and other professional binds, one employee noted that it did not solve the problems in their workplaces. Many career civil servants explained and rationalized that leaving could result in being replaced by newer, less-experienced hires who lacked traditional loyalties to public administration and the democratic state and who were more loyal to the administration's agenda. While such rationalizations can justify civil servants' staying on during the deterioration of the state and their short-term compliance to such an agenda, as some political scientists recognize,[26] the ceding of power to a new presidential administration through senior officials' voluntary exits is also real and can reduce both short- and long-term state capacity and functioning.

Some senior career civil servants changed jobs internally to move away from vindictive appointees and particularly tense work units in their agency. This introduced the possibility of using voice through conventional channels (e.g., the Office of Inspector General) for some like Blackburn. These opportunities were more likely to open for those feeling supported by colleagues and supervisors, in conditions in which they thought using their voice might be efficacious in supporting democratic functioning and public interest.

I witnessed the testing of democratic norms and the weakening of the spirit of public administration, as well as growing chasms between the camps of politicals and career employees, but I rarely witnessed eruptions of overt and sustained conflict or resistance in which career civil servants breached the bounds of their official position's duties and professional norms of responsiveness or fought openly with appointed leaders. Midlevel managers sometimes expressed anger and frustration at their own supervisors for their compliance and failure to exercise speak up with their senior appointed leaders. But given the power differentials, such incidents seemed mostly to blow over, although they could contribute to growing resentment among midlevel managers and staff.

As an outsider trying to understand career civil servants' perspectives, it became more apparent to me, as I considered their experiences embedded in these deteriorating conditions, how easy it is for career employees to opt not to speak up. It was also surprisingly easy for autocratic leaders to gain power gradually through these accumulated sources of uncertainty, professional risk, and the slippery slopes of democratic decline they incited.

It seemed that career civil servants working in the most politicized locations simply did not have good options. It seemed especially challenging for career civil servants to protect democratic norms and structures rooted in the Constitution and intended to prevent tyranny,[27] which they swore to defend, and to stymie political elites' autocratic and corrupt practices under an illiberal presidency able to sideline those who raised questions. It was even more difficult for career civil servants to navigate loyalty traps and other ethical professional binds amid a wider populist uprising and circulating misinformation accusing them of being political elites part of a deep state, especially when most outsiders do not understand the complex structure of the state or the demanding ethical obligations of public service. Political scientists decry such accusations of a U.S. deep state on the grounds that such hyperbolic claims fail to recognize the notable transparency in the United States compared to other states, and the many ways the state continues to serve citizens effectively.[28]

# IV

## CIVIL SERVANT
## RESISTANCE

# 10

## COVERT RESISTANCE

Longtime Environmental Protection Agency (EPA) scientist Jeffrey Thompson met me at a coffee shop wearing an outdoorsy dark green plaid shirt and dark jeans. As someone about to retire from decades of dedicated service at the EPA, he had a lot to say. He reminded me of older professors, happy to share life-learned wisdom and crack some witty jokes along the way. He watched me attentively as he spoke, double-checking to see if I understood what he was saying. I could tell, at this stage of life, that transmitting what he knew and his legacy of work was important to him.

The EPA was a particularly contested agency during Donald Trump's first administration. Trump was known for calling climate change "a hoax invented by the Chinese," and administrator Scott Pruitt was Oklahoma's former attorney general who represented the state in a lawsuit trying to stop President Barack Obama's clean power plan to reduce greenhouse gas emissions from coal-fired power plants.[1] Various EPA employees reported during this time that the administration was prioritizing business interests over the agency's core mission of protecting human health and the environment and scientific evidence. By 2018, the Trump administration was having a direct impact on Thompson's work. He showed me a mainstream newspaper article with his team in the White House on the front cover to prove it. He disapproved of the direction appointees had taken the EPA. Even so, he felt his avenues for responding were limited. Like many others in the civil service, he was risk averse. For the most part, he expressed his discontent obliquely, through meandering stories and poignant metaphors, rather than directly.

Thompson felt compelled to uphold the ethical mandates of his position. But it seemed from his perspective that any dissent or dissatisfaction would need to be subtle, if not imperceptible to others. In his office at the EPA, he told me, "We remain . . . underneath the radar . . . just so your hairs don't show up out of water. If you were a fish, you don't want your dorsal fin to be out of the water, like a porpoise, because you want them to know that the waters are still. But there's something beneath the surface, and that's the easiest way." Thompson's spirit of resistance was tied to his devotion to science; this commitment, he said, was shared by his colleagues. As long as the career civil servants hired in his agency were committed to "good science," Thompson surmised that they would be inclined to engage in covert resistance.[2] "They're not going to do what you ask them to do . . . if it's an issue of a denial of something that affects climate change, or a policy that . . . isn't based on good science," he said. For many EPA employees, such requests would challenge not only their professional integrity but also their personal code of ethics. Thompson said, "I don't think I would raise my hand and say I'm going to be politically part of that kind of decision to make. My ethics wouldn't let me do that."

Rather than directly resist the administration, Thompson suggested that EPA employees he knew were more likely to neglect their work and avoid tasks and initiatives they fundamentally opposed. Thompson described a form of covert political conflict where members of an organization can resist leadership through individualistic disorganized action within their work, executed in ways designed to be unseen and undetected by those in power.[3]

How does one distinguish resistance from compliance? Past sociological research defines resistance in terms of two "core elements" of action and opposition.[4] At face value, one might assume that action is simple to distinguish as a measurable behavior that an actor does or does not do. Opposition similarly can be identified based on an actor's intent to combat something exerting power over them, whether it be an ideology, authority, structure, or system in place.[5] Resistance by this definition (whether overt or covert) is distinguishable from speaking up or using one's voice in Albert O. Hirschman's sense because voice uses established organizational channels to communicate members' dissatisfaction to superiors, while resistance seeks instead to pressure the organization to change its ways.[6] Covert political resistance is more likely to seek to undermine organizational operations from within; it can occur through sabotaging material operations of an organization or by symbolic means, such as efforts to "subvert dominant meanings, ideologies, and discourses."[7]

In practice, however, distinguishing covert resistant action and intent from exercising voice or compliance became more complicated as the Trump years wore on and the ethical landscape of the state changed. The administration's suspicion widened the window of expected "loyal" behavior to the administration. Understandings of what resistance was broadened at the same time. A Department of Energy (DOE) midlevel manager said by the middle of Trump's first term that he had come to believe that even having critical thoughts about the Trump administration felt like resistance. "I don't know that people are willing to *do* as many explicit things," he said. "It tends to be—we count whenever we disagree with a political appointee's decision" [emphasis added]. As described by this manager, however, this spirit of resistance was seemingly unconnected to externally discernible forms of resistance. Some scholars, such as Yale political scientist James C. Scott, author of *Weapons of the Weak: Everyday Forms of Peasant Resistance*, and Black feminist scholars may disagree. Black feminist scholar Mel Monier suggests, for example, that defiant thoughts, or even taking naps, can be powerful seeds of resistance in the face of unrelenting and systemic oppression.[8]

Assessing opposition can be even more challenging. Assessments of compliance and/or resistance in a civil servant's action should take into account the multiple dimensions of possible compliance or resistance. First, analysts should ground assessments of actors' behavior in the institutional context in which it is evoked. In the case of civil servants, compliance could be assessed in relation to any of their ethical obligations. Is the action, or tactic as social movement scholars would say, used under normal conditions or not? Is it in keeping with habitual action over the long term (e.g., an act of conformity) from this perspective?[9] This may be tricky to discern because there is typically a degree of normal tension between political leadership and career bureaucrats, particularly when administrations change.[10] When does "resistance" transcend typical baseline organizational friction tied to conflicting role responsibilities and professional self-interest? In speaking with longtime career civil servants who had worked under prior contentious leadership, such as in the Department of Justice (DOJ) Civil Rights Office or in the EPA under Anne Gorsuch's leadership, they were more likely to presume that some periods of evident conflict between political leadership and the career corps was just part and parcel of their job. Younger career civil servants without this prior work experience or those working in less historically contentious locations were more likely to interpret career civil servant anger, antipathy, and resistance to the Trump administration as unusual.

Whether an *external analyst* discerns an actor's resistance to those in positions of power or organizational power in a given act is an additional factor to consider.[11] Such opposition may be palpable to an observer through evidence collected or such action's impact in challenging or undermining authorities, even if the actor is not consciously aware of it or publicly acknowledging having a resistant intent. Career public servants may have good reason not to acknowledge resistant thoughts or action because of the pressure to maintain their professional face and their requisite professional ethical obligations. In the context of resistance at work, another point is whether an employee's action breaches the confines of their roles and/or professional norms. Such transgressions may provide evidence of resistance to authority to an external observer.

A related point to consider is whether the authorities being opposed believe that career civil servants' beliefs or actions are resistant. In the case of the Trump administration, those appointees with a suspicious autocratic and authoritarian bent do not seem to be reliable reporters based on the accounts of the civil servants with whom I spoke. As established in prior chapters, some appointees' overzealous accusations of "leaking" and targeting of allegedly resistant career employees in the unfortunate position of working on Obama-era projects far exceeded the bounds of a typical administration, as well as the law. Some members of the Trump administration also diagnosed some career civil servant behavior as resistant or disloyal, even if such employees lacked an oppositional intent and merely slowed or obstructed appointee plans in order to adhere to the law or standard operating procedures (such as in Adele Sullivan's case). Even when inaccurate, these accusations had tangible impacts on subsequent interactions between appointees and civil servants and affected civil servants' careers. While I do not have primary data from the appointees referenced in most cases, I acknowledge such data would strengthen my and others' analyses.

Once they take these different dimensions of compliance and resistance into account, an analyst can step back and assess the degrees of compliance and resistance inherent in a select action and how they are interrelated. A combination of resistant intent, resistant action, and visibility of opposition should be interpreted as particularly clear-cut evidence of resistance. A belief or action that appears to contradict the aims of those in power or organizational power but lacks an actor's oppositional intent— or an invisible oppositional belief and action—can be argued to be, by comparison, weaker forms of resistance, depending on the particular circumstances of such actions.[12]

It is also important to recognize that believing people will stand up for their professional and personal values because they say so and evidence that they actually have done so are two very different things and crucial to distinguish.[13] This is especially critical when leaders use their political power to pressure and sometimes even threaten employees to adhere to their agendas, and the perceived opportunity to use one's voice closes. As the midlevel manager suggested above, and scholarship on the "weapons of the weak" indicates, under such conditions, it can *feel* like resistance, and perhaps be resistant given the circumstances, just to have a resistant thought.[14] But it is questionable if such thoughts, especially if kept private, have any tangible impact on these employees' larger organizations. However, they may provide seeds for future action.

Although we can theoretically distinguish between resistance and compliance, and many people may assume these two seemingly antithetical concepts are distinct and separate, in practice, it is a much more challenging and perhaps impossible endeavor to categorize civil servants' thoughts or actions as in either binary categories of resistance or compliance over time. Theoretically, their actions could be fully resistant or compliant, but in practice, many actions seemed to be a combination of both under the Trump administration. Among those who revealed some form of resistant belief or action, their resistance always coincided with other forms of compliance to the other long-standing ethical obligations of their position and/or their commitments to serving appointed and elected leadership. They also recognized and reported almost always adhering to the limited power of their own positions. For example, Jeffrey Thompson said:

> We all want to be consistent . . . The professionals have a conversation regularly about being consistent and understanding what we can and cannot do. Or what we feel is, on the basis of how some of the messages then [are] at least disseminated from the top down, what we are allowed to do and what we're not allowed to do . . . that kind of gives you a way of understanding that it's not important for you to promote a particular process as much as it is to continue to sustain an ultimate process because this process works and has worked better than the new one. [laughs]
>
> And beyond that, . . . unless and until there are fixed acceptable executive decisions on the basis of where people have been placed and access to an executive authority, you don't have to follow that rule. Think about how this administration has still got to fill so many gaps in their executive authority . . . There's a buffer about who can tell you what to do. [laughs]

Thompson exudes a spirit of resistance, a bit gleefully, although he takes care to act within the lines of his position and established ways of working. Rather than acting quickly to advance the new administration's agenda, Thompson and others act consistently and deliberately. Until the chain of command is apparent and they are told otherwise, he suggests his office will continue to operate as they have been.

Others similarly mentioned how they viewed maintaining government stability as a central part of their role in the state bureaucracy. An employee at the National Institutes of Health (NIH) said that career civil servants' "job is not to make changes. It's to steer the ship straight until they're told to make changes," which he added, "hampers the administration's ability to make their decisions." Thompson and others like him rely on the core structures of the state bureaucracy to slow down changes they view as driven by politicals' private, political, and business interests, which they see as antithetical to their agency mission, professional expertise, and professional ethics. They are operating as a check on executive power and thus as they are supposed to in a functioning democratic state when leadership is perceived as corrupt and self-serving.[15]

It is important to acknowledge how compliance and resistance coincided in the behaviors and ethical calculations of the more concerned and unswerving civil servants in chaotic and politicized areas and in other parts of the government. To do so, I propose both resistance and compliance should be recognized as being employed in often overlapping and interrelated ways in practice to justify resistance to different forms of authority within formal institutions like the state. Much resistance against a certain form of authority is couched as compliance with other forms of authority and ethical obligations. This was evident not only in Thompson's case but also in the narratives of experiences shared by every person in my study who expressed engaging in any form of resistance against the administration. It is also important, however, to take seriously the many cases in which institutional actors earnestly insist that they are *not* seeking to be resistant, even as some of their actions are interpreted as such by those in power or even by their colleagues. Discernment of resistance is thus a delicate and often shifting dynamic process over time, aided but also complicated by triangulating data across sources.

Given these theoretical starting points, how did civil servants employ covert resistant action against Trump leadership? To what extent did these subtle efforts undermine the efficacy of Trump leadership? As Thompson suggested, some career civil servants engaged in covert acts of resistance to defend their organizational missions, professional practices, and values; ease their consciences; and express their disagreement with leadership changes. Their subtle acts of resistance included (1) acts of surreptitious subversion, such as how they framed or described their work, covertly continued unauthorized work against the administration's agenda, and/or neglected work; (2) stretching work boundaries and activating allies' support in informal gatherings; and (3) documenting perceived transgressions as a backstop.

As the Trump administration wore on, and considerable numbers of civil servants engaged in some form of covert resistance, it became evident that this was not bold activist resistance. Instead, this form of professional resistance almost always occurred within the constraints of career civil servants' stipulated roles at work. Intent aside, many acts of covert resistance were difficult to distinguish from colleagues' work lacking such a resistant intent, especially when productivity was already dipping due to confusion or fear in many locations. In addition, the ever-present intent to comply with state ethical obligations among the people with whom I spoke, no doubt moderated the subversive acts some career civil servants reported.

## ACTS OF SURREPTITIOUS SUBVERSION

Because of civil servants' risk-averse tendencies,[16] they are more likely to engage in covert conflict or "guerilla government" within the institutions of government[17] than openly confront senior leadership. In her book, *The Ethics of Dissent: Managing Guerilla Government*, public administration scholar Rosemary O'Leary argues that four conditions tend to provoke covert resistance: (1) when there are limited, or declining, means for bureaucrats to voice discontent; (2) when the perceived cost of vocal resistance is higher than that of using covert resistance; (3) when grievances are tied to personal issues or esteemed values; and (4) when quitting is viewed as more harmful to the work at issue than staying. All these factors coalesced to give rise to a burst of covert resistance among career civil servants during the Trump administration.

Civil servants reported engaging in the following forms of surreptitious subversion: they altered the framing of their work to align, at face value, with leadership goals; they secretly continued work without disclosing it to leadership; they neglected and slow-walked their work; they let leadership fail; and sometimes they outstrategized them. Civil servants used these tactics to do "valuable damage control," as an EPA employee told me, and to "steer jobs" to align with agency missions and professional goals against the grain of appointed leadership's agenda.

Many of these tactics are not new; former and current civil servants with a long tenure of federal service under various administrations described how these tactics had been used under contentious leadership in prior administrations, both Democrat and Republican.[18] Scholarly literature on public administration has long acknowledged the "normal" baseline friction between career civil servants and politicals. Conflicts between civil servants and appointed political leadership can simmer and erupt based on clashing ideologies, policy disagreements, bureaucrats' distaste for and resistance to change, preferences for autonomy and discretion, and efforts to protect budgets and turf.[19]

During the beginning and middle of the first Trump administration, covert tactics were a relatively low-risk way by which some career bureaucrats tried to cope and confront a leadership agenda that cut against their ethical obligations and seemed to capture and/or subvert the state. Chaos early in the administration gave greater latitude for civil servant "resistance" because they could take advantage of leadership vacuums and novice or ineffective appointees. But over time, some of these advantages shrank. As more appointees took office, clearer directives were handed down, and career civil servants who failed to build trusting relationships with appointed leaders were excised from decision-making processes.

## Gradations of Compliant and Resistant Framing

Activists and institutional changemakers often employ framing techniques to build support and consensus around their causes and projects.[20] A frame, as depicted by sociologist Erving Goffman, is a "schemata of interpretation," which imbues occurrences with meaning and social significance and can be used to categorize and organize such events as well as guide future actions.[21] While activists typically use framing to build alignment between members' interests, values, and beliefs and their movement's activities, goals and ideology,[22] socially skilled actors in institutions may also use framing to align with dominant institutional structures and professional norms in an effort to appeal to leaders and build support for their work.[23]

Framing is a valued skill set in the government. With frequent changes to appointed leadership and presidential administration turnover every four to eight years, framing serves to provide continuity in policies and procedures across political difference. During the first Trump administration, many civil servants I spoke with argued that employing these skills was a normal part of doing their job. Others with a more resistant inclination in particularly contested locations suggested that framing was a valuable tactic for preserving work they thought was important, even if appointed political leaders thought otherwise. As you will see, whether one might view a specific instance of framing as resistance depends on the intent and interpretation of the framer. Such variation in how framing can be interpreted creates an ethical or moral gray area, which can enable actor discretion.[24] This ambiguity is apparent not only in the use of framing in government work but in other covert resistant tactics as well.

Civil servants across agencies commonly used framing techniques during normal presidential transitions to align policy agendas, project work, and tools with an incoming administration's goals. In accordance with the literature on social skill among bureaucrats,[25] several civil servants said that framing was not inherently a subversive act but one that demonstrated their skillful ability to facilitate smooth leadership transitions and continuity in the federal bureaucracy. As Office of Management and Budget (OMB) employee Lewis Waters described, "This is not unique to the Trump administration. When leadership shifts from the top, civil servants need to incorporate things from the past, but in a way not tainted by the past." He said that his team would do "small things . . . in an attempt to avoid bias," such as "when you are writing something and the sentence is from the previous administration—if I can say it in a different way, I will do that to not trigger the antibodies." He reiterated, "That is not peculiar to this administration. Similar things happened [from George W.] Bush to Obama. I feel this is like an inside baseball thing. We aren't trying to cook the books, but [we] are in service to doing our jobs and making sure leaders make decisions based on the best facts."

As a senior civil servant, Waters seeks to be a ballast during the tumultuous shifts between presidential administrations and sees framing as a means of maintaining some continuity and doing his job well. He does not describe using it here as an act of resistance, although some Trump appointees in his agency might view such an approach as resistant. At face value, Waters's example seems mainly one of compliance; he is seeking to aid appointees as he had always done.

Other senior civil servants attested to how calculated framing of issues in federal service is a highly valued skill set. Supervisors reported teaching newer staff members the importance of skillful framing, and mentees reported learning it from esteemed senior civil servants. Lawyers, in particular, described how knowing your audience or judge and building convincing arguments based on legal precedents was a core part of their job.

When the Trump administration tried to alter legal interpretations and the enforcement of civil rights, lower-level DOJ lawyer Brandon Kelley earnestly described his work to preserve legal precedents and commonplace interpretations of civil rights as in keeping with normative legal best practices in his unit and *not* as a form of resistance against the presidential administration. Kelley repeatedly described himself as an apolitical person over the years I spoke with him, a person who did not have strong political preferences or allegiances. He expressed little personal concern about the Trump administration's impact on work in his area on human rights during both our meetings in 2017 and 2018 and sought to do his job ethically and loyally above all.

Given the contentious division he worked in and his seeming emotional neutrality, I asked him various kinds of questions across our interviews to see if I would get some kind of political response. But he earnestly maintained that he was not a political person, and like a typical technocrat, he emphasized that he was not bothered or really affected by the administration, in part because of the long-term duration of the cases he worked on.

Kelley seemed to prefer to fly under the radar of the administration's heated political rhetoric and do his job as he thought he was supposed to, which involved protecting "an expansive definition" of clauses protecting human rights, in keeping with the previous administration and a longer history of office precedents, despite fears that the Trump administration "would have more contracted views." Kelley did acknowledge more fully using the framing tactics in concert with others in his office to protect some basic human rights during the early years of the Trump administration after he changed offices in the middle of the administration: "Because we still tried to profess a relatively expanded view, but without highlighting it in such a way that [it] would be an obvious problem for the incoming administration." He justified the use of these efforts to protect the established working consensus on human rights in his former office without any personal animosity or spirit of resistance against the administration. He wanted above all to serve in a politically neutral dispassionate manner. He acknowledged knowing that this approach cut against the preferred agenda of the Trump administration and that politicals would likely call the approach resistance. Although this lawyer's actions under most other administrations, in keeping with the policy norms in his office, would be largely viewed as compliance, under the Trump administration, with its markedly different priorities, this lawyer's work might be thought by some external observers to exhibit some resistance.

I heard about other examples in which career civil servants viewed some proposed changes as bad decisions and used overtly polite, respectful framing to deny such changes. For example, when one midlevel manager's agency proposed a rule to support a program favored by industry that would increase environmental pollution, he heard from colleagues at their "sister agency that actually handled that rule-making request" that the civil servants there, who tended to be politically neutral, "felt insulted that that was even being proposed because it doesn't remotely make sense in terms of economics or good policy decisions . . . And they were pleasantly surprised when that rule was rejected." He reported that the other organization seemed to be trying to "placate" his agency through professional platitudes: "it was like 'oh this is a good idea and we need to look into it more, but we're not going to issue the rule as proposed.' And I think the idea was just to act like it was a good idea and that they support the [program] without actually having to do anything about it."

When I asked if the the administration ever noticed and reacted, he responded, "I can't think of a situation in anything I've worked on that they have." Thus, to employees using such framing techniques as vaguely aligning work content with the presidential administration's goals and using polite, deferential language seemed to be a low-risk means of trying to protect the work they cared most about. And it likely had notably low visibility to the administration.

Other lawyers working on progressive issues emphasized the importance of using framing "to thread" the "very small needle" between standing up for the progressive causes they believed in and avoiding being "seen as a crazy radical rebel," as one lawyer put it. This was seen as a necessary skill in being "a good lawyer" and also a means of aligning their professional ethical obligations and personal moral commitments. Those incorporating their progressive political beliefs into their decision making would generally be considered resistant to the Trump administration by administrators, but again, it is important to consider the institutional and professional context of any given act.

Some civil servants did strategically frame contentious policy issues as a way to directly resist leadership's efforts to initiate change. When I first spoke to him in 2017, one lawyer in a particularly contested agency said that he had frequent conversations with his colleagues on how to "preserve things we've worked up under the Obama administration or the prior administration and repackage them so that they're palatable for this administration." Like many others working in tumultuous agencies, he said that it was common for people to "globally change things like climate change to energy independence. So there's sort of word games that are used frequently to rebrand Obama ideas in a vocabulary that's going to be more acceptable to Trump people." Although this lawyer had more of a spirit of resistance, thus far, this is seemingly close in practice to Waters's approach to using framing as a way to maintain continuity and preserve what bureaucrats viewed as established good practices across administrations.

This lawyer took it a step farther, however, elucidating several ways in which attorneys and policy experts drew on their expertise and tinkered with language to protect the integrity of work they cared most about. They added detail to "provide more nuanced perspective" in the hope that "you can get them to see the pieces that they may not see" or they adjusted "the political tone of a report." Federal civil servants also tried to enact "damage control" to minimize the scope of policy and program rollbacks through adding "alternative solutions, arguments, etc.," or toning down recommendations, he said. They could also broaden political appointees' agendas or scope to make it more inclusive than leadership would have. Through these tactics, career civil servants edited work to reduce changes that they thought were based on inaccurate information; were detrimental to the public; or ran counter to their professional identities, their agency's mission, and/or sometimes their personal moral compass. These actions were infused with a spirit of resistance and were intended to undermine the administration's agenda and preserve the administrative state as they knew it. While these examples of framing would likely be called resistance by Trump appointees and some respondents, they could also comfortably be assessed as seeking to preserve the continuity of what was largely viewed as quality work under prior administrations, far beneath the administration's political rhetoric.

Reflecting on the covert framing tactics career that bureaucrats used over the course of the administration, some career civil servants questioned not only their efficacy but also their true purpose. Were covert framing tactics efficacious in undercutting the Trump administration agenda? Or were civil servants' covert tactics more of a psychological salve and means of reducing moral dissonance than an effective strategy to preserve their work and how they thought the state should function? From speaking to some civil servants using framing as a form of covert resistance, it seemed that various conditions in the Trump administration and facets of the state bureaucracy limited the efficacy of such approaches. Their use seemed to decline by the end of the administration.

Across agencies, public servants committed to climate change work engaged in linguistic gymnastics with a spirit of resistance. Yet such efforts did not seem to matter when programs were dramatically cut by leadership and midlevel managers anyway. In the office of Lisa Pearce, an entry-level EPA employee, for example, career civil servants tried to preserve their work on climate change by removing all references to climate change. Instead, they alluded to climate change work through a variety of vague euphemisms, such as calling climate change "adaption work," "community resilience, or community planning. Efficiency if that was applicable," she said. She also referred to climate change work as "regional collaboration," "sharing information and that kind of thing." Some projects in the EPA and elsewhere were completely renamed, shifting from references to climate to words referring to resilience.[26]

The rephrasing of specific scientific or policy language to more vague, politically palatable euphemisms is not without its costs. As Yale historian Timothy Snyder warns, weakening language is a common response of many people eager to please those in power.[27] When bureaucrats and civilians obey authoritarian leaders in advance by altering language without being required to do so, they may unintentionally allow, if not exacerbate, processes of democratic decline.

The civil servants at the EPA had a different goal. In an effort to preserve climate change work they knew was antithetical to the Trump administration's agenda, they renamed it. In doing so, however, they decentered the climate and regulatory focus of their work and eliminated direct references to them, which inadvertently complied in part with Trump administration goals to weaken these areas. Without using proper terminology or being willing to advocate for climate change or regulatory programs, as had occurred in the past, it was likely they would continue to atrophy.

Pearce acknowledged that, with the reframing of terms and titles, "we were still working but they weren't as climate focused anymore, which was not—didn't feel the same." Her work had "slowed down really significantly," she said. "The amount of projects that could actually be reframed were definitely fewer

than my full workload," and "most of my EPA calls were can-
celled or postponed indefinitely, so our national workgroups
were pretty much at a halt."

This occurred in part because Pearce's supervisor was particularly responsive to appointed political leadership. Although
her supervisor was passionate about the environment and climate change work and had been engaged in innovative project
work under the Obama administration when such work was
supported, her supervisor made an "immediate switch" to being
more cautious when Trump was elected. She communicated to
her team that "we can't really do anything without headquarters
saying it's okay, and I don't think they're going to say it's okay
right now." In their office, "everything was kind of put on hold,"
Pearce recalled, "which was very frustrating as a staffer." New
initiatives were shut down "as soon as the election happened
just because the agency didn't want to put time and effort into
things that were no longer going to be programs to work on." In
the months that followed, "it seemed like pretty much all communication was shut down as soon as the new administration
came in. And . . . then my manager would not make any moves,"
Pearce said.

Pearce also explained that it was easier for Trump appointees
to roll back project work on climate change because there was
"not a regulatory or statutory background in climate change in
the EPA." For air and water regulation, which was grounded in
federal laws, noncompliance could lead to lawsuits, but climate
change work could simply be stopped. With less work, Pearce
got bored. In addition, as a newer employee, her sense of vulnerability and fear of getting laid off increased. She eventually left
federal civil service for a private firm.

Others described how the efficacy of using "creative" framing tactics was limited by appointed political leaders' use of

administrative presidency tactics to wrest power from career civil servants. Because the president and his political appointees controlled agenda setting and decision making, they could effectively usurp a considerable amount of career bureaucrats' power and influence. One higher-level foreign affairs expert told me that, in his office at the State Department under the Trump administration, other career leaders stayed at first:

> Because they wanted to be in the room to make the arguments, even if the argument didn't win the day . . . but what I found is that those meetings have actually never taken place because there is such a distrust of the career officers that we aren't invited into those conversations. So I think a lot of people wanted to stay in to be uniquely positioned at the right place and the right time to help shape a different outcome, but we've never had a chance . . . So that's when I think my friends and I started looking for other jobs.

These examples suggest that resistant framing can come with unintended consequences. It can initiate a slippery slope of language degradation, which then can lead to weakening and disassociating important program content. As Pearce's experience reveals, framing content to align with leadership-prioritized cuts and rollbacks to preserve important work enacts resistance, but it can unintentionally come with compromises that aid leadership's initiatives, as Snyder suggested.[28] Moreover, if elected leadership and their appointees have primary agenda-setting and decision-making power, then framing efforts may prove futile. Leadership can simply ignore civil servants' feedback, cut their resources, or change policy to undercut their abilities to do their jobs.

Despite these limitations, using framing techniques seemed to provide civil servants with a modicum of relief from guilt tied to compliance with leadership initiatives they abhorred. Through these small acts of resistance, they could justify to themselves that they were trying to save their work and adhere to their professional values and missions, while also, at face value, building relationships with new leaders. This likely made framing quite an attractive approach under divergent or domineering leadership.

## Covertly Continuing Work
## Unsupported by Politicals

As explained in chapter 9, many civil servants reported "staying under the radar" as a strategy to avoid negative attention from Trump administrators. An EPA employee in a regional office described this as a "common strategy": "You simply try not to draw attention and do your work and hope nobody interferes with you. I think there's a whole lot of that going on at EPA." Because "a lot of . . . regulations are still . . . being developed," and "a lot of risk assessments are being done," he said that "there may not be a whole lot of interference with that sort of machinery of what goes on. So you sort of try and keep doing it, trying not to become too visible politically, and go on."

Although this hunkering-down approach was a pragmatic means of merely doing their job as they had always done in the absence of new guidance for many civil servants, others intimated that they brought a spirit of resistance to this approach under the Trump administration. A Department of Health and Human Services (HHS) midlevel manager described in 2018 that his program was "under the radar, which I think right now is good for programs." Appointees lacked "a vision" for his program, he said, which gave them "some freedom."

Some reported that this strategy enabled them to continue work that they thought the Trump administration disapproved of. For example, a DOJ lawyer described how, at the start of the administration, "Everything was kind of in flux. There were so many fires going on within the new administration that focusing on our particular issues wasn't the highest priority. So we were able to squeeze a lot of things in just because there were more pressing things to deal with."

Others were more candid about their approach, saying that they were preserving their work with a stronger spirit of resistance. In 2018, a midlevel manager in another agency dismissed some Trump appointees as incompetent and tried to preserve work by disguising it with vague, accommodating, and/or technical language. "We tend to wait it out knowing the political appointees will change out, or they'll lose focus on something," he said. "And we've definitely proposed things that are worded to give the appearance they align perfectly with the administration's priorities, and we're counting on the fact they won't read enough into details to know it's something we've been doing, you know, multiple administrations now, and it's good for the department, and hoping that it just flies under the radar."

This manager expressed low regard for some lower-level Schedule C political appointees with whom he had interacted. They did not seem to understand his work, and "there's definitely a few that have undefined portfolios," he said. To avoid getting further involved with them, he reported that in his workgroup, "our main goal, whenever we have to meet with those types of people, is to make our work sound boring enough that they stay away . . . Because we don't trust that their involvement wouldn't negatively impact our programs." This midlevel manager alludes to both oppositional intent and resistant action intended to undercut the administration's influence. Even so, in this example, this work group was seeking to protect and continue projects valued under prior administrations through covert resistance in an effort to preserve continuity and the quality of their programs.

A midlevel National Science Foundation (NSF) manager also reported that her office was trying to preserve the good work they believed themselves to be doing. They were careful to present data that were unlikely to provoke an unwanted reaction from the administration:

> What we do is we try to find data that tell people what they want to hear. And we draw attention away from the stuff they don't want to hear. And so we have all this great data on race and gender and wage gaps for women and minorities, [but] we draw our attention to things like foreign markets, which aren't really relevant to the interests in the current administration. If we draw attention away from the stuff they don't like, they won't notice it, and they won't try to squash it, so it will still be there for people who want to use it. There are all of these researchers who are just like, do whatever you need to so we can still use it.

In this example, this NSF manager described how her office selectively presented more politically neutral content, or content of interest to the administration, in an effort to hide data they collected that they thought the administration would disapprove of and safeguard them for researchers who rely on them.

Quietly continuing to do work in contested areas was a low-risk means of resisting leadership's rollbacks, especially among lower and midlevel civil servants who did not regularly work with politically appointed leadership. They sought to lay low in order to preserve as much of their valued preexisting work as they could.

## Neglect and Slow-Walking

Much research suggests that when loyal employees think that their organizations are being led in the wrong direction by management and that management is unlikely to respond favorably to their feedback, they can lose a sense of positive affiliation with the organization. As a result, they may disengage and become detached from their work, leading them to neglect their duties.[29]

Through slow-walking (slowing things down or making them harder) or neglect (minimally complying with distasteful political directives), career civil servants could reconcile powerful conflicting imperatives and loyalties. Deliberately neglecting their work was uncommon among the civil servants with whom I spoke. Most civil servants felt very strongly about serving their country and the public to the best of their ability. Nearly all avoided active sabotage because of professional norms and ethics. A few described sabotage as a last resort, to be used only in the most dire of circumstances.[30]

It is also important to acknowledge how, under the Trump administration, career civil servants across politicized locations reported a decline in their productivity because of a host of other reasons. A climate of suspicion or fear in some locations, a lack of strong leadership in many offices, leadership's focus on rollbacks in regulations and budget cuts, and a lack of communication on priorities for new project work all contributed to employees' reports of declining efficacy, productivity, and control over their work. Those working in contested agencies intent on complying with political leadership and those resistant in spirit alike said that leaders' lack of trust in their expertise and work stymied rather than fostered good work and innovation, as described in chapter 8. Civil servants across agencies reported that, in a climate of mistrust, leaders required that they fill out more tedious request forms as part and parcel of their everyday work. This caused frustration *and* lowered productivity.

For many career civil servants working under the Trump administration, productivity had already fallen, so deliberately neglecting their work was a low-risk way of expressing their discontent with leadership priorities. Career civil servants tended to report neglecting their work individually.[31] For example, in response to serving under leadership he thought acted in corrupt and self-serving ways, one midlevel Department of Housing and Urban Development (HUD) employee described taking a "personal," "private" approach, which included sometimes choosing not to do certain tasks. Another EPA employee told me that one of the few things she could do to stymie leadership was "get lazy." She took this tactic when she did not believe in the work or when leadership cut material incentives like overtime. "If the government isn't giving overtime, you get lazier," she said.

Civil servants also reported neglect among their coworkers and supervisors. A midlevel manager said that she had been working very hard to compensate for her supervisor. Her direct supervisor, "who's a career fed and has been in the government for decades is used to not necessarily working as hard in a Republican administration," and "no one had really held her [supervisor] accountable yet."

Slow-walking was another low-risk means of resisting certain political initiatives. The normal bureaucratic feedback process was slow by design, and typically required input from multiple stakeholders. This made it difficult for others to determine if career civil servants were doing their job well or moving slow on purpose. Under the Trump administration, some career civil servants took solace in this lengthy, collaborative decision-making process. As a midlevel HHS civil servant said when facing budget cuts, "the plus of many, many layers to things getting done is there will often be someone along the way who will question it and you have to kind of hope that it slows things down." He noted the "positive to that: it requires thinking and you have to have good arguments."

Civil servants seemed inclined to slow-walk when asked to do something that they did not want to do, based on their professional knowledge or on ethical or legal grounds. When an EPA lawyer was asked "to provide cover for certain things" he thought were "bad decisions for the agency," even though he did not feel threatened and did not think the requests were illegal or unethical, he decided to push back and slow-walk his response. He knew that his "advice on many matters was unwanted or ignored" by appointed senior leadership, and with the collaboration of other colleagues, he also "engaged other people to avoid things being done." Another DOJ lawyer reported that in his agency, when people were asked to do something "abhorrent," instead of quitting, they might similarly "just drag their feet along and do it."

In these examples, slow-walking seems to have been used as a resistance tactic to mitigate what career civil servants perceived as bad decisions or wrongdoing. Contrary to what some might think, most of the career civil servants I spoke with who mentioned using slow-walking did so precisely because they cared about the quality of their work. They also knew they could lean on the collaborative bureaucratic decision-making process of the state, which is designed to elicit different perspectives, build consensus, and diffuse power.

## Failing to Support and Outstrategizing Leadership

Some senior career employees reported letting appointees fail on purpose or outstrategizing them. These tactics tended to be used by higher-level bureaucrats under extenuating circumstances. They might use these tactics as a last resort, when it seemed leadership was not listening to them anyway, despite their efforts to build those relationships. Because career civil servants took their professional duties to serve the administration and the American public very seriously, most career civil servants were wary about admitting they had deliberately failed to support appointed leaders. They started talking about this tack as something career employees around them might do. A few midlevel and senior career employees then admitted that they had engaged in these forms of covert resistance.

A top career official at the EPA described how, under normal conditions, career executives could aid appointed officials' decisions by doing the following: "You can find a way to communicate it to your staff so they understand it. You can help develop talking points that put it in a favorable light for press questions. You can try to convince some people that, although it may not be perfect, it's not a bad decision. You can be involved in finding middle ground positions." Yet, when senior leadership do not develop trusting, open, collaborative relationships and instead instill a climate of suspicion and fear, he said, "passive resistance" is more likely:

I think once people feel disaffected, they don't help find middle ground. They're like, "Fine, make a terrible decision. It'll get leaked to the press and you'll get slammed because you didn't listen to us." So I think it can be—I don't know that it's really active, but I think it's the lack of support, the lack of standing by the decision maker and defending him, maybe even [making] subtle suggestions that the decision is not legitimate. That stuff can start to hurt morale and productivity. And I think disaffected senior people can result in a lot of those negative things happening when they don't feel they're involved and respected and consulted.

Brian Taylor was one of the most transparent career civil servants when it came to resistance. A mid- to upper-level manager in a very contentious agency, he described the difficulty in building trusting and open working relationships with Trump appointees, and he admitted that, in his agency, civil servants had let leaders fail. "Sometimes," he said, "you can sort of not brief on the full range of things—not educate the principals about everything." He explained:

> It's just like—is there an upcoming opportunity or event which your principal could use to advance a policy that you think is going to be harmful to the United States? Maybe you don't have to really flag it. Like you don't have to get everybody riled up and stirred up and you just let it pass. Or there were a few times that I've seen people at [his agency], I can't really say that people deliberately set up this person to fail, but it certainly is on our minds. Because it's never phrased like, "Should we set them up to fail?" It's more—the way I talk about it with other civil servants is like, "How much do we mitigate the bad effects of their decisions? How much do we shield them from the consequences of their decisions?" Because it's like when parents talk about children, and you have to let them go make their own mistakes; otherwise they'll never learn from them . . . Or it's like yeah, we can run interference for you all day long, but how about we just like stand on the sidelines for this one and let you crash and burn a little bit, which you are going to do anyway. But we're not making them crash. But we're just like not trying to help right now because maybe then you'll learn a little bit next time to listen to our advice.

When I asked if he had done that, he said, "Sometimes, and sometimes you find yourself hoping."

It was clear that civil servants, even in the most contested agencies, did not take choosing to withhold support from leadership lightly. They tended to use this tactic when experiencing a loyalty trap, when they were stuck between their loyalty to serving what they thought was for the good of the country based on their expertise and knowledge and their duty to serve appointees. It was also described as a form of giving up after repeated efforts to work with appointees constructively. As Taylor revealed in discussing this tactic, civil servants were careful about justifying their seeming dereliction of duty by framing their actions as intended to reduce the damaging consequences of bad leadership decisions for the public and the country.

Even so, the consequences of failing to support leaders weighed on career civil servants like Taylor. He acknowledged his parent-child analogy ultimately fell apart because of the consequential nature of government decisions. He wondered, in the end, "Who is being damaged?" He concluded, "There's broader repercussions to the [agency], to the United States, to the national security, to our effectiveness in international institutions, so people view it as like a really dicey proposition." But then he reflected upon the conditions under which he worked. Under the Trump administration, with its evident leadership incompetence and seemingly rash decision making, it was particularly difficult to support leadership fully.

Taylor also described how career civil servants could outstrategize and outmaneuver appointed political leadership. For example, civil servants could "try to create the situations where this administration has to respond or listen to you." If his team could convince top leaders to talk about certain morally laden issues, like Christians' human rights, which some Trump appointees cared about, then the career civil servants could thereby open opportunities to advance their broader human rights agendas. According to his logic: "If you're going to talk about them [civil and human rights issues], you have to say the right things. And if you are saying the right things, then you're on the record and you have to have policies maybe to back them up, and then you have to ask the experts to tell you what those policies should look like. So it's almost like backwardly creating the opportunity to advance policy."

HHS midlevel manager Nick Pratt, who struggled under a particularly unprofessional political appointee, also discussed using his knowledge about his program and the state bureaucratic decision-making processes strategically to try to attain what he thought were the best possible outcomes. As an experienced professional, he said that he knew how his program and "how the government works better than they [political appointees] do." This was, he suggested, career civil servants' "best asset" and could work to their advantage under contested leadership.[32] For projects "where I'm not a big fan," he said, "I try to find the least harmful option, right?" While he admitted that some Trump-backed initiatives would "still look bad" to the public, as an expert in human services, he knew "we can do it in a way that would be a lot worse or more forceful, but, if they don't know it, then . . . we can try to . . . cushion the blow a little bit."

For some career civil servants, letting their leaders fail was not really a choice; it was more of an acknowledgment of the reality that, in their position, under leadership that mistrusted them and often disregarded their feedback, all they could do was let the leadership act as they would and take some comfort in knowing that poor policies might face political checks elsewhere. One senior official shared the realization that, even though she could not stop an ideological appointee above her, he would likely "go down in court with some of his very extreme theories." As a more supportive political appointee in her agency said to her, "'Look, you can't stop it,' nonetheless. Or he has said to me that he and I both know that once this gets into the federal courts that [the ideological appointee] will lose and lose big time. And almost like the best way for him to learn from his outrageous behavior is to let him light himself on fire and watch it happen . . . so that he learns now in order to stop a lot more bad activity after."

For this senior career official, letting the politically appointed leader fail was not a deliberate resistance tactic; it was a mere acknowledgement of the situation she faced at work. This gave her some satisfaction and release of a sense of responsibility and personal failure. As she said, it "actually helps me to let go and not feel like I have to try to stop the unstoppable." In this example, she trusted the law and the democratic system to provide a check against the appointee's transgressive behaviors, as they were supposed to.

## STRETCHING WORK BOUNDARIES AND ACTIVATING ALLIES' SUPPORT IN INFORMAL GATHERINGS

Some civil servants stretched the boundaries of their work by seeking information and support about how to respond best to the Trump administration through backroom discussions or in other gatherings outside work. Their discussions ranged from friendly chatter on administration-led political developments and challenges to meetings that provided strategic support and informed career civil servants about how they could stand up to appointee malfeasance. For many respondents, such information sharing and networking fit comfortably within the parameters of their work while also providing support in navigating unwelcome changes in their agencies during a time of questionable leadership and weak vertical communication. Yet these seemingly "normal part(s) of the job" could serve new purposes and take on new meanings in the unsettled environment of the Trump administration.

Those most likely to take part in these types of gatherings tended to be bothered by the administration privately and in the course of their work. On average, they were among the younger federal servants with whom I spoke (in their mid-thirties), had approximately five to ten years of federal work experience, and ranked at fairly high General Schedule levels (GS-13 to GS-15). They also often engaged in other resistance tactics in and outside work, including the other forms of covert resistance discussed in this chapter, speaking up directly to their supervisors, and/or engaging in other forms of more overt resistance such as attending protests outside work. These ancillary resistant behaviors suggest that the informal discussions such civil servants engaged in may have helped support their oppositional conduct, psychologically or otherwise.

Some career civil servants leaned on each other merely as a means of letting off steam. They described the strain of working for the government in the Trump mediascape and chaos. During lunch breaks out of the office or after hours, they vented and commiserated with colleagues and friends. While hanging out, they could express their incredulity and concern about media accounts of the Trump administration's radical policy priorities; process the administration's reported ethical transgressions, foibles, and other daily happenings; and gather information. Such acts can be viewed as resistant in thought and perhaps in action because such spaces develop groups with shared grievances that can support future action.[33] Many participants reported that such meetings did not seem tied, however, to collective strategizing or action. They were instead described more as casual gatherings where gossip could be shared with friends and colleagues, as happens in many workplaces.

In some of the most politicized agencies, career civil servants were supported by allies in their efforts to push back against leadership initiatives they disagreed with. Support from colleagues seemed to provide emotional support primarily. In some cases, these safe spaces also enabled information sharing and brainstorming about how to work with controversial appointed leadership strategically and possibly engage in covert resistance. Several civil servants working on policy areas facing cuts and other radical changes from Trump leadership said that they shared information and brainstormed with colleagues about how to focus their work on areas where they had more control. One Department of the Treasury (USDT) employee, for example, mentioned that in his workgroup, people had "sidebar meetings: discussions on how can we structure our work product in a way to promote our priorities" and preserve work from prior administrations. While he "wouldn't have those with my boss," he had those discussions with his colleagues frequently. Even though he knew the strategies they devised "may not be very successful," such conversations helped him cope with rapid leadership changes and provided a sense of camaraderie and emotional support.

It was common to hear allusions to such resistance expressed in vague, carefully veiled language from risk-averse longtime career technocrats who had survived multiple and sometimes contentious administration changes by keeping their heads down and grounding their actions in the core ethical obligations of public administration. EPA scientist Jeffrey Thompson was a case in point. Thompson's spirit of resistance to an administration insufficiently incorporating science into their policy agenda was grounded in the relationships in his office and agency after working there for decades *and* the bureaucratic and ethical foundation of his agency. Thompson's experience shows that groups

and networks of career bureaucrats who kept lines of communication open could covertly maintain preexisting ethical and
procedural norms that otherwise may have been discarded in the
face of leadership pressures. Their continuing mutual support
allowed them to maintain a long-term perspective, distinguish
clearer bounds for the actions they were allowed to take, and act
accordingly. From his network of supportive colleagues, Thompson gained not only information that helped him critically
decide what leadership agendas he had to follow but some social
support and affirmation that it was alright not to support leadership agendas as much as he could have. Such a covert collective
response clearly combines both multiple forms of organizational
compliance and some resistance to the Trump administration.

For a subset of career bureaucrats with more of an inclination
to resist the administration, convening with colleagues afforded
an opportunity to discuss how they could combat the administration more directly by standing up for their rights. A group of
international affairs experts, for example, shared their experiences
and provided support to others who had witnessed appointed
leaders' legal and ethical transgressions. In this network, civil
servants encouraged each other to stand up for their individual
rights by reporting appointees' illegal behavior so that at least it
would be documented in the historical government record. In
a few rare cases, civil servants admitted to deliberately sharing
information about leadership transgressions with the media and
congressional staff in the hope that it would aid further inquiries.

Not a single civil servant, however, discussed using organized collective acts of resistance to confront appointed leadership about illegal, unethical, or poor decision making during
the Trump administration in the course of their daily work.
Ben Lopez, who I discussed in chapter 1, acknowledged that
civil servants ultimately had few means of holding leadership

accountable for their transgressions, despite how important he thought collective action and support were in the face of appointee malfeasance. Although a few long-standing and former employees in contested agencies admitted to engaging in rare collective acts of dissent, such as several members of a division at the DOJ sending a cosigned letter to appointed leadership under a prior administration, I did not speak with anyone under the Trump administration who reported engaging in overt collective acts of resistance at work during that time.[34]

Some civil servants with wide-ranging areas of expertise and long tenure at their agencies mentioned increased use of pre-existing relationships with allies in other agencies or outside the federal government. In response to weakened trust between senior leaders and civil servants, some of the latter admitted to taking problems that had always been dealt with internally in the past and instead reaching out to colleagues in other federal agencies for advice about how to respond and sometimes how to resist leadership requests or initiatives. One midlevel manager reported in 2017:

> I no longer trust our internal systems to resolve these [issues]. I'm much more willing to share information outside of the department, obviously within the bounds. I'm fortunate I work in an open environment so it's not like I'm dealing with anything that's sensitive that would have limitations that couldn't be shared, other than the fact it's just internal agency discussions. If I saw something inappropriate, I would be more comfortable seeking help outside of the normal channels to get it resolved rather than the normal channels I would've used a year ago.

Such accounts document how communication and deliberations changed, in part because of the lack of trust in the Trump administration. Rather than communications flowing through typical channels, in some of the most tumultuous parts of the government, career civil servants developed more informal and diffuse networks of communication and support to continue their work as they saw fit and uphold state functioning. Some viewed such channels as a necessary part of doing their work under chaotic leadership, while others intimated a spirit of resistance to such communications.

Some career civil servants discussed deliberately focusing on their work with external groups, such as state programs, in an effort to support work they viewed as valuable and knew the Trump administration did not approve of. Because these collaborations tended to occur outside the radar of politicals' attention, career civil servants viewed supporting external actors in their local work as an opportunity to safeguard "good" work. HHS midlevel manager Nick Pratt's area of programming had been dramatically contracted under the Trump administration. He said that the career civil servants in his work group were careful not to push their own agenda too much and instead incorporated elements of Trump's agenda into their work. In this context, they "really focused on minimums" and supporting "best practices." If their initiatives were not backed by "actual regulation, we can't force it on the policy side," he said. He reported that his work group aligned their stated work with the Trump administration's priorities such as cutting "red tape and all these buzz things that they talk about."

While they felt more constrained in their internal work, Pratt said that his team hoped to develop relationships with state partners to "move them in a way that maybe . . . the politicals wouldn't want us to, [but] not that it's outside of the bounds." So while Pratt covertly leaned on his partnerships with state programs to continue doing what he saw as good work, which may have stretched the bounds a bit of what his political leadership might have wanted, he also took care to adhere simultaneously to their explicit instructions, which commanded them to pare down his program. Here again we see a resistant spirit seeking covertly to maintain "good work" in their program in the face of undesirable, executive-led policy shifts. This resistant spirit, however, is set against a backdrop of largely compliant action that reduced his program in alignment with the administration's goals.

Aside from state partnerships, some offices had relationships with nonprofit organizations and advocacy groups with shared interests and work. Although some research suggests that such partnerships can aid civil servant resistance from within,[35] some career civil servants, like Pratt, suggested that this did not seem plausible in their work for several reasons. Pratt described his division's partnerships with progressive advocacy groups as so damaged under the first Trump administration that they were nearly nonexistent. Former partners had less access than conservative groups to senior appointed leadership and thus had nearly no impact on appointed leadership's policy agenda in his program area. "That makes it hard because we don't really have people to reach out to," he said. Even though they had enough funding to work with outside partners, considering the mixed support from political appointees and the dampened ties with outside advocacy groups and policy experts, he said that "even if we were allowed to invite them, . . . we will not be able to get the best people in our field." This was true, he thought, even if the event was given extensive promotion, such as a White House summit. He did not think that the top experts in his program area would "want any part of" such an event associated with the presidency, "at least not publicly . . . So that's hard."

Other advocacy and lobby groups supportive of the mission of certain agencies tried to support efforts at accountability and transparency in government from the outside. However, some career civil servants alluded to their inability to uphold such work from the inside during the first Trump administration. For example, EPA scientist Jeffrey Thompson said that "we couldn't be as transparent" as lobby groups requested "because we didn't have the resources to be that transparent." In addition, EPA employees were restrained in their ability to review cases and enforce environmental regulation because it was antithetical to political leadership's agenda. Thompson reported political leadership simply would not "let you get this particular aspect done because it's not in the interest of our administration to exact that requirement on industry."

Working with allies and sharing information within the government and across the public sector were two of the primary tactics midlevel civil servants discussed for maintaining the quality of their work and sometimes for strategizing about how to push back in subtle ways against politically appointed leadership. These tactics remained discreet and seemed to incur little risk to career civil servants. In some rare cases, gatherings of allies supported individual bureaucrats in reporting leadership transgressions through conventional channels, like Congress and the Inspector General's office, as well as through leaking to outside media sources; however, these actions largely remained private and individual rather than public or collective efforts for accountability.

Senior-level executives generally presented themselves as even more cautious when it came to sharing information with fellow Senior Executive Service (SES) and staff members working below them. As one senior executive in the EPA told me, communications with other career senior executives became "a little bit" more "guarded . . . partly to protect each other." When "one person who did resign in protest made a big splash and was in a lot of press, and she talked to several of us on her way out about . . . trying to build a little network of us who are still here to be working together—and maybe work with her from the outside," he said, "we were all—and I was extremely nervous about that because—for obvious reasons." Senior executives were generally more cautious and tried not to incite the suspicion of political appointees. Even if they had somewhat resistant tendencies, most buried such tendencies under carefully veiled language and actions they could reasonably explain away as staying within appropriate bounds of their roles.

## DOCUMENTING PERCEIVED TRANSGRESSIONS AS A BACKSTOP

Merely by doing some of the basic functions of their jobs, civil servants sometimes seemed at odds with the Trump administration. When they found themselves in loyalty traps, these civil servants quietly documented their work so that, should it come under scrutiny, they would have a contemporaneous record. Such a practice was not new. Some of my respondents maintained these kinds of records during prior administrations.[36] Multiple respondents indicated much wider use of the practice during the first Trump administration, however, especially those working in politicized areas or with particularly contentious appointees. While these career civil servants saw this kind of documentation as part of doing their job, they also recognized that some Trump-appointed leadership would view such actions as resistance or disloyalty.

When relationships between appointed leadership and career civil servants deteriorated, I found career civil servants conscientiously preserved records and documented leadership transgressions they witnessed. Some did so before leaving government service or transferring to other safer, less volatile positions in federal civil service. Others sought to preserve records of important information that might disappear under Trump's leadership or to document leaders' ethical and legal transgressions privately in the hope that it might someday help hold leaders accountable.[37] Even if they did nothing else, by staying in their positions, safeguarding important information, and documenting the malfeasance they had seen, these civil servants felt that they were upholding a baseline of professional integrity and accountability in the state. They felt better knowing that their documentation could contribute to holding leaders accountable in the future should the opportunity arise. Even those who took the time to document leaders' transgressions, however, suggested that they had little realistic hope that appointed leaders would ever be held accountable for all their ethical and legal transgressions by inspector generals, Congress, or anyone else.

In some cases, career bureaucrats worked to preserve data and scientific analyses on controversial content, such as climate change, as soon as Trump was elected. A senior EPA official said that when agency leaders learned about the election, "we worked to back up everything in the climate science . . . so there are archives so we would not lose that." A midlevel EPA scientist said that "quietly we all figure that our databanks are what we're gonna protect . . . we then arm ourselves." He continued, "our data are something that's gonna keep us in a kind of assertive focus, [knowing] that at some point in time, we gotta release that data so we can challenge whatever that authority is."

Others documented leaders' unethical and/or illegal behavior. Such documentation is part of civil servants' jobs, but it could be risky and interpreted as disloyal and subversive behavior by appointed leaders. It seemed as if the bureaucrats who took the time to document leaders' transgressions suspected their colleagues were not taking similar actions. Some of the federal civil servants who admitted to documenting leadership transgressions were remarkably tight-lipped about doing so with their colleagues: they did not want to draw attention to themselves as possibly acting disloyal to leadership. It is also likely that the people willing to speak with me were more likely than most to take such actions.

Near the end of my second interview with him in 2018, one senior career official at the EPA who had witnessed corrupt appointee behavior discussed at length the importance of documenting such egregious leadership behavior. When he heard that a political appointee blatantly prioritized the reelection of a specific politician over and above public health, which is at the core of the EPA mission, the senior career official said that, at first, he "couldn't believe what they were telling us, and we were all stunned. And no one was writing it down."[38] In the face of evident corruption, he said emphatically, "I wrote down every word. And I was just thinking, 'This is something that is stunning that shouldn't be happening, and I want to have a record of it.'"

"Did you write it down there or after the meeting?" I asked.

"No, I wrote it down right there, as it was happening," he responded.

"And did anyone else there do that then?"

"No," he said.

"Did it feel risky to do that then, because you were breaking that norm?" I asked.

"It did feel risky," he said. "Because if we do get a FOIA [Freedom of Information Act] request, it's something we probably wouldn't release because we could probably claim a privilege, like internal deliberative process or something, but it would go to—people in the agency would then know that I had written that down." Despite the risks, he "just felt like this is so shockingly wrong that I don't care what the consequences are: I'm writing this down."

This career official also said that, in the unlikely case he ever "was asked to do something that I really couldn't [ethically] do," then he would "have some information, and if I decided to be a whistleblower—then that might have been in the back of my mind as I wrote this down. And there is some possibility, [but] hopefully not—that I would have to leave the agency as a whistleblower. And if so, then I would want to be able to rely on more than just my memory."

Rumors of appointee corruption also swirled at HUD. A midlevel HUD civil servant reported hearing that recently hired appointees had been granted benefits that it typically took career bureaucrats years to earn. He had also seen senior leaders taking costly foreign trips, which were unprecedented in his agency. As one of few Black people in his workgroup, along with other people of color, he had felt increasing tension and even experienced some discrimination. As "my own personal and private thing," he said, he had "informally" documented the discrimination he had experienced. He was not alone in experiencing and documenting racial discrimination at his agency. He referenced a Black female employee at the Federal Home Loan Mortgage Corporation (also known as Freddie Mac) who had worked with their union to confront the agency with a discrimination case and had been awarded a substantial settlement nearing $1 million. He had yet to make any reports about discrimination to the union because he was seeking a promotion and wanted to be in leadership's good graces. But he admitted that he kept "some files that, you know, if pushed, I could collect a little something."

While these career civil servants began discussing their documentation of leadership transgressions as an ethical duty to resist corrupt leadership, documentation could serve multiple purposes. Such documentation also served as a hedge. The employees realized that leadership had crossed standard ethical and legal bounds. They felt it was wrong and were compelled to do something. Realizing that their actions were risky under vindictive leadership and could bring them unwelcome attention, however, they decided to hold their information privately in case they needed to use it in the future should their situations in their agencies deteriorate further.

A few of the civil servants I spoke with who reported suffering from different forms of political retribution under Trump's appointees submitted information to official grievance channels such as the inspector general's offices in their agencies and to congressional oversight committees. According to Albert O. Hirschman's definition, this would be a use of appropriate voice rather than resistant action.[39] Some federal employees might call this loyal dissent. Those who made official reports, however, seemed sensitive to how external observers might view such actions as forms of resistance to the administration.

A few career civil servants I spoke with recognized "the limits of our influence and ability" but took some solace in that "at least it's in the record," as one State Department official told me. "And maybe people find out about it twenty-five years down the record, and at least it's there, even if its classified . . . I can give you the information and ultimately you're going to make the decision and the record is going to show that I did that." This seemed like a private ethical stand that these career bureaucrats felt they could take to uphold this form of historical accountability within the state.

## PSYCHOLOGICAL SALVE BUT QUESTIONABLE EFFICACY

The limited impact of using covert resistance tactics led some civil servants to question whether such tactics were mainly efficacious in assuaging bureaucrats' troubled professional and moral consciences by the end of the administration. In speaking with those who engaged in covert resistance, many noted on reflection that it made them feel better, but they wondered about its efficacy over the course of the administration.

Sometimes they noted that they had helped appointees considerably, more, in fact, than they may have intended. Although HHS employee Nick Pratt engaged in some covert resistance tactics discussed in this chapter, he admitted that he had the tendency to offer a bit too much support to policies he actually disagreed with. As a normal part of his job, he had gotten used to trying to support leaders' policy initiatives as "an intellectual exercise" rather than as a "realistic piece of policy," he said. "When you know something really well, one of those skills is you should be able to argue the other side." While working on a recent piece of policy, to his own chagrin, he ended up making an argument that his boss thought might be "too strong" in favor of a poor policy. "It's easy," Pratt said, "in those situations to fall into like, well: . . . how would I argue this [idea] on the other side? . . . So that was funny when we [he and his supervisor] were like, 'Let's calm down, let's not get too far.' But then, when I wrote it, and my political director was like, 'Oh this is great'— then I was a little concerned it was maybe a little too strong. So that piece is kind of hard."

In another agency office where a career civil servant reported covert resistance in 2018, he questioned whether the unit overstated their own self-importance and impact. He said that "some people," such as his supervisor, believe and think "that the impact of the work of the office is greater than it is." He thought his colleagues and immediate supervisors "bury their heads in the sand" and fail to recognize the terrible state of disrepair in the agency as a whole. Even though they might have small wins in their office, given the limited scope of their agency, the impact of their local resistance efforts, he thought, were small.

When I spoke with USDT employee Andrew Williams in 2018, he acknowledged that some career staff in his agency working under less knowledgeable appointees could have some influence on the most important and ideological issues in his agency, but overall he had the sense that "there's very little opportunity to . . . change the train tracks." Williams suggested that even if civil servants dramatically reframed content in their areas of expertise based on more credible sources or perspectives, it had little impact when political appointees did not value their feedback and take it into account. In 2020, with respect to covert resistance tactics, he reflected that:

> I think they're largely ineffective . . . over the course of four years, there's really no opportunity to slow-walk projects. I mean I certainly still make the comments that I would like to make on documents, for example, when I think that important policy goals are not being raised. But that doesn't have any impact, and I don't really anticipate it will. I do that more for my own . . . peace of mind than I have any expectations it will change anything.

Engaging in small acts of covert resistance did help assuage career civil servants' consciences, allowing them to make the case to themselves, or to me, that they were doing what they could. Subtle acts of resistance could provide career civil servants with some sense of control in the face of the uncertainty, chaos, and fear that had infiltrated the top of the federal government and many of its agencies. Having a sense of control can reduce fear and its physiological responses[40] as well as increase tolerance for adverse events.[41] Situating the most subtle forms of covert resistance in a long-term perspective might lead some discerning career civil servants and external critics alike to wonder whether it is more of a variation of long-term coping and compliance than a means of efficacious resistance. In certain circumstances, civil servants' covert tactics may aid their cause, but some public servants' reports, like Williams's, near the end of the Trump administration suggested that covert tactics may have limited efficacy over the course of a four-year presidential term or a longer time period.

## CONCLUSION

Through small covert acts of resistance, civil servants stood up for their personal, professional, and agency values and missions while avoiding egregious breaches of their duties to serve appointed senior leadership. Civil servants' repertoire of surreptitious subversive tactics included: framing alignment with the Trump administration's goals, neglecting or slow-walking their work, letting leadership fail, and outstrategizing them.

Although career civil servants who engaged in such tactics largely believed such actions were better than doing nothing, their impact was limited by the government hierarchy and power structure. When Trump and his administration effectively implemented tactics of an administrative presidency through reliance on politically appointed officials rather than civil servants to write reports or policy briefs, feedback from civil servants was dramatically reduced and sometimes even excised. In these cases, tactics such as framing, slow-walking, and failing to support leaders were of little use. Appointed leaders simply were not relying on them or listening.

During trying times, many career civil servants reported relying on their informal networks of friends and colleagues in their offices and across the government. These networks relayed information, provided emotional support, and sometimes provided a place for civil servants to strategize collectively about how to respond to difficult leadership and policy agendas they found abhorrent. Even though these groups could strategize about internal resistance, it seemed that they mainly supported individuals in crafting their own personal responses to political appointees rather than planning collective action.

Others tried to maintain the integrity of the state by documenting appointee transgressions in the case they would be useful in future inquiries. They described keeping these records mainly on their own.

How resistant were these civil servants in the end? Did their actions have an impact, or were they merely ways to soothe their moral and professional consciences? In some cases, covert resistance likely helped protect elements of project or policy work in contested political terrain, but in many cases, the impacts of such subtle resistance seemed like a drop in the bucket compared to appointed leaders' power to set agendas, influence resource distribution, instill fear and caution in their peers, and weaken relationships between agencies and some of their former external allies in the nonprofit sector. Given these limiting factors, one wonders whether such low-risk forms of resistance were inevitably also low-impact tactics, especially over longer periods of time. A more cynical person might also wonder if covert tactics, and the apparent still waters Thompson alluded to, signaled to some Trump appointees that the coast was clear and that they could simply lead as they saw fit, through hell or high water.

# 11

## MORAL COURAGE

A s discussed in previous chapters, most civil servants are reluctant to challenge appointed leadership in the federal bureaucracy overtly. So who *is* willing to exhibit moral courage and overt resistance, if deemed necessary? Psychologist Ervin Staub defines moral courage as "the ability and willingness to act according to one's most important values even in the face of opposition, disapproval, and the danger of ostracism."[1] In this chapter, I examine the following questions: Among career civil servants, who stood up for their personal and/or professional values in the face of opposition, disapproval, or potential ostracism from agency leadership? Under what conditions did they do so?[2]

American civil servants under Donald Trump's first administration described continually trying to adhere to their duties to support political leadership, which aligns in part with post–World War II scholarship on obedience.[3] The accounts of the civil servants I spoke with suggest, however, that under emergent autocratic and authoritarian conditions, people differ in their interpretations and responses based on a combination of their personal characteristics and situational conditions.[4] Although some people are more predisposed to challenge authority than others, the particular circumstances they encounter, which can either enable them to act or hinder their perceived ability to do so, are critical factors in how they respond to authority in democracies in decline.

Rather than being led by a single moral compass, public servants under the Trump administration grappled with different moral compasses tied to their different role identities—say, as civil servants, technical experts, parents, devotees of their religion, and so on. Civil servants made different calculations based on the specific conditions in their workplace, with real incentives or costs for adhering to certain personal or professional values, which were subject to change over the course of the four-year Trump administration. Potential costs were likely to be especially daunting for civil servants in more precarious economic positions or working under vindictive leadership willing to engage in political retribution for perceived disloyalty.

## EXERCISING MORAL COURAGE

During Trump's first presidency, I witnessed civil servants grappling in real time with the moral and ethical implications of his autocratic turn in governance. Career civil servants juggled their contested loyalties working in their positions in relation to those working above, beside, and below them in their respective locations, in emergent and sometimes chaotic situations. The rare civil servants who engaged in acts of moral courage against the grain of the administration were not always the people I would have expected based on my first impressions of them. Some people who had a history of activism and who seemed quite disturbed by Trump and his administration's early policy agendas, such as some outspoken staffers in regional offices in

MORAL COURAGE • 283

2017, largely quieted down over the course of the administration, settling into their everyday routines. Some in lower and midlevel positions suggested that the administration was not as bad as they had feared. Their work had been less affected than they had expected, and they had carried on, for the most part, as they had before.

The very rare civil servants who exhibited observable acts of moral courage discussed in this chapter reveal not only the deeply situational nature of their moral action but also how conditions of rapid change can evoke more conscious moral deliberation than typically expected by some social psychologists.[5] The most visible and vocal resisters thought carefully about their roles and actions in a rapidly changing and tumultuous work environment through the duration of the administration, as shared with me at multiple points in time.

I sometimes saw them changing in front of my very eyes, as they unexpectedly experienced new realizations through the course of our conversations and the reflective and sometimes critical questions I asked. Their responses to difficult circumstances at work were certainly not all premeditated; they discussed situations in which they acted habitually, other circumstances in which they deliberated how to respond, as well as contexts in which they spontaneously erupted in ways even they had not anticipated because of converging pressures. I witnessed considerable changes in some of their situations and responses over the course of the administration. These changes served as situational natural experiments across civil servants' careers.

It is also important to acknowledge that most people with whom I spoke who were troubled by the first Trump administration's leadership in their agencies did not speak up or resist appointed leadership in ways the political leadership would be able to discern, despite perceptible organizational decline. What distinguished those who stood their ground more overtly or, in certain situations, pushed back against political encroachments in their areas of work? I compared the very small group of those who acted in the most evident morally courageous ways, despite attendant professional risks, to those who expressed an interest in resistance but ultimately quieted down and acquiesced at work. In doing so, I identified nine situational and personal characteristics that contributed to a heightened consideration of the moral implications of career civil servants' actions and to their resistant acts of moral courage. These characteristics are described in table 11.1.[6] While considerable proportions of my

## TABLE 11.1 WORKPLACE CONDITIONS AND PERSONAL CHARACTERISTICS FOSTERING MORAL COURAGE

| Workplace Conditions | Personal Characteristics and Perspectives |
| --- | --- |
| 1. *Threat to professional expertise:* Work unit's area of expertise was particularly threatened by appointed leadership. | 1. *Alarm and urgency:* Actors perceived changing workplace conditions with alarm and a sense of urgency in their responses. |
| 2. *Threatened agency missions:* Work unit experienced direct, deleterious leadership influence in agencies threatened with cuts and/or major leadership changes that deviated from agency missions. | 2. *Capability and efficacy:* Actors perceived themselves as competent and capable enough to resist leadership in certain situations efficaciously and tended to occupy some privileged positions. |
| 3. *Professional universal values:* Key professional values involved working for universal equality and justice, and benevolence for all. | 3. *Long-term moral self-assessments:* Actors evaluated the morality of their actions from a long-term perspective and/or evaluated how their future selves would interpret their actions. |

4. *Supportive colleagues, who contribute to a sense of psychological safety:* Work units and actor networks included supportive colleagues and mentors who helped actors strategize; affirmed their perspectives, professional commitments, and values; and protected them psychologically, and in some cases within the organizational hierarchy.

4. *Commitment to moral integrity despite risks:* Despite the risks that came with resistance, actors thought taking action was worth it and that it was important to uphold their moral conceptions of themselves.

5. *Alternative moral communities:* Outside work, actors' personal relationships; families; and participation in nonprofit, religious, educational, and other civic groups were sources of alternative moral ideas to those espoused by Trump and some of his appointed administrators, as well as sources of additional affirmation and support.

sample fit any one of the criteria outlined above, the combination of the nine factors in particular situations together seemed to predispose the most vocal civil servants to take a stand based on their convictions.

To have the opportunity to enact moral courage, career civil servants had to work in a location in which employees felt, as Staub theorized, opposition, disapproval, and/or fear of ostracism.[7] The federal civil servants I identified who engaged in acts of moral courage worked in locations where their area of professional expertise and related work was at risk of being cut or, from their view, changed for the worse, without leaders sufficiently heeding professional advice. The most morally courageous also tended to be located in agencies marked by distrust in appointee–career civil servant relationships, where appointees sought cuts or to deviate from agency missions or the law.

Those who exhibited the most moral courage worked in professions where their expertise grounded them not only in knowledge about structures of inequality and violations of such rights but in professional values and norms espousing universal equality and justice, and a sense of benevolence for all.[8] Such values seemed particularly salient to them professionally and personally. They were likely a self-selected group who chose their profession in alignment with prior commitments to justice, human rights, and service. Their prior histories of activism and community involvement suggest as much.

Those who engaged in acts of moral courage also mentioned how much having a network of supportive colleagues and mentors mattered. They relied on these networks for advice and affirmation of their professional commitments and ethical obligations. It seemed that such support from others around them, and often above them, helped provide them with a degree of psychological safety. As management scholars Abraham Carmeli and Jody Hoffer Gittell suggest, high-quality relationships, in which participants share goals, knowledge, and mutual respect, nurture psychological safety. Such relationships also help organizational members cope with challenging situations and learn from failures.[9] Psychological safety has been tied to greater use of voice, even when it involves pointing out errors to a supervisor, or may lead to disagreements.[10]

Along with these aforementioned workplace conditions, certain personal perspectives and characteristics seemed to contribute to one's likelihood of engaging in acts of moral courage. Those who engaged in moral courage interpreted workplace conditions as dire and urgent and as requiring a response intending to right the situation. The most vocal resisters identified as Democrats and were bothered by elements of the Trump administration's policy agenda, which they thought would cause harm to the state and the American public. They were dismayed by appointees' aberrant behaviors that disregarded bureaucratic standard operating procedures and ethical obligations.

Those exhibiting moral courage evaluated whether they should speak up or act against authority and considered whether such acts could be efficacious in the circumstances they faced. Ultimately, they believed in their own ability to respond efficaciously. The bureaucrats who exercised moral courage and the most vocal resistance at work had considerable status and privileges, which likely contributed to their sense of self-efficacy: they were more likely to be men than women and to have completed terminal degrees such as a PhD or JD, which put these civil servants well above the average level of education in the United States. As Marissa M. Golden conveys in her account of civil servant resistance and compliance under the Reagan administration, it is more customary for lawyers to argue in support of their expert opinions with their superiors than others.[11] Those exhibiting moral courage also earned more than the average American household income. General Schedule level 14 (GS-14) starting pay, for example, was $90,621 per year in 2019.[12] The most vocal and resistant civil servants tended to have worked in federal service for fewer years than others, clustering around just under ten years, although several had between twenty-five and thirty years of federal experience. Those engaged in overt resistance at work were also particularly likely to use some of the covert resistance tactics described in chapter 10.

The career civil servants who engaged in acts of moral courage thoughtfully considered the professional and personal costs of acting or failing to act based on their convictions. They evaluated the morality of their actions from a long-term perspective and/or evaluated how their future selves would evaluate their actions. Should their actions lead to poor professional outcomes, they concluded that taking action was worth the associated risks and important to upholding their moral conception of themselves.

Those willing to engage in acts of moral courage also reported having support from alternative moral communities. In alignment with Timothy Snyder's advice to those facing tyranny, in their private life, they remained active in communities contributing to good causes, such as nonprofits and/or religious congregations. Snyder recognized the power of belonging to such groups because they were places where trust can be built and learning engendered; such communities created "points of light . . . against a darkening sky."[13] He noted how "anticommunist dissidents of Eastern Europe, facing a situation more extreme than ours, recognized the seemingly nonpolitical activity of civil society as an expression and safeguard of freedom."[14]

In this chapter, I profile a civil rights lawyer and a human rights lawyer who were the most willing of the civil servants I met to engage in acts of moral courage and vocal resistance in the course of their everyday work. Both were relatively high-ranking civil servants (Senior Executive Service [SES] and GS-14) working on areas of expertise with attendant values, knowledge, and relationships that opposed the Trump administration's policy agenda and that experienced considerable challenges across agencies. The experiences of the two lawyers reveal how the particularities of their different circumstances working in especially tumultuous agencies on hot-button issues threatened by the Trump agenda influenced when and how they responded to perceived threats to their workplaces. Marie Glassman exemplified how a senior career civil servant can exercise voice and contestation after developing a strong working relationship with a senior appointed official. In contrast, in the absence of appointed leadership, Brian Taylor, a midlevel manager, stretched beyond his official role to continue doing his job as he saw fit, even if it ran counter to the direction appointed leaders were taking his agency.

## Exercising Voice and Confrontation as a Seasoned Leader of the Civil Service

Marie Glassman exemplified how, under certain conditions in which one is supported by senior appointed leadership, a high-ranking lawyer can push back against a presidential administration's agenda through the use of loyal dissent. A senior lawyer, Glassman had risen through the ranks of federal service over several decades. Glassman came across as confident, affable, and at ease while also being a direct, cut-to-the-chase kind of person. She seemed extremely knowledgeable, competent, and very passionate about her work.

After spending most of her career in civil rights work in the federal government, she realized that it was "unfortunately, just a really volatile area." Unlike most of the other civil servants I spoke with, Glassman had experience working in an office decimated by the appointed leadership under a prior administration. Faced with a presidential administration at odds with their work and appointee mistrust, her vibrant, hardworking, collegial former office had convened under threat and sent a collective grievance letter to one of the top leaders in their agency to raise concerns that normal deliberative processes eliciting their feedback were not being upheld by appointed leaders. This was one of the very few examples of career civil servants' collective action that I encountered in speaking with a wide range of civil servants, many of whom had worked for the federal government for decades. In response, managers in Glassman's former office, including her, were swiftly "removed." Going from being "really respected to becoming a pariah overnight," she said, was "a really tough thing to go through."

By the beginning of the first Trump administration, Glassman was working as a senior executive in another agency. Her portfolio included some work expanding civil rights that was a pet project of former president Barack Obama and that the new administration sought to rescind shortly after Trump was inaugurated. Glassman reported working closely with several "extremely out there, right-wing" appointees whose agendas came "at the expense of civil rights basically," she said. In comparison to prior administrations she had served under, Glassman thought the Trump administration was "the worst." Many appointees' extreme ideological views struck Glassman as different from prior administrations—whether Democrat or Republican. The appointees' socially conservative ideological bent personally and professionally bothered Glassman. As an "openly lesbian" married parent, the Trump administration's aims to roll back lesbian, gay, bisexual, and transgender (LGBTQ) rights "hits pretty close to home for me," she said.

Glassman was not only personally at odds with the Trump administration's political agenda and appointees' ideological views. She was also disturbed on a professional level by their failure to adhere to bureaucratic norms and standard operating procedures and by their threats to civil rights. She described the administration as unique in not caring "about procedure as much" or about "getting everything right." Instead, they were just "shredding up" preexisting policies and procedures.

Glassman depicted the appointees she worked with as contentious and combative. She said that they displayed overt distrust of career civil servants and hid important information from her team. They played games, such as giving them overwhelming amounts of information to review at the last minute at inopportune times, including during holidays when most people were not expected to work.

Nonetheless, in 2017, Glassman's response was typical of career civil servants: she acknowledged (somewhat apologetically) that "I think for me, I've actually been a little surprised by my own approach because, if you remember, I told you when I was much younger, that I was really one of the people who kind of fought, right?" As a senior career civil servant, she told me, her perspective had changed. She was juggling multiple duties and responsibilities, such as sharing her expertise and knowledge with political appointees to help them advance their agendas, protecting her staff, and maintaining her professional and personal commitments to protecting civil rights. As a senior career manager, she said, "You don't just have the work on your mind. You also have the health of your office in mind. It's important to buffer and protect other people, to kind of take hits for them. That's I think what good career managers do. I'm the one who's most exposed . . . That means that I should be taking on the stress of this more than my people do, right?"

As a lawyer, she initially believed she would be able to balance these responsibilities while remaining within the bounds of her position by distinguishing between legal questions and policy questions. "When it comes to legal stuff," she said, "I have superiors too, obviously, that can reverse me, but I definitely have the power to say no. If I say something is unlawful, I can stop it for the most part . . . [However] if something doesn't have a legal consequence but is a pure policy choice, even if it's a terrible one, it really isn't my job to go say—I mean I can go and say, 'I think this is terrible policy and these are things I think you should think about,' but I don't have the power to be like 'no.'"

Glassman told me early in the administration that her approach was "not coming from a desire to obstruct them. It's coming from a desire to do my job faithfully." She believed that doing her job well meant being direct but ultimately deferential to leadership. To avoid a "credibility gap," she said that she "took it up with people . . . straight up, and then to try to do my job everyday with integrity. So I do go to my superiors sometimes and say to them, 'What's your choice?'" knowing "they run the show." Sometimes she would tell appointed leadership, "I can't be with you on this, here are the reasons why, and, I know you'll make the final decision, and feel free to overrule me." As she tried to walk this moral tightrope, constrained by her obligation to serve appointed leadership and navigating her own sense of personal integrity, professional credibility, and her desire to protect those working under her, she was left with "very conflicting feelings about it."[15] In 2017, she reflected that her efforts to work with political appointees had:

definitely been a compartmentalized effort because it's not like I've lost my very deep commitment to civil rights. I don't feel good about a lot of what's happening around me, and I know I can't control it. And I think it will be an ongoing thing for me about, whether it will make sense to stay or go. But right now, I have no plan to go. And one final quick thing: the other reason that weighs on my mind heavily about not going is that, if I do go, then the next [person in my position] will probably be someone with a very different ideological perspective than I have, and that person could be here for, you know, twenty to thirty years. So you do start to have that sense of—if you depart, who's going to fill your slot?

Glassman's perspective in 2017 echoes narratives that Hannah Arendt documented among Nazi bureaucrats during World War II. One of the most common civil servant justifications for service to the Hitler regime, Arendt suggests, was that "we who appear guilty today were in fact those who stayed on the job to prevent worse things from happening; only those who remained inside had a chance to mitigate things and to help at least some people."[16] Glassman expressed that she continued to care about civil rights; that she planned to stay, with the hope that she could reduce the damage; and that she would be better than a more socially conservative ideologue who might fill her place. She also noted the limited power she had in her position in the bureaucracy, and how it felt like the damage from executive agendas were beyond her control.

When I interviewed Glassman in 2018 and 2020, she seemed different. She described regularly engaging in acts of moral courage in which she overtly confronted—and even fought with—appointed leaders at work. And she seemed more at ease in doing so. By 2018, she had successfully opposed several items on the Trump administration's agenda. She had saved civil rights protections that retained government services for millions of disadvantaged people from proposed cuts and softened several decisions coming from White House leaders.

She sought to protect the integrity of her office, the morale of those working under her, and the quality of their work by standing up to appointees over hiring decisions. Like many other offices in the Trump administration, some leaders of Glassman's office were partial to hiring job candidates from relatively low-ranking institutions, like Liberty University, which were known for their conservative ideology and which, under a more typical administration, would not have been considered well-trained, high-quality recruits. Glassman fought against such hires. She confronted appointees in her efforts to maintain her job responsibilities and rights in hiring processes, and to counter appointees' attempts to roll over her decisions and to influence senior appointed leadership by perpetuating what she thought were lies.

She was aware that such confrontations were "the kind of thing that could cause somebody to lose their job," she said. However, based on her prior work experience in an office that had suffered nearly complete turnover under a prior administration, she had seen what a detrimental long-term impact hiring poor job candidates could have, and she sought to avoid that in her current role to the best of her ability.

In addition, Glassman conscientiously documented concerns about the Trump administration's policy prerogatives undermining the civil rights of certain underprivileged groups in an effort to benefit their own, more affluent constituencies. Including their actions in a written historical and legal institutional record, which could be accessed by civil servants in future administrations, gave her great satisfaction and pride.

On several occasions, when political appointees altered reports she had written on key policy issues, changing their meaning to state the opposite of what she had originally written, after "a few sleepless nights," she "refused to sign" the final documents. In facing the appointees, she said, "I thought really carefully about the how and the way that I did it, [which] was basically [to] say, 'Look, I am happy to help you in any way I can; that's my job. I'm happy to have my team help you, but you have to also understand that the views that are here in this memo are not views that I share and I don't want my name associated with it, so please take my name off.'"

As a lawyer, she also exercised voice when illegal behavior was proposed. She acknowledged that she was able to do this in part because of her seniority and in part because it aligned with her official role and professional expertise:

> People below me can't really do this, but looking at senior people and saying like, 'Basically you're so off and you've got so many problems . . . the answer is what you want to do is not legal and if you or people above you want to take the risks and go forward and do X, that's not legal, that's not my decision, go make it. You're not gonna change our advice to you.' So the implications of what we have to say—other people can make those decisions, I'm fine with that. That's an appropriate position for me to take. But fundamentally, when we're giving people advice, it's very good advice, very well thought out, there's research behind it and it's valuable, and the only issue is whether they'll listen.

Here Glassman stood up for what she thought was ethical professionally and personally and in alignment with her expert professional opinion, her role, and the law.

Throughout 2018 and through the rest of the administration, Glassman experienced her work as "stressful" but "doable," she said. "I don't feel like there's no way to get anything done." She expressed pride in her work history and felt that she had struck a good balance between her professional ethical and personal moral guideposts. "I have nothing to hide, and I don't let my personal ideology impact my legal work," she said, "but I'm also absolutely not afraid to go after my superiors and tell them when I think they're doing unlawful things. Like I am no shrinking violet; otherwise, I don't see a point in being there." This was possible in part, she said, because as a lawyer in her particular position, it was her job to give voice to legal concerns with policy agendas.

That being said, I had also spoken with two other lawyers in similar positions in two other agencies who were much more deferential to appointed leadership. And, the prior year, in 2017, Glassman had felt far less certain. What had changed for Glassman in the interim, that helped her transition from fitfully trying to navigate the new administration to feeling capable of navigating her personal and professional moral and ethical conundrums more confidently, skillfully, and successfully? And what contributed to her increased use of voice in alignment with her professional and personal convictions, while so many others had grown quiet at work in the face of real risks to their careers?

Glassman attributed her increased comfort in resisting the new administration to the appointment of a reasonable, experienced supervisor who valued quality legal work and who supported her. Despite their considerable ideological and political differences, Glassman "established a really good working relationship" with the new Republican appointee. "If I did not have support from above vertically, . . . I'd be in huge trouble," she said. She told me her supervisor was:

> willing to allocate that time to work with us, support us, hear from us because I think he's trying to help us stabilize [a relationship with an appointee, specific details removed] that he knows is extremely challenged, and who challenges him and insults him, too. If those things were not there, my guess is that this conversation would be some form of I'm being pushed out, I'm in deep trouble, or my entire team is being imploded. It could've gone in that direction, and it hasn't because of [Glassman's supervisor], and it also hasn't because I think I'm pretty strategic.

For Glassman, developing good working relationships with some appointed senior leadership in her agency was a turning point. In her work on other areas outside civil rights, she found points of convergence and agreement with other leaders who could "evaluate the craziness of their own administration" and serve as "spots of a little bit more order." Glassman's experiences reveal how having top-level support at work could enable other high-ranking civil servants to stand up to political leadership.

Due to building a good working relationship with a senior appointee, and her subsequent perceived ability to confront other political appointees more directly, Glassman's trajectory diverged from others over the latter two years of the administration. Although she was able to exercise more voice without getting fired and had more efficacy in her efforts to uphold legal procedures, integrity in her work, and protect civil rights work in her unit, her interpersonal relationships with some appointees deteriorated considerably. Communication between an adversarial political appointee's team and her office broke down. When her team met with the appointee's team, conflict ensued. "We don't meet as much as we used to to discuss our concerns because the meeting turns literally to screaming, which is extremely unprofessional and stressful and my lawyers started to feel attacked by them," she said in 2020. "So I think that the way our [adversarial appointee] has responded definitely has included personal attacks behind my back a lot." She reported that high-ranking appointees had told top agency officials "what a terrible lawyer I am and what a lazy workforce we are. And then you've got us working twenty-four hours a day because there's so much to do. It's just very, very different perspectives. And so yes, the working relationships are terrible, like they've never been worse," she said.

But even as her relationships with some political adversaries became increasingly strained by 2020, under these conditions— and perhaps because of them—she maintained a strong relationship with her own team and chain of command above her. She said that her team was able to maintain open communication and a sense of camaraderie: "I can talk about those challenges with my team, so we can assure that our team is strong and that we have [a] really good flow of information with each other," she told me in 2020. "And I also give a lot of opportunities to my staff to bring concerns to me to vent to help them figure out how best to work with the [appointee]. And then we've had many, many, many discussions with our political superiors."

Even amid signs of organizational decline, it sounded like Glassman managed to keep her team intact and functioning in a way that upheld the law, meritocratic standards of hiring, and typical ethical obligations of public administration to the best of their ability. They seemed to function, as political scientists of developing nations might say, as a bureaucratic "pocket" or "island of excellence" rooted in civil servants' technical competence and professionalism, even in an agency with other distinguishable signs of declining capacity and functioning.[17]

Glassman also stood out because she engaged in bolder forms of resistance outside the office compared to many other senior executives. For example, in a fit of frustration after a particularly "horrific day" at work, Glassman stormed out of her office "pissed . . . walking right out of my job," she said, to attend a protest with friends on the steps of the Supreme Court. Compared to many senior executives with whom I spoke, who generally avoided attending public protests in the Capitol where they might be recognized by colleagues, Glassman's decision to leave work to attend a nearby protest on an issue related to her work seemed like an exceptionally rare, public act of dissent for a senior executive service member who regularly worked with political appointees.

Glassman was predisposed to act on her convictions against leadership because she had engaged in civic, political, and workplace resistance in the past—both in and outside work. She was the only person I spoke with who had taken part in a collective act of protest at work under a prior administration. She had also attended fourteen protests and worked with ten different civic organizations prior to Trump's election. These figures were markedly higher than for most others with whom I spoke. Her involvement continued after Trump's election. During the first two years of the Trump administration, she attended another four protests and had been involved with six nonprofit organizations, which again distinguished her as among the most civically active people with whom I spoke.

Grounding and reinforcing her moral commitments and actions was a particularly rich network of social support from a variety of alternative moral communities that shared her value commitments. With her typically heavy workload and the "emotionally exhausting" nature of her job, which on some days, she said, felt "like an ideological meat grinder," Glassman was aware that she really needed the social support of others. As a result, she made a deliberate effort to prioritize her relationships outside work. Her partner provided a supportive moral and strategic sounding board at home. Glassman built "in buffers," many of which involved maintaining her relationships, like going to "see a friend" or volunteering "at my kid's school." She regularly attended religious services with her family. These kinds of activities helped her "get back out into the world." In alignment with historian Timothy Snyder's advice, Glassman had learned the importance of taking time to leave her job behind and develop her personal life in interaction with others in different communities.[18] This helped her maintain her own resilience and put her work in perspective.

Glassman also maintained relationships with leaders of past Democratic administrations "that [she] was really close with," who provided advice and support. They reiterated that she was "successful" in "just being able to stand down in your job through this torrent. If you take that perspective, being able to do that is kind of an accomplishment."[19] The support and alternative perspectives gained from her various relationships helped sustain her sense of efficacy during her most challenging times at work.

Glassman's grounding in various personal and professional networks outside her everyday work, which supported her values, aligns with past research on activism and altruism. A long tradition of scholarship on activism and benevolent action under authoritarian governments suggests that people with ties to others who share similar sociopolitical attitudes and values, and have engaged in collective action for causes they believe in, are more likely to engage in activism or to resist authoritarianism.[20]

Compared to others, Glassman felt particularly resilient, competent, and capable of action during the middle and second half of the first Trump administration.[21] As a seasoned senior civil servant who worked with appointees and as a lawyer, she was able to give voice to her concerns directly to leadership. She was willing to take on the associated risks of speaking truth to power because she felt supported by a top appointee and thought she would land on her feet regardless of what transpired. After all, she had survived being pushed out of federal service in the past:

I've made very careful choices about this, and I definitely give in on some things, [but] it's not like I'm clueless . . . but my personality is just of a nature where I feel like if the cost of being honest with these people is that I'm gonna be thrown out of my job, then do it. It's a big world. You always recover, and my personal integrity is much more important to me than holding my job, and I think that allows me to feel more space to go after people when I want to . . . I think if you've gone through the experience of losing control over your career . . . and you survived it and you have some perspective on that . . . it's made me feel much more comfortable taking risks now and I just don't see how I could do it any other way.

Glassman had developed resilience by surviving what many civil servants would view as the worst possible scenario under a former presidential administration. In response to being vocal and engaging in collective action with colleagues to confront political appointees, she had been pushed out of her dream job. Yet she had gained practical experience confronting authority under the mentorship of an unusual, dedicated, and supportive cadre of experienced civil servants, came out of it on her feet, and "learned from it in hindsight," which later helped her navigate her work in the Trump administration courageously and skillfully when she believed she had sufficient support from above.

Glassman also evaluated the morality of her actions from a long-term perspective. When experiencing potentially morally compromising situations at work, she said that she "made calculated choices," taking into account how she would evaluate her actions years later. For example, in choosing not to sign certain documents, she had reflected that, "ten years from now my name would be on something that is the absolute opposite of my own views, and I'm not gonna let that happen. There's no way." In this way, despite feeling like she "definitely had my arm twisted," she said that "somehow I seem to have survived it."

It is also important to recognize that, despite how Glassman stood out among federal civil servants for a seemingly strong use of voice in critique of some Trump appointees' leadership, she took care to do so within the purview of her role. She was not pressuring appointees through leaking or mobilizing other forces outside the purview of her job or institution. She acted within the bounds of her position and sought to maintain support to leadership while recognizing the need sometimes to check their decisions when they were illegal or she thought they would bring harm to her work unit or to the American public.

Glassman was rare in her ability to act on her convictions both inside and outside work in a way that was markedly more transparent and aligned with her personal and professional moral compass than the vast majority of career civil servants I met. Of course, some readers may question whether she truly acted in as moral and courageous a manner as she could have and the extent to which she was complicit in aiding the Trump administration in their civil rights rollbacks. Glassman touched on the question of complicity during multiple interviews. "Still, of course, I think every day of my life there that many things that they're doing are completely immoral, are repugnant to me, truly disgusting, mean-spirited," she said to me in 2018. She had to work on the civil rights consequences of some of their "really horrific" policies. "It's not a great scene overall," she said. "There are still civil rights losses left and right every week, but compared to what it was, I think it's a little bit better." Justifying her involvement, she said, "the way that I have been able to work on those issues is by limiting the damage." She continued, "And it's never building positive things—it's limiting damage . . . So I can't say we feel strongly motivated, . . . but when you can get them, you'll often be able to take a proposal that was horrific and narrow it." In the end, she concluded that the limited impact she could have in resisting the Trump administrations' rollbacks of civil rights was worth staying for.

She acknowledged that "at other times I have had to work on things that are the opposite of my own commitments, but there was no real legal problem with them, and so integrity means that I don't get to obstruct what they do. And . . . I think maybe one reason why they haven't gone after me is because I've also really helped them." Glassman adhered to varying value systems under different situations; sometimes she followed her own moral compass, while at other times she prioritized adhering to the responsibilities and ethics of her professional position, which contradicted her own beliefs and values. This aligns with the "moral creativeness" that management scholar Chester Barnard championed among executives.[22]

For Glassman, different value systems became salient and activated across her specific circumstances and were affected by the institutional systems of power and hierarchies in which they were embedded. Although she had many personal and social characteristics that would make her likely to engage in morally courageous action from the start of the Trump administration, it was only after she had developed strong working relationships with select political appointees that she more boldly and regularly confronted other political appointees whose behavior she found problematic.

## Expanding One's Role in a Vacuum of Power

Of all the civil servants with whom I spoke, lawyer Brian Taylor struck me as the boldest in his efforts to protect human rights work from the Trump administration's cuts. He exemplified how, in the absence of appointed leadership oversight and in working among enterprising and supportive colleagues, career civil servants could carve out pockets where they tried to do their jobs as they saw fit, even when doing so cut against the grain of the administration or stretched beyond the bounds of their prescribed roles.

At first sight, in a sharp, stylish dark suit, Taylor appeared youthful and energetic as he approached me. It was only as he got closer that I noticed small crevices lining his face, making

304 • CIVIL SERVANT RESISTANCE

it seem more weathered up close than his years seemed to war-
rant. Although Taylor had not been working in federal service
as long as some of the others profiled, with the support of an
"encouraging," "indefatigable," and "inspiring" mentor who
had taken him under his wing and brought him along to his
meetings and supported his overall development, he had been
promoted to be a midlevel manager. His mentor had fostered
a collegial, supportive space in which members of his workgroup felt empowered, competent, and capable of taking what
they viewed as appropriate and necessary actions. Taylor's unit
had learned what he called a spirit of "entrepreneurialism and
self-initiative," which struck me as rare in federal service. When
his mentor departed the agency, he left in his wake a vacuum
of power, which expanded with Trump's election into office. For
several years, Taylor worked under a series of acting directors.

Taylor had learned bureaucratic skills and tricks of the trade
from some of his former supervisors. Like nearly all the civil servants I spoke with, he had learned to prioritize serving the mission of his agency, to be "prudent" during leadership transitions,
and to make every effort to work with and support appointed
senior leadership. He told me in 2018:

> We shouldn't assume that the politicals are uneducable. And part
> of your job is simply to educate them about the complexity of the
> choices they face. That part of your obligation and duty is to make
> the best argument you can. That doesn't mean being antagonistic
> necessarily; you have to find different ways to make your argu-
> ments. He [his mentor] taught us that there are moderating influ-
> ences that should necessarily emerge and [not to] get too alarmed.

Early in the first Trump administration, however, notable
alarm bells began ringing. The prior rules did not seem to be

operating. Even the supervisor Taylor referenced, who had told him to develop good working relationships with political appointees and not to get too alarmed by their policy agendas because of the moderating influence of the bureaucracy and its expert advisers, changed his tune. "So, for example, one thing he told me was *to be alarmed* because there are not always moderating influences in this administration [emphasis added]." Taylor's supervisor had indicated that a specific radical decision related to a high-profile ally could be read as a "key test of whether this administration can be educated and moderated in this issue because . . . any dispassionate security policy expert will dispense advice that this is a bad idea and that it is untenable and will damage the prospects for advancing our interests." Yet under Trump's appointed leadership, this "bad" decision came to pass, breaching this suggested problematic threshold. When I asked him where he could go from this point onward, Taylor replied, "It can always get fucking worse."

Taylor worked in a particularly contentious agency under the Trump administration. Like other civil servants I spoke with working on civil and human rights, Taylor found some appointees' ideological bent, lack of expertise, and seeming disregard for adverse consequences alarming. He said that these appointees lacked basic diplomatic skills and strategic ability, such as precision in timing when and how they shared their perspectives and policy agendas, and skill in their framing of issues. Their international policy preferences and actions also seemed to contradict each other. In short, he reported that appointees appeared unable to comprehend the complex social landscape of international relations, making them unable to use such knowledge to their advantage. The ability to "have multiple things in your mind at once, to be able to do more than one fucking thing at once," he said, was a trait of a good civil servant. "And that's the kind of advice that only really good civil servants can give; that is nonpartisan advice. That is just like, 'Here is how this works.'"

Yet appointees largely failed to listen to their career support teams in his agency and continued to commit egregious blunders. He said that the process of communication between career civil servants and political appointees had largely collapsed in his agency; the Trump administration's leadership seemed set against listening to career bureaucrats' advice. Taylor had also heard of threats and retribution from appointed senior leadership in his agency and was acutely aware of the vindictive nature of politically appointed leadership there. These conditions increased his sense of urgency in working to protect and extend what he believed to be the good work in his unit.

During the first two years of the administration, without being able to communicate effectively up to senior management through conventional channels and lacking proper supervision and oversight, Taylor described taking the reins in his own hands and overstepping the bounds of his role. "I just will go out and pretend to be more important than I am," he said. "Or make the connections and use the connections that I have" from working under his former supervisor "to just try and make things happen and do some of the work." Even in the absence of his former supervisor, which led to his area of work being "deprioritized and amid the larger dysfunction" of his agency, he thought, "we're still able to get a fair amount done. And if I weren't able to do that, then I would leave tomorrow." He later added that he did not "want to overstate" it, but in some ways, he had stopped caring about potential repercussions. Taylor's professed overstepping beyond his official role was a rare demonstration of moral courage and resistance that sharply cut against most civil servants' normative risk-averse, rule-following nature and their commitments to being responsive in serving appointed leadership. Taylor knew his work resisted the direction senior leadership was moving his agency, and he continued to do it anyway. "In some ways," Taylor told me, having no leadership "was a blessing because we just kept on doing a lot of the things we were doing."

Like some others I spoke with, Taylor justified this approach to his colleagues. He would say to them, "'Look, in the absence of countervailing policies, our assumption should be that we have the same policy as we did before,' which is the only logical way you can operate. That is not an attempt to subvert the administration we're serving; that is an attempt to have a rational way of knowing what you're supposed to do when you wake up and go to work. Because if that is not true, then nobody has any idea what the fuck you're supposed to be doing."

Taylor's approach in 2018 was possible mostly because of the "safe space" he described having in his workgroup. There, at least, he was confident in his colleagues' support and in their shared, long-standing, "entrepreneurial" office culture and support of human rights work. "We speak very openly with each other," he said. Together they discussed troubling developments under the Trump administration's leadership and strategized "about ways in which we think we can present arguments to decision makers that will get them to see a different perspective or understand some of the negative consequences, maybe, of some of their decisions." At times, as occurred in Glassman's office, his team realized that "certain decision makers are not persuadable on logic or reason or prudence and there's just an ideological disregard for that dispassionate presentation of policy consequences."

When it became apparent that some appointed senior leadership's policy agendas would "be harmful to the United States" and that they were not open to listening to feedback from career bureaucrats, Taylor and his colleagues used other strategies to "mitigate the bad effects" of leaders' decisions. They tried to outstrategize leaders and let leadership fail by not fully briefing them or by not flagging certain problematic issues, as discussed in chapter 10.

In this setting, in which career civil servants felt like senior leadership was incompetent, arrogant, irrational, and hostile to bureaucrats and the well-being of the nation, leaking occurred more frequently than was typical in government service. When necessary, Taylor felt he had "to play it dirty" and leak information. He acknowledged that this was not a good long-term strategy—it engendered internal organizational warfare, which could operate as a race to the bottom of sorts. But when threats to shut down his area of work surfaced, he thought leaking was the only option available. It "was not the first outlet we pursued," he said. They had tried to communicate through official channels, and it had not worked because senior leadership would not listen to them. Consequently, as "a last-ditch effort," he had leaked nonclassified information to former high-level officials, contacts working for Congress and the media.

Taylor's daily work situation was considerably different when we spoke in early 2020. By then, his office was supervised by a political appointee. Although Taylor worked in an agency he feared was being used as a tool of a presidency with authoritarian tendencies, he acknowledged, "in my personal office I've maybe had it better than some." The political appointee leading his office, he said, "by and large was good . . . thoughtful, smart on policy, open to suggestions and ideas, not inherently distrustful of career civil service, fought for positions that I believed in, and still gives me a significant degree of autonomy and ownership of my job."

In alignment with his description of his position and professed commitment to building relationships with appointees, he thought he had fostered a good working relationship with his new supervisor by finding "the areas that you think that they will be interested in and agree on and emphasize those" and avoiding "any kind of political talk, statements or chatter." He felt "lucky . . . because my political appointee actually valued my expertise and my competency. He had built trust with his supervisor by quickly helping him on a particular issue he cared about. "That's the kind of thing where he's gonna be very appreciative and think, well, this person really is working for me; they're loyal, they're responsive," he told me.

In shifting from a leadership vacuum to working under this appointed leader, Taylor thought that the conditions in his office had deteriorated. His particular area of work was "subverted by presidential politics, frankly." He said:

> There are certain just no-go areas for me that I don't see the administration is still having a useful policy that does anything right. So overall, everything was terrible in my own little corner. I was still able to fight for things, but it gets exhausting, and it gets tiring to do that and [you] feel like you're always pushing a boulder uphill . . . Everything's [within his policy remit] being sidelined. It's very difficult to even get what should be pretty run-of-the-mill public statements out about certain things because it just doesn't get any priority. And then just the decision-making process and the policy-making process is totally broken. I work in a functional [location] and I think it's been especially frustrating for [offices like his at his agency] because we're so disempowered.

His sense of efficacy had diminished, and he was burned out. "I also lose all the time, so that's kind of part and parcel of the job. But at least I get to fight and express my opinions and advocate for policy outcomes without fear of repercussion," he said in 2020.

Even though he worked with "largely the same group of people," he said that "our dynamic changed because we had a political appointee in the office heading us and so *we had to sort of rebuke ourselves* a little bit or be more strategic about what we engaged on and how we engaged on it, like I said, *to align ourselves* [emphasis added]. I also observed steady depressions or degradation of morale. I mean there's a lot more people closing the door to their office and just holing up."

Two of the nine proposed criteria for supporting morally courageous action in a democracy in decline were reduced. His perceived capability and efficacy to do what he saw fit diminished with an appointed leader in place. His group, as he stated, had to align with the direction the leader and administration wanted to take his agency. The supportive, entrepreneurial, and collegial workplace he had previously described was no more. Instead, he described each person working separately on projects they no longer believed in. Morale plummeted.

This is the opposite of what occurred in Glassman's office. After building a relationship with her senior appointee, she gained more of a sense of capability and efficacy. Under such conditions, she described communication and relationships within her office as strong. Instead of falling apart under the perceived harmful direction other appointees were taking her agency, Glassman's team, under her protective leadership, banded together.

Taylor, in contrast, described a sense that things were falling apart. Reflecting on his situation in 2020, he said:

> I always joke to people I'm the frog that has boiled. Things are still really bad at [his agency] and there are policies that I find

abhorrent. Overall morale is terrible, and our secretary sells out
our own career [bureaucrats], and the rest of the department is in
complete dysfunction, disarray, and shambles. No policy making
process has actually been functional. The NSC [National Security Council] can best be described as a raging dumpster fire with
absolutely no direction, no coherent thinking. The [agency] has
no functional process to make decisions to have policy fights . . .
I think there's just been no strategic thinking, focus, or prioritiza-
tion of what our policy is and how it can be holistic.

As a result of his new working conditions and "in part because
I was sick of this administration and getting very frustrated and
burned out, [and] in part just because it was a great professional
development opportunity," Taylor chose to leave his position
near the end of Trump's first term in office. "I needed to get out
of the pressure cooker," he said. Instead he moved to a position
where he thought he could hold the executive branch accountable.

Like the others in this section, Taylor had several personal
and professional characteristics that predisposed him to resisting the administration and standing up for human rights. He
was a lawyer who specialized in human rights and had a history
of protest attendance and volunteering in civic and nonprofit
organizations. He had attended about two dozen protests and
rallies since high school, the highest number I recorded among
any government employees with whom I spoke. In addition to
a career of working in human rights law around the world, he
served in and/or donated to over a dozen nonprofits, including
those advocating for civil rights and human rights and doing
work to prevent hate crimes.

Throughout the Trump administration, Taylor also consistently reflected on the moral and ethical implications of his

thoughts and actions in a long-term historical context. During the transition to the Trump administration, he read intellectual work on the history of human rights under authoritarian regimes and spoke with colleagues about moral and ethical issues with respect to working under Trump appointees' leadership. He had read "a whole series of intellectual articles written in 2017 about the ethical questions facing the civil servants in this adminis- tration." In one such article, in the spirit of Hannah Arendt, a Georgetown professor "came out very severely," he said, likening the Trump administration to "Nazis" and drawing attention to the "moral justifications that Nazi bureaucrats used." In particu- lar, he reported that the article referenced an example of a lawyer whose "job inside the Third Reich as a bureaucrat was to review the racial purification laws." This lawyer justified continuing to do his job by saying he was "softening" the laws "here" and "mitigating it there, and if I weren't here than" it would be worse. Taylor acknowledged how the professor had critiqued such a justification, arguing that the bureaucrats referenced were pro- viding a "self-serving" justification that "ultimately legitimizes a morally bankrupt project."

Although Taylor thought such a perspective was "too abso- lutist," he pondered it seriously in 2018. As an experienced civil servant, he recognized the "value of having people who care about doing the right thing and who want to educate" others with their expertise. "But it is, I think, a useful cautionary les- son that you have to be wary of self-serving justifications. And the other lesson is that there's always, even in the most extreme circumstances, the possibility of making that argument. You can always say I think I'm doing a little bit more good by being here, even [with] the Nazis."

Taylor had talked with other colleagues and pondered what his moral and ethical redline would be early in the Trump administration. He had "prepared some contingency plans" and "mentally prepared myself for the decision of leaving," in case he was put in a bad position by leadership and pressured to cross his moral and ethical boundaries.

In the end, Taylor acknowledged his own fallibility. Reflecting on his work in his agency in 2020, Taylor noted, as did Glassman, how he had tried to act to the best of his ability under the constraints of his role and obligations to serve the administration, but it was difficult to assess his moral efficacy under the torrent of challenges and changes wrought in his agency under the Trump administration:

> I still think the policies that I sort of had to go along with or implement that I thought were bad or harmful to the United States or morally offensive didn't outweigh the positive that I was able to add. But I'm less sure, you know. I don't know. I just know that I was able to keep fighting for certain things I wanted and then a lot of really, really immoral policies were put forward and enacted and a lot of policy decisions based purely on party politics and the personal enrichment of the president were put forward, and so I don't know.

Although Taylor felt overwhelmed by the deterioration he witnessed in his workplace and agency, he continued to engage in acts of moral courage throughout his time serving the administration. How he did so differed, however, based on whether a political appointee was leading his office and if he perceived he had efficacy to do what he thought he should in his role. In the absence of close oversight by the administration, he felt empowered to stretch his role by leveraging his networks and knowledge and to operate outside the lines by leaking information in an effort to save his office. Acts of overt resistance like these, stretching his role and leaking information, were extremely rare among the people I spoke with. When conditions changed and the supervision over his unit increased, he chose to leave his office in the end to work in a temporary position where he felt like he could hold the administration accountable. Despite his use of the analogy of the frog in boiling water that slowly becomes accustomed to the heat, Taylor's perception of his situation and response to it deviated from the fable. When Taylor felt less efficacious in his job and became more morally troubled by the conditions of his workplace, he chose to leave rather than boil in the water in perpetuity. Given the size and differentiated structure of the American federal government, it was big enough for him to find a place to go where he could do work that was more morally aligned with his personal and professional values and could resist the deleterious direction he perceived the Trump administration leading the government.

Taylor's experiences depict the federal government more as an ocean experiencing climate change than a single boiling pot.[23] While members of the Trump administration had certain policy agendas and breaches of standard operating procedures that shifted the government writ large toward autocracy and authoritarian tendencies, appointed and elected leadership altered some parts of the government more than others. Even in areas with the most turmoil, where appointees changed over the course of the administration, conditions evolved in distinct trajectories. These situational variations affected civil servants differently. Given their professional credentials, work experience, networks, and biographies, civil servants gave unique interpretations to changing situations and their ability to exercise voice or resistance or to change jobs in the context of changing work situations.

In summary, Glassman and Taylor shared various characteristics that both heightened the salience of their moral deliberations and emboldened them to engage in more overt acts of speaking up and resistance at work. They worked in particularly contentious locations that were affected by the chaos, ineptitude, and confusion of the Trump administration earlier than most. They were both high-level lawyers specializing in human and civil rights who found important critical support from immediate colleagues and supervisors with whom they regularly interacted, which at certain junctures enabled their efficacious actions resisting the Trump administration's leadership in the course of their everyday work. As would be predicted by scholarship on social movement activism—which suggests that prior activism, membership in social movement organizations, and involvement in other civic groups make people more likely to engage in resistance[24]—these two people had attended far more prior protests than most of the civil servants with whom I spoke. They also reflected regularly on the morality of their actions in their particular positions, both from a short- and a long-term perspective on their own and in conversation with others, and they were willing to leave should they have to.

It is important to contextualize Glassman's and Taylor's acts of moral courage in their everyday work. Both acknowledged that they sometimes stood their ground and spoke up, but at other times, as their roles and profession norms commanded, they helped the administration in policies they thought were harmful in accordance with their duties as career civil servants.

The circumstances in which they felt they could do their job as they saw fit, even if it diverged from leadership priorities, differed based on their rank and particular circumstances. As a senior civil servant and lawyer, and after building a strong working relationship with a senior political appointee, Glassman felt she could use her voice in a more direct, confrontational way with other appointees. Taylor, as a midlevel manager with far fewer years of experience and a lower rank, lost his sense of efficacy and esprit de corps with his coworkers and opted to leave when leadership was appointed to his office.

## A CONSTELLATION OF CONTRIBUTING CAUSES: MORAL SALIENCE, COURAGE, AND RESISTANCE

Based on my conversations with dozens of federal bureaucrats, Glassman and Taylor were rare exceptions. They noticed alarming signs under the first Trump administration, were particularly prone to acting in accordance with their personal beliefs and values, and worked in locations where they thought they had the ability to act against administrators' agenda. It was extremely rare for federal civil servants to confront senior leadership directly about their potentially harmful policies and/or poor leadership behavior in the course of their daily work; such acts took courage and operated against career civil servants' deeply ingrained, risk-averse professional culture; commitment to being nonpartisan and loyally serving senior leadership; and apprehensions about vindictive leaders' retaliatory actions.

Those who repeatedly engaged in acts of moral courage involving explicit pushback against appointees despite the professional risks tended to work in locations greatly affected by appointed leadership's influence. They described agencies in turmoil and decline under appointed officials who did not seem to adhere to agency missions. They perceived changing conditions with alarm and had a sense of urgency in how they responded.

The most morally courageous people I spoke with also tended to specialize in professional areas of expertise that were intrinsically related to values of universal equality, justice, and benevolence, all of which ran counter to the Trump administration's policy agenda. These people had supportive networks of career colleagues who helped them strategize and affirmed their perspectives.

Those who most often engaged in acts of moral courage evaluated the morality of their actions from a long-term perspective and considered how their future self would judge their actions. They believed themselves to be efficacious and able to resist leadership in their positions and were willing to lose their jobs to uphold their moral conceptions of themselves.[25] They also tended to have a history of activism and/or civic engagement, and they were part of alternative moral communities outside work that affirmed their personal and professional moral codes.

Glassman, Taylor, and others similar to them had earned impressive academic degrees; tended to be in privileged, professional positions; and lived in relatively financially secure households. Those most willing to speak up tended to be middle-aged civil rights or human rights lawyers who either felt secure in their particular positions and/or were willing to leave their jobs if necessary. These contributing factors were often interrelated and jointly seemed to increase civil servants' likelihood of speaking up against perceived leadership transgressions.

Glassman and Taylor are notable because they were likely to engage in discernible acts of moral courage at work. They differed from those who agonized over what they perceived to be an abysmal, destructive presidential administration but who preferred to engage only in discreet subversive tactics like those discussed in chapter 10, such as modifying the framing and the language of certain contentious project work in order to align it with the priorities of the Trump administration.

Some scholars of authoritarianism have warned that it is all too easy for those who engage in the corruption of language, using the vague, euphemistic language of leadership, to become complicit; this can reduce their likelihood of engaging in further resistance.[26] In contrast to many other bureaucrats I spoke with who were working in particularly threatened positions and agencies, the most morally courageous and vocal dissenters seemed less apt to weaken their language, replacing their professional vocabularies with vague or euphemistic language that aligned more clearly with that of senior leadership compared to other civil servants with whom I spoke. Instead, they seemed prone to express their perspective directly from where they stood or to avoid an area of work and say nothing at all.

Both Glassman's and Taylor's experiences suggest that the particular conditions in which public servants work matter a great deal. As an SES who believed herself to be protected by key appointees, Glassman used her voice more often and sometimes engaged in direct conflict with appointees as part of her efforts to convey her professional expertise, defend the bounds of her role, and try to soften negative impacts of the administration's policy agenda. Taylor's stretching of his role only seemed possible in the absence of appointed senior leadership. Morale and solidarity among his colleagues dropped when a leader was appointed to his office, and he chose to exit his position as his heroic self-narrative lost plausibility, his sense of efficacy declined, and moral confusion set in. Their experiences underscore the powerful influence of particular situations in enabling or depressing resistance to authority.

While the career civil servants in this chapter stood up to the first Trump administration in some way, their lack of engagement in collective action at work is notable. Like other federal civil servants who used more covert resistance tactics, it seemed that the most vocal and morally courageous spoke up to preserve some good work or prevent rollbacks that they thought would cause harm. But even the civil servants in this latter group were notably constrained by the bounds of their role and by their professional ethical obligations.

# V

# CONCLUSION

# 12

## AMERICAN DEMOCRACY
## AT A CROSSROADS

hen I started writing this book, I truly did not anticipate the extent to which Donald Trump's first administration would challenge the country's democratic foundations. Despite warning signs from historians and political scientists, I began this study wondering if career civil servants would comply or resist an administration I imagined would be more like former president Ronald Reagan's, which was anti-bureaucratic and mistrustful of career civil servants.[1]

To get past what felt like a torrent of emotional sound bites from the mainstream media in early 2017, I wanted to hear directly from career civil servants about their everyday work experiences under the Trump administration. I wanted to speak to a spectrum of midlevel and senior career civil servants across the executive branch and independent agencies and to include a subset more likely to resist the administration. I admit that I would have liked to speak to Republicans as well as political centrists and Democrats, and did my best to reach them, but the former would not speak with me. In spite of the progressive political skew of my sample, as I recount in this book, I was incredibly impressed by the conscientious forbearance of most of the career civil servants I spoke with; by their professionalism;

their impressive technocratic, scientific, and legal knowledge; and their evident deep commitments to the many ethical obligations of public administration under trying circumstances.[2] And as a sociologist who was an outsider to this political world, I confess that I was surprised to a degree.

It is debatable if loyalty to the president is as or is less important than the combination of career civil servants' twelve other ethical obligations explained by Dwight Waldo, which include adhering to the Constitution; law; the country; democracy; organizational and bureaucratic norms; one's profession and professionalism; public interest and welfare; middle-range collectives; humanity as a whole; and then family, friends and self.[3] The Trump administration weighed loyalty to the president more heavily, which is notably absent from Waldo's list of ethical obligations.

Most of the people I spoke with during the first year of the administration were not yet directly affected by the Trump administration's autocratic and chaotic leadership approach and policy agenda. By the end of the administration, however, far more people in my sample were affected in their everyday work by loyalty traps, other professional binds, and personal moral conflicts than I had expected. By the end of the administration, more senior career civil servants also concluded that the government was proving its resilience under the Trump administration than I expected. They thought government structures had stayed largely intact throughout the presidency and were optimistic for the future of the country, despite how a considerable number thought Trump might win a second term.

Even though he acknowledged the government was experiencing a "shock test," for example, senior Department of Defense (DOD) official Ralph McCafferty thought in 2018 that the state was proving its resilience. Although he had "concern about a constitutional crisis," he attributed "our current checks and balances" to why the country had not had "a coup d'état or . . . an authoritarian government, like Russia . . . If there's something positive to be taken away from the current situation," he said, "it's that democracy works. And this is a shock test of democracy, but so far it's working." International affairs expert Steve Marsh similarly described in early 2020 that:

> Our democracy is going through an extreme stress test right now. [But] I think it's important to realize that what we are seeing right now is an aberration; it is not normal. Other Republican administrations and Democratic administrations operated within certain guardrails: they respected the rule of law. They generally would respond to subpoenas or public information requests. They would testify when compelled to testify by Congress. These guys are not doing that: they're operating outside the bounds of the rule of law. So, I don't have a crystal ball. I don't know if they're gonna be held accountable. I sure hope they will be because, I tell you, if, if he gets away with it, then I shudder to think what a future autocrat might do, which is why I worry about the health of our democracy.
>
> All that said, I am hopeful and optimistic that we will ultimately survive, but I think there's a lot of damage that's being done to the environment, to the climate and public health, and to the economy that we will spend decades paying for. The debt that we're incurring; this administration has been just, you know, very wasteful. And the damage that we're doing just to our institutions, it's going to be very hard to restore in short order. And then the damage that the administration is doing to our credibility and our trust around the world, that will take a long time to restore, probably beyond my lifetime. Because people can understand if there's a policy difference, but when you have an administration come in that just wantonly rips up previous agreements, like the one with Iran or like the Paris Agreement, that tells other countries that we are no longer a reliable, democratically driven country. And that worries me greatly.

After four years working in the Trump administration, lawyer and senior official Marie Glassman described her position as embedded in an agency where "I don't feel fundamentally like all of our processes have been torn to shreds. I feel like they've been pushed, I feel like they've been played with." She had witnessed decisions made by top appointed agency officials overturned by those in lower positions with connections to the White House, which she said differed from her prior work experience: "Sometimes the politics are overtaking the legal decisions," she said.

She continued to have faith in the courts, however: "The courts don't care if some political powerful person in the administration says we're gonna do it," she said. "The courts are gonna evaluate whether it's legal or not . . . I feel like our structures have been pushed, but they haven't been torn apart, and if a Democratic team comes in, it's not like they're gonna have to rebuild all the structure. What they're gonna have to do is undo a lot of the actual substantial damage, and that takes a huge amount of work—like they're gonna have to write new regulations." Glassman's perspective seemed accurate at the end of Trump's first administration. By April 2021, 200 of the 259 (77 percent) of the regulations, guidance documents, and agency memos that the Trump administration issued and that were challenged in court failed to stand up to scrutiny. In these cases, either a court ruled against the agency action, or the agency was sued and subsequently withdrew the action.[4] This statistic starkly contrasts with other administrations, which the Massachusetts Institute of Technology (MIT) Institute for Policy Integrity suggested tended to lose about 30 percent of the time.[5]

Some of those career civil servants who were most explicit in describing the democratic state as being in decline had a graduate education in government and worked in midlevel management in some areas of government that were moderately or less contested than other areas. They were more removed from some of the most dynamic and politicized areas of the government.

As Department of Housing and Urban Development (HUD) midlevel manager Stuart Erving disclosed in 2020, he thought the foundation of the democratic state remained, but "my view of the government has really changed" during the first Trump administration. He said that his loyalties to the state remained strong, but he did not see the government operating as it should:

> I totally believe in the three branches of government. I totally believe that there are checks and balances . . . and I don't see it happening now at all. I do think the Senate has abdicated their [*sic*] duties . . . I think there are so many institutional norms that have been eclipsed, eradicated almost, I don't know how we go back . . . I think what we call a democratic republic, which we are, I think that paradigm has shifted. Good, bad, indifferent, but has shifted. I don't think it's the same. I don't think the foundational blocks are the same. Maybe the foundation is, but the second, third and fourth floor has shifted.

When I asked him how he would describe it now, he responded, "It's a mess. I almost want to say I just don't recognize it as the form of government I've studied, the form of government I thought we had. I don't want to say corrupt . . . but I just think that people are complacent and people are not doing their jobs and not living up to their oath and their duties. And to me that's unpatriotic. If you're patriotic, you place the country before yourself, and people are not placing the country before themselves."

When I asked Erving if he would describe the current changes as moving toward an authoritarian or semiauthoritarian system," he said, "Oh yes, I think. Complacent, and so that's where we're going, more authoritarian, more dictatorship, yes." He cited how the Senate had not taken up bills passed by the House. "It's like no one wants to sign their name to anything. They don't want to be on record for an official position. I think also that people are on such party lines . . . what you say in private you should be able to say in public." He also noted the confusion caused by the president communicating through Twitter. "Maybe I'm just a little bit more conservative than I thought. But that just is astonishing to me. And I think all of that should be on the public record." Circling back to his intrinsic care for the government, Erving concluded, "I'm very disappointed in the state of government. But I'm very proud to be a federal government worker, and I'm very proud of the civil servants and definitely in the impeachment hearings in the House—those are civil servants who put themselves on the line."

There were a few select others, who were working in the most contentious areas in civil rights or human rights and were knowledgeable about what autocratic or authoritarian regimes looked like elsewhere. They also identified the state of the democratic government as being in peril of a shift to authoritarianism.

After conducting 127 interviews over the course of the first Trump administration with current and former career civil servants and observing how easily so many of them could be excised from key decision-making processes and intimidated into silence, I am sobered by the fragility of the U.S. government in the face of a leader seeking autocratic power. Political leadership had sufficient power to set an agenda, enact an autocratic leadership style, and sideline those who obstructed their aims in some of the most contested parts of the government. Despite the naïve popular patriotism of many that conceive of our government as an exception because of the founders' efforts to protect the government against such a leader, it is clear from the many incremental and interrelated processes of organizational decline I document in this book that the downfall of democracy is not only possible but can happen more quickly and more seamlessly in the United States than most Americans would suppose. It may well go down with less of a bang and more of a whimper.

The public servants' professional culture, which they deeply revered and which could safeguard the democracy in stable times, seemed woefully insufficient in preserving the democratic state under an autocratic leader. In certain situations, it could even enable the further crumbling of democracy. Career civil servants' risk aversion, antipathy toward intemperance, and commitment to serving appointed leadership seemed to contribute to some complacency: this all coalesced to allow for a continued stigmatization of using loaded language to describe the deterioration of the government during the period in which I studied it.

In contrast, the Trump administration was quite comfortable with using loaded language. When bureaucrats and citizens adopt authoritarian leaders' vague, oversimplistic, politically infused, and often manipulative stock phrases and clichés, it can lead their society down a slippery slope, wherein linguistic precision is lost, and truth is undermined. This is especially likely to occur if people adopt what historian Timothy Snyder calls "dangerous words," which tilt people's perspectives to emphasize the "exception" rather than the norm,[6] such as focusing on "terrorism" and "extremism," and the "treacherous use of patriotic vocabulary." Other techniques that can lead people to stray from the truth include the repetition of untruths so often that they become accepted as truth—and make criminal behavior plausible—and adopting "magical" logic that embraces contradictory statements at the same time, even though they cannot both be true.[7] All this transpired under Trump's leadership in the government.

Career civil servants' reluctance to call out and collectively organize to combat politicals' readiness to transgress the law, enact political retaliation, and dismiss factual evidence and reason likely contributed to some of the civil servants' own isolated suffering and islands of declining organizational capacity. This and the adaptation of language to accommodate the administration's preferences could foster rather than resist a changing workplace culture of loyalty to the administration above all. It could also fail to stymie undue suspicion of employees and foreclose employees' sense that the appropriate use of voice or collective mobilization in the face of appointees' inappropriate behavior is possible as long as the latter were in power. This all further marginalized some of the most knowledgeable and experienced career civil servants who were loyal to the spirit of public administration and pushed them to the exits. Many of these accomplished technocrats could find more appealing positions in other locations in the government or in other sectors. In their stead, less competent and more ostensibly ideological and loyal replacements could step in and advance among the ranks, or exiters might not be replaced at all. Over the course of the administration, these cyclical pathways of organizational decline and others that I discuss throughout the book then led to palpable institutional decline in parts of the government.

The spirit of public administration needs to be protected, as Dwight Waldo, James Comey, Joseph Biden, Liz Cheney, and others across the political spectrum have warned.[8] The ethical obligations of civil servants are reinforced through the civil servant oath and ethics training, but when the president and his appointed leaders regularly disregard them and start to alter the norms of offices and agencies, democratic ethics can be superseded all too easily by a climate of fear, suspicion, and self-serving behavior. This, combined with the imposition of structural holes across levels, then fortifies the leadership of an autocrat, weakens the influence of the meritocratic civil service system, and can lead to the regulatory capture of agencies. This has happened in many other countries, such as Hungary and Turkey, and can happen in the United States.[9]

Although some very rare career civil servants, such as Marie Glassman, who was protected by appointees from above and worked within a supportive workgroup, could stand up to appointees' transgressions in select efficacious acts of moral courage, many more, such as senior Environmental Protection Agency (EPA) official Adele Sullivan, were removed from power and pushed to the exits. Others were more cowed by such acts of retribution and thus silenced.

With Biden's election to the presidency in 2020, the legal system for a time began to hold Trump and his supporters accountable for legal transgressions. As this book goes to press, twelve hundred people have been arrested by the Federal Bureau of Investigation (FBI) for crimes related to the January 6, 2021 insurrection. Trump himself faces multiple investigations related to January 6, 2021, and his efforts to influence the 2020 presidential election results. Thus far, about nine hundred people have pled guilty or been convicted of crimes ranging from assaulting the police to bringing a gun onto the Capitol grounds and breaching the Capitol building, to obstructing Congress, to seditious conspiracy,[10] and 454 defendants have been incarcerated for their crimes.[11] Given Trump's re-election to be the 47th president of the United States, it is likely he will pardon and "free" January 6 defendants and cease the remaining January 6 investigations.[12]

Trump and other Republicans claim that federal law enforcement has been "weaponized" and is "'persecuting' conservatives."[13] I have also heard Trump aides and appointees lament that the many career civil servants who engaged in "policy resistance" obstructed the Trump administration's ability to pursue their agenda effectively.[14] James Sherk, director of the Center for American Freedom at America First Policy Institute and special assistant to the president in the Trump administration, has complained of civil servant deception, subterfuge, and slow-walking,[15] citing Deborah Birx's tell-all book and actions in the Civil Rights Division in the Department of Justice (DOJ).[16]

My book documents the different forms of covert and overt resistance some career civil servants engaged in, particularly in the most politicized areas of the government, such as in the Department of State, Department of Health and Human Services (HHS), and EPA, which indeed includes some slow-walking, subterfuge, and deception. The magnitude and the scale of resistance claimed by Trump and his allies by far overstates, however, the recalcitrance of senior career civil servants and that of the so-called deep state as a whole. It is important to recognize that a great many career civil servants across all levels of govenment were fully compliant with the presidential administration, even to the point where some senior officials like Rick Anderson worked deeply on themselves to serve the administration loyally, even after experiencing political retribution.

The covert tactics employed need to be considered in context, which I document in painstaking detail to convey these actors' stories in their own voices (at the cost of frustrating some impatient readers). Career civil servants described trying to do the best they thought they could amid the competing obligations of public administration—and accounting for the law, the Constitution, democratic norms and practices, and serving the public interest—as a culture of perceived apprehension, silencing, and subordination increasingly encircled them. Career employees always positioned their use of resistance as justified in standing up for these other tenets of the American state and as enacted in consideration of the bounds of their role. The career civil servants I spoke with might resist if an order was seen as illegal. They were more likely to exercise voice with a spirit of resistance to the administration's policy agenda prior to a decision if they viewed a policy was insufficiently developed, antithetical to their mission, illegal, or not serving public interest because they saw such truth telling as central to their duties and purpose.

But they were careful to serve political leadership after legitimate decisions were made within a transparent chain of command. Covert and overt resistance were coupled in practice with much compliance and helping the presidential administration achieve its goals. At times, some career civil servants referred to covert resistance when they were merely disgruntled and frustrated with the administration—but they did not act to obstruct it. And overt resistance was quite rare.

Covert tactics were the most common forms of resistance employed in politicized areas, but they seemed largely ineffective over Trump's first four-year term. By the end of the administration, covert tactics seemed to be useful mainly in helping reduce moral dissonance and assuage career civil servants' consciences. Even the career civil servants most engaged in covert or overt resistance reported aligning themselves with presidential appointees' leadership in many ways, such as by following legitimate orders, not promoting their programs to adhere to leaders' wishes, cutting their programs, and/or weakening the descriptions of their work. A considerable number quit when they felt they could not serve dispassionately or in alignment with the policies and agenda of the presidential administration because of their troubled consciences.

Taken together, the use of covert tactics and the quite rare use of overt resistance I document in this book seem largely ineffective and insufficient in stymieing the many autocratic assaults on the state by Trump appointees and their allies. I watched and tracked the spreading breadth and depth of the first Trump administration's disruption of offices across the executive branch and independent agencies, including through the incidents that were conveyed to me during the administration and the many others that have been documented in the historical record through court proceedings and the media since the end of the administration.

As I complete the book, Trump has just been elected the 47th president of the United States. It is apparent one of his first objectives when he enters office in 2025 will be to try to dismantle the admininstrative state and weaken checks and balances that constrain his presidential power. In short, he hopes to irrevocably harm the fundamental democratic and meritocratic structures of the state. At present, Trump plans to appoint entrepreneur Elon Musk and former pharmaceutical executive Vivek Ramaswamy to create a new department seemingly operating outside of the formal government called the Department of Government Efficiency to help. Musk suggests he will try to cut $2 trillion from the federal budget, and Ramaswamy has promised to eliminate the Education Department, the Federal Bureau of Investigation (FBI), and the Internal Revenue Service (IRS).[17] While such claims seem full of bluster, and challenging, if not impossible to implement, it is more likely the next Trump administration will be more successful in replacing many senior experienced and knowledgeable career civil servants with ideologues and presidential loyalists. Trump and others are eager to reinstate Schedule F, an executive order that weakens civil service protections among senior career leadership (including many of the policy experts and lawyers with whom I spoke). As Trump has already vowed, he will start by removing career civil servants from national security and law enforcement agencies. This will make it easier to turn this tier of career civil servants into another partisan tool rather than a technocratic force of stability and repository of expert knowledge.[18] Given the evidence I have shared from Trump's first administration of appointees' suspicion; readiness to enact political retribution; and disregard for facts, science, and law, I especially worry about further damage during his second term.

It is unclear from the first Trump administration's estimates exactly how many career civil servants could be replaced with a reinstatement of Schedule F. Advocates of Schedule F suggest fifty thousand federal employees could lose civil service protections. (It is not evident how they derived this statistic.) Under Trump's executive order, the Office of Management and Budget (OMB) was one of the first to comply. OMB director Russell Vought recommended that 88 percent of his agency workforce be converted to Schedule F employees.[19] This raises questions about how many more career civil servants in other agencies could be affected and indicates the potential for this to be more than the estimated amount.

In the years since the first Trump term, a massive organizational apparatus, including the Center for Renewing America, Steven Miller's American First Legal, Trump's America First Policy Institute, American Moment, the Conservative Partnership Institute, the Personnel Policy Organization, and the Heritage Foundation (under Kevin Robert's leadership), have raised millions of dollars from conservative donors and organized lists of potential new and more loyal recruits to serve as future appointees and career civil servants.[20] These recruits would likely be less experienced and less competent than typical public servant recruits from reputable universities through established and respected pipelines, such as the Presidential Management Fellows Program, where they are trained in a public service culture that prizes serial partisanship and political neutrality. In addition, they would be more radically ideological and right wing. As Miles Taylor, the former chief of staff at the Department of Homeland Security under Trump put it, "the next Trump will install only devout loyalists in top positions, while purging dissenters from the executive branch . . . From the start, he or she will populate the administration with a 'D Team' of political operatives who pledge allegiance to a cult of personality, not the Constitution."[21]

Despite Trump's federal indictment in June 2023, in which he was the first president to be charged with thirty-seven criminal offenses in a federal court, and even more serious charges in August 2023 tied to the January 6 uprising and an attempt to subvert the 2020 presidential election results, Trump's re-election shows his popular support has grown stronger. Trump's embattled nature and fights with the courts are rallying his base, despite considerable evidence of his disregard for the law.

Trump supporters are not the only ones who have lost trust in the federal government. Pew Research Center polls from the spring of 2022 show that American popular trust in the federal government is not only at all-time lows among Republicans but continues to be low even among Democrats (and younger Democrats in particular).[22]

It is also important to recognize, however, that U.S. citizens' contempt for the government at large has existed since the founding of the nation. The American Revolution itself was a reaction against the perceived "administrative misdeeds of [English king] George III" and his bureaucracy.[23] This cultural imaginary has become more salient at particular junctures in American history ever since. President Andrew Jackson, a president particularly critical of federal civil service, argued anyone "of average intelligence" could easily learn and do the duties of federal officials.[24] Bashing government bureaucrats then declined during the Progressive Era, when a meritocratic-based system rooted in administrative expertise and executive oversight were developed as remedies to government corruption. Since the 1970s, however, distrust and criticism of waste and inefficiencies in government have proliferated. Citizens mistrust elected officials and feel powerless with respect to the policy-making process.[25]

Rising populism and frustration with the federal government in the United States is likely in part a result of many citizens' lack of understanding about what the state does to help them and protect them from risks,[26] as well as the palpable high levels of inequality and corporate influence in American governance.[27] Perhaps it is time to fundamentally reassess the structure of American governance and imagine structural changes to voting and democratic checks and balances to help the government better support and represent the public as a whole. However, a shift away from support for enforcing the law and toward an autocratic leader supported by a government careening toward authoritarianism will likely lead to more, not less, corruption and regulatory capture.[28]

Public administration scholars describe the "paradox of distance" in popular opinion about American government. At the heart of this paradox is that many Americans tend to think negatively of the government and politicians in the abstract, but they have positive specific experiences with particular public servants and government programs. Thus, as David G. Frederickson and H. George Frederickson summarize, "while people trust and even revere those government officials who are near at hand, they believe that government officials who are far away are lazy, incompetent and probably dishonest," in part because of incendiary political rhetoric that can aid political candidates on the campaign trail.[29]

A 2022 study from the Partnership for Public Service suggests that the paradox of distance continues today. Only four of ten people in its national U.S. survey said that they "trust the federal government to do what is right." Yet a majority of the public had positive views of most specific federal agencies named. The National Park Service (NPS) was the most popular, with 84 percent of respondents supporting it. Parks maintained by the NPS typically have about 300 million visitors per year. Other popular agencies, such as the Social Security Administration (SSA), with 69 percent of respondents' support; the Centers for Disease Control and Prevention (CDC), with 65 percent of respondents' support; and Veteran's Affairs (VA), with 64 percent support, also tend to interact frequently with the public.[30]

Most Americans continue to desire a government of scale that supports the bulk of its citizens. In 2022, most Americans reported wanting more government support for lower-income (66 percent) and middle-income people (69 percent), as well as retired people (65 percent). Most Americans also believe the government should do more to support disabled people and children (54 percent each, with Democrats more likely to support policies for children). Sixty-one percent of Americans also think the government is doing too much for high-income people. Similar proportions of Democrats (56 percent) and Republicans (52 percent) think the state is doing too little for "people like you."[31]

In a time of heightened partisan polarization, collective work needs to be done to heal and bind the nation.[32] The collective foundations of democracy need to be fortified. To achieve this goal, the United States needs to invest in more civics education. Public education can do more to inform citizens about how the government works, how they can be involved in the public sphere, and how to better distinguish between reliable news reports and false information. More systematic efforts need to address income and wealth inequality, and federal regulation needs to restrict partisan engines of misinformation, such as those promoting narratives that the 2020 presidential election was stolen from Trump.

The precision of language and development of a new common narrative in pursuit of the common good is also crucial to fortifying the democratic state. During the period of rapid change in the federal government under the first Trump administration, career civil servants held onto old narratives of governance at a time when appointed leadership advanced alternative narratives of how to run the government and about the state's future. While relying on the old narratives of American democracy and the ethical bedrock of public administration helped steady some career employees in this storm, it also may have led some career civil servants to underestimate the threats posed by the Trump administration. Career civil servants lacked a clear and cohesive shared narrative around these potential threats. This is to be expected, and perhaps is due to an ever-present weakness in human social psychology; people have bounded rationality and it takes time to analyze complex institutions undergoing rapid change. Forbearance also, of course, remains essential among career bureaucrats.[33]

Moving forward, it is my hope that assessments of the Trump administration, such as this book, will help career civil servants and the American public alike better understand the subtle ways in which democracy dies, even when hundreds of thousands of government employees are trying to preserve it and when the public is watching. Much of what I have reported in this book has been published in popular media, to their credit. Such reports are scattered across many outlets, however, and most concerned citizens do not have the time or systemic understandings about how the government works to hold it all together and make lucid sense of it. It is my hope that this book helps toward this end.

I hope Americans can build strong, new collective narratives and rituals that account more conscientiously for the real threats of the ideological capture of the state so that they can face ongoing threats and prepare for possible future recurrences. As Yale cultural sociologist Jeffrey Alexander demonstrates with how the Holocaust came to be publicly understood as a horrific and "evil" genocidal event, such cultural narratives must be produced, supported, and collectively maintained as cautionary tales.[34] By no means should anyone take it for granted that this occurs naturally in society. The development and memorialization of such new narratives will take a large and well-resourced collective effort from the state and concerned citizens.[35] Calling out autocratic and authoritarian practices as they are is important, even if it makes some people uncomfortable. While some of this has happened under Joseph Biden's administration and through the bipartisan January 6th Commission, the country has continued to splinter culturally. Given Trump's re-election, I also urge federal civil servants to consider trying to stay in the government for as long as they can. Create spaces where you can support each other and develop responses to Trump's looming assault on democratic structures and norms together. For some, having support from colleagues, mentors, and loved ones may make the difference in their perceived ability to speak up when it counts. Try to maintain what important structures and work you can, and as Timothy Snyder (2017) has advised, "Do not obey in advance." You may not have sufficient power to respond as you think would be best. Even so, continue to document legal and other normative transgressions witnessed.

The U.S democratic republic remains an ongoing experiment. The administrative state has evolved far beyond what the country's founders anticipated. Some key values and beliefs revered by many Americans today, such as support for a government run in accordance with the insights of science and public servant knowledge and merit—and even democracy—are not legally enshrined in the Constitution.[36] As an American public—and as federal civil servants—we have to keep choosing what kind of government we want. We do that by voting and by speaking up for what we—individually and collectively—want. It is critical that we do not take these things for granted. As some of the federal civil servants' experiences under the first Trump administration demonstrate, our government can be administered in many other, less favorable ways. We stand on the brink of seeing the foundational structure of democracy get tested again. May we all work to build a better government to serve all American citizens from here.

# APPENDIX A

Study Participants' Sociodemographic Backgrounds

### TABLE A.1 RESPONDENTS BY AGENCY

| gency | Respondents' Agency Service over Career[a] | Percent of Total Sample ($n = 77$) | Respondents' Agency During the Trump Administration | Percent of Sample Employed in Agency Under the Trump Administration ($n = 66$) |
|---|---|---|---|---|
| nvironmental Protection gency (EPA) | 20 | 26.0 | 13 | 19.7 |
| epartment of State (DOS) | 14 | 18.2 | 7 | 10.6 |
| epartment of Defense )OD) | 12 | 15.6 | 4 | 6.1 |
| epartment of Justice (DOJ) | 11 | 14.3 | 5 | 7.6 |
| ealth and Human Services IHS) | 9 | 11.7 | 7 | 10.6 |
| epartment of Agriculture JSDA) | 5 | 6.5 | 3 | 4.5 |
| eneral Services dministration (GSA) | 5 | 6.5 | 3 | 4.5 |
| ffice of Management and 1dget (OMB) | 5 | 6.5 | 3 | 4.5 |
| ace Corps | 5 | 6.5 | 0 | 0.0 |
| epartment of Energy )OE) | 4 | 5.2 | 3 | 4.5 |
| epartment of the Interior | 3 | 3.9 | 2 | 3.0 |
| eterans Affairs (VA) | 3 | 3.9 | 2 | 3.0 |

(continued)

| Agency | Respondents' Agency Service over Career[a] | Percent of Total Sample ($n = 77$) | Respondents' Agency During the Trump Administration | Percent of Sample Employed in Agency Under the Trump Administration ($n = 6$ |
|---|---|---|---|---|
| Census Bureau | 2 | 2.6 | 1 | 1.5 |
| Department of Homeland Security (DHS) | 2 | 2.6 | 2 | 3.0 |
| Department of Labor | 2 | 2.6 | 1 | 1.5 |
| Department of the Treasury (USDT) | 2 | 2.6 | 2 | 3.0 |
| National Science Foundation (NSF) | 2 | 2.6 | 2 | 3.0 |
| Commodity Futures Trading Commission | 1 | 1.3 | 0 | 0.0 |
| Department of Education | 1 | 1.3 | 1 | 1.5 |
| Department of Housing and Urban Development (HUD) | 1 | 1.3 | 1 | 1.5 |
| Equal Employment Opportunity Commission (EEOC) | 1 | 1.3 | 0 | 0.0 |
| Federal Deposit Insurance Corporation (FDIC) | 1 | 1.3 | 1 | 1.5 |
| Federal Emergency Management Agency (FEMA) | 1 | 1.3 | 1 | 1.5 |
| Food and Drug Administration (FDA) | 1 | 1.3 | 0 | 0.0 |
| National Biological Survey | 1 | 1.3 | 0 | 0.0 |
| National Foundation on the Arts and Humanities | 1 | 1.3 | 0 | 0.0 |
| National Oceanic and Atmospheric Administration (NOAA) | 1 | 1.3 | 0 | 0.0 |
| Office of National Drug Control Policy | 1 | 1.3 | 0 | 0.0 |
| United States Agency for International Development (USAID) | 1 | 1.3 | 1 | 1.5 |
| U.S. Securities and Exchange Commission (SEC) | 1 | 1.3 | 1 | 1.5 |

[a] Work experience in legislative and judicial branch offices is not included.

## TABLE A.2 SOCIODEMOGRAPHIC COMPARISON OF MY PARTICIPANTS WITH THE FEDERAL WORKFORCE

| | Summary Statistics for Research Participants | | Summary Statistics for Non-Postal Federal Civil Employees |
|---|---|---|---|
| *Education* (*n* = 69) | | | |
| Bachelor's degree | 15% | | 35%[a] |
| Master's degree | 46% | | 27%[a] |
| Doctoral/professional degree (PhD, JD, MD) | 39% | | 10%[a] |
| *Position* (n = 76) | | | |
| General Schedule (GS) level Average | 14 | Range = 11 to 15 | 10[b] |
| GS-11 | 9% | | |
| GS-12 | 11% | | |
| GS-13 | 21% | | |
| GS-14 | 28% | | |
| GS-15 | 28% | | |
| GS rank (*n* = 53) | 69% | | 88%[a] |

a   Data from 2020 Governmentwide Management Report.
b   2017 data from the U.S. Office of Personnel Management (OPM) website: https://www
    .opm.gov/policy-data-oversight/data-analysis-documentation/federal-employment
    -reports/reports-publications/profile-of-federal-civilian-non-postal-employees/.

*Note*: Sample sizes vary because reported data are based on information disclosed by
    participants in their interviews, correspondence, and what was available online.
    Sometimes respondents did not wish to answer specific questions; in some cases, they
    ran out of time and ended interviews, and I did not get to ask all questions on my
    interview guide.
Missing data included one GS level civil servant who said that he did not want to report
    his level. Based on his position, education, location, and years of experience, it was
    likely the lowest level in my sample. Four respondents did not disclose their GS
    or Senior Executive Service (SES) level and I could not reach them in subsequent
    correspondence. I guessed their likely GS level based on their position title, agency,
    education level, and years of experience.
For members of the military, approximate equivalents to GS level were included. One
    respondent was counted both as a contractor and as holding a GS-ranked position.

# APPENDIX B

## Methodological Background Information

I lived for the greater part of 2017 to 2019 in Washington, DC, while conducting the research for this book. This helped me get a pulse on the city while conducting this study. To support my time in DC and transcription costs, I used my research start-up fund and additional funding from the Dean of Faculty office at Hamilton College. I was also supported by a Franklin Research Grant from the American Philosophical Society.

I began this study by surveying protesters at the March for Science and the People's Climate March in Washington, DC, in the spring of 2017. Of the 391 surveys my team collected, however, only twelve participants identified as current or former federal civil servants, and only seven followed up and completed interviews. This signaled to me from the start how cautious federal civil servants were at the time, even among those willing to attend public protests in the heart of the Capitol. At this point, I widened the net. I contacted four more federal employees who were named in national media for attending protests and one who identified as a whistleblower.

Because of these early challenges in recruiting participants for the study, I relied heavily on personal and professional networks—and my network's social connections—through universities, which connected me with an additional thirty-five participants who worked for Donald Trump's first administration but who were not necessarily unhappy with it. This approach likely led to some social similarity bias, with a disproportionate number of highly educated professionals with graduate education.[1] From initial contacts, I snowball-sampled to contact additional participants. I recruited one additional participant at an academic conference and another via a Facebook post made by a study participant on a private listserv.

The study has Institutional Review Board (IRB) oversight at Hamilton College (approval number S17–108). While my collaborator Yvonne Zylan and I initially planned a one-year study, based on recommendations both from respondents and from the editorial team of the *American Journal of Sociology* (*AJS*), we extended our study with modification forms to collect data for a second and third set of interviews. To provide further protection, I obtained a National Institutes of Health (NIH) Certificate of Confidentiality for the study as well, based on a recommendation from Director of Sponsored Programs Jeff Ritchie at Hamilton College.

I sought to interview all participants again in a second set of interviews in 2018, and others joined the study as my networks grew. The third round of data collection focused on those most likely to experience change, such as those working with political appointees and in Washington, DC. This third set of interviews was cut short by COVID-19. In my third round of interviews, I discussed with participants in particularly risky and specific situations what they would be comfortable with me disclosing publicly. Erring on the side of caution, I altered and omitted some details in describing some of their experiences in this book.

Additional information on our methods and analysis are provided in Yvonne Zylan and my co-written article on our early findings: "Walking the Moral Tightrope: Federal Civil Servants' Loyalties, Caution, and Resistance Under the Trump Administration."[2] After the article was published, I sent it to study participants interested in reading the results of the study. I received favorable responses to the article, which suggested that our interpretations were on track. I also started sharing that article with other federal civil servants, who further affirmed our portrayal of career civil servants' experiences working under the first Trump administration.

I presented a preliminary version of my findings at Dana Fisher's colloquium through the Program for Society and the Environment at the University of Maryland, College Park, and at the Interdisciplinary Collaborative Workshop's Democracy Under Threat in Times of Populism and Racial Nationalism conference at the University of Minnesota. I received helpful feedback after both presentations. I also presented results at the 2018 European Consortium for Political Research in Hamburg, Germany, where I was interested to learn about similar populist and political shifts across Europe. I received very helpful feedback from several panel presentations for the political sociology section at the American Sociological Association and from a presentation for the European Group for Public Administration's Permanent Study Group VII on Ethics and Integrity as well.

# NOTES

## 1. WALKING THE MORAL TIGHTROPE

1.  Such tactics were not new; they have been used under presidential transitions in the past. For example, see: Marissa M. Golden, "Exit, Voice, Loyalty, and Neglect: Bureaucratic Responses to Presidential Control During the Reagan Administration," *Journal of Public Administration Research and Theory* 2, no. 1 (1992): 29–62; William G. Resh, *Rethinking the Administrative Presidency: Trust, Intellectual Capital and Appointee-Careerist Relations in the George W. Bush Administration* (Baltimore, MD: Johns Hopkins University Press, 2015).

2.  See also Miles Taylor, *Blowback: A Warning to Save Democracy from the Next Trump* (New York: Atria, 2024).

3.  U.S. Department of Labor, "Federal Employers," accessed June 26, 2023, http://www.dol.gov/agencies/odep/program-areas/employers/federal -employment. Different political scientists and public administration scholars have various ways of describing the complexity of the administrative state. Dwight Waldo, for example, divides the government into five parts, which include the constitutional elements of the legislative, executive, and judicial branches and the administrative and electoral apparatus. Dwight Waldo, *The Enterprise of Public Administration* (Novato, CA: Chandler and Sharp, 1980), 68. John Kingdon portrays the government as having three streams of processes, including the problems the state faces, the policies at hand, and politics. John Kingdon, "A Model of Agenda-Setting, with Applications," *Law Review M.S.U—D.C.L*, no. 2 (Summer 2001), 331–38.

4. John Anthony Rohr, *To Run a Constitution: The Legitimacy of the Administrative State* (Lawrence: University Press of Kansas, 1986), xi.

5. Ari Hoogenboom, "The Pendleton Act and the Civil Service," *American Historical Review* 64, no. 2 (1959): 301–18, https://doi.org/10.1086/ahr/64.2.301. The merit-based system continued to be developed through 1940. George H. Frederickson, *The Spirit of Public Administration*, 1st ed. (San Francisco: Jossey-Bass, 1997), 64.

6. "Upholding Civil Service Protections and Merit System Principles," *Federal Register* 88, no. 179 (September 18, 2023): 63862–85, https://www.federalregister.gov/documents/2023/09/18/2023-19806/upholding-civil-service-protections-and-merit-system-principles.

7. Francis Fukuyama, "In Defense of the Deep State," *Asia Pacific Journal of Public Administration* 46 (August 25, 2023): 1, https://doi.org/10.1080/23276665.2023.2249142; Eloy Oliveira, Gordon Abner, Shinwoo Lee, Kohei Suzuki, Hyunkang Hur, and James L. Perry, "What Does the Evidence Tell Us About Merit Principles and Government Performance?," *Public Administration* 102, no. 2 (2023): 1–23, https://doi.org/10.1111/padm.12945.

8. Dwight Waldo, *The Administrative State: A Study of the Political Theory of American Public Administration* (Piscataway, NJ: Transaction, 2006).

9. Larry Jay Diamond, *The Spirit of Democracy: The Struggle to Build Free Societies Throughout the World*, 1st ed. (New York: Times Books/Henry Holt, 2008); John Stuart Mill, *Considerations on Representative Government*, 1861, https://www.gutenberg.org/files/5669/5669-h/5669-h.htm. Democracy is a value not stipulated in the Constitution. See Waldo. *The Enterprise of Public Administration*, 79.

10. Martin Wolf, *The Crisis of Democratic Capitalism* (New York: Penguin Random House, 2023).

11. Steven Levitsky and Daniel Ziblatt, *How Democracies Die* (New York: Broadway, 2018), 102–7.

12. Frederickson, *The Spirit of Public Administration*; Hugh Heclo, "The Spirit of Public Administration," *PS: Political Science & Politics* 35, no. 4 (2002): 689–94; Waldo, *The Administrative State*. See also Rohr, *To Run a Constitution*, x. Rohr describes the Constitution as a "covenant as well as contract."

13. James Comey, *A Higher Loyalty: Truth, Lies, and Leadership* (New York: Flatiron, 2018), 54.

14. I have also heard the importance of trust between career civil servants and politicals from others. For example, former principal deputy director of national intelligence Sue Gordon mentioned this repeatedly on a virtual panel called "Speaking Truth to Power: Lessons in Administrative Courage," hosted by the American Political Science Association, November 30, 2023.

15. Joel D. Aberbach and Bert A. Rockman, *In the Web of Politics: Three Decades of the U.S. Federal Executive* (Washington, DC: Brookings Institution Press, 2000), 3. See also Rachel Augustine Potter, *Bending the Rules: Procedural Politicking in the Bureaucracy* (Chicago: University of Chicago Press, 2019).

16. Dimitar Bechev, *Turkey Under Erdoğan: How a Country Turned from Democracy and the West* (New Haven, CT: Yale University Press, 2022).

17. I was not alone. In submitting an early draft of a paper to a reputable sociology journal during the middle of the Trump administration, an editor at the journal raised a question about using emergent "authoritarianism" to describe the Trump administration's early years.

18. Michael W. Bauer, "Administrative responses to democratic backsliding: When is bureaucratic resistance justified?," *Regulation & Governance* (2023).

19. Nancy Bermeo, "On democratic backsliding." *Journal of democracy* 27, no. 1 (2016): 156; Bauer, "Administrative responses to democratic backsliding."

20. Bauer, "Administrative responses to democratic backsliding"; Levitsky and Ziblatt, *How Democracies Die.*

21. See also James N. Druckman and Lawrence R. Jacobs's discussion of Trump as a "unitary executive": James N. Druckman and Lawrence R. Jacobs, *Who Governs? Presidents, Public Opinion, and Manipulation* (Chicago: University of Chicago Press, 2015), chap. 3.

22. Peter D. Harms, Dustin Wood, Karen Landay, Paul B. Lester, and Gretchen Vogelgesang Lester, "Autocratic Leaders and Authoritarian Followers Revisited: A Review and Agenda for the Future," *Leadership Quarterly* 29, no. 1 (2018): 105–22.

23. Robert Alan Dahl, *Polyarchy: Participation and Opposition* (New Haven, CT: Yale University Press, 1972), 3; Joseph A. Schumpeter, *Capitalism, Socialism, and Democracy* (London: Harper and Brothers, 1942), 260, 271.

24. Harms et al., "Autocratic Leaders and Authoritarian Followers Revisited."

25. Marlies Glasius, "What Authoritarianism Is . . . and Is Not: A Practice Perspective," *International Affairs* 94, no. 3 (2018): 515–33, https://doi.org/10.1093/ia/iiy060; Levitsky and Ziblatt, *How Democracies Die.*

26. Levitsky and Ziblatt, *How Democracies Die,* 5.

27. Ruth Ben-Ghiat, *Strongmen: Mussolini to the Present* (New York: Norton, 2020); Heather Cox Richardson, *Democracy Awakening: Notes on the State of America,* 1st ed. (New York: Viking, 2023); Marissa M. Golden, "Exit, Voice, Loyalty, and Neglect: Bureaucratic Responses to Presidential Control During the Reagan Administration"; Marissa M. Golden, *What Motivates Bureaucrats? Politics and Administration During the Reagan Years* (New York: Columbia University Press, 2000); Donald Moynihan, "Populism and the Deep State: The Attack on Public Service Under Trump," in *Democratic Backsliding and Public Administration,* ed. Michael W. Bauer, B. Guy Peters, Jon Pierre, Kutsal Yesilkagit, and Stefan Becker (Cambridge: Cambridge University Press, 2021), 151–77; Taylor, *Blowback.*

28. I am grateful to Yvonne Zylan for her help on this chapter, chapter 2, and chapter 5, and her many contributions to this project, some of which are evident in our cowritten article: Jaime Kucinskas and Yvonne Zylan, "Walking the Moral Tightrope: Federal Civil Servants' Loyalties, Caution, and Resistance Under the Trump Administration," *American Journal of Sociology* 128, no. 6 (2023).

29. Fukuyama, "In Defense of the Deep State."

30. Andrew L. Whitehead, Samuel L. Perry, and Joseph O. Baker, "Make America Christian Again: Christian Nationalism and Voting for Donald Trump in the 2016 Presidential Election," *Sociology of Religion* 79, no. 2 (2018): 147–71.

31. Paul Dans and Steven Groves, eds., *Mandate for Leadership: The Conservative Promise* (Washington, DC: Heritage Foundation, 2023).

32. Dans and Groves, *Mandate for Leadership.*

33. Hannah Arendt, *The Origins of Totalitarianism* (New York: Schocken, 1951); Hannah Arendt, *Eichmann in Jerusalem: A Report on the Banality of Evil* (New York: Viking, 1963); Hannah Arendt, "Personal Responsibility Under Dictatorship," in Arendt, *Responsibility and Judgment* (New York: Schocken, 2003 [1964]), 17–48; Craig Haney and Philip G. Zimbardo, "Persistent Dispositionalism in Interactionist Clothing: Fundamental Attribution Error in Explaining Prison Abuse," *Personality and*

*Social Psychology Bulletin* 35, no. 6 (2009): 807–14; Stanley Milgram, *Obedience to Authority: An Experimental View* (New York: Harper and Row, 1974); Philip G. Zimbardo, Craig Haney, W. Curtis Banks, and David Jaffe, "The Stanford Prison Experiment," 1971.

34. Christopher Browning, *Ordinary Men: Reserve Police Battalion 101 and the Final Solution in Poland* (New York: Harper Collins, 1992); Haney and Zimbardo, "Persistent Dispositionalism in Interactionist Clothing"; Sam McFarland and Thomas Carnahan, "A Situation's First Powers Are Attracting Volunteers and Selecting Participants: A Reply to Haney and Zimbardo," *Personality and Social Psychology Bulletin* 35, no. 6 (2009): 815–18.

35. See, for example, Arendt, *Eichmann in Jerusalem*; Ludy T. Benjamin Jr. and Jeffry A. Simpson, "The Power of the Situation: The Impact of Milgram's Obedience Studies on Personality and Social Psychology," *American Psychologist* 64, no. 1 (2009): 12–19; Browning, *Ordinary Men*; David Cesarini, *Eichmann: His Life and Crimes* (London: Vintage, 2005); Haney and Zimbardo, "Persistent Dispositionalism in Interactionist Clothing"; Yaacov Lozowick, *Hitler's Bureaucrats: The Nazi Security Police and the Banality of Evil* (New York: Continuum, 2003); David R. Mandel, "The Obedience Alibi," *Analyze & Kritik* 20, no. 1 (1998): 74–94; McFarland and Carnahan. "A Situation's First Powers."

36. Arendt, "Personal Responsibility Under Dictatorship," 17–48.

37. Arendt, *Eichmann in Jerusalem*, 6.

38. William Brustein, *The Logic of Evil: The Social Origins of the Nazi Party, 1925–1933* (New Haven, CT: Yale University Press, 1998).

39. Amos Elon, "Introduction," in *Eichmann in Jerusalem: A Report on the Banality of Evil*, by Hannah Arendt (New York: Penguin Classics, 2006), vii–xxiii.

40. Arendt, *Eichmann in Jerusalem*.

41. Elon, "Introduction."

42. Judith Butler, "Hannah Arendt's Challenge to Adolf Eichmann," Opinion, *The Guardian*, August 29, 2011, https://www.theguardian.com /commentisfree/2011/aug/29/hannah-arendt-adolf-eichmann-banality -of-evil.

43. Milgram, *Obedience to Authority*.

44. Stanley Milgram, "Obedience to Criminal Orders: The Compulsion to Do Evil," *Patterns of Prejudice* 1, no. 6 (1967): 3–7.

45. Mandel, "The Obedience Alibi."
46. As Harms et al., "Autocratic Leaders and Authoritarian Followers Revisited," 118, report in their review on autocratic leaders and authoritarian followers published in the second year of my data collection. Although scholarship on autocratic leadership was once popular, scholarly interest had rapidly declined by the 1980s. They argue more studies on "the effects of such leadership styles within and across varying situational contexts is necessary." In my effort to examine the reception of an autocratic presidential administration by midlevel bureaucrats, I use open-ended qualitative methods (in contrast to much of the research they review).
47. Ronald S. Burt, "The Network Structure of Social Capital," *Research in Organizational Behavior* 22 (2000): 345–423, https://doi.org/10.1016/S0191-3085(00)22009-1.
48. Ronald S. Burt, "The Social Structure of Competition," in *Networks and Organizations: Structure, Form, and Action*, ed. N. Nohria and Robert G. Eccles (Boston: Harvard Business School Press, 1992); Mark Granovetter, "The Strength of Weak Ties: A Network Theory Revisited," *Sociological Theory* 1 (1983): 201. https://doi.org/10.2307/202051.
49. For the danger of diluting language as such, see Timothy Snyder, *On Tyranny: Twenty Lessons from the Twentieth Century* (New York: Tim Duggan, 2017).
50. Political appointees were excluded from the sample.
51. Hun Myoung Park and James L. Perry, "The Transformation of Governance: Who Are the New Public Servants and What Difference Does It Make for Democratic Governance?," *American Review of Public Administration* 43, no. 1 (2013): 26–49, https://doi.org/10.1177/0275074011433814.
52. See also Kucinskas and Zylan, "Walking the Moral Tightrope."

## 2. A LURCH TOWARD AUTOCRACY

1. For example, see Miles Taylor, *Blowback: A Warning to Save Democracy from the Next Trump* (New York: Atria, 2024); Marie L. Yovanovitch, *Lessons from the Edge: A Memoir* (New York: Mariner, 2022), 256–57, 286; Paul Dans and Steven Groves, eds., *Mandate for Leadership: The Conservative Promise* (Washington, DC: Heritage Foundation, 2023).

2. Dominico Montanaro, "6 Strongmen Trump Has Praised—And the Conflicts It Presents," *NPR*, May 2, 2017, https://www.npr.org/2017/05/02/526520042/6-strongmen-trumps-praised-and-the-conflicts-it-presents.

3. Steven Levitsky and Daniel Ziblatt, *How Democracies Die* (New York: Broadway, 2018), 78–81.

4. Heather Cox Richardson, *Democracy Awakening: Notes on the State of America*, 1st ed. (New York: Viking, 2023).

5. Brett Samuels, "Trump Ramps up Rhetoric on Media, Calls Press 'the Enemy of the People,'" *The Hill*, April 5, 2019, https://thehill.com/homenews/administration/437610-trump-calls-press-the-enemy-of-the-people/.

6. Levitsky and Ziblatt, *How Democracies Die*, 181.

7. Levitsky and Ziblatt, *How Democracies Die*, 65–67, 176.

8. Levitsky and Ziblatt, *How Democracies Die*, 183–84; National Archives. "Presidential Advisory Commission on Election Integrity—The White House," July 13, 2017, https://trumpwhitehouse.archives.gov/articles/presidential-advisory-commission-election-integrity/.

9. Levitsky and Ziblatt, *How Democracies Die*, 102–7.

10. Bob Woodward and Carl Bernstein, "Woodward and Bernstein Thought Nixon Defined Corruption: Then Came Trump," *Washington Post*, June 3, 2022, https://www.washingtonpost.com/outlook/2022/06/05/woodward-bernstein-nixon-trump/.

11. Josh Dawsey, Rosalind S. Helderman, and David A. Fahrenthold. "How Trump Abandoned His Pledge to 'Drain the Swamp,'" *Washington Post*, October 24, 2020, https://www.washingtonpost.com/politics/trump-drain-the-swamp/2020/10/24/52c7682c-0a5a-11eb-9be6-cf25fb429f1a_story.html.

12. For example, see Taylor, *Blowback*; Yovanovitch, *Lessons from the Edge*, 256–57, 286.

13. David A. Fahrenthold, Joshua Partlow, and Carol D. Leonnig, "Trump's Children Brought Secret Service Money to the Family Business with Their Visits, Records Show," *Washington Post*, October 12, 2020, https://www.washingtonpost.com/politics/secret-service-spending-trump-kids/2020/10/12/ffc1c330-ff31-11ea-9ceb-061d646d9c67_story.html.

14. Bauer, "Administrative responses to democratic backsliding," 3.

15. Taylor, *Blowback*.

16. Tom Gjelten, "Peaceful Protesters Tear-Gassed to Clear Way for Trump Church Photo-Op," *NPR*, June 1, 2020, https://www.npr.org/2020/06 /01/867532070/trumps-unannounced-church-visit-angers-church-officials.

17. Richardson, *Democracy Awakening*; Aaron C. Davis, "How Trump Amassed a Red State Army in the Nation's Capitol," *Washington Post*, October 1, 2020, https://www.washingtonpost.com/investigations/how -trump-amassed-a-red-state-army-in-the-nations-capital--and -could-do-so-again/2020/10/01/2f10e17c-f9d6-11ea-a275-1a2c2d36e1f1 _story.html?_pml=1

18. Lauren Leatherby, Arielle Ray, Anjali Singhvi, Christiaan Triebert, Derek Watkins, and Haley Willis, "How A Presidential Rally Turned In-to a Capitol Rampage," *New York Times*, January 12, 2021, https://www .nytimes.com/interactive/2021/01/12/us/capitol-mob-timeline.html.

19. For a summary of the hearings, see *New York Times*, "The Jan. 6 Capi-tol Attack: Inquiries and Fallout," accessed July 19, 2022, https://www .nytimes.com/news-event/jan-6-committee.

20. Oona A. Hathaway, "Reengaging on Treaties and Other International Agreements (Part I): President Donald Trump's Rejection of Interna-tional Law," *Just Security*, October 2, 2020, https://www.justsecurity .org/72656/reengaging-on-treaties-and-other-international-agreements -part-i-president-donald-trumps-rejection-of-international-law/.

21. Jonah E. Bromwich and Ben Protess, "Trump Guilty on All Counts in Hush-Money Case," *New York Times*, May 30, 2024, https://www .nytimes.com/live/2024/05/31/nyregion/trump-news-guilty-verdict.

22. Forty additional charges were dismissed by Judge Aileen Cannon in the U.S. District Court for the Southern District of Florida, but are being appealed by special counsel Jack Smith. Kaela Malig and Kristina Abovyan, "A Guide to the Criminal Cases Against Donald Trump," *Front-line*, September 11, 2024, https://www.pbs.org/wgbh/frontline/article /a-guide-to-the-criminal-cases-against-donald-trump/.

23. Levitsky and Ziblatt, *How Democracies Die*; Timothy Snyder, *On Tyr-anny: Twenty Lessons from the Twentieth Century* (New York: Tim Dug-gan, 2017); Bob Woodward, *Fear: Trump in the White House* (New York: Simon and Schuster, 2018; Woodward and Bernstein, "Woodward and Bernstein Thought Nixon Defined Corruption."

24. Levitsky and Ziblatt, *How Democracies Die*, 65.

25. Edward Luce, "Historian Heather Cox Richardson: 'Now People See What's Happening. Thank God!,'" *Financial Times*, July 16, 2021, https://www.ft.com/content/08f3728c-bbff-493f-aa66-a1aa35dd3924; Taylor, *Blowback*.

## 3. THE SPIRIT AND INHERENT CHALLENGES OF PUBLIC ADMINISTRATION

1. See "Neoclassical" at the *Architect of the Capitol* government website: Architect of the Capitol, "Neoclassical," accessed July 8, 2023, https://www.aoc.gov/explore-capitol-campus/buildings-grounds/neoclassical.

2. Parts of this chapter draw upon Jaime Kucinskas and Yvonne Zylan, "Walking the Moral Tightrope: Federal Civil Servants' Loyalties, Caution, and Resistance Under the Trump Administration," *American Journal of Sociology* 128, no. 6 (2023), https://doi.org/10.1086/725313; Albert O. Hirschman, *Exit, Voice, and Loyalty: Responses to Decline in Firms, Organizations, and States* (Cambridge, MA: Harvard University Press, 1970), 4.

3. Hugh Heclo, "The Spirit of Public Administration," *PS: Political Science & Politics* 35, no. 4 (2002): 692.

4. George H. Frederickson, *The Spirit of Public Administration*, 1st ed. (San Francisco: Jossey-Bass, 1997), 64; Heclo, "The Spirit of Public Administration," 692; Johan P. Olsen, "Maybe It Is Time to Rediscover Bureaucracy," *Journal of Public Administration Research and Theory* 16, no. 1 (2006): 1–24.

5. Heclo, "The Spirit of Public Administration," 691.

6. James L. Perry, Annie Hondeghem, and Lois Recascino Wise, "Revisiting the Motivational Bases of Public Service: Twenty Years of Research and an Agenda for the Future," *Public Administration Review* 70, no. 5 (2010): 681–90.

7. Olsen, "Maybe It Is Time to Rediscover Bureaucracy."

8. Heclo, "The Spirit of Public Administration," 689.

9. Frederickson, *The Spirit of Public Administration*, 234.

10. Peggy A. Thoits, "On Merging Identity Theory and Stress Research," *Social Psychology Quarterly* 54, no. 2 (1991): 104.

11. Thoits, "On Merging Identity Theory and Stress Research," 104.

12. Peggy A. Thoits, "Multiple Identities and Psychological Well-Being: A Reformation and Test of the Social Isolation Hypothesis," *American Sociological Review* 48, no. 2 (1983): 174–87; Philip E. Crewson, "Public Service Motivation: Building Empirical Evidence of Incidence and Effect," *Journal of Public Administration Research and Theory* 7, no. 4 (1997): 499–518, https://doi.org/https://doi.org/10.1093/oxfordjournals.jpart.a024363.

13. Erving Goffman, *The Presentation of Self in Everyday Life* (Reprint, London: Penguin, 1959).

14. See also Stuart Shapiro, *Trump and the Bureaucrats: The Fate of Neutral Competence* (Cham, Switzerland: Springer International, 2023), on the importance of neutral competence to federal civil servants, and their experiences working in the Office of Management and Budget, Government Accountability Office, Congressional Budget Office, and Economic Research Service at the U.S. Department of Agriculture.

15. This model of socialization builds on the varied accounts of people with whom I spoke: each particular piece does not apply to every civil servant; rather, I draw on the rich accounts of particular civil servants who spoke on each piece in turn, and combine them into this model depicting the many mechanisms through which socialization into becoming a professional civil servant can occur. Although this process does not occur in this particular way for every civil servant, this general model largely depicts the contours of the careers of many civil servants with whom I spoke. See also Alex Bitektine, Patrick Haack, Joel Bothello, and Johanna Mair, "Inhabited Actors: Internalizing Institutions Through Communication and Actorhood Models," *Journal of Management Studies* 57, no. 4 (2020): 885–97, https://doi.org/https://doi.org/10.1111/joms.12560; Benjamin Schneider, Harold W Goldstein, and D. Brent Smith, "The ASA Framework: An Update," *Personnel Psychology* 48, no. 4 (1995): 747–73. See also James L. Perry, *Managing Organizations to Sustain Passion for Public Service* (Cambridge: Cambridge University Press, 2020).

16. I interpret these narratives as such, not as accurate causal representations. It is likely that in working as civil servants, their patriotism and civil values have become more salient. See Shel Stryker and Richard T. Serpe, "Commitment, Identity Salience, and Role Behavior: A Theory

and Research Example," in *Personality, Roles and Social Behavior*, ed. W. Ickes and Eric S. Knowles (New York: Springer-Verlag, 1982), 199–218. They also may present themselves as particularly loyal to these values to me as a researcher to create a positive impression.

17.  Others also mentioned how foundational their parents' influence continued to be in their moral assessments. For a public account, see Maria L. Yovanovitch, *Lessons from the Edge: A Memoir* (New York: Mariner, 2022), xviii, 121.

18.  Sean T. Lyons, Linda E. Duxbury, and Christopher A. Higgins, "A Comparison of the Values and Commitment of Private Sector, Public Sector, and Parapublic Sector Employees," *Public Administration Review* 66, no. 4 (2006): 605–18, https://doi.org/10.1111/j.1540-6210.2006.00620.x; James L. Perry and Lyman W. Porter, "Factors Affecting the Context for Motivation in Public Organizations," *Academy of Management Review* 7, no. 1 (1982): 89–98, https://doi.org/10.2307/257252; James L. Perry and Lois Recascino Wise, "The Motivational Bases of Public Service," *Public Administration Review*, 1990, 367–73; Wouter Vandenabeele, Gene A. Brewer, and Adrian Ritz, "Past, Present, and Future of Public Service Motivation Research," *Public Administration* 92, no. 4 (2014): 779–89.

19.  U.S. Census Bureau, "U.S. Census Data," 2020, https://www.census.gov /data/tables/2020/demo/educational-attainment/cps-detailed-tables .html.

20.  See the sociodemographic summary of respondents in appendix A of this book.

21.  I am grateful to Alfred Kelly for pointing this out in a Hamilton Sociology colloquium. See also Perry, *Managing Organizations to Sustain Passion for Public Service*, 109–10.

22.  Carolyn Chen, *Work Pray Code: When Work Becomes Religion in Silicon Valley* (Princeton, NJ: Princeton University Press, 2022); Jaime Kucinskas, *The Mindful Elite: Mobilizing from the Inside Out* (New York: Oxford University Press, 2019); Lauren A. Rivera, *Pedigree: How Elite Students Get Elite Jobs* (Princeton, NJ: Princeton University Press, 2015).

23.  Neil Fligstein, "Social Skill and the Theory of Fields," *Sociological Theory* 19, no. 2 (2001): 105–25; Everett C. Hughes, "Work and Self," in *The Sociological Eye: Selected Papers* (Abingdon: Routledge, 1984 [1951]);

Charles Tilly, *Why? What Happens When People Give Reasons . . . and Why* (Princeton, NJ: Princeton University Press, 2008).

24. Cornell Law School/Legal Information Institute, "5 U.S. Code § 3331—Oath of Office," accessed September 8, 2021, https://www.law.cornell.edu/uscode/text/5/3331.

25. See also Yovanovitch, *Lessons from the Edge.*

26. U.S. Office of Special Counsel, "Federal Employee Hatch Act Information," accessed June 20, 2022, https://osc.gov/Services/Pages/HatchAct-Federal.aspx#tabGroup12|tabGroup31.

27. Because of Trump's running for reelection, one career civil servant, who was an outlier, said something that ran counter to what nearly everyone else I spoke said: "Mostly I think it's nearly impossible to adhere to the Hatch Act. The law says that we can't talk about it on social media or instant messenger or anything, and that's just not possible. The Hatch Act applies to people who are running for office and if Trump weren't running for office right now, we would be allowed to talk about these things, but him running for office and announcing that so early effectively is designed to like squash our ability to just talk about the news. So that's stupid and if the FBI comes in and reads my chat logs and they want to fire me, fuck it, I don't care." Notably, I met this employee while they were on break during a day when they were working at home. Following the social media protocols would likely be more challenging while working from home.

28. Dwight Waldo, *The Enterprise of Public Administration* (Novato, CA: Chandler and Sharp, 1980). For the figure, see Rosemary O'Leary, *The Ethics of Dissent: Managing Guerrilla Government* (Washington, DC: CQ Press, 2020), 22.

29. Waldo, *The Enterprise of Public Administration,* 100.

30. Richard Stillman, "A Tribute to Dwight Waldo," *Institute of Governmental Studies Public Affairs Report* 42, no. 1 (2001).

31. Waldo, *The Enterprise of Public Administration,* 100–101.

32. George Lowery and Dana Cook, "Dwight Waldo Started It All," Maxwell School of Public Affairs, Syracuse University, December 12, 2019, https://www.maxwell.syr.edu/news/article/dwight-waldo-started-it-all.

33. Waldo, *The Enterprise of Public Administration,* 113.

34. Marissa M. Golden, *What Motivates Bureaucrats? Politics and Adminis-tration During the Reagan Years* (New York: Columbia University Press, 2000); William G. Resh, *Rethinking the Administrative Presidency: Trust, Intellectual Capital and Appointee-Careerist Relations in the George W. Bush Administration* (Baltimore, MD: Johns Hopkins University Press, 2015).

35. Although Waldo does not make this comparison, it would be interest-ing to compare salient professional values with other sectors, such as the nonprofit and the business sectors. Career civil servants have more salient and varied competing professional ethical values than employees of other sectors.

36. Golden, *What Motivates Bureaucrats?* See also Yovanovitch, *Lessons from the Edge*, 215–17.

37. Max Weber, *Economy and Society: An Outline of Interpretive Sociology*, vol. 1 (Berkeley: University of California Press, 1978).

38. Katherine Schlosser Bersch, Sérgio Praça, and Matthew M. Taylor, "An Archipelago of Excellence? Autonomous Capacity Among Brazilian State Agencies," paper presented at the Princeton University–Universidade de São Paulo Conference on "State Capacity in the Developing World," São Paulo, Brazil, February 2012.

39. Harry Kopp, "Members of the Foreign Service Regularly Grapple with the Professional and Moral Dilemma of Dissent," The State of Dissent in the Foreign Service, September 2017, https://afsa.org/state-dissent-foreign-service; Miller Center, University of Virginia, "McCarthyism and the Red Scare," accessed June 29, 2022. https://millercenter.org/the-presidency/educational-resources/age-of-eisenhower/mcarthyism-red-scare.

40. Kopp, "Members of the Foreign Service Regularly Grapple with the Professional and Moral Dilemma of Dissent."

41. Kopp, "Members of the Foreign Service Regularly Grapple with the Professional and Moral Dilemma of Dissent."

42. Marissa M. Golden, "Exit, Voice, Loyalty, and Neglect: Bureaucratic Responses to Presidential Control during the Reagan Administration," *Journal of Public Administration Research and Theory* 2, no. 1 (1992): 30. This was also a period in which political appointees engaged in historic levels of corruption, as discussed in Frederickson, *The Spirit of Public Administration*, 190.

43. Golden, "Exit, Voice, Loyalty, and Neglect."
44. Richard P. Nathan, *The Administrative Presidency* (New York: Wiley, 1983); Resh, *Rethinking the Administrative Presidency*; Bert A. Rockman, "The Modern Presidency and Theories of Accountability: Old Wine and Old Bottles," *Congress & the Presidency* 13, no. 2 (1986): 525–47.
45. Perry, *Managing Organizations to Sustain Passion for Public Service*, 184–5.
46. Albert Bandura, "Social Cognitive Theory of Self-Regulation," *Organizational Behavior and Human Decision Processes* 50, no. 2 (1991), https://doi.org/https://doi.org/10.1016/0749-5978(91)90022-L.; Albert Bandura, "Social Cognitive Theory of Personality," in *The Coherence of Personality: Social-Cognitive Bases of Consistency, Variability, and Organization*, ed. D. Cervone and Y. Shoda (New York: Guilford Press, 1999), 185–241; Timothy Snyder, *On Tyranny: Twenty Lessons from the Twentieth Century* (New York: Tim Duggan, 2017); Jo-Ann Tsang, "Moral Rationalization and the Integration of Situational Factors and Psychological Processes in Immoral Behavior," *Review of General Psychology* 6, no. 1 (2002): 25–50, https://doi.org/10.1037/1089-2680.6.1.25.
47. Keith Dowding, Peter John, Thanos Mergoupis, and Mark Vugt, "Exit, Voice and Loyalty: Analytic and Empirical Developments," *European Journal of Political Research* 37, no. 4 (2000): 469–95, https://doi.org/10.1111/1475-6765.00522; Golden, *What Motivates Bureaucrats?*; John P. Meyer and Natalie Jean Allen, *Commitment in the Workplace: Theory, Research, and Application* (Thousand Oaks, CA: Sage, 1997); Perry, *Managing Organizations to Sustain Passion for Public Service*.

## 4. "TOO EARLY TO TELL": RATIONALIZING FORBEARANCE

1. Matt Broomfield, "Women's March Against Donald Trump Is the Largest Day of Protests in US History, Say Political Scientists," *Independent*, January 23, 2017, https://www.independent.co.uk/news/world/americas/womens-march-anti-donald-trump-womens-rights-largest-protest-demonstration-us-history-political-scientists-a7541081.html.
2. Craig J. Jenkins, *The Politics of Insurgency: The Farm Worker Movement in the 1960s* (New York: Columbia University Press, 1985); Frances Fox Piven and Richard A. Cloward *Poor People's Movements: Why They Succeed, How They Fail* (New York: Vintage, 1979).

3. Albert O. Hirschman, *Exit, Voice, and Loyalty: Responses to Decline in Firms, Organizations, and States* (Cambridge, MA: Harvard University Press, 1970); Jaime Kucinskas, "The Unobtrusive Tactics of Religious Movements," *Sociology of Religion* 75, no. 4 (2014): 537–50, https://doi.org/10.1093/socrel/sru055; Jaime Kucinskas, *The Mindful Elite: Mobilizing from the Inside Out* (New York: Oxford University Press, 2019).

4. Brakkton Booker, "With 'Pussyhats' at Women's Marches, Headwear Sends a Defiant Message," *NPR*, January 22, 2017, https://www.npr.org/2017/01/22/511048762/with-pussyhats-at-womens-marches-headwear-sends-a-defiant-message; *Trump on Tape: I Grab Women "By the Pu\*\*y,"* *YouTube*, accessed June 27, 2023, https://www.youtube.com/watch?v=WhsSzIS84ks.

5. Michael Lewis, *The Fifth Risk* (New York: Norton, 2018).

6. From 2010 to 2012, Congress passed legislation supporting presidential transitions. These laws provide free office space for presidential nominees, reduce the number of presidential appointments requiring Senate confirmation, and require the sitting president to prepare for the transition to the next president. See Lewis, *The Fifth Risk*, 27. Given these developments, civil servants I spoke with who were working on the transition thought the chaos of the first Trump transition was particularly notable.

7. Lewis, *The Fifth Risk*.

8. McKay Coppins, "The Man Who Broke Politics," *Atlantic*, October 15, 2018, https://www.theatlantic.com/magazine/archive/2018/11/newt-gingrich-says-youre-welcome/570832/.

9. Dana R. Fisher, *American Resistance: From the Women's March to the Blue Wave* (New York: Columbia University Press, 2019).

10. Leon Festinger, *A Theory of Cognitive Dissonance*, vol. 2 (Stanford, CA: Stanford University Press, 2001 [1962, 1985]), 3.

11. Ervin Staub, *The Psychology of Good and Evil: Why Children, Adults, and Groups Help and Harm Others* (Cambridge: Cambridge University Press, 2003), 123.

12. Philip Zimbardo, *The Lucifer Effect: How Good People Turn Evil* (London: Rider, 2007), 219–20.

13. See also the moral dissonance model in Hans Te Brake and Bart Nauta, "Caught Between Is and Ought: The Moral Dissonance Model," *Frontiers in Psychiatry* 13 (2022): 4, https://doi.org/10.3389/fpsyt.2022.906231.

14. Florence Rockwood Kluckhohn, "Cultural Factors in Social Work Practice and Education," *Social Service Review* 25, no. 1 (1951): 38–47; Milton Rokeach, *The Nature of Human Values* (New York: Free Press, 1973).

15. Jo-Ann Tsang, "Moral Rationalization and the Integration of Situational Factors and Psychological Processes in Immoral Behavior," *Review of General Psychology* 6, no. 1 (March 2002): 25–50, https://doi.org/10.1037/1089-2680.6.1.25.

16. Michael L. Benson, "Denying the Guilty Mind: Accounting for Involvement in a White Collar Crime," *Criminology* 23, no. 4 (1985): 583–607, https://doi.org/10.1111/j.1745-9125.1985.tb00365.x; April McGrath, "Dealing with Dissonance: A Review of Cognitive Dissonance Reduction," *Social and Personality Psychology Compass* 11, no. 12 (2017): e12362, https://doi.org/10.1111/spc3.12362; W. William Minor, "Techniques of Neutralization: A Reconceptualization and Empirical Examination," *Journal of Research in Crime and Delinquency* 18, no. 2 (1981): 295–318, https://doi.org/10.1177/002242788101800206; Marvin B. Scott and Stanford M. Lyman, "Accounts," *American Sociological Review* 33, no. 1 (1968): 46–62, https://doi.org/10.2307/2092239; David Shepherd and Mark Button, "Organizational Inhibitions to Addressing Occupational Fraud: A Theory of Differential Rationalization," *Deviant Behavior* 40, no. 8 (2019): 971–91, https://doi.org/10.1080/01639625.2018.1453009; Graham M. Sykes and David Matza, "Techniques of Neutralization: A Theory of Delinquency," *American Sociological Review* 22, no. 6 (1957): 664–70, https://doi.org/10.2307/2089195.

17. This aligns with some public administration research on the risk-averse federal bureaucracy and psychological research on how people respond to threats. See Don Bellante and Albert N. Link, "Are Public Sector Workers More Risk-Averse Than Private Sector Workers?," *Industrial and Labor Relations Review* 34, no. 3 (n.d.): 408–12; Marissa M. Golden, *What Motivates Bureaucrats? Politics and Administration During the Reagan Years* (New York: Columbia University Press, 2000); Shelley E. Taylor and Marci Lobel, "Social Comparison Activity Under Threat: Downward Evaluation and Upward Contacts," *Psychological Review* 96, no. 4 (1989): 569–75, https://doi.org/10.1037/0033-295X.96.4.569.

18. Herbert A. Simon, *Administrative Behavior* (New York: Simon and Schuster, 1947).

19. Festinger, *A Theory of Cognitive Dissonance*; McGrath, "Dealing with Dissonance."

20. After this interview, this civil servant's area of work became even more politicized, and she dropped out of my study.

21. See Albert Bandura, "Social Cognitive Theory of Self-Regulation," *Organizational Behavior and Human Decision Processes* 50, no. 2 (1991), https://doi.org/10.1016/0749-5978(91)90022-L; Albert Bandura, "Social Cognitive Theory of Personality," in *The Coherence of Personality: Social-Cognitive Bases of Consistency, Variability, and Organization*, ed. D Cervone and Y Shoda, 185–241 (New York: Guilford, 1999); Tsang, "Moral Rationalization."

22. He had influence, however, over environmental policy that shaped health consequences for millions of people. This included influence over some environmental pollutants that were harming people under his jurisdiction. He did attempt to intervene to aid these people during the Trump administration, but I do not have further information on whether he was efficacious or not. He seemed to imply that, by raising the issue as high as he could in his agency, he had done his due diligence.

23. Tsang, "Moral Rationalization."

24. Zimbardo, *The Lucifer Effect*.

25. Taylor and Lobel, "Social Comparison Activity Under Threat," 569.

26. McCafferty was consistent across interviews in 2017 and 2018. In 2018, he said, "No, under the Hatch Act that's kind of prohibited. No, I'm not involved in political activities outside of work. We are neutral instruments."

## 5. SPLIT LIVES AND EXTERNAL ENGAGEMENT

1. It is important to acknowledge that, upon asking at the end of each of my first interviews with informants, each informant privately identified as politically ranging from centrists to Democrats. At work, however, they all espoused the importance of being impartial and nonpartisan.

2. Political commentator and former communications director for Jeb Bush's 2016 presidential campaign Tim Miller identified compartmentalization as a key psychological mechanism enabling populist

Republicans to take part in democratic backsliding and the moral decline of the Republican Party under Trump. See Tim Miller, *Why We Did It: A Travelogue from the Republican Road to Hell*, 1st ed. (New York: HarperCollins, 2022). Marie Yovanovitch also mentions it in her book; see Maria L. Yovanovitch, *Lessons from the Edge: A Memoir* (New York, Mariner, 2022), 31.

3. Cvetan Todorov, *Facing the Extreme: Moral Life in the Concentration Camp.* (New York: Holt, 1997), 129. See also Jo-Ann Tsang, "Moral Rationalization and the Integration of Situational Factors and Psychological Processes in Immoral Behavior," *Review of General Psychology* 6, no. 1 (March 2002): 25–50, https://doi.org/10.1037/1089-2680.6.1.25.

4. Tsang, "Moral Rationalization," 44.

5. It is likely that their protests increased again after George Floyd was killed in 2020 because mass protests spiked thereafter. See Larry Buchanan, Quoctrung Bui, and Jugal K. Patel, "Black Lives Matter May Be the Largest Movement in U.S. History," *New York Times*, July 3, 2020, https://www.nytimes.com/interactive/2020/07/03/us/george-floyd -protests-crowd-size.html.

6. For example, here are some of many media articles on Environmental Protection Agency (EPA) protests during 2017: David Abel, "EPA Workers Protest Budget Cuts in March to Boston Common," *Boston Globe*, May 24, 2017, https://www.bostonglobe.com/metro/2017/05/24 /protest/PkybDk5esowmHOkmzUGQiL/story.html; Coral Davenport, "E.P.A. Workers Try to Block Pruitt in Show of Defiance," *New York Times*, February 16, 2017, https://www.nytimes.com/2017/02/16/us/politics /scott-pruitt-environmental-protection-agency.html; Ross Levitt, "Two Resign in Protest from EPA Subcommittee," *CNN*, May 12, 2017, https:// www.cnn.com/2017/05/12/politics/epa-resignation-protest-review -board/index.html.

7. Keith Dowding and Peter John, "The Three Exit, Three Voice and Loyalty Framework: A Test with Survey Data on Local Services," *Political Studies* 56, no. 2 (2008): 288–311, https://doi.org/10.1111/j.1467 -9248.2007.00688.x; Marissa M. Golden, "Exit, Voice, Loyalty, and Neglect: Bureaucratic Responses to Presidential Control During the Reagan Administration," *Journal of Public Administration Research and Theory* 2, no. 1 (1992).

8. Marissa M. Golden, "Exit, Voice, Loyalty, and Neglect: Bureaucratic Responses to Presidential Control During the Reagan Administration," *Journal of Public Administration Research and Theory* 2, no. 1 (1992): 29–62; and Marissa M. Golden, *What Motivates Bureaucrats? Politics and Administration During the Reagan Years* (New York: Columbia University Press, 2000).

## 6. APPOINTEES' MISTRUST

1. See Michael Lewis, *The Fifth Risk* (New York: Norton, 2018) on the chaos and incompetence of Donald Trump's transition teams. They also did not adhere to standards of leadership that many civil servants assumed to be characteristic of high-quality leaders, such as making efforts to act professional, show respect for staff, listen to subject matter experts, use collective decision-making processes, and earnestly seek to serve the American public.

2. Mark Granovetter, "The Strength of Weak Ties: A Network Theory Revisited," *Sociological Theory* 1 (1983): 201, https://doi.org/10.2307/202051.

3. As Marissa M. Golden (*What Motivates Bureaucrats? Politics and Administration During the Reagan Years* [New York: Columbia University Press, 2000]) documents under the Reagan administration, in an effort to control the bureaucracy, presidential appointees can transfer and demote high-level bureaucrats and use jigsaw puzzle management by giving work typically done by careerists to appointees, excluding career civil servants from decision-making processes. See also P. M. Benda and C. H. Levine, "Reagan and the Bureaucracy: The Bequest, the Promise, and the Legacy," in *The Reagan Legacy: Promise and Performance* (Chatham, NJ: Chatham House, 1988), 102–42; Patricia Ingraham, *The Foundation of Merit: Public Service in American Democracy* (Baltimore, MD: Johns Hopkins University Press, 1995). While Reagan's administration was known for its aggressive stance against career civil servants, such tactics have been used since by various presidents. See William G. Resh, *Rethinking the Administrative Presidency: Trust, Intellectual Capital and Appointee-Careerist Relations in the George W. Bush Administration* (Baltimore, MD: Johns Hopkins University Press, 2015). See also Eloy Oliveira, Gordon Abner, Shinwoo Lee, Kohei Suzuki, Hyunkang Hur,

and James L. Perry, "What Does the Evidence Tell Us About Merit Principles and Government Performance?," *Public Administration* 102, no. 2 (2023): 1–23, https://doi.org/10.1111/padm.12945.

4. Many critics have questioned whether he was most committed to "draining the swamp" of the federal bureaucracy or the appearance of doing so. In a telling example, President Trump reversed his executive order from January 2017 prohibiting employees in executive agencies from lobbying agencies where they had previously worked for the following five years after leaving their positions. See Steve Benen, "In the Middle of the Night, Trump Takes Step to Refill the Swamp," *MSNBC*, *MaddowBlog* (blog), January 20, 2021, https://www.msnbc.com/rachel -maddow-show/maddowblog/middle-night-trump-takes-step-refill -swamp-n1254872.

5. Brian Naylor, "'A Huge Attack': Critics Decry Trump Order That Makes Firing Federal Workers Easier," *NPR*, October 31, 2020, https:// www.npr.org/2020/10/31/929597578/a-huge-attack-critics-decry -trump-order-that-makes-firing-federal-workers-easier; Lisa Rein, "Trump Takes Aim at Federal Bureaucracy with New Executive Orders Rolling Back Civil-Service Protections," *Washington Post*, May 26, 2018, https://www.washingtonpost.com/politics/trump-takes-aim-at-federal -bureaucracy-with-new-executive-orders-altering-civil-service-protections /2018/05/25/3ed8bf84-6055-11e8-9ee3-49d6d4814c4c_story.html.

6. "Schedule F and the Future of the Public Service, virtual panel hosted by the National Academy of Public Administration, June 29, 2023.

7. Erich Wagner, "White House Revives Controversial Retirement Cut Proposals," *Government Executive*, February 10, 2020, https://www .govexec.com/pay-benefits/2020/02/white-house-revives-controversial -retirement-cut-proposals/163015/.

8. See also Maria L. Yovanovitch, *Lessons from the Edge: A Memoir* (New York, Mariner, 2022), 234, 239.

9. W. Muno and H. Briceño, "Autocratization and Public Administration: The Revolutionary-Populist Regime in Venezuela in Comparative Perspective," *Asia Pacific Journal of Public Administration* 45, no. 1 (2023): 73–92.

10. See also Resh, *Rethinking the Administrative Presidency*, on how lacking trust between political appointees and career bureaucrats can be

detrimental to a presidential administration; Hugh Heclo, *A Government of Strangers: Executive Politics in Washington* (Washington, DC: Brookings Institution, 1977).

11. David E. Pozen, "The Leaky Leviathan: Why the Government Condemns and Condones Unlawful Disclosures of Information," *Harvard Law Review* 127, no. 2 (2013), 521.

12. Susan Hennessey and Helen Klein Murillo, "The Law of Leaks," *Law-Fare* (blog), February 15, 2017, https://www.lawfareblog.com/law-leaks.

13. See also Miles Taylor, *Blowback: A Warning to Save Democracy from the Next Trump*, (New York: Atria, 2024).

14. Emily Tamkin, "Here's What Happened to a USAID Official Who Ran Afoul of Mike Pence," *BuzzFeed News*, September 18, 2018, https://www.buzzfeednews.com/article/emilytamkin/usaid-christians-aid-iraq-pence-interference.

15. McFarlane was convicted for illegal behavior aiding Nicaraguan rebels in the Iran Contra affair during his tenure as national security advisor during the 1980s: Neil A. Lewis, "Robert C. McFarlane, Top Reagan Aide in Iran-Contra Affair, Dies at 84," *New York Times*, May 13, 2022, https://www.nytimes.com/2022/05/13/us/robert-c-mcfarlane-dead.html.

16. Tamkin, "Here's What Happened to a USAID Official."

17. Tamkin, "Here's What Happened to a USAID Official."

18. A few other study participants stopped responding to my attempts to contact them during the second set of interviews in 2018. Although losing some respondents is typical in longitudinal research, the people who dropped out of the study tended to work in particularly contentious departments or program areas, and some expressed discomfort about continuing interviews because of the increasing suspicion and risk associated with speaking out.

19. See Jim Sciutto, "Exclusive: Vindman to Retire from Military. His Lawyer Blames White House 'Campaign of Bullying, Intimidation and Retaliation,'" *CNN*, July 8, 2020, https://www.cnn.com/2020/07/08/politics/vindman-retiring-alleged-white-house-retaliation/index.html.

20. Sciutto, "Exclusive." See also Kaitlin Collins, Zachary Cohen, Kylie Atwood, and Kevin Liptak, "Bolton Manuscript Revelations Thrust Little-Known White House Office into Spotlight," *CNN*, January 27, 2020,

https://www.cnn.com/2020/01/27/politics/nsc-records-management
-division-bolton-manuscript/index.html.

21. Sciutto, "Exclusive," 1.

22. See, for example, Danielle Schulkin and Julia Brooks, "Loyalty Above
All: The 'Shallow State' of the Trump Administration," *Just Security*,
November 2, 2020, https://www.justsecurity.org/73226/loyalty-above-all
-the-shallow-state-of-the-trump-administration/; Taylor, *Blowback*;
Yovanovitch, *Lessons from the Edger*.

23. Michael S. Schmidt, "In a Private Dinner, Trump Demanded Loyalty.
Comey Demurred," *New York Times*, May 12, 2017, https://www.nytimes
.com/2017/05/11/us/politics/trump-comey-firing.html.

24. James Comey, *A Higher Loyalty: Truth, Lies, and Leadership* (New York:
Flatiron, 2018), 7.

25. For primary documents, see "The Impeachment of Donald John
Trump Evidentiary Record from the House of Representatives (116th)"
House Committee on the Judiciary, Chairman Jerrold Nadler, accessed
July 28, 2022, https://judiciary.house.gov/the-impeachment-of-donald
-john-trump/.

26. "Exhibit, Investigative Committees, Alexander Vindman Deposition
Complete Exhibits, October 29, 2019," accessed July 28, 2022, https://
judiciary.house.gov/uploadedfiles/2019-10-29_deposition_of_vindman
_exhibits.pdf

27. See also Yovanovitch, *Lessons from the Edge*, 279, 281.

28. Daniel Carpenter and David A. Moss, eds., *Preventing Regulatory Capture: Special Interest Influence and How to Limit It* (New York: Cambridge University Press, 2013); Lindsey Dillon, Christopher Sellers,
Vivian Underhill, Nicholas Shapiro, Jennifer Liss Ohayon, Marianne
Sullivan, Phil Brown, Jill Harrison, Sara Wylie, and the EPA Under
Siege Writing Group, "The Environmental Protection Agency in the
Early Trump Administration: Prelude to Regulatory Capture," *American Journal of Public Health* 108, no. S2 (2018): S89–S94, https://doi.org
/10.2105/AJPH.2018.304360.

29. Joel D. Aberbach and Bert A. Rockman, *In the Web of Politics: Three
Decades of the U.S. Federal Executive* (Washington, DC Brookings Institution Press, 2000), 6.

30. Federal Register, "Reducing Regulation and Controlling Regulatory
Costs," February 3, 2017, https://www.federalregister.gov/documents

/2017/02/03/2017-02451/reducing-regulation-and-controlling-regulatory
-costs.

31. There are many public accounts of State Department appointees' transgressions, one of the most egregious being Frederico Klein's ten convictions on felony charges based on obstructing the electoral vote count
and six violent encounters with law enforcement officers on January 6,
2021, in the U.S. Capitol. See Spencer S. Hsu and Tom Jackman, "Former Trump State Dept. Appointee Guilty in Jan. 6 Tunnel Assaults,"
*Washington Post*, July 20, 2023, https://www.washingtonpost.com/dc-md
-va/2023/07/20/federico-klein-guilty-jan-6-trump-appointee/.

32. Resh, *Rethinking the Administrative Presidency*.

# 7. LOYALTY TRAPS

1. See Maria L. Yovanovitch, *Lessons from the Edge: A Memoir* (New York:
Mariner, 2022), chaps. 13–15.

2. Stephen K. Bailey, "Ethics and the Public Service," *Public Administration
Review* 24, no. 4 (1964): 234–43. See also Dwight Waldo, *The Enterprise of
Public Administration* (Novato, CA: Chandler and Sharp, 1980), 66.

3. Chester I. Barnard, *The Functions of the Executive* (Cambridge, MA:
Harvard University Press, 1947), chap. 17.

4. Coral Davenport, Lisa Friedman, and Maggie Haberman, "E.P.A.
Chief Scott Pruitt Resigns Under a Cloud of Ethics Scandals," *New
York Times*, July 5, 2018, accessed July 19, 2022, https://www.nytimes
.com/2018/07/05/climate/scott-pruitt-epa-trump.html

5. Steven Levitsky and Daniel Ziblatt, *How Democracies Die* (New York:
Broadway, 2018), 177–78.; Michael S. Schmidt, "In a Private Dinner,
Trump Demanded Loyalty. Comey Demurred," *New York Times*, May 12,
2017, sec. U.S. https://www.nytimes.com/2017/05/11/us/politics/trump
-comey-firing.html.

6. As Ines Blackburn conveyed also in 2018: "The president is elected by
the people and can define his or her own foreign policy and our job as
career officers of the State Department is to enact that person's policy.
So I have no problem—I have my own moral questions about what
the president's foreign policy choices are—but from a commitment and
service oath that I've taken to work at the State Department, is it my
job to implement the intent of the president and the Secretary of State."

7. Dan Froomkin, "Impeachment Witnesses Highlight Plight of Career Civil Servants Under Trump," *Press Watch*, November 22, 2019, https:// presswatchers.org/2019/11/impeachment-witnesses-highlight-plight -of-career-civil-servants-under-trump/.

8. Karl A. Racine and Elizabeth Wilkins, "Enforcing the Anti-Corruption Provisions of the Constitution," *Harvard Law & Policy Review* 13, no. 2 (2019); Miles Taylor, *Blowback: A Warning to Save Democracy from the Next Trump* (New York: Atria, 2024).

9. The perspective of this midlevel manager aligns with a Weberian view of public servant responsibilities and loyalties. Max Weber, *Economy and Society: An Outline of Interpretive Sociology*, Vol. 1 (Berkeley: University of California Press, 1978).

10. United States Environmental Protection Agency, "Our Mission and What We Do," January 29, 2013, https://www.epa.gov/aboutepa/our -mission-and-what-we-do.

11. Joana Story, Gabriela Lotta, and Gustavo M Tavares, "(Mis)Led by an Outsider: Abusive Supervision, Disengagement, and Silence in Politicized Bureaucracies," *Journal of Public Administration Research and Theory* 33, no. 4 (2023): 549–62, https://doi.org/10.1093/jopart/muad004.

12. Gabriela Lotta, Gustavo M. Tavares, and Joana Story, "Political Attacks and the Undermining of the Bureaucracy: The Impact on Civil Servants' Well-Being," *Governance* (2023), gove.12792. https://doi.org/10.1111 /gove.12792.

13. Kanybek Nur-Tegin and Hans J. Czap, "Corruption: Democracy, Autocracy, and Political Stability," *Economic Analysis and Policy* 42, no. 1 (2012): 51–66; Eloy Oliveira, Gordon Abner, Shinwoo Lee, Kohei Suzuki, Hyunkang Hur, and James L. Perry, "What Does the Evidence Tell Us About Merit Principles and Government Performance?," *Public Administration* 102, no. 2 (2023): 1–23, https://doi.org/10.1111/padm.12945.

14. Jason Ditton, "Alibis and Aliases: Some Notes on the Motives' of Fiddling Bread Salesman," *Sociology* 11, no. 2 (1977): 233, https://doi.org /https://doi.org/10.1177/003803857701100201.

15. Zolan Kanno-Youngs, Maggie Haberman, Michael D. Shear, and Eric Schmitt, "Kirstjen Nielsen Resigns as Trump's Homeland Security Secretary," *New York Times*, April 7, 2019, https://www.nytimes.com/2019/04/07 /us/politics/kirstjen-nielsen-dhs-resigns.html; Robin Lindsay, "Homeland Security Secretary Kirstjen Nielsen Exits Trump's Cabinet," *New York*

*Times* video transcript, 2019, https://www.nytimes.com/video/us/politics /100000006213836/kirstjen-nielsen-resigns-dhs.htm; Geneva Sands, "Kirstjen Nielsen Says She Left DHS Because 'Saying No' Wasn't Enough," *CNN*, October 22, 2019, https://www.cnn.com/2019/10/22 /politics/kirstjen-nielsen-speech/index.html. See also James Comey, *A Higher Loyalty: Truth, Lies, and Leadership* (New York: Flatiron, 2018); Cassidy Hutchinson, "Testimony to the Select Committee to Investigate the January 6th Attack on the U.S. Capitol," *PBS Newshour*, December 22, 2022, https://www.pbs.org/newshour/politics/read-the-transcripts-of -cassidy-hutchinsons-closed-door-jan-6-testimony.

16. Marissa M. Golden, "Exit, Voice, Loyalty, and Neglect: Bureaucratic Responses to Presidential Control During the Reagan Administration," *Journal of Public Administration Research and Theory* 2, no. 1 (1992): 30; William G. Resh, *Rethinking the Administrative Presidency: Trust, Intellectual Capital and Appointee-Careerist Relations in the George W. Bush Administration* (Baltimore, MD: Johns Hopkins University Press, 2015).

17. Hannah Arendt, *The Origins of Totalitarianism* (New York: Schocken, 1951), 474.

## 8. SIGNS OF ORGANIZATIONAL DECLINE

1. Michael Lewis, *The Fifth Risk* (New York: Norton, 2018).

2. For additional evidence of Trump's incompetence, see also Miles Taylor, *Blowback: A Warning to Save Democracy from the Next Trump* (New York: Atria, 2024).

3. "Energy Secretary Swearing-in Ceremony," *C-SPAN*, March 2, 2017, https:// www.c-span.org/video/?424865-2/energy-secretary-swearing-ceremony.

4. Sarah Farmer's perspective aligned with another, more generous career employee at the Department of Energy (DOE), who described the administrator as "very reasonable" but "much less engaged than prior secretaries." This employee said that Rick Perry emailed "at a much lower frequency than other secretaries," and he didn't know what was important to him because "he's not very communicative . . . I don't know. This is my impression based on reading newspapers. These aren't official proclamations . . . I guess to the extent that he can, he is toeing the administration lines."

5. See also Maria L. Yovanovitch, *Lessons from the Edge: A Memoir* (New York: Mariner, 2022), 245–46.

6. See also Taylor, *Blowback*; Yovanovitch, *Lessons from the Edge*.

7. Umair Irfan, "Trump's EPA Just Replaced Obama's Signature Climate Policy with a Much Weaker Rule," *Vox*, June 19, 2019, https://www .vox.com/2019/6/19/18684054/climate-change-clean-power-plan-repeal -affordable-emissions.

8. In 2018, another Environmental Protection Agency (EPA) employee in that office took comfort in the fact that "we have a regional administrator now." She expressed faith it would be better and that "he will lead us in some direction." She thought their regional administrator was "a strong leader. He seems to be good." But as she struggled to express why he seemed good, she seemed to waver. "He has goals," she said, but "I don't know what they are. But they don't concern my program, so I'm okay."

9. For more about bounded rationality in administrative organizations, see Herbert A. Simon, *Administrative Behavior* (New York: Simon and Schuster, 1947).

10. See also Taylor, *Blowback*.

11. This deviates from an administrative presidency leadership approach. See William G. Resh, *Rethinking the Administrative Presidency: Trust, Intellectual Capital and Appointee-Careerist Relations in the George W. Bush Administration* (Baltimore, MD: Johns Hopkins University Press, 2015).

12. Nancy Cook, "Trump's Staffing Struggle: After 3 Years, Unfilled Jobs Across the Administration," *Politico*, January 20, 2020, https://www .politico.com/news/2020/01/20/trumps-staffing-struggle-unfilled-jobs -100991.

13. Zolan Kanno-Youngs, Maggie Haberman, Michael D. Shear, and Eric Schmitt, "Kirstjen Nielsen Resigns as Trump's Homeland Security Secretary," *New York Times*, April 7, 2019, https://www.nytimes.com/2019/04/07 /us/politics/kirstjen-nielsen-dhs-resigns.html. See also Taylor, *Blowback*.

14. Kanno-Youngs et al., "Kirstjen Nielsen Resigns."

15. In 2018, the Trump administration disregarded a similar recommendation by the Office of Special Counsel to fire Senior Counselor Kellyanne Conway for violating the Hatch Act. Such behavior demonstrated the Trump administration's flagrant dismissal of legal restrictions that checked their power and their protection and rewarding of loyalists. See Michael D. Shear, "Top Homeland Security Officials Are Serving Illegally, G.A.O. Says," *New York Times*, August 14, 2020, https://www .nytimes.com/2020/08/14/us/politics/homeland-security-illegal-gao.html.

16. See also Taylor, *Blowback*; Yovanovitch, *Lessons from the Edge.*

17. See also Taylor, *Blowback.*

18. For more on hiring inexperienced sycophantic appointees, see Tim Miller, *Why We Did It: A Travelogue from the Republican Road to Hell*, 1st ed. (New York: HarperCollins, 2022).

19. See also Taylor, *Blowback.*

20. Heather Cox Richardson, *Democracy Awakening: Notes on the State of America* (New York: Viking, 2023). See also Ruth Ben-Ghiat, *Strongmen: Mussolini to the Present* (New York: Norton, 2020); Taylor, *Blowback*, 76.

21. Kimberly D. Elsbach, and C. B. Bhattacharya, "Defining Who You Are by What You're Not: Organizational Disidentification and the National Rifle Association," *Organization Science* 12, no. 4 (2001): 393–413, https://www.jstor.org/stable/3085979.

22. See also Yovanovitch, *Lessons from the Edge*, 251–53, 270, 289, 304.

23. See also a *New York Times* report on this by Julian E. Barnes and Matthew Rosenberg, "Charges of Ukrainian Meddling? A Russian Operation, U.S. Intelligence Says," *New York Times*, November 22, 2019, https://www.nytimes.com/2019/11/22/us/politics/ukraine-russia-interference.html and Yovanovitch, *Lessons from the Edge*, 288–89.

24. Legal scholars disagree on this point. See Karl A. Racine and Elizabeth Wilkins, "Enforcing the Anti-Corruption Provisions of the Constitution," *Harvard Law & Policy Review* 13, no. 2 (2019): 449–69.

25. Thanks to Al Kelly for highlighting this point. See also Richard Stillman, "A Tribute to Dwight Waldo," *Institute of Governmental Studies Public Affairs Report* 42, no. 1 (2001).

26. Robert Reich, *Supercapitalism: The Transformation of Business, Democracy and Everyday Life* (New York: First Vintage, 2007).

27. See Miranda Green, "Pruitt Faces Resistance from Ethanol Groups During Midwest Trips," *The Hill* (blog), June 13, 2018, https://thehill.com/policy/energy-environment/392076-pruitt-met-with-resistance-from-ethanol-groups-during-midwest-trips/.

28. Michael R. Bashshur, Ana Hernández, and Vicente González-Romá, "When Managers and Their Teams Disagree: A Longitudinal Look at the Consequences of Differences in Perceptions of Organizational Support," *Journal of Applied Psychology* 96, no. 3 (2011): 558–73, https://doi.org/10.1037/a0022675.

29. John D. Kammeyer-Mueller, Lauren S. Simon, and Bruce L. Rich, "The Psychic Cost of Doing Wrong: Ethical Conflict, Divestiture Socialization, and Emotional Exhaustion," *Journal of Management* 38, no. 3 (2012): 784–808. https://doi.org/10.1177/0149206310381133.

30. Devina Upadhyay and Anu Gupta, "Morale, Welfare Measures, Job Satisfaction: The Key Mantras for Gaining Competitive Edge," *International Journal of Physical and Social Sciences* 2, no. 7 (2012): 80–94.

31. Yovanovitch, *Lessons from the Edge*, 270.

32. For example, Sarah Farmer also noted how difficult it was to do everyday work without sufficient guidance under a suspicious administration:

> People are very nervous because they would like time to prepare for things, and it's hard when you have no idea what their [appointed leaders'] priorities are. People keep trying to work as normal, but everyone, especially managers, have to do everything cautiously. Because even if they've been in their role for twenty, thirty years, they have this new political appointee that's going to ask questions about everything they do. If it's not something that has to be done now, they consider: do I want to wait until the dust settles and then I have a better idea of how this is going to be received?

> But in Farmer's case, further guidance never came. She reported at the time trying not to "sound political," but being frustrated by "things not moving forward and also not getting direction." Another problem that arose working in conditions of uncertainty about what the administration wanted, she reported, was that people lacked the willingness to take a stand. "Instead of saying, 'Our policy is. we discourage this,' we just don't say yes," she said. "That's where we are now: things aren't getting rejected. It'll just sit on someone's desk for three months, and you sort of get the hint that that's not going any further."

33. Herbert M. Lefcourt, "The Function of the Illusions of Control and Freedom," *American Psychologist* 28, no. 5 (1973): 417–25, https://doi.org/10.1037/h0034639; Ervin Staub, *The Psychology of Good and Evil: Why Children, Adults, and Groups Help and Harm Others* (Cambridge: Cambridge University Press, 2003), 122.

34. Marissa M. Golden, "Exit, Voice, Loyalty, and Neglect: Bureaucratic Responses to Presidential Control During the Reagan Administration," *Journal of Public Administration Research and Theory* 2, no. 1 (1992).

## 9. TO STAY OR GO?

1. Political scientists and legal experts acknowledge there is a baseline of tension between presidential administrations and career bureaucrats, and the latter can at times speak truth to power or resist illegal, unscientific, or undemocratic political decisions. They also suggest, as shown in my book, that Trump's conspiracy-like claims of an American deep state run by shadowy unresponsive bureaucrats with their own independent agenda are overstated and a means of scapegoating. In contrast to some other countries where it might be more applicable, like Egypt and Turkey, U.S. agencies are "rule-bound," and seek to operate in a "transparent, egalitarian" manner. As Jon D. Michaels argues (and as I suggest throughout this book), the American state is more of a defensive "bulwark," in keeping with the constitutional importance of having a separation of powers and checks on executive power, than a "battering ram." See Jon D. Michaels, "Trump and the 'Deep State': The Government Strikes Back," *Foreign Affairs* 96, no. 5 (2017): 52–56, https://www.jstor.org/stable/44821868; Jon D. Michaels, "The American Deep State," *Notre Dame Law Review* 93, no. 4 (March 1, 2018): 1653, https://scholarship.law.nd.edu/ndlr/vol93/iss4/10; Donald Moynihan, "Populism and the Deep State: The Attack on Public Service Under Trump," in *Democratic Backsliding and Public Administration*, 1st ed., ed. Michael W. Bauer, B. Guy Peters, Jon Pierre, Kutsal Yesilkagit, and Stefan Becker, 151–77 (Cambridge: Cambridge University Press, 2021), https://doi.org/10.1017/9781009023504.008.

2. Parts of this chapter draw upon Jaime Kucinskas and Yvonne Zylan, "Walking the Moral Tightrope: Federal Civil Servants' Loyalties, Caution, and Resistance Under the Trump Administration," *American Journal of Sociology* 128, no. 6 (2023); Albert O. Hirschman, *Exit, Voice, and Loyalty: Responses to Decline in Firms, Organizations, and States* (Cambridge, MA: Harvard University Press, 1970), 4.

3. Calvin Morrill, Mayer N. Zald, and Hayagreeva Rao, "Covert Political Conflict in Organizations: Challenges from Below," *Annual Review of Sociology* 29, no. 1 (2003): 391–415; Hirschman, *Exit, Voice, and Loyalty.*

4. Hirschman, *Exit, Voice, and Loyalty*, 78.

5. Soo-Young Lee and Andrew B. Whitford, "Exit, Voice, Loyalty, and Pay: Evidence from the Public Workforce," *Journal of Public Administration Research and Theory* 18, no. 4 (October 17, 2007): 647–71, https://doi.org/10.1093/jopart/mum029.

6. Lee and Whitford, "Exit, Voice, Loyalty, and Pay;" Birgitta Niklasson, Peter Munk Christiansen, and Patrik Öhberg, "Speaking Truth to Power: Political Advisers' and Civil Servants' Responses to Perceived Harmful Policy Proposals," *Journal of Public Policy* 40, no. 3 (2020): 492–512, https://doi.org/10.1017/S0143814X18000508.

7. See also William G. Resh, *Rethinking the Administrative Presidency: Trust, Intellectual Capital and Appointee-Careerist Relations in the George W. Bush Administration* (Baltimore, MD: Johns Hopkins University Press, 2015).

8. Rosemary O'Leary, *The Ethics of Dissent: Managing Guerrilla Government* (Washington, DC: CQ Press, 2020).

9. For an example of this, see Andreas Glaeser, *Political Epistemics: The Secret Police, the Opposition, and the End of East German Socialism* (Chicago: University of Chicago Press, 2011).

10. These are my terms, not my respondents' language.

11. The American Foreign Service Association also has Constructive Dissent Awards.

12. Other documents supported his story, but I do not want to specify them in an effort to maintain his confidentiality.

13. See also Talia Shiff, "A Sociology of Discordance: Negotiating Schemas of Deservingness and Codified Law in US Asylum Status Determinations," *American Journal of Sociology* 127, no. 2 (2021): 337–75, on how U.S asylum workers navigate the "ordinary" moral discordance when their ideas of client deservingness do not match codified definitions of asylum eligibility.

14. Sociologist Arlie Hochschild refers to this deep emotional self-work in service of one's job and its associated values and goals as "deep acting." In doing such intrapersonal work, employees such as Anderson try so earnestly to meet the emotional and moral commitments of

their roles that they go beyond front-stage performances and come to embody such roles as manifestations of who they are. See Arlie Russell Hochschild, *The Managed Heart: Commercialization of Human Feeling*, updated ed. (Berkeley: University of California Press, 2012). Another alternative social psychological explanation might interpret his behavior as reaffirming the positive attributes of his job in the face of cognitive dissonance and cognitive threats in order to reduce dissonance. See Blake E. Ashforth, Glen E. Kreiner, Mark A. Clark, and Mel Fugate, "Normalizing Dirty Work: Managerial Tactics for Countering Occupational Taint," *Academy of Management Journal* 50, no. 1 (2007): 149–74; Amanda S. Hinojosa, William L. Gardner, H. Jack Walker, Claudia Cogliser, and Daniel Gullifor, "A Review of Cognitive Dissonance Theory in Management Research: Opportunities for Further Development," *Journal of Management* 43, no. 1 (2017): 170–99, https://doi.org/10.1177/0149206316668236.

15. Samuel P. Oliner and Pearl M. Oliner, *The Altruistic Personality: Rescuers of Jews in Nazi Europe* (New York: The Free Press, 1988, 146.

16. I am grateful to Yvonne Zylan, in particular, for her help analyzing this section. See also Kucinskas and Zylan, "Walking the Moral Tightrope."

17. Alexander Bolton, John M. De Figueiredo, and David E. Lewis, "Elections, Ideology, and Turnover in the US Federal Government," *Journal of Public Administration Research and Theory* 31, no. 2 (2021): 451–66.

18. Exits increased each year during the Trump administration, especially among entry-level employees and older employees who opted for retirement. During the COVID-19 pandemic, however, resignations decreased considerably, likely because of the pandemic, which depressed the administration's average voluntary separation rate. Exit rates may also have been slightly higher because of a demographic shift, with baby boomers retiring. See Partnership for Public Service, "The Federal Workforce and the Trump Administration," 2023, https://ourpublicservice.org/fed-figures/the-federal-workforce-and-the-trump-administration/.

19. Partnership for Public Service, "Who Is Quitting and Retiring: Important Fiscal 2021 Trends in the Federal Government," 2023, https://ourpublicservice.org/fed-figures/attrition/.

20. Bolton, De Figueiredo, and Lewis, "Elections, Ideology, and Turnover;" Kathleen M. Doherty, David E. Lewis, and Scott Limbocker,

"Executive Control and Turnover in the Senior Executive Service," *Journal of Public Administration Research and Theory* 29, no. 2 (2019): 159–74.

21. Bolton, De Figueiredo, and Lewis, "Elections, Ideology, and Turnover."

22. The one exception was whistleblower Joel Clement (see chapter 6), who was removed from his position, along with a number of others at the Department of Interior, and quit shortly thereafter. For more on resistant exit, see Jennet Kirkpatrick, "Resistant Exit," *Contemporary Political Theory* 18, no. 2 (June 2019): 135–57, https://doi.org/10.1057/s41296-018-0252-1.

23. See John W. Kingdon, "A Model of Agenda-Setting, with Applications," *Law Review M.S.U—D.C.L*, no. 2 (Summer 2001): 331–38, on how failures can lead to greater attention and policy change.

24. Bolton, De Figueiredo, and Lewis, "Elections, Ideology, and Turnover."

25. Katherine Bersch, Sérgio Praça, and Matthew M. Taylor, "Bureaucratic Capacity and Political Autonomy Within National States: Mapping the Archipelago of Excellence in Brazil," in *States in the Developing World*, ed. Miguel A. Centeno, Atul Kohli, and Deborah J. Yashar, 157–83 (Cambridge: Cambridge University Press, 2017).

26. Doherty, Lewis, and Limbocker, "Executive Control and Turnover;" Richard A. Harris and Sidney M. Milkis, *The Politics of Regulatory Change: A Tale of Two Agencies* (New York: Oxford University Press, 1989); Francis E. Rourke, "Executive Responsiveness to Presidential Policies: The Reagan Presidency," *Congress & the Presidency* 17, no. 1 (1990): 1–11.

27. Dwight Waldo, *The Enterprise of Public Administration* (Novato, CA: Chandler and Sharp, 1980), 66.

28. Michaels, "Trump and the 'Deep State'"; Moynihan, "Populism and the Deep State;" Francis Fukuyama, "In Defense of the Deep State," *Asia Pacific Journal of Public Administration* 46 (August 25, 2023): 1, https://doi.org/10.1080/23276665.2023.2249142.

## 10. COVERT RESISTANCE

1. Lauren Gambino, "Scott Pruitt Confirmation Hearing for Environmental Protection Agency: The Key Points," *The Guardian*, January 18, 2017, https://www.theguardian.com/us-news/2017/jan/18/scott-pruitt-confirmation-hearing-epa-key-points.

2. Adhering to science is a value not stipulated in the Constitution. Dwight Waldo, *The Enterprise of Public Administration* (Novato, CA: Chandler and Sharp, 1980), 79.

3. Calvin Morrill, Mayer N. Zald, and Hayagreeva Rao, "Covert Political Conflict in Organizations: Challenges from Below," *Annual Review of Sociology* 29, no. 1 (2003): 391–415.

4. Jocelyn A. Hollander and Rachel L. Einwohner, "Conceptualizing Resistance," *Sociological Forum* 19, no. 4 (2004), 538; Jaime Kucinskas and Yvonne Zylan, "Walking the Moral Tightrope: Federal Civil Servants' Loyalties, Caution, and Resistance Under the Trump Administration," *American Journal of Sociology* 128, no. 6 (2023): 1770.

5. See James C. Scott, *Weapons of the Weak: Everyday Forms of Peasant Resistance* (New Haven, CT: Yale University Press, 1985).

6. Albert O. Hirschman, *Exit, Voice, and Loyalty: Responses to Decline in Firms, Organizations, and States* (Cambridge, MA: Harvard University Press, 1970).

7. Morrill, Zald, and Rao, "Covert Political Conflict in Organizations," 394.

8. Mel Monier, "'Rest as Resistance': Black Cyberfeminism, Collective Healing and Liberation on @TheNapMinistry," *Communication, Culture & Critique* 16, no. 3 (August 25, 2023): 119–25, https://doi.org/10.1093/ccc/tcad022; Scott, *Weapons of the Weak*.

9. Some past definitions of resistant action distinguish resistance as behavior that inverts a status quo. For example, Victoria Pitts defines resistance as "expressive behavior that inverts, contradicts, abrogates, or prevents alternatives to cultural codes." If the extant cultural code is Heclo's spirit of public administration in a Weberian state, then career civil servants' actions might be seen as trying to protect the status quo rather than subvert it. See Victoria L. Pitts, "Reclaiming the Female Body: Embodied Identity Work, Resistance and the Grotesque," *Body & Society* 4, no. 3 (1998): 67–84.

10. Joel D. Aberbach and Bert A. Rockman, *In the Web of Politics: Three Decades of the U.S. Federal Executive* (Washington, DC: Brookings Institution Press, 2000).

11. See past definitions of resistance as rooted in insubordination to authority, such as Weitz: "actions that not only reject subordination but do so by challenging the ideologies that support that subordination;" Rubin:

actions involving consciousness, collective action, and direct challenges to structures of power; Prasad and Prasad: "either any kind of organized, collective opposition or any subversive action directly intended to damage and/or disrupt the functioning of an organization. See Anshuman Prasad and Pushkala Prasad, "Everyday struggles at the Workplace: The Nature and Implications of Routine Resistance in Contemporary Organizations," *Research in the Sociology of Organizations* 15, no. 2 (1998): 226; Jeffrey W. Rubin, "Defining Resistance: Contested Interpretations of Everyday Acts," *Studies in Law, Politics, and Society* 15 (1996): 24; Rose Weitz, "Women and Their Hair: Seeking Power Through Resistance and Accommodation," *Gender & Society* 15, no. 5 (2001): 670. See also Hollander and Einwohler, "Conceptualizing Resistance."

12. See the discussion of recognition and visibility in Hollander and Einwohler, "Conceptualizing Resistance." Career civil servants have some power, and including this facet recognizes that.

13. C. Wright Mills, "Situated Actions and Vocabularies of Motive," *American Sociological Review* 5, no. 6 (1940): 904–13; Ann Swidler, *Talk of Love: How Culture Matters* (Chicago: University of Chicago Press, 2001); Daniel Winchester and Kyle D. Green, "Talking Your Self into It: How and When Accounts Shape Motivation for Action," *Sociological Theory* 37, no. 3 (2019): 257–81, https://doi.org/10.1177/0735275119869959.

14. Scott, *Weapons of the Weak*.

15. John Anthony Rohr, *To Run a Constitution: The Legitimacy of the Administrative State* (Lawrence: University Press of Kansas, 1986): 66.

16. Don Bellante and Albert N. Link, "Are Public Sector Workers More Risk-Averse Than Private Sector Workers?," *Industrial and Labor Relations Review* 34, no. 3 (1981): 408–12.

17. Morrill, Zald, and Rao, "Covert Political Conflict in Organizations;" Rosemary O'Leary, *The Ethics of Dissent: Managing Guerrilla Government* (Washington, DC: CQ Press, 2020)

18. See also Marissa M. Golden, "Exit, Voice, Loyalty, and Neglect: Bureaucratic Responses to Presidential Control During the Reagan Administration," *Journal of Public Administration Research and Theory* 2, no. 1 (1992); Marissa M. Golden, *What Motivates Bureaucrats? Politics and Administration During the Reagan Years* (New York: Columbia University Press, 2000); O'Leary, *The Ethics of Dissent*.

19. J. D. Aberbach and B. A. Rockman, "Clashing Beliefs Within the Executive Branch: The Nixon Administration Bureaucracy," *American Political Science Review* 70, no. 2 (1976): 456–68; Frederick C. Mosher, *Democracy and the Public Service*, 2nd ed. (New York: Oxford University Press, 1982; William Niskanen, *Bureaucracy and Representative Government* (Chicago: Aldine Atherton, 1971); O'Leary, *The Ethics of Dissent*; Benjamin Page and Mark Petracca, *The American Presidency* (New York: McGraw Hill, 1983); Richard M. Pious, *The American Presidency* (New York: Basic Books, 1979); Aaron B. Wildavsky, *The Politics of the Budgetary Process*, 4th ed. (Boston: Little, Brown, 1984).

20. Robert D. Benford and David A. Snow, "Framing Processes and Social Movements: An Overview and Assessment," *Annual Review of Sociology* 26 (2000): 611–39; Neil Fligstein and Doug McAdam, *A Theory of Fields* (Oxford: Oxford University Press, 2012); David N. Pellow, "Framing Emerging Environmental Movement Tactics: Mobilizing Consensus, Demobilizing Conflict," *Sociological Forum* 14, no. 4 (1999): 659–83; D. A. Snow and R. D. Benford, "Ideology, Frame Resonance, and Participant Mobilization," *International Social Movement Research* 1, no. 1 (1988): 197–217; D. A. Snow and R. D. Benford, "Master Frames and Cycles of Protest," in *Frontiers in Social Movement Theory*, ed Aldon Morris and Carol McClung Mueller (New Haven, CT: Yale University Press, 1992); David A. Snow, E. Burke Rochford, Steven K. Worden, and Robert D. Benford, "Frame Alignment Processes, Micromobilization, and Movement Participation," *American Sociological Review* 51, no. 4 (1986): 464–81.

21. Erving Goffman, *Frame Analysis: An Essay on the Organization of Experience* (Cambridge, MA: Harvard University Press, 1974), 21.

22. Snow et al., "Frame Alignment Processes."

23. Fligstein and McAdam, "Toward a General Theory of Strategic Action Fields;" Jaime Kucinskas, *The Mindful Elite: Mobilizing from the Inside Out* (New York: Oxford University Press, 2019).

24. Kimberly Kay Hoang, *Spiderweb Capitalism: How Global Elites Exploit Frontier Markets* (Princeton, NJ: Princeton University Press, 2022).

25. Fligstein and McAdam, "Toward a General Theory of Strategic Action Fields."

26. With the Trump administration's emphasis on rollbacks, regulations and project work were renamed as well to avoid provoking ire from

appointed officials. An entry-level employee in a different Environmental Protection Agency (EPA) office said that they were "trying to not use the word 'regulations' anymore."

27. Timothy Snyder, *On Tyranny: Twenty Lessons from the Twentieth Century* (New York: Tim Duggan, 2017).

28. Snyder, *On Tyranny*.

29. C. Caldwell and M. Canuta-Carranco, "'Organizational Terrorism' and Moral Choices—Exercising Voice When the Leader Is the Problem," *Journal of Business Ethics* 97, no. 1 (2010): 159–71. See also Dan Farrell, "Exit, Voice, Loyalty, and Neglect as Responses to Job Dissatisfaction: A Multidimensional Scaling Study," *Academy of Management Journal* 26, no. 4 (1983): 596–607; Caryl E. Rusbult, Dan Farrell, Glen Rogers, and Arch G. Mainous III, "Impact of Exchange Variables on Exit, Voice, Loyalty, and Neglect: An Integrative Model of Responses to Declining Job Satisfaction," *Academy of Management Journal* 31, no. 3 (1988): 599–627.

30. Golden, "Exit, Voice, Loyalty, and Neglect."

31. As shown in this chapter, my understanding of employees using "neglect" as a subversive strategy against leadership initiatives is based on the civil servants' own accounts. It differs from Golden's concept, which she articulates as not being a form of resistance. See Golden, *What Motivates Bureaucrats?*

32. Aberbach and Rockman, *In the Web of Politics*.

33. Larry W. Isaac, Anna W. Jacobs, Jaime Kucinskas, and Allison R. McGrath, "Social Movement Schools: Sites for Consciousness Transformation, Training, and Prefigurative Social Development," *Social Movement Studies* 19, no. 2 (March 3, 2020): 160–82, https://doi.org/10.1080/14742837.2019.1631151.

34. Golden also found that collective acts of resistance among federal bureaucrats was rare. See Golden, "Exit, Voice, Loyalty, and Neglect."

35. O'Leary, *The Ethics of Dissent*.

36. For example, when asked to use a "remedy" in her work that she knew "was no longer effective" by supervisors who "didn't understand the technical details in my letter" and who "didn't think the upper management would understand," one EPA career employee under the Obama administration tried to have her job transferred. When her request was

not granted, she asked for the initial request "in writing" to document that they were making her approve the decision.

37. As one person suggested, such documentation might be useful should their personal situation at work deteriorate or should they be targeted by leadership.

38. He described as a baseline that, in his role, "sometimes, when something is really sensitive, then we won't write it down;" "that's usually if we're talking about 'we want to do this,' but there is some litigation risk," and they are discussing "what the risk is." He said that, because they are "subject to FOIA [Freedom of Information Act]," they may opt not to write something down because they "don't want to give helpful material to someone who is going to challenge us in court." But, he argued, that context of discussing something that is "the right thing to do," which he thought undergirded those prior examples, was quite different than the situation concerning corruption at hand.

39. Hirschman, *Exit, Voice, and Loyalty.*

40. E. Staub, B. Tursky, and G. E. Schwartz, "Self-Control and Predictability: Their Effects on Reactions to Aversive Stimulation," *Journal of Personality and Social Psychology* 18, no. 2 (1971): 157.

41. Ervin Staub, *The Psychology of Good and Evil: Why Children, Adults, and Groups Help and Harm Others* (Cambridge: Cambridge University Press, 2003), 122.

## 11. MORAL COURAGE

1. Ervin Staub, *The Psychology of Good and Evil: Why Children, Adults, and Groups Help and Harm Others* (Cambridge: Cambridge University Press, 2003), 8.

2. Compared to social psychological studies, such as Oliner and Oliner's study of rescuers of Jew during World War II or Ervin Staub's work on the psychology of good and evil, I take a more sociological perspective, paying more attention to the social and situational factors than focusing on psychological characteristics. See Samuel P. Oliner and Pearl M. Oliner, *The Altruistic Personality: Rescuers of Jews in Nazi Europe* (New York: The Free Press, 1988); Staub, *The Psychology of Good and Evil.*

3. Arendt, *Eichmann in Jerusalem; a Report on the Banality of Evil*; Stanley Milgram, "Obedience to Criminal Orders: The Compulsion to Do Evil," *Patterns of Prejudice* 1, no. 6 (1967): 3–7.

4. This builds on criticism of the conformist situational obedience model and aligns in some ways with an interactionist model as posited both by critics who acknowledge that they are "interactionists" (810) while continuing to stress how powerful situational influence can be. Psychologists S. Alexander Haslam and Stephen Reicher suggest, however, that people's likelihood of following authorities "is conditional on identification with the authority and an associated belief that the authority is right." As I explain in this chapter and throughout the book, this is not what I find among a considerable number of my respondents who feel obligated, out of loyalty to the state and the public, to serve elected leadership, even when they do not identify with the president and believe his agenda to be harmful. See S. Alexander Haslam and Stephen D. Reicher, "Contesting the 'Nature' of Conformity: What Milgram and Zimbardo's Studies Really Show," *PLoS Biology* 10, no. 11 (2012): 1; David R. Mandel, "The Obedience Alibi," *Analyze & Kritik* 20, no. 1 (1998): 74–94; Sam McFarland and Thomas Carnahan, "A Situation's First Powers Are Attracting Volunteers and Selecting Participants: A Reply to Haney and Zimbardo," *Personality and Social Psychology Bulletin* 35, no. 6 (2009): 815–18; Thomas Carnahan and Sam McFarland, "Revisiting the Stanford Prison Experiment: Could Participant Self-Selection Have Led to the Cruelty?," *Personality and Social Psychology Bulletin* 33, no. 5 (2007): 603–14; S. Alexander Haslam and Stephen D. Reicher, "Beyond the Banality of Evil: Three Dynamics of an Interactionist Social Psychology of Tyranny," *Personality and Social Psychology Bulletin* 33, no. 5 (2007): 615–22; Craig Haney and Philip G. Zimbardo, "Persistent Dispositionalism in Interactionist Clothing: Fundamental Attribution Error in Explaining Prison Abuse," *Personality and Social Psychology Bulletin* 35, no. 6 (2009): 807–14.

5. Jonathan Haidt, "The Emotional Dog and Its Rational Tail: A Social Intuitionist Approach to Moral Judgment," *Psychological Review* 108, no. 4 (2001): 814–34; Jonathan Haidt, "The New Synthesis in Moral Psychology," *Science* 316, no. 5827 (2007): 998–1002.

6. Only a handful of civil servants I spoke with engaged in the most visibly overt and potentially risky forms of resistance during the Trump administration. Given the small sample size of people engaging in such actions, I share their narratives in hopes of contributing to theory building. Some details have been altered to maintain anonymity. In an earlier draft of this book, I compared the most overt resisters to those who I thought would resist more to show the utility of this framework. In the interest of brevity and partly because of how the other chapters developed, I cut this comparison and integrated the latter group's experiences throughout the other chapters of the book.

7. Staub, *The Psychology of Good and Evil*, 8.

8. Holding universalist values of equality and justice has been predictive of acts of moral courage and resistance to authoritarianism in the past. Samuel Oliner and Pearl Oliner found that the rescuers of Jews during the Holocaust were more committed to universal ethical values extended to all human beings (39 percent versus 15 percent of nonrescuers and 13 percent of bystanders). Nonrescuers tended to apply ethical obligations more exclusively to family, friends, elders, church, and country. In particular, rescuers valued justice, equality, and respect for all, and were troubled that innocent people were being unjustly persecuted. Rescuers also tended to have more egalitarian views and considered Jews co-citizens rather than different from themselves. See Oliner and Oliner, *The Altruistic Personality*, 165–66, 169, 170; Robert Braun, "Religious Minorities and Resistance to Genocide: The Collective Rescue of Jews in the Netherlands During the Holocaust," *American Political Science Review* 110, no. 1 (2016): 127–47. This also accords with H. George Frederickson's emphasis on the importance of benevolence in public service. See H. George Frederickson, *The Spirit of Public Administration*, 1st ed. (San Francisco: Jossey-Bass, 1997), 195–208, 234.

9. Abraham Carmeli and Jody Hoffer Gittell, "High-Quality Relationships, Psychological Safety, and Learning from Failures in Work Organizations," *Journal of Organizational Behavior* 30, no. 6 (2009): 709–29.

10. Alexander Newman, Ross Donohue, and Nathan Eva, "Psychological Safety: A Systematic Review of the Literature." *Human resource management review* 27, no. 3 (2017): 521–35.

11.  Marissa M. Golden, *What Motivates Bureaucrats? Politics and Adminis-tration During the Reagan Years* (New York: Columbia University Press, 2000).

12.  Federal Pay, "GS-14 Pay Scale—General Schedule 2019," 2019, https://www.federalpay.org/gs/2019/GS-14.

13.  Timothy Snyder, *On Tyranny: Twenty Lessons from the Twentieth Cen-tury* (New York: Tim Duggan, 2017), 93.

14.  Snyder, *On Tyranny*, 94.

15.  The civil servants' understandings of their experiences align with social action theories advanced by symbolic interactionists and identity the-orists, as well as by organizational scholars of culture. Such theorists maintain that the self is composed of multiple identities linked through interactions with one's networks of social relationships and roles, where one learns how to act appropriately by situation. Social psychologist Shel Stryker defines identities as "self-cognitions tied to roles and thus to positions in organized social relations." The more likely an identity is invoked trans-situationally—and "will come into play in a variety of sit-uations as a function of its properties as a cognitive schema," the more salient it is. Given identities' ability to be applied trans-situationally, their motivational aspect, which can move them to action based on a salient identity, and their self-reinforcing nature over time (as the more they are salient, the more they can lead to associated behavior, which can then strengthen one's initial identity), in any given situation, "These identities are potential competitors in producing behavioral choices." Thus, human action can be a fraught, stressful process through which people negotiate consciously and unconsciously among various identi-ties, as I witnessed among some of the civil servants I spoke with under the Trump administration. See Mustafa Emirbayer and Ann Mische, "What Is Agency?," *American Journal of Sociology* 103, no. 4 (1998): 962–1023; Stanley G. Harris, "Organizational Culture and Individual Sen-semaking: A Schema-Based Perspective," *Organization Science* 5, no. 3 (1994): 309–21; George H. Mead, *Mind, Self, and Society*, vol. 3 (Chicago: University of Chicago Press, 1934); Sheldon Stryker, "Identity Com-petition: Key to Differential Social Movement Participation?," in *Self, Identity, and Social Movements* (Minneapolis: University of Minnesota Press, 2000), 21, 28; Sheldon Stryker, Timothy J. Owens, and Robert W.

White, eds., *Self, Identity, and Social Movements*, vol. 13 (Minneapolis: University of Minnesota Press, 2000.

16. Hannah Arendt, "Personal Responsibility Under Dictatorship," in *Responsibility and Judgment* (New York: Schocken, 2003 [1964]), 34.

17. Katherine Schlosser Bersch, Sérgio Praça, and Matthew M. Taylor, "An Archipelago of Excellence? Autonomous Capacity Among Brazilian State Agencies," paper presented at the Princeton University–Universidade de São Paulo Conference on "State Capacity in the Developing World," São Paulo, Brazil, February 2012, 1.

18. Snyder, *On Tyranny*.

19. Early in the Trump administration, Glassman attended several federal resistance meetup groups, which she thought could be "really great" for younger employees. "As a more seasoned civil servant," she said, "I wasn't getting a lot out of them . . . I think if I were younger probably, if I were in my old position, they would have more benefit to me, but I think after you've gone through this a few times, you kind of just find your own way of navigating."

20. Oliner and Oliner found that rescuers of Jews tended to emphasize learning ethical values significantly more than nonrescuers and bystanders (70 percent of rescuers compared to 56 percent of nonrescuers and 57 percent of bystanders) in their biographical histories. They mentioned the importance of being caring, which they learned from their parents and other esteemed role models (44 percent of rescuers compared to 25 percent of nonrescuers and 21 percent of bystanders). Generosity and expansiveness rather than fairness and reciprocity were also significantly more important to rescuers' parents. See Bert Klandermans and Dirk Oegema, "Potentials, Networks, Motivations, and Barriers: Steps Towards Participation in Social Movements," *American Sociological Review* 52, no. 4 (1987): 519–31; Doug McAdam, *Freedom Summer* (New York: Oxford University Press, 1988); Oliner and Oliner, *The Altruistic Personality*; Heidi Ravven, *The Self Beyond Itself: An Alternative History of Ethics, the New Brain Sciences, and the Myth of Free Will* (New York: The New Press, 2013).

21. Along similar lines, Oliner and Oliner's rescuers were more likely to have a stronger sense of an internal rather than external locus of control over their actions and lives than nonrescuers. On average, rescuers had a

stronger sense of self-efficacy, self-responsibility, and control over their actions, as well as more of a willingness to risk failure than nonrescuers, who viewed themselves more "at the mercy of external circumstances." See Oliner and Oliner, *The Altruistic Personality*, 177.

22. Chester I. Barnard, *The Functions of the Executive* (Cambridge, MA: Harvard University Press, 1947).

23. I am grateful to Yagmur Karakaya for sharing this perceptive insight.

24. Klandermans and Oegema, "Potentials, Networks, Motivations, and Barriers;" McAdam, *Freedom Summer*.

25. For research on self-verification, see Elizabeth C. Pinel and William B. Swann Jr, "Finding the Self Through Others: Self-Verification and Social Movement Participation," in Stryker, Owens, and White, *Self, Identity, and Social Movements*, 132–52. For research on identity work, see David A. Snow and Leon Anderson, "Identity Work Among the Homeless: The Verbal Construction and Avowal of Personal Identities," *American Journal of Sociology* 92, no. 6 (1987): 1348, which refers to the "range of activities individuals engage in to create, present and sustain personal identities that are congruent with and supportive of their self-concept." See also David A. Snow and Doug McAdam, "Identity Work Processes in the Context of Social Movements: Clarifying the Identity/Movement Nexus," in Stryker, Owens, and White, *Self, Identity, and Social Movements*, which discusses how identity work can contribute to activism.

26. Snyder, *On Tyranny*.

## 12. AMERICAN DEMOCRACY AT A CROSSROADS

1. Marissa M. Golden, *What Motivates Bureaucrats? Politics and Administration During the Reagan Years* (New York: Columbia University Press, 2000). I later learned that the Reagan administration had a notably high rate of fraud, waste, and abuse among appointees. See H. George Frederickson, *The Spirit of Public Administration* (San Francisco: Jossey-Bass, 1997), 190.

2. See also Michael Lewis, *The Fifth Risk* (New York: Norton, 2018).

3. Dwight Waldo, *The Enterprise of Public Administration* (Novato, CA: Chandler and Sharp, 1980).

4. Institute for Policy Integrity, "Roundup: Trump-Era Agency Policy in the Courts," 2021, https://policyintegrity.org/trump-court-roundup.

5. Olga Khazan, "The Unraveling of the Trump Era," *The Atlantic*, July 28, 2021, https://www.theatlantic.com/politics/archive/2021/07/which-trump -regulations-were-overturned-biden/619583/.

6. Timothy Snyder, *On Tyranny: Twenty Lessons from the Twentieth Century* (New York: Tim Duggan, 2017), 99–100.

7. Snyder, *On Tyranny*, 66–67.

8. Liz Cheney, *Oath and Honor: A Memoir and a Warning* (New York: Little, Brown, and Co, 2023); James Comey, *A Higher Loyalty: Truth, Lies, and Leadership* (New York: Flatiron, 2018); Waldo, *The Enterprise of Public Administration*.

9. Mihály Fazelas and István János Tóth, "From Corruption to State Capture: A New Analytical Framework with Empirical Applications from Hungary," *Political Research Quarterly* 69, no. 2 (2016): 320–34, https:// doi.org/10.1177/1065912916639137; David White and Marc Herzog, "Examining State Capacity in the Context of Electoral Authoritarianism, Regime Formation and Consolidation in Russia and Turkey," *Southeast European and Black Sea Studies*, 16, no.4 (2016): 551–69, https:// doi.org/10.1080/14683857.2016.

10. Tom Dreisbach and Noah Caldwell, "The Trump Campaign Embraces Jan. 6 Rioters with Money and Pardon Promises," *NPR*, January 4, 2024, https://www.npr.org/2024/01/04/1218672628/the-trump-campaign -embraces-jan-6-rioters-with-money-and-pardon-promises.

11. United States Attorney's Office, District of Columbia, "35 Months Since the Jan. 6 Attack on the Capitol," December 6, 2023, https:// www.justice.gov/usao-dc/33-months-jan-6-attack-capitol-0.

12. Dreisbach and Caldwell, "The Trump Campaign Embraces Jan. 6 Rioters."

13. Erich Wagner, "Trump Vows to 'Shatter the Deep State,' Revive Schedule F and Move More Agencies Out of DC," *Government Executive*, March 21, 2023, https://www.govexec.com/workforce/2023/03/trump -vows-shatter-deep-state-revive-schedule-f-and-move-more-agencies -out-dc/384266/.

14. James Sherk and Michael Rigas, "Schedule F and the Future of the Public Service," presented at the National Academy of Public Administration, Washington, DC, June 29, 2023.

15. Sherk and Rigas, "Schedule F and the Future of the Public Service."
16. Deborah Birx, *Silent Invasion: the Untold Story of the Trump Administration, Covid-19, and Preventing the Next Pandemic Before It's Too Late* (New York: HarperCollins, 2022).
17. Michael D. Shear and Eric Lipton, "Trump Taps Elon Musk and Vivek Ramaswamy to Slash Government," *New York Times*, November 12, 2024, https://www.nytimes.com/2024/11/12/us/politics/elon-musk-vivek-ramaswamy-trump.html.
18. Wagner, "Trump Vows to 'Shatter the Deep State.'"
19. Erich Wagner, "OMB Reportedly Designates 88 percent of Its Employees for Schedule F," *Government Executive*, November 23, 2020, https://www.govexec.com/management/2020/11/omb-reportedly-designates-88-its-employees-schedule-f/170275/.
20. Donald Moynihan, "Trump Got Burned by a Major Mistake in His First Term. He Won't Make It Again," *Slate*, July 27, 2022, https://slate.com/news-and-politics/2022/07/donald-trump-schedule-f-civil-service-authoritarian.html; Jonathan Swan, "A Radical Plan for Trump's Second Turn," *Axios*, July 22, 2022, https://www.axios.com/2022/07/22/trump-2025-radical-plan-second-term. Project 2025 is a coalition of over eighty organizations led by the Heritage Foundation that has raised $22 million to prepare a transition plan, including lists of personal and policies, to recommend should a Republican candidate win the 2024 election. For more information about it, see its website at https://www.project2025.org/about/advisory-board and see Jonathan Swan, Charlie Savage, and Maggie Haberman, "Trump and Allies Forge Plans to Increase Presidential Power in 2025," *New York Times*, July 17, 2023, https://www.nytimes.com/2023/07/17/us/politics/trump-plans-2025.html.
21. Miles Taylor, *Blowback: A Warning to Save Democracy from the Next Trump* (New York: Atria, 2024), 70, 72.
22. Reem Nadeem, "Americans' Views of Government: Decades of Distrust, Enduring Support for Its Role," *Pew Research Center–U.S. Politics & Policy* (blog), June 6, 2022, https://www.pewresearch.org/politics/2022/06/06/public-trust-in-government-2/.
23. Richard J. Stillman II, *Preface to Public Administration: A Search for Themes and Directions* (New York: St. Martin's Press, 1990), 20.

24. Frederick C. Mosher, *Democracy and the Public Service* (New York: Oxford University Press, 1982). See also David G. Frederickson and H. George Frederickson, "The Paradox of Distance and the Problem of Differentiation," in *The Spirit of Public Administration*, ed. H. George Frederickson, 183–94 (San Francisco: Jossey-Bass, 1997), 184.

25. Frederickson and Frederickson, "The Paradox of Distance."

26. Frederickson and Frederickson, "The Paradox of Distance;" Forrest David Mathews, *Politics for People: Finding a Responsible Public Voice* (Urbana: University of Illinois Press, 1999); Lewis, *The Fifth Risk*.

27. Thomas Piketty, *Capital in the Twenty-First Century* (Cambridge, MA: The Belknap Press of Harvard University Press, 2014); Robert Reich, *Supercapitalism: The Transformation of Business, Democracy and Everyday Life* (New York: First Vintage, 2007).

28. Nur-Tegin, Kanybek, and Hans J. Czap. "Corruption: Democracy, Autocracy, and Political Stability." *Economic Analysis and Policy* 42, no. 1 (2012): 51–66; Eloy Oliveira, Gordon Abner, Shinwoo Lee, Kohei Suzuki, Hyunkang Hur, and James L. Perry, "What Does the Evidence Tell Us About Merit Principles and Government Performance?," *Public Administration* 102, no. 2 (2023): 1–23, https://doi.org/10.1111/padm.12945.

29. Frederickson and Frederickson, "The Paradox of Distance," 187. For specific cases and data analysis, see Charles T. Goodsell, *The Case for Bureaucracy: A Public Administration Polemic*. 3rd ed. (Chatham, NJ: Chatham House, 1995). For more on the impact of such rhetoric, see also George W. Downs and Patrick D. Larkey, *The Search for Government Efficiency: From Hubris to Helplessness* (New York: Random House, 1986), 241; Robert L. Kahn, Daniel Katz, Barbara Gutek, and Eugenia Barton, "Bureaucratic Encounters—An Evaluation of Government Services," *Journal of Applied Behavioral Science* 12, no. 2 (1976): 178–98, https://doi.org/10.1177/002188637601200203.

30. Loren DeJonge Schulman, Paul Hitlin and Nadzeya Shutava, "Trust in Government: A Close Look at Public Perceptions of the Federal Government and Its Employees," *Partnership for Public Service*. March 23, 2022: https://ourpublicservice.org/video/trust-in-government-public-perceptions-of-the-federal-government/

31. Nadeem, "Americans' Views of Government."

32. See, for example, Ruth Braunstein, "A (More) Perfect Union? Religion, Politics, and Competing Stories of America," *Sociology of Religion* 79, no. 2 (2018): 172–95.

33. Herbert A. Simon, *Administrative Behavior* (New York: Simon and Schuster, 1947).

34. Jeffrey Alexander, "On the Social Construction of Moral Universals: The 'Holocaust' from War Crime to Trauma Drama," *European Journal of Social Theory* 5, no. 1 (2022): 5–85; Daniel Levy and Natan Sznaider, "The Institutionalization of Cosmopolitan Morality: The Holocaust and Human Rights," *Journal of Human Rights* 3, no. 2 (2004): 143–57.

35. Lauren A. Rivera, "Managing 'Spoiled' National Identity: War, Tourism, and Memory in Croatia," *American Sociological Review* 73, no. 4 (2008): 613–34; Leanne White and Elspeth Frew, *Dark Tourism and Place Identity: Managing and Interpreting Dark Places* (New York: Routledge, 2013).

36. Waldo, *The Enterprise of Public Administration*, 79.

## APPENDIX B. METHODOLOGICAL BACKGROUND INFORMATION

1. Others note that, in contrast to the British and French government, the U.S. government tends to have a notably representative workforce that reflects the nation's diversity. See James N. Druckman and Lawrence R. Jacobs. *Who Governs? Presidents, Public Opinion, and Manipulation* (Chicago: University of Chicago Press, 2015); Stephen Skowronek, John A. Dearborn, and Desmond S. King, *Phantoms of a Beleaguered Republic: The Deep State and the Unitary Executive* (New York: Oxford University Press, 2021), 16.

2. Jaime Kucinskas and Yvonne Zylan, "Walking the Moral Tightrope: Federal Civil Servants' Loyalties, Caution, and Resistance Under the Trump Administration," *American Journal of Sociology* 128, no. 6 (2023).

# REFERENCES

Abel, David. "EPA Workers Protest Budget Cuts in March to Boston Common." *Boston Globe*, May 24, 2017. https://www.bostonglobe.com/metro/2017/05/24/protest/PkybDk5esowmHOkmzUGQiL/story.html.

Aberbach, J. D., and B. A. Rockman. "Clashing Beliefs Within the Executive Branch: The Nixon Administration Bureaucracy." *American Political Science Review* 70, no. 2 (1976): 456–68.

Aberbach, Joel D., and Bert A. Rockman. *In the Web of Politics: Three Decades of the U.S. Federal Executive*. Washington, DC: Brookings Institution Press, 2000.

Alexander, Jeffrey. "On the Social Construction of Moral Universals: The 'Holocaust' from War Crime to Trauma Drama." *European Journal of Social Theory* 5, no. 1 (2022): 5–85.

Architect of the Capitol. "Neoclassical." Accessed July 8, 2023. https://www.aoc.gov/explore-capitol-campus/buildings-grounds/neoclassical.

Arendt, Hannah. *Eichmann in Jerusalem: A Report on the Banality of Evil*. New York: Viking, 1963.

——. *The Origins of Totalitarianism*. New York: Schocken, 1951.

——. "Personal Responsibility Under Dictatorship." In *Responsibility and Judgment*, 17–48. New York: Schocken, 2003 [1964].

Ashforth, Blake E., Glen E. Kreiner, Mark A. Clark, and Mel Fugate. "Normalizing Dirty Work: Managerial Tactics for Countering Occupational Taint." *Academy of Management Journal* 50, no. 1 (2007): 149–74.

Bailey, Stephen K. "Ethics and the Public Service." *Public Administration Review* 24, no. 4 (1964): 234–43.

Bandura, Albert. "Social Cognitive Theory of Personality." In *The Coherence of Personality: Social-Cognitive Bases of Consistency, Variability, and Organization*, ed. D Cervone and Y. Shoda, 185–241. New York: Guilford, 1999.

——. "Social Cognitive Theory of Self-Regulation." *Organizational Behavior and Human Decision Processes* 50, no. 2 (1991). https://doi.org/10.1016/0749-5978(91)90022-L.

Barnard, Chester I. *The Functions of the Executive*. Cambridge, MA: Harvard University Press, 1947.

Barnes, Julian E., and Matthew Rosenberg. "Charges of Ukrainian Meddling? A Russian Operation, U.S. Intelligence Says." *New York Times*, November 22, 2019. https://www.nytimes.com/2019/11/22/us/politics/ukraine-russia-interference.html.

Bashshur, Michael R., Ana Hernández, and Vicente González-Romá. "When Managers and Their Teams Disagree: A Longitudinal Look at the Consequences of Differences in Perceptions of Organizational Support." *Journal of Applied Psychology* 96, no. 3 (2011): 558–73. https://doi.org/10.1037/a0022675.

Bechev, Dimitar. *Turkey Under Erdoğan: How a Country Turned from Democracy and the West*. New Haven, CT: Yale University Press, 2022.

Bellante, Don, and Albert N. Link. "Are Public Sector Workers More Risk-Averse Than Private Sector Workers?" *Industrial and Labor Relations Review* 34, no. 3 (1981): 408–12.

Benda, P. M., and C. H. Levine. "Reagan and the Bureaucracy: The Bequest, the Promise, and the Legacy." In *The Reagan Legacy: Promise and Performance*, ed. Charles O. Jones. Chatham, NJ: Chatham House, 1988. 102–42.

Benen, Steve. "In the Middle of the Night, Trump Takes Step to Refill the Swamp." *MaddowBlog* (blog). *MSNBC*, January 20, 2021. https://www.msnbc.com/rachel-maddow-show/maddowblog/middle-night-trump-takes-step-refill-swamp-n1254872.

Benford, Robert D., and David A. Snow. "Framing Processes and Social Movements: An Overview and Assessment." *Annual Review of Sociology* 26 (2000): 611–39.

Ben-Ghiat, Ruth. *Strongmen: Mussolini to the Present*. New York: Norton, 2020.

Benjamin, Ludy T., Jr., and Jeffry A. Simpson. "The Power of the Situation: The Impact of Milgram's Obedience Studies on Personality and Social Psychology." *American Psychologist* 64, no. 1 (2009): 12.

Benson, Michael L. "Denying the Guilty Mind: Accounting for Involvement in a White Collar Crime." *Criminology* 23, no. 4 (November 1985): 583–607. https://doi.org/10.1111/j.1745-9125.1985.tb00365.x.

Bersch, Katherine Schlosser, Sérgio Praça, and Matthew M. Taylor. "An Archipelago of Excellence? Autonomous Capacity Among Brazilian State Agencies." Paper presented at the Princeton University–Universidade de São Paulo Conference on "State Capacity in the Developing World," São Paulo, Brazil, February 2012.

——. "Bureaucratic Capacity and Political Autonomy Within National States: Mapping the Archipelago of Excellence in Brazil." In *States in the Developing World*, ed. Miguel A. Centeno, Atul Kohli, and Deborah J. Yashar, 157–83. Cambridge: Cambridge University Press, 2017.

Birx, Deborah L. *Silent Invasion: The Untold Story of the Trump Administration, Covid-19, and Preventing the Next Pandemic Before It's Too Late*. New York: HarperCollins, 2022.

Bitektine, Alex, Patrick Haack, Joel Bothello, and Johanna Mair. "Inhabited Actors: Internalizing Institutions Through Communication and Actorhood Models." *Journal of Management Studies* 57, no. 4 (2020): 885–97. https://doi.org/10.1111/joms.12560.

Bolton, Alexander, John M. De Figueiredo, and David E. Lewis. "Elections, Ideology, and Turnover in the US Federal Government." *Journal of Public Administration Research and Theory* 31, no. 2 (2021): 451–66.

Booker, Brakkton. "With 'Pussyhats' at Women's Marches, Headwear Sends a Defiant Message." *NPR*, January 22, 2017. https://www.npr.org/2017/01 /22/511048762/with-pussyhats-at-womens-marches-headwear-sends-a -defiant-message.

Braun, Robert. "Religious Minorities and Resistance to Genocide: The Collective Rescue of Jews in the Netherlands During the Holocaust." *American Political Science Review* 110, no. 1 (2016): 127–47.

Braunstein, Ruth. "A (More) Perfect Union? Religion, Politics, and Competing Stories of America." *Sociology of Religion* 79, no. 2 (2018): 172–95.

Bromwich, Jonah E., and Ben Protess. "Trump Guilty on All Counts in Hush-Money Case." *New York Times*, May 30, 2024. https://www.nytimes .com/live/2024/05/31/nyregion/trump-news-guilty-verdict.

Broomfield, Matt. "Women's March Against Donald Trump Is the Largest Day of Protests in US History, Say Political Scientists." *Independent*, January 23, 2017. https://www.independent.co.uk/news/world/americas /womens-march-anti-donald-trump-womens-rights-largest-protest -demonstration-us-history-political-scientists-a7541081.html.

Browning, Christopher. *Ordinary Men: Reserve Police Battalion 101 and the Final Solution in Poland*. New York: Harper Collins, 1992.

Brustein, William. *The Logic of Evil: The Social Origins of the Nazi Party, 1925–1933*. New Haven, CT: Yale University Press, 1998.

Buchanan, Larry, Quoctrung Bui, and Jugal K. Patel. "Black Lives Matter May Be the Largest Movement in U.S. History." *New York Times*, July 3, 2020. https://www.nytimes.com/interactive/2020/07/03/us/george-floyd -protests-crowd-size.html.

Burt, Ronald S. "The Social Structure of Competition." In *Networks and Organizations: Structure, Form, and Action*, ed. N. Nohria and Robert G. Eccles. Boston: Harvard Business School Press, 1992.

——. "The Social Structure of Competition." *Networks and Organizations: Structure, Form, and Action* 4, no. 3 (1992): 57–91.

Butler, Judith. "Hannah Arendt's Challenge to Adolf Eichmann." Opinion, *The Guardian*, August 29, 2011. https://www.theguardian.com/commentisfree /2011/aug/29/hannah-arendt-adolf-eichmann-banality-of-evil.

Caldwell, C., and M. Canuta-Carranco. "'Organizational Terrorism' and Moral Choices—Exercising Voice When the Leader Is the Problem." *Journal of Business Ethics* 97, no. 1 (2010): 159–71.

Carmeli, Abraham, and Jody Hoffer Gittell. "High-Quality Relationships, Psychological Safety, and Learning from Failures in Work Organizations." *Journal of Organizational Behavior* 30, no. 6 (2009): 709–29.

Carnahan, Thomas, and Sam McFarland. "Revisiting the Stanford Prison Experiment: Could Participant Self-Selection Have Led to the Cruelty?" *Personality and Social Psychology Bulletin* 33, no. 5 (2007): 603–14.

Carpenter, Daniel, and David A. Moss, eds. *Preventing Regulatory Capture: Special Interest Influence and How to Limit It*. New York: Cambridge University Press, 2013.

Cesarini, David. *Eichmann: His Life and Crimes*. London: Vintage, 2005.

Chen, Carolyn. *Work Pray Code: When Work Becomes Religion in Silicon Valley*. Princeton, NJ: Princeton University Press, 2022.

Cheney, Liz. *Oath and Honor: A Memoir and a Warning*. New York: Little, Brown, 2023.

Collins, Kaitlin, Zachary Cohen, Kylie Atwood, and Kevin Liptak. "Bolton Manuscript Revelations Thrust Little-Known White House Office into Spotlight." *CNN*, January 27, 2020. https://www.cnn.com/2020/01/27 /politics/nsc-records-management-division-bolton-manuscript/index.html.

Comey, James. *A Higher Loyalty: Truth, Lies, and Leadership*. New York: Flatiron, 2018.

Cook, Nancy. "Trump's Staffing Struggle: After 3 Years, Unfilled Jobs Across the Administration." *Politico*, January 20, 2020. https://www.politico.com /news/2020/01/20/trumps-staffing-struggle-unfilled-jobs-100991.

Coppins, McKay. "The Man Who Broke Politics." *The Atlantic*, October 15, 2018. https://www.theatlantic.com/magazine/archive/2018/11/newt-gingrich -says-youre-welcome/570832/.

Cornell Law School/Legal Information Institute. "5 U.S. Code § 3331—Oath of Office." Accessed September 8, 2021. https://www.law.cornell.edu/uscode /text/5/3331.

Crewson, Philip E. "Public Service Motivation: Building Empirical Evidence of Incidence and Effect." *Journal of Public Administration Research and Theory* 7, no. 4 (1997): 499–518. https://doi.org/10.1093/oxfordjournals .jpart.a024363.

Dahl, Robert Alan. *Polyarchy: Participation and Opposition*. New Haven, CT: Yale University Press, 1972.

The Daily Conversation. "Trump on Tape: I Grab Women 'by the Pu**y.'" *YouTube*, October 7, 2017. Accessed June 27, 2023. https://www.youtube .com/watch?v=WhsSzIS84ks.

Davenport, Coral. "E.P.A. Workers Try to Block Pruitt in Show of Defiance." *New York Times*, February 16, 2017. https://www.nytimes.com/2017/02/16 /us/politics/scott-pruitt-environmental-protection-agency.html.

Davenport, Coral, Lisa Friedman, and Maggie Haberman. "E.P.A. Chief Scott Pruitt Resigns Under a Cloud of Ethics Scandals." *New York Times*, July 5, 2018. https://www.nytimes.com/2018/07/05/climate/scott-pruitt-epa -trump.html.

Davis, Aaron C. "How Trump Amassed a Red State Army in the Nation's Capitol." *Washington Post*, October 1, 2020. https://www.washingtonpost.com /investigations/how-trump-amassed-a-red-state-army-in-the-nations -capital--and-could-do-so-again/2020/10/01/2f10e17c-f9d6-11ea-a275 -1a2c2d36e1f1_story.html.

Dawsey, Josh, Rosalind S. Helderman, and David A. Fahrenthold. "How Trump Abandoned His Pledge to 'Drain the Swamp.'" *Washington Post*, October 24, 2020. https://www.washingtonpost.com/politics/trump-drain -the-swamp/2020/10/24/52c7682c-0a5a-11eb-9be6-cf25fb429f1a_story.html.

DeJonge Schuman, Loren, Paul Hitlin, and Nadzeya Shutava. "Trust in Government: A Close Look at Public Perceptions of the Federal Government and Its Employees." *Partnership for Public Service*. March 23, 2022. https://

ourpublicservice.org/video/trust-in-government-public-perceptions-of
-the-federal-government/.

Diamond, Larry Jay. *The Spirit of Democracy: The Struggle to Build Free Societies Throughout the World.* 1st ed. New York: Times Books/Henry Holt, 2008.

Dillon, Lindsey, Christopher Sellers, Vivian Underhill, Nicholas Shapiro, Jennifer Liss Ohayon, Marianne Sullivan, Phil Brown, Jill Harrison, Sara Wylie, and the "EPA Under Siege" Writing Group. "The Environmental Protection Agency in the Early Trump Administration: Prelude to Regulatory Capture." *American Journal of Public Health* 108, no. S2 (April 2018): S89–S94. https://doi.org/10.2105/AJPH.2018.304360.

Ditton, Jason. "Alibis and Aliases: Some Notes on the 'Motives' of Fiddling Bread Salesman." *Sociology* 11, no. 2 (1977): 233–55. https://doi.org/10.1177/003803857701100201.

Doherty, Kathleen M., David E. Lewis, and Scott Limbocker. "Executive Control and Turnover in the Senior Executive Service." *Journal of Public Administration Research and Theory* 29, no. 2 (2019): 159–74.

Dowding, Keith, and Peter John. "The Three Exit, Three Voice and Loyalty Framework: A Test with Survey Data on Local Services." *Political Studies* 56, no. 2 (June 2008): 288–311. https://doi.org/10.1111/j.1467-9248.2007.00688.x.

Dowding, Keith, Peter John, Thanos Mergoupis, and Mark Vugt. "Exit, Voice and Loyalty: Analytic and Empirical Developments." *European Journal of Political Research* 37, no. 4 (June 2000): 469–95. https://doi.org/10.1111/1475-6765.00522.

Downs, George W., and Patrick D. Larkey. *The Search for Government Efficiency: From Hubris to Helplessness.* New York: Random House, 1986.

Dreisbach, Tom, and Noah Caldwell. "The Trump Campaign Embraces Jan. 6 Rioters with Money and Pardon Promises." *NPR*, January 4, 2024. https://www.npr.org/2024/01/04/1218672628/the-trump-campaign
-embraces-jan-6-rioters-with-money-and-pardon-promises.

Druckman, James N., and Lawrence R. Jacobs. *Who Governs? Presidents, Public Opinion, and Manipulation.* Chicago: University of Chicago Press, 2015.

Elon, Amos. "Introduction." In *Eichmann in Jerusalem: A Report on the Banality of Evil,* by Hannah Arendt, vii–xxiii. New York: Penguin Classics, 2006.

Elsbach, Kimberly D., and C. B. Bhattacharya. "Defining Who You Are by What You're Not: Organizational Disidentification and the National

Rifle Association." *Organization Science* 12, no. 4 (2001): 393–413. https://www.jstor.org/stable/3085979.

Emirbayer, Mustafa, and Ann Mische. "What Is Agency?" *American Journal of Sociology* 103, no. 4 (1998): 962–1023.

"Energy Secretary Swearing-in Ceremony." *C-SPAN*, March 2, 2017. https://www.c-span.org/video/?424865-2/energy-secretary-swearing-ceremony.

Fahrenthold, David A., Joshua Partlow, and Carol D. Leonnig. "Trump's Children Brought Secret Service Money to the Family Business with Their Visits, Records Show." *Washington Post*, October 12, 2020. https://www.washingtonpost.com/politics/secret-service-spending-trump-kids/2020/10/12/ffc1c330-ff31-11ea-9ceb-061d646d9c67_story.html.

Farrell, Dan. "Exit, Voice, Loyalty, and Neglect as Responses to Job Dissatisfaction: A Multidimensional Scaling Study." *Academy of Management Journal* 26, no. 4 (1983): 596–607.

Fazekas, Mihály, and István János Tóth. "From Corruption to State Capture: A New Analytical Framework with Empirical Applications from Hungary." *Political Research Quarterly* 69, no. 2 (2016): 320–34. https://doi.org/10.1177/1065912916639137.

Federal Pay. "GS-14 Pay Scale—General Schedule 2019." *Federal Pay*, 2019. https://www.federalpay.org/gs/2019/GS-14.

Federal Register. "Reducing Regulation and Controlling Regulatory Costs." *Federal Register*, February 3, 2017. https://www.federalregister.gov/documents/2017/02/03/2017-02451/reducing-regulation-and-controlling-regulatory-costs.

Festinger, Leon. *A Theory of Cognitive Dissonance.* Vol. 2. Stanford, CA: Stanford University Press, 2001.

Fisher, Dana R. *American Resistance: From the Women's March to the Blue Wave.* New York: Columbia University Press, 2019.

Fligstein, Neil. "Social Skill and the Theory of Fields." *Sociological Theory* 19, no. 2 (2001): 105–25.

Fligstein, Neil, and Doug McAdam. *A Theory of Fields.* Oxford: Oxford University Press, 2012.

——. "Toward a General Theory of Strategic Action Fields." *Sociological Theory* 29, no. 1 (2011): 1–26.

Frederickson, David G., and H. George Frederickson. "The Paradox of Distance and the Problem of Differentiation." In *The Spirit of Public*

*Administration*, ed. H. George Frederickson, 183–94. San Francisco: Jossey-Bass, 1997.

Frederickson, H. George. *The Spirit of Public Administration*. 1st ed. San Francisco: Jossey-Bass, 1997.

Froomkin, Dan. "Impeachment Witnesses Highlight Plight of Career Civil Servants Under Trump." *Press Watch*, November 22, 2019. https://press-watchers.org/2019/11/impeachment-witnesses-highlight-plight-of-career-civil-servants-under-trump/

Fukuyama, Francis. "In Defense of the Deep State." *Asia Pacific Journal of Public Administration* 46 (August 25, 2023): 1–12. https://doi.org/10.1080/23276665.2023.2249142.

Gambino, Lauren. "Scott Pruitt Confirmation Hearing for Environmental Protection Agency: The Key Points." *The Guardian*, January 18, 2017. https://www.theguardian.com/us-news/2017/jan/18/scott-pruitt-confirmation-hearing-epa-key-points.

Gjelten, Tom. "Peaceful Protesters Tear-Gassed to Clear Way for Trump Church Photo-Op." *NPR*, June 1, 2020. https://www.npr.org/2020/06/01/867532070/trumps-unannounced-church-visit-angers-church-officials.

Glaeser, Andreas. *Political Epistemics: The Secret Police, the Opposition, and the End of East German Socialism*. Chicago: University of Chicago Press, 2011.

Glasius, Marlies. "What Authoritarianism Is . . . and Is Not: A Practice Perspective." *International Affairs* 94, no. 3 (May 1, 2018): 515–33. https://doi.org/10.1093/ia/iiy060.

Goffman, Erving. *Frame Analysis: An Essay on the Organization of Experience*. Cambridge, MA: Harvard University Press, 1974.

——. *The Presentation of Self in Everyday Life*. Reprint, London: Penguin, 1959.

Golden, Marissa M. "Exit, Voice, Loyalty, and Neglect: Bureaucratic Responses to Presidential Control During the Reagan Administration." *Journal of Public Administration Research and Theory* 2, no. 1 (1992): 29–62.

——. *What Motivates Bureaucrats? Politics and Administration During the Reagan Years*. New York: Columbia University Press, 2000.

Goodsell, Charles T. *The Case for Bureaucracy: A Public Administration Polemic*. 3rd ed. Chatham, NJ: Chatham House, 1995.

Gordon, Sue. "Speaking Truth to Power: Lessons in Administrative Courage." Virtual panel presentation at the American Political Science Association, November 30, 2023.

Granovetter, Mark. "The Strength of Weak Ties: A Network Theory Revisited." *Sociological Theory* 1 (1983): 201. https://doi.org/10.2307/202051.

Green, Miranda. "Pruitt Faces Resistance from Ethanol Groups During Midwest Trips." *The Hill* (blog), June 13, 2018. https://thehill.com/policy/energy-environment/392076-pruitt-met-with-resistance-from-ethanol-groups-during-midwest-trips/.

Haidt, Jonathan. "The Emotional Dog and Its Rational Tail: A Social Intuitionist Approach to Moral Judgment." *Psychological Review* 108, no. 4 (2001): 814.

——. "The New Synthesis in Moral Psychology." *Science* 316, no. 5827 (2007): 998–1002.

Haney, Craig, and Philip G. Zimbardo. "Persistent Dispositionalism in Interactionist Clothing: Fundamental Attribution Error in Explaining Prison Abuse." *Personality and Social Psychology Bulletin* 35, no. 6 (2009): 807–14.

Harms, Peter D., Dustin Wood, Karen Landay, Paul B. Lester, and Gretchen Vogelgesang Lester. "Autocratic Leaders and Authoritarian Followers Revisited: A Review and Agenda for the Future." *Leadership Quarterly* 29, no. 1 (2018): 105–22.

Harris, Richard A., and Sidney M. Milkis. *The Politics of Regulatory Change: A Tale of Two Agencies.* New York: Oxford University Press, 1989.

Harris, Stanley G. "Organizational Culture and Individual Sensemaking: A Schema-Based Perspective." *Organization Science* 5, no. 3 (1994): 309–21.

Haslam, S. Alexander, and Stephen D. Reicher. "Beyond the Banality of Evil: Three Dynamics of an Interactionist Social Psychology of Tyranny." *Personality and Social Psychology Bulletin* 33, no. 5 (2007): 615–22.

Haslam, S. Alexander, and Stephen D. Reicher. "Contesting the 'Nature' of Conformity: What Milgram and Zimbardo's Studies Really Show." *PLoS Biology* 10, no. 11 (2012): e1001426.

Hathaway, Oona A. "Reengaging on Treaties and Other International Agreements (Part I): President Donald Trump's Rejection of International Law." *Just Security*, October 2, 2020. https://www.justsecurity.org/72656/reengaging-on-treaties-and-other-international-agreements-part-i-president-donald-trumps-rejection-of-international-law/.

Heclo, Hugh. *A Government of Strangers: Executive Politics in Washington.* Washington, DC: Brookings Institute, 1977.

——. "The Spirit of Public Administration." *PS: Political Science & Politics* 35, no. 4 (2002): 689–94.

Hennessey, Susan, and Helen Klein Murillo. "The Law of Leaks." *LawFare* (blog), February 15, 2017. https://www.lawfareblog.com/law-leaks.

Heritage Foundation. "Mandate for Leadership: The Conservative Promise." Eds. Paul Dans and Steven Groves. Project 2025, 2023.

Hinojosa, Amanda S., William L. Gardner, H. Jack Walker, Claudia Cogliser, and Daniel Gullifor. "A Review of Cognitive Dissonance Theory in Management Research: Opportunities for Further Development." *Journal of Management* 43, no. 1 (2017): 170–99. https://doi.org/10.1177/0149206316668236.

Hirschman, Albert O. *Exit, Voice, and Loyalty: Responses to Decline in Firms, Organizations, and States.* Cambridge, MA: Harvard University Press, 1970.

Hoang, Kimberly Kay. *Spiderweb Capitalism: How Global Elites Exploit Frontier Markets.* Princeton, NJ: Princeton University Press, 2022.

Hochschild, Arlie Russel. *The Managed Heart: Commercialization of Human Feeling.* Updated ed. Berkeley: University of California Press, 2012.

Hollander, Jocelyn A., and Rachel L. Einwohner. "Conceptualizing Resistance." *Sociological Forum* 19, no. 4 (2004): 533–54.

"Homeland Security Secretary Kirstjen Nielsen Exits Trump's Cabinet." *New York Times* Video Transcript, April 8, 2019. https://www.nytimes.com/video/us/politics/100000006213836/kirstjen-nielsen-resigns-dhs.html.

Hoogenboom, Ari. "The Pendleton Act and the Civil Service." *American Historical Review* 64, no. 2 (1959): 301–18. https://doi.org/10.1086/ahr/64.2.301.

Hsu, Spencer S., and Tom Jackman. "Former Trump State Dept. Appointee Guilty in Jan. 6 Tunnel Assaults." *Washington Post,* July 20, 2023. https://www.washingtonpost.com/dc-md-va/2023/07/20/federico-klein-guilty-jan-6-trump-appointee/.

Hughes, Everett C. "Work and Self." In *The Sociological Eye: Selected Papers.* Abingdon, Oxon: Routledge, 1951.

Hutchinson, Cassidy. Testimony to the Select Committee to Investigate the January 6th Attack on the U.S. Capital. *PBS*, September 14, 2022. https://www.pbs.org/newshour/politics/read-the-transcripts-of-cassidy-hutchinsons-closed-door-jan-6-testimony.

Ingraham, Patricia W. *The Foundation of Merit: Public Service in American Democracy.* Baltimore, MD: Johns Hopkins University Press, 1995.

Institute for Policy Integrity. "Roundup: Trump-Era Agency Policy in the Courts." *Policy Integrity*, 2021. https://policyintegrity.org/trump-court-roundup.

Irfan, Umair. "Trump's EPA Just Replaced Obama's Signature Climate Policy with a Much Weaker Rule." *Vox*, June 19, 2019. https://www.vox.com/2019/6/19/18684054/climate-change-clean-power-plan-repeal-affordable-emissions.

Isaac, Larry W., Anna W. Jacobs, Jaime Kucinskas, and Allison R. McGrath. "Social Movement Schools: Sites for Consciousness Transformation, Training, and Prefigurative Social Development." *Social Movement Studies* 19, no. 2 (March 3, 2020): 160–82. https://doi.org/10.1080/14742837.2019.1631151.

Jenkins, Craig J. *The Politics of Insurgency: The Farm Worker Movement in the 1960s.* New York: Columbia University Press, 1985.

Kahn, Robert L., Daniel Katz, Barbara Gutek, and Eugenia Barton. "Bureaucratic Encounters—An Evaluation of Government Services." *Journal of Applied Behavioral Science* 12, no. 2 (1976): 178–98. https://doi.org/10.1177/002188637601200203.

Kammeyer-Mueller, John D., Lauren S. Simon, and Bruce L. Rich. "The Psychic Cost of Doing Wrong: Ethical Conflict, Divestiture Socialization, and Emotional Exhaustion." *Journal of Management* 38, no. 3 (May 2012): 784–808. https://doi.org/10.1177/0149206310381133.

Kanno-Youngs, Zolan, Maggie Haberman, Michael D. Shear, and Eric Schmitt. "Kirstjen Nielsen Resigns as Trump's Homeland Security Secretary." *New York Times*, April 7, 2019. https://www.nytimes.com/2019/04/07/us/politics/kirstjen-nielsen-dhs-resigns.html.

Khazan, Olga. "The Unraveling of the Trump Era." *The Atlantic*, July 28, 2021. https://www.theatlantic.com/politics/archive/2021/07/which-trump-regulations-were-overturned-biden/619583/.

Kingdon, John W. "A Model of Agenda-Setting, with Applications." *Law Review M.S.U—D.C.L*, no. 2 (Summer 2001): 331–38.

Kirkpatrick, Jennet. "Resistant Exit." *Contemporary Political Theory* 18, no. 2 (June 2019): 135–57. https://doi.org/10.1057/s41296-018-0252-1.

Klandermans, Bert, and Dirk Oegema. "Potentials, Networks, Motivations, and Barriers: Steps Towards Participation in Social Movements." *American Sociological Review* 52, no. 4 (1987): 519–31.

Kluckhohn, Florence Rockwood. "Cultural Factors in Social Work Practice and Education." *Social Service Review* 25, no. 1 (1951): 38–47.

Kopp, Harry. "Members of the Foreign Service Regularly Grapple with the Professional and Moral Dilemma of Dissent." *Foreign Service Journal*, 2017. https://afsa.org/state-dissent-foreign-service.

Kucinskas, Jaime. *The Mindful Elite: Mobilizing from the Inside Out*. New York: Oxford University Press, 2019.

———. "The Unobtrusive Tactics of Religious Movements." *Sociology of Religion* 75, no. 4 (2014): 537–50. https://doi.org/10.1093/socrel/sru055.

Kucinskas, Jaime, and Yvonne Zylan. "Walking the Moral Tightrope: Federal Civil Servants' Loyalties, Caution, and Resistance Under the Trump Administration." *American Journal of Sociology* 128, no. 6 (2023). https://doi.org/10.1086/725313.

Leatherby, Lauren, Arielle Ray, Anjali Singhvi, Christiaan Triebert, Derek Watkins, and Haley Willis. "How a Presidential Rally Turned into a Capitol Rampage." *New York Times*, January 12, 2021. https://www.nytimes.com/interactive/2021/01/12/us/capitol-mob-timeline.html.

Lee, Soo-Young, and Andrew B. Whitford. "Exit, Voice, Loyalty, and Pay: Evidence from the Public Workforce." *Journal of Public Administration Research and Theory* 18, no. 4 (October 17, 2007): 647–71. https://doi.org/10.1093/jopart/mum029.

Lefcourt, Herbert M. "The Function of the Illusions of Control and Freedom." *American Psychologist* 28, no. 5 (1973): 417–25. https://doi.org/10.1037/h0034639.

Levitsky, Steven, and Daniel Ziblatt. *How Democracies Die*. New York: Broadway, 2018.

Levitt, Ross. "Two Resign in Protest from EPA Subcommittee." *CNN*, May 12, 2017. https://www.cnn.com/2017/05/12/politics/epa-resignation-protest-review-board/index.html.

Levy, Daniel, and Natan Sznaider. "The Institutionalization of Cosmopolitan Morality: The Holocaust and Human Rights." *Journal of Human Rights* 3, no. 2 (2004): 143–57.

Lewis, Michael. *The Fifth Risk*. New York: Norton, 2018.

Lotta, Gabriela, Gustavo M. Tavares, and Joana Story. "Political Attacks and the Undermining of the Bureaucracy: The Impact on Civil Servants' Well-Being." *Governance*, 2023. https://doi.org/10.1111/gove.12792.

Lowery, George, and Dana Cook. "Dwight Waldo Started It All." Maxwell School of Public Affairs, Syracuse University, December 12, 2019. https://www.maxwell.syr.edu/news/article/dwight-waldo-started-it-all.

Lozowick, Yaacov. *Hitler's Bureaucrats: The Nazi Security Police and the Banality of Evil*. New York: Continuum, 2003.

Luce, Edward. "Historian Heather Cox Richardson: 'Now People See What's Happening. Thank God!'" *Financial Times*, July 16, 2021. https://www.ft .com/content/08f3728c-bbff-493f-aa66-a1aa35dd3924.

Lyons, Sean T., Linda E. Duxbury, and Christopher A. Higgins. "A Comparison of the Values and Commitment of Private Sector, Public Sector, and Parapublic Sector Employees." *Public Administration Review* 66, no. 4 (July 2006): 605–18. https://doi.org/10.1111/j.1540-6210.2006.00620.x.

Mandel, David R. "The Obedience Alibi." *Analyze & Kritik* 20, no. 1 (1998): 74–94.

Mathews, Forrest David. *Politics for People: Finding a Responsible Public Voice*. Urbana: University of Illinois Press, 1999.

Malig, Kaela and Kristina Abovyan. "A Guide to the Criminal Cases Against Donald Trump." *Frontline*, September 11, 2024. https://www.pbs.org/wgbh /frontline/article/a-guide-to-the-criminal-cases-against-donald-trump/.

McAdam, Doug. *Freedom Summer*. New York: Oxford University Press, 1988.

McFarland, Sam, and Thomas Carnahan. "A Situation's First Powers Are Attracting Volunteers and Selecting Participants: A Reply to Haney and Zimbardo." *Personality and Social Psychology Bulletin* 35, no. 6 (2009): 815–18.

McGrath, April. "Dealing with Dissonance: A Review of Cognitive Dissonance Reduction." *Social and Personality Psychology Compass* 11, no. 12 (2017): e12362. https://doi.org/10.1111/spc3.12362.

Mead, George H. *Mind, Self, and Society*. Chicago: University of Chicago Press, 1934.

Meyer, John P., and Natalie Jean Allen. *Commitment in the Workplace: Theory, Research, and Application*. Thousand Oaks, CA: Sage, 1997.

Michaels, Jon D. "The American Deep State." *Notre Dame Law Review* 93, no. 4 (March 1, 2018): 1653. https://scholarship.law.nd.edu/ndlr/vol93/iss4/10.

——. "Trump and the 'Deep State': The Government Strikes Back." *Foreign Affairs* 96, no. 5 (2017): 52–56. https://www.jstor.org/stable/44821868.

Milgram, Stanley. "The Dilemma of Obedience." *Phi Delta Kappan* 55, no. 9 (1974): 603–6.

——. *Obedience to Authority: An Experimental View*. New York: Harper and Row, 1974.

——. "Obedience to Criminal Orders: The Compulsion to Do Evil." *Patterns of Prejudice* 1, no. 6 (1967): 3–7.

Miller Center and the University of Virginia. "McCarthyism and the Red Scare." Accessed June 29, 2022. https://millercenter.org/the-presidency /educational-resources/age-of-eisenhower/mcarthyism-red-scare.

Miller, Tim. *Why We Did It: A Travelogue from the Republican Road to Hell.* 1st edition. New York: HarperCollins, 2022.

Mills, C. Wright. "Situated Actions and Vocabularies of Motive." *American Sociological Review* 5, no. 6 (1940): 904–13.

Minor, W. William. "Techniques of Neutralization: A Reconceptualization and Empirical Examination." *Journal of Research in Crime and Delinquency* 18, no. 2 (1981): 295–318. https://doi.org/10.1177/002242788101800206.

Monier, Mel. "'Rest as Resistance:' Black Cyberfeminism, Collective Healing and Liberation on @TheNapMinistry." *Communication, Culture & Critique* 16, no. 3 (August 25, 2023): 119–25. https://doi.org/10.1093/ccc/tcad022.

Montanaro, Dominico. "6 Strongmen Trump Has Praised—and the Conflicts It Presents." *NPR*, May 2, 2017. https://www.npr.org/2017/05/02 /526520042/6-strongmen-trumps-praised-and-the-conflicts-it-presents.

Morrill, Calvin, Mayer N. Zald, and Hayagreeva Rao. "Covert Political Conflict in Organizations: Challenges from Below." *Annual Review of Sociology* 29, no. 1 (2003): 391–415.

Mosher, Frederick C. *Democracy and the Public Service*, 2nd ed. New York: Oxford University Press, 1982.

Moynihan, Donald. "Populism and the Deep State: The Attack on Public Service Under Trump." In *Democratic Backsliding and Public Administration*, ed. Michael W. Bauer, B. Guy Peters, Jon Pierre, Kutsal Yesilkagit, and Stefan Becker, 151–77. New York: Cambridge University Press, 2021. https://doi.org/10.1017/9781009023504.008.

——. "Trump Got Burned by a Major Mistake in His First Term. He Won't Make It Again." *Slate*, July 27, 2022. https://slate.com/news-and -politics/2022/07/donald-trump-schedule-f-civil-service-authoritarian.html.

Muno, W., and H. Briceño. "Autocratization and Public Administration: The Revolutionary-Populist Regime in Venezuela in Comparative Perspective." *Asia Pacific Journal of Public Administration* 45, no. 1 (2023): 73–92.

Nadeem, Reem. "Americans' Views of Government: Decades of Distrust, Enduring Support for Its Role." *Pew Research Center—U.S. Politics & Policy* (blog), June 6, 2022. https://www.pewresearch.org/politics/2022/06/06 /public-trust-in-government-2/.

Nathan, Richard P. *The Administrative Presidency.* New York: Wiley, 1983.

National Archives. "Presidential Advisory Commission on Election Integrity—The White House," July 13, 2017. https://trumpwhitehouse .archives.gov/articles/presidential-advisory-commission-election-integrity/.

Nawaz, Amna, and Matt Loffman. "New Poll Reveals What Voters Think of Trump's Federal Indictment." *PBS NewsHour*, June 16, 2023. https:// www.pbs.org/newshour/show/new-poll-reveals-what-voters-think -of-trumps-federal-indictment.

Naylor, Brian. "'A Huge Attack': Critics Decry Trump Order That Makes Firing Federal Workers Easier." *NPR*, October 31, 2020. https://www.npr .org/2020/10/31/929597578/a-huge-attack-critics-decry-trump-order-that -makes-firing-federal-workers-easier.

Newman, Alexander, Ross Donohue, and Nathan Eva. "Psychological Safety: A Systematic Review of the Literature." *Human Resource Management Review* 27, no. 3 (2017): 521–35.

*New York Times.* "The Jan. 6 Capitol Attack: Inquiries and Fallout." Accessed July 19, 2022. https://www.nytimes.com/news-event/jan-6-committee.

Niklasson, Birgitta, Peter Munk Christiansen, and Patrik Öhberg. "Speaking Truth to Power: Political Advisers' and Civil Servants' Responses to Perceived Harmful Policy Proposals." *Journal of Public Policy* 40, no. 3 (September 2020): 492–512. https://doi.org/10.1017/S0143814X18000508.

Niskanen, William. *Bureaucracy and Representative Government.* Chicago: Aldine Atherton, 1971.

Nur-Tegin, Kanybek, and Hans J. Czap. "Corruption: Democracy, Autocracy, and Political Stability." *Economic Analysis and Policy* 42, no. 1 (2012): 51–66.

O'Leary, Rosemary. *The Ethics of Dissent: Managing Guerrilla Government.* Washington, DC: CQ Press, 2020.

Oliner, Samuel P., and Pearl M. Oliner. *The Altruistic Personality: Rescuers of Jews in Nazi Europe.* New York: The Free Press, 1988.

Oliveira, Eloy, Gordon Abner, Shinwoo Lee, Kohei Suzuki, Hyunkang Hur, and James L. Perry. "What Does the Evidence Tell Us About Merit Principles and Government Performance?" *Public Administration* 102, no. 2 (2023): 1–23. https://doi.org/10.1111/padm.12945.

Olsen, Johan P. "Maybe It Is Time to Rediscover Bureaucracy." *Journal of Public Administration Research and Theory* 16, no. 1 (2006): 1–24.

Page, Benjamin, and Mark Petracca. *The American Presidency*. New York: McGraw Hill, 1983.

Park, Hun Myoung, and James L. Perry. "The Transformation of Governance: Who Are the New Public Servants and What Difference Does It Make for Democratic Governance?" *American Review of Public Administration* 43, no. 1 (2013): 26–49. https://doi.org/10.1177/0275074011433814.

Partnership for Public Service. "The Federal Workforce and the Trump Administration." *Our Public Service*, 2023. https://ourpublicservice.org/fed-figures/the-federal-workforce-and-the-trump-administration/.

——. "Who Is Quitting and Retiring: Important Fiscal 2021 Trends in the Federal Government." *Our Public Service*, 2023. https://ourpublicservice.org/fed-figures/attrition/.

Pellow, David N. "Framing Emerging Environmental Movement Tactics: Mobilizing Consensus, Demobilizing Conflict." *Sociological Forum* 14, no. 4 (1999): 659–83.

Perry, James L. *Managing Organizations to Sustain Passion for Public Service*. Cambridge: Cambridge University Press, 2020.

Perry, James L., Annie Hondeghem, and Lois Recascino Wise. "Revisiting the Motivational Bases of Public Service: Twenty Years of Research and an Agenda for the Future." *Public Administration Review* 70, no. 5 (2010): 681–90.

Perry, James L., and Lyman W. Porter. "Factors Affecting the Context for Motivation in Public Organizations." *Academy of Management Review* 7, no. 1 (January 1982): 89–98. https://doi.org/10.2307/257252.

Perry, James L., and Lois Recascino Wise. "The Motivational Bases of Public Service." *Public Administration Review* 50, no. 3 (1990): 367–73.

Piketty, Thomas. *Capital in the Twenty-First Century*. Cambridge, MA: Belknap Press of Harvard University Press, 2014.

Pinel, Elizabeth C., and William B. Swann Jr. "Finding the Self Through Others: Self-Verification and Social Movement Participation." In *Self, Identity, and Social Movements*, ed. Sheldon Stryker, Timothy J. Owens, and Robert W. White, 132–52. Minneapolis: University of Minnesota Press, 2000.

Pious, Richard M. *The American Presidency*. New York: Basic Books, 1979.

Pitts, Victoria L. "Reclaiming the Female Body: Embodied Identity Work, Resistance and the Grotesque." *Body & Society* 4, no. 3 (1998): 67–84.

Piven, Frances Fox, and Richard A. Cloward. *Poor People's Movements: Why They Succeed, How They Fail*. New York: Vintage, 1979.

Potter, Rachel Augustine. *Bending the Rules: Procedural Politicking in the Bureaucracy*. Chicago: University of Chicago Press, 2019.

Pozen, David E. "The Leaky Leviathan: Why the Government Condemns and Condones Unlawful Disclosures of Information." *Harvard Law Review* 127, no. 2 (2013): 512–635.

Prasad, Anshuman, and Pushkala Prasad. "Everyday Struggles at the Workplace: The Nature and Implications of Routine Resistance in Contemporary Organizations." *Research in the Sociology of Organizations* 15, no. 2 (1998): 225–57.

Racine, Karl A., and Elizabeth Wilkins. "Enforcing the Anti-Corruption Provisions of the Constitution." *Harvard Law & Policy Review* 13, no. 2 (2019): 449–69.

Ravven, Heidi. *The Self Beyond Itself: An Alternative History of Ethics, the New Brain Sciences, and the Myth of Free Will*. New York: New Press, 2013.

Reich, Robert. *Supercapitalism: The Transformation of Business, Democracy and Everyday Life*. New York: First Vintage, 2007.

Rein, Lisa. "Trump Takes Aim at Federal Bureaucracy with New Executive Orders Rolling Back Civil-Service Protections." *Washington Post*, May 26, 2018. https://www.washingtonpost.com/politics/trump-takes-aim-at-federal-bureaucracy-with-new-executive-orders-altering-civil-service-protections/2018/05/25/3ed8bf84-6055-11e8-9ee3-49d6d4814c4c_story.html.

Resh, William G. *Rethinking the Administrative Presidency: Trust, Intellectual Capital and Appointee-Careerist Relations in the George W. Bush Administration*. Baltimore, MD: Johns Hopkins University Press, 2015.

Richardson, Heather Cox. *Democracy Awakening: Notes on the State of America*. New York: Viking, 2023.

Rivera, Lauren A. "Managing 'Spoiled' National Identity: War, Tourism, and Memory in Croatia." *American Sociological Review* 73, no. 4 (2008): 613–34.

——. *Pedigree: How Elite Students Get Elite Jobs*. Princeton, NJ: Princeton University Press, 2015.

Rockman, Bert A. "The Modern Presidency and Theories of Accountability: Old Wine and Old Bottles." *Congress & the Presidency* 13, no. 2 (1986): 525–47.

Rohr, John Anthony. *To Run a Constitution: The Legitimacy of the Administrative State*. Lawrence: University Press of Kansas, 1986.

Rokeach, Milton. *The Nature of Human Values*. New York: Free Press, 1973.

Rourke, Francis E. "Executive Responsiveness to Presidential Policies: The Reagan Presidency." *Congress & the Presidency* 17, no. 1 (1990): 1–11.

Rubin, Jeffrey W. "Defining Resistance: Contested Interpretations of Everyday Acts." *Studies in Law, Politics, and Society* 15 (1996): 237–60.

Rusbult, Caryl E., Dan Farrell, Glen Rogers, and Arch G. Mainous III. "Impact of Exchange Variables on Exit, Voice, Loyalty, and Neglect: An Integrative Model of Responses to Declining Job Satisfaction." *Academy of Management Journal* 31, no. 3 (1988): 599–627.

Samuels, Brett. "Trump Ramps Up Rhetoric on Media, Calls Press 'The Enemy of the People.'" *The Hill*, April 5, 2019. https://thehill.com/homenews/administration/437610-trump-calls-press-the-enemy-of-the-people/.

Sands, Geneva. "Kirstjen Nielsen Says She Left DHS Because 'Saying No' Wasn't Enough." *CNN*, October 22, 2019. https://www.cnn.com/2019/10/22/politics/kirstjen-nielsen-speech/index.html.

Schmidt, Michael S. "In a Private Dinner, Trump Demanded Loyalty. Comey Demurred." *New York Times*, May 12, 2017. https://www.nytimes.com/2017/05/11/us/politics/trump-comey-firing.html.

Schneider, Benjamin, Harold W Goldstein, and D. Brent Smith. "The ASA Framework: An Update." *Personnel Psychology* 48, no. 4 (1995): 747–73.

Schulkin, Danielle, and Julia Brooks. "Loyalty Above All: The 'Shallow State' of the Trump Administration." Reiss Center on Law and Security at New York University School of Law. Just Security, November 2, 2020. https://www.justsecurity.org/73226/loyalty-above-all-the-shallow-state-of-the-trump-administration/.

Schumpeter, Joseph A. *Capitalism, Socialism, and Democracy*. London: Harper and Brothers, 1942.

Sciutto, Jim. "Exclusive: Vindman to Retire from Military. His Lawyer Blames White House 'Campaign of Bullying, Intimidation and Retaliation.'" *CNN*, July 8, 2020. https://www.cnn.com/2020/07/08/politics/vindman-retiring-alleged-white-house-retaliation/index.html.

Scott, James C. *Weapons of the Weak: Everyday Forms of Peasant Resistance*. New Haven, CT: Yale University Press, 1985.

Scott, Marvin B., and Stanford M. Lyman. "Accounts." *American Sociological Review* 33, no. 1 (1968): 46–62. https://doi.org/10.2307/2092239.

Shapiro, Stuart. *Trump and the Bureaucrats: The Fate of Neutral Competence*. Cham, Switzerland: Springer International, 2023. https://doi.org/10.1007/978-3-031-22079-1.

Shear, Michael D. "Top Homeland Security Officials Are Serving Illegally, G.A.O. Says." *New York Times*, August 14, 2020. https://www.nytimes.com/2020/08/14/us/politics/homeland-security-illegal-gao.html.

Shepherd, David, and Mark Button. "Organizational Inhibitions to Addressing Occupational Fraud: A Theory of Differential Rationalization." *Deviant Behavior* 40, no. 8 (2019): 971–91. https://doi.org/10.1080/01639625.2018.1453009.

Sherk, James, and Michael Rigas. "Schedule F and the Future of the Public Service." Virtual presentation at the National Academy of Public Administration, Washington, DC, June 29, 2023.

Shiff, Talia. "A Sociology of Discordance: Negotiating Schemas of Deservingness and Codified Law in US Asylum Status Determinations." *American Journal of Sociology* 127, no. 2 (2021): 337–75.

Simon, Herbert A. *Administrative Behavior*. New York: Simon and Schuster, 1947.

Skowronek, Stephen, John A. Dearborn, and Desmond S. King. *Phantoms of a Beleaguered Republic: The Deep State and the Unitary Executive*. New, expanded ed. New York: Oxford University Press, 2021.

Snow, D. A., and R. D. Benford. "Ideology, Frame Resonance, and Participant Mobilization." *International Social Movement Research* 1, no. 1 (1988): 197–217.

——. "Master Frames and Cycles of Protest." In *Frontiers in Social Movement Theory*, ed. Aldon Morris and Carol McClung Mueller. New Haven, CT: Yale University Press, 1992.

Snow, David A., and Leon Anderson. "Identity Work Among the Homeless: The Verbal Construction and Avowal of Personal Identities." *American Journal of Sociology* 92, no. 6 (1987): 1336–71.

Snow, David A., and Doug McAdam. "Identity Work Processes in the Context of Social Movements: Clarifying the Identity/Movement Nexus." In *Self, Identity, and Social Movements*, ed. Sheldon Stryker, Timothy J. Owens, and Robert W. White, 41–67. Minneapolis: University of Minnesota Press, 2000.

Snow, David A., E. Burke Rochford, Steven K. Worden, and Robert D. Benford. "Frame Alignment Processes, Micromobilization, and Movement Participation." *American Sociological Review* 51, no. 4 (1986): 464–81.

Snyder, Timothy. *On Tyranny: Twenty Lessons from the Twentieth Century.* New York: Tim Duggan, 2017.

Staub, E., B. Tursky, and G. E. Schwartz. "Self-Control and Predictability: Their Effects on Reactions to Aversive Stimulation." *Journal of Personality and Social Psychology* 18, no. 2 (1971): 157.

Staub, Ervin. *The Psychology of Good and Evil: Why Children, Adults, and Groups Help and Harm Others.* Cambridge: Cambridge University Press, 2003.

Stillman, Richard. "A Tribute to Dwight Waldo." *Institute of Governmental Studies Public Affairs Report* 42, no. 1 (2001).

Stillman, Richard J., II. *Preface to Public Administration: A Search for Themes and Directions.* New York: St. Martin's Press, 1990, 20.

Story, Joana, Gabriela Lotta, and Gustavo M Tavares. "(Mis)Led by an Outsider: Abusive Supervision, Disengagement, and Silence in Politicized Bureaucracies." *Journal of Public Administration Research and Theory* 33, no. 4 (March 29, 2023): 549–62. https://doi.org/10.1093/jopart/muad004.

Stryker, Sheldon. "Identity Competition: Key to Differential Social Movement Participation?" In *Self, Identity, and Social Movements*, ed. Sheldon Stryker, Timothy J. Owens, and Robert W. White, 21–40. Minneapolis: University of Minnesota Press, 2000.

Stryker, Sheldon, and Richard T. Serpe. "Commitment, Identity Salience, and Role Behavior: A Theory and Research Example." In *Personality, Roles and Social Behavior*, ed. W. Ickes and Eric S. Knowles, 199–218. New York: Springer-Verlag, 1982.

Stryker, Sheldon, Timothy J. Owens, and Robert W. White, eds. *Self, Identity, and Social Movements.* Vol. 13. Minneapolis: University of Minnesota Press, 2000.

Stuart Mill, John. *Considerations on Representative Government*, 1861. https://www.gutenberg.org/files/5669/5669-h/5669-h.htm.

Swan, Jonathan. "A Radical Plan for Trump's Second Turn." *Axios*, July 22, 2022. https://www.axios.com/2022/07/22/trump-2025-radical-plan-second-term.

Swan, Jonathan, Charlie Savage, and Maggie Haberman. "Trump and Allies Forge Plans to Increase Presidential Power in 2025." *New York Times*,

July 17, 2023. https://www.nytimes.com/2023/07/17/us/politics/trump
-plans-2025.html.

Swidler, Ann. *Talk of Love: How Culture Matters*. Chicago: University of Chicago Press, 2001.

Sykes, Gresham M., and David Matza. "Techniques of Neutralization: A Theory of Delinquency." *American Sociological Review* 22, no. 6 (1957): 664–70. https://doi.org/10.2307/2089195.

Tamkin, Emily. "Here's What Happened to a USAID Official Who Ran Afoul of Mike Pence." *BuzzFeed News*, September 18, 2018. https://www.buzzfeednews.com/article/emilytamkin/usaid-christians-aid-iraq-pence-interference.

Taylor, Miles. *Blowback: A Warning to Save Democracy from the Next Trump*. New York: Atria, 2024.

Taylor, Shelley E., and Marci Lobel. "Social Comparison Activity Under Threat: Downward Evaluation and Upward Contacts." *Psychological Review* 96, no. 4 (1989): 569–75. https://doi.org/10.1037/0033-295X.96.4.569.

Te Brake, Hans, and Bart Nauta. "Caught Between Is and Ought: The Moral Dissonance Model." *Frontiers in Psychiatry* 13 (2022): 906231. https://doi.org/10.3389/fpsyt.2022.906231.

Thoits, Peggy A. "Multiple Identities and Psychological Well-Being: A Reformation and Test of the Social Isolation Hypothesis." *American Sociological Review* 48, no. 2 (1983): 174–87.

——. "On Merging Identity Theory and Stress Research." *Social Psychology Quarterly* 54, no. 2 (1991).

Tilly, Charles. *Why? What Happens When People Give Reasons . . . and Why*. Princeton, NJ: Princeton University Press, 2008.

Todorov, Cvetan. *Facing the Extreme: Moral Life in the Concentration Camp*. New York: Henry Holt, 1997.

Tsang, Jo-Ann. "Moral Rationalization and the Integration of Situational Factors and Psychological Processes in Immoral Behavior." *Review of General Psychology* 6, no. 1 (March 2002): 25–50. https://doi.org/10.1037/1089-2680.6.1.25.

United States Attorney's Office, District of Columbia. "35 Months Since the Jan. 6 Attack on the Capitol." Department of Justice, December 6, 2023. https://www.justice.gov/usao-dc/33-months-jan-6-attack-capitol-0.

United States Environmental Protection Agency. "Our Mission and What We Do." January 29, 2023. https://www.epa.gov/aboutepa/our-mission-and -what-we-do.

Upadhyay, Devina, and Anu Gupta. "Morale, Welfare Measures, Job Satisfaction: The Key Mantras for Gaining Competitive Edge." *International Journal of Physical and Social Sciences* 2, no. 7 (2012): 80–94.

"Upholding Civil Service Protections and Merit System Principles." *Federal Register* 88, no. 179 (September 18, 2023): 63862–85. https://www.federalregister .gov/documents/2023/09/18/2023-19806/upholding-civil-service-protections -and-merit-system-principles.

U.S. Census Bureau. "U.S. Census Data," 2020. https://www.census.gov/data /tables/2020/demo/educational-attainment/cps-detailed-tables.html.

U.S. Department of Labor. "Federal Employers." Accessed June 26, 2023. http://www.dol.gov/agencies/odep/program-areas/employers/federal -employment.

U.S. Office of Special Counsel. "Federal Employee Hatch Act Information." Accessed June 20, 2022. https://osc.gov/Services/Pages/HatchAct-Federal .aspx#tabGroup12|tabGroup31.

Vandenabeele, Wouter, Gene A. Brewer, and Adrian Ritz. "Past, Present, and Future of Public Service Motivation Research." *Public Administration* 92, no. 4 (2014): 779–89.

Wagner, Erich. "OMB Reportedly Designates 88 Percent of Its Employees for Schedule F." *Government Executive*, November 23, 2020. https:// www.govexec.com/management/2020/11/omb-reportedly-designates -88-its-employees-schedule-f/170275/.

——. "Trump Vows to 'Shatter the Deep State,' Revive Schedule F and Move More Agencies Out of DC." *Government Executive*, March 21, 2023. https://www.govexec.com/workforce/2023/03/trump-vows-shatter -deep-state-revive-schedule-f-and-move-more-agencies-out-dc/384266/.

——. "White House Revives Controversial Retirement Cut Proposals." *Government Executive*, February 10, 2020. https://www.govexec.com/pay-benefits/2020 /02/white-house-revives-controversial-retirement-cut-proposals/163015/.

Waldo, Dwight. *The Administrative State: A Study of the Political Theory of American Public Administration*. Piscataway, NJ: Transaction, 2006.

——. *The Enterprise of Public Administration*. Novato, CA: Chandler and Sharp, 1980.

Weber, Max. *Economy and Society: An Outline of Interpretive Sociology*. Vol. 1. Berkeley: University of California Press, 1978.

Weitz, Rose. "Women and Their Hair: Seeking Power Through Resistance and Accommodation." *Gender & Society* 15, no. 5 (2001): 667–86.

White, David, and Marc Herzog. "Examining State Capacity in the Context of Electoral Authoritarianism, Regime Formation and Consolidation in Russia and Turkey." *Southeast European and Black Sea Studies*, 16, no.4 (2016): 551–69. https://doi.org/10.1080/14683857.2016.

White, Leanne, and Elspeth Frew. *Dark Tourism and Place Identity: Managing and Interpreting Dark Places*. New York: Routledge, 2013.

Whitehead, Andrew L., Samuel L. Perry, and Joseph O. Baker. "Make America Christian Again: Christian Nationalism and Voting for Donald Trump in the 2016 Presidential Election." *Sociology of Religion* 79, no. 2 (2018): 147–71.

Wildavsky, Aaron B. *The Politics of the Budgetary Process*. 4th ed. Boston: Little, Brown, 1984.

Winchester, Daniel, and Kyle D. Green. "Talking Your Self into It: How and When Accounts Shape Motivation for Action." *Sociological Theory* 37, no. 3 (September 2019): 257–81. https://doi.org/10.1177/0735275119869959.

Wolf, Martin. *The Crisis of Democratic Capitalism*. New York: Penguin Random House, 2023.

Woodward, Bob. *Fear: Trump in the White House*. New York: Simon and Schuster, 2018.

Woodward, Bob, and Carl Bernstein. "Woodward and Bernstein Thought Nixon Defined Corruption: Then Came Trump." *Washington Post*, June 3, 2022. https://www.washingtonpost.com/outlook/2022/06/05/woodward -bernstein-nixon-trump/.

Yovanovitch, Maria L. *Lessons from the Edge: A Memoir*. New York: Mariner, 2022.

Zimbardo, Philip. *The Lucifer Effect: How Good People Turn Evil*. London: Rider, 2007.

Zimbardo, Philip G., Craig Haney, W. Curtis Banks, and David Jaffe. "The Stanford Prison Experiment," 1971.

# INDEX

4-H Clubs, 45

Abadi, Yasin, 10, 59–60, 123–24, 154–55, 160–61, 186–90, 198–200, 207–8, 220–21
Aberbach, Joel, 10
*Access Hollywood*, television program, 64
Alexander, Jeffrey, 339
America First, 33–34, 335
American Moment, 335
Anderson, Rick, 200–204, 224–26, 332
Arendt, Hannah, 14–15, 147, 293, 312
Army, 57

Bailey, Stephen, 137
Bannon, Steve, 115
Barnard, Chester, 137, 303
Barr, William, 33
Bernstein, Carl, 32
Biden, Hunter, 128
Biden, Joseph, President, 32, 218–19
Birx, Deborah, 332

Black Lives Matter (BLM), 33
Blackburn, Ines, 140–41, 183, 208–15, 218, 224, 228, 371n,
BLM. *See* Black Lives Matter (BLM)
Boy Scouts of America, 45
Breitbart News, 115
Bureau of Alcohol, Tobacco, Firearms and Explosives. *See* United States Bureau of Alcohol, Tobacco, Firearms and Explosives
Burt, Ronald, 16–17
Bush, George W., President, 43, 125, 144, 164, 169, 245
Bush, Jeb, 365n
Butler, Judith, 14–15
Butler, Sean, 52, 60, 83–86, 90, 102–3, 105, 111–13, 116, 181

Carmeli, Abraham, 286
Carson, Ben, 133
CBP. *See* United States Customs and Border Protection

CDC. *See* Centers for Disease Control and Prevention (CDC)

Census Bureau. *See* United States Census Bureau

Center for American Freedom at America First Policy Institute, 332

Center for Renewing America, 335

Centers for Disease Control and Prevention (CDC), 338

Cheney, Liz, 330

Chertoff, Michael, 164

Civil Rights Act of 1965, 46

Civil Rights Division of the United States Department of Justice, 45

Civil Rights Office, 236

Civil Service Reform Act (CSRA) of 1978, 7

Clean Power Plan, 158

Clement, Joel, 125, 380n

Clinton, Hilary, 32, 128

Comey, James, 9, 126–27, 330

Conservative Partnership Institute, 335

Conway, Kellyanne, 374n

Cook, Nancy, 162

CSRA. *See* Civil Rights Reform act (CSRA) of 1978

Cuccinelli,Kenneth T., 164–65

Customs and Border Protection. *See* United States Customs and Border Protection (CBP)

Cybersecurity and Infrastructure Security Agency. *See* United States Cybersecurity and Infrastructure Security Agency

DEA. *See* United States Drug Enforcement Administration (DEA)

Department of Agriculture. *See* United States Department of Agriculture

Department of Commerce. *See* United States Department of Commerce (DOC)

Department of Defense. *See* United States Department of Defense

Department of Energy. *See* United States Department of Energy (DOE)

Department of Health and Human Services. *See* United States Department of Health and Human Services

Department of Homeland Security. *See* United States Department of Homeland Security

Department of Housing and Urban Development. *See* United States Department of Housing and Urban Development

Department of Interior. *See* United States Department of Interior

Department of Justice. *See* United States Department of Justice (DOJ)

Department of Labor. *See* United States Department of Labor (DOL)

Department of State. *See* United States Department of State (DOS)

Department of the Treasury. *See*
    United States Department of
    the Treasury (USDT)
Department of Transportation. *See*
    United States Department of
    Transportation
DiFranco, Elaine, 78–79
Dissent Channel, 197
DOC. *See* United States
    Department of Commerce
    (DOC)
DOE. *See* United States
    Department of Energy (DOE)
DOJ. *See* United States Department
    of Justice (DOJ)
DOL. *See* United States
    Department of Labor (DOL)
DOS. *See* United States
    Department of State (DOS)
Drug Enforcement Administration.
    *See* United States Drug
    Enforcement Administration
    (DEA)
Duterte, Rodrigo, 30

Eichmann, Adolf, 14–15
Environmental Protection
    Agency. *See* United States
    Environmental Protection
    Agency (EPA)
EPA. *See* United States
    Environmental Protection
    Agency (EPA)
Erdogan, Recep Tayyip, 30
Erving, Stuart, 327–28
Executive Order 13771, 134

Farmer, Sarah, 150, 158–61, 207, 373n,
    376n
FBI. *See* United States Federal
    Bureau of Investigation (FBI)
Federal Bureau of Emergency
    Management Agency.
    *See* United States Federal
    Emergency Management
    Agency (FEMA)
Federal Bureau of Investigation.
    *See* United States Federal
    Bureau of Investigation (FBI)
Federal Home Loan Mortgage
    Corporation. *See* United
    States Federal Home Loan
    Mortgage Corporation
    (Freddie Mac)
Federal Vacancies Reform Act,
    164–65
FEMA. *See* United States Federal
    Emergency Management
    Agency (FEMA)
Festinger, Leon, 69
FOIA. *See* Freedom of Information
    Act (FOIA)
Foster, Annette, 43–44, 49, 59, 75–76,
    129–30, 164, 175–76
Freddie Mac. *See* United
    States Federal Home Loan
    Mortgage Corporation
    (Freddie Mac)
Frederickson, David G., 337
Frederickson, H. George, 337
Freedom of Information Act
    (FOIA), 273, 385n
Future Farmers of America, 45

GAO. *See* United States Government Accountability Office (GAO)

General Schedule Levels, 220, 223, 264, 287

General Services Administration. *See* United States General Services Administration (GSA)

Gingrich, Newt, 65

Gittell, Jody Hoffer, 286

Glassman, Marie, 289–303, 307, 310, 313, 315–18, 326, 331, 389n

Goffman, Erving, 42, 243

Golden, Marissa M., 56, 104, 196, 287

Gorsuch, Anne, 236

Government Accountability Office. *See* United States Government Accountability Office (GAO)

GSA. *See* United States General Services Administration (GSA)

Hailwood, Gail, 103

Hatch Act, 24, 51–53, 70, 87, 93–94, 98–99, 101, 106, 360n, 365n, 374n

Hathaway, Oona, 34

Heclo, Hugh, 39–41

Heritage Foundation, 13, 172, 335, 392n

HHS. *See* United States Department of Health and Human Services (HHS)

Hill, Fiona, 175

Hirschman, Albert O., 39, 194–95, 224, 226, 235, 275

Hitler, Adolf, 293

Holocaust, 3, 14, 20, 95, 340, 387n

Homeland Security. *See* United States Department of Homeland Security

HUD. *See* United States Department of Housing and Urban Development

Hungary, 331

ICE. *See* United States Immigration and Customs Enforcement (ICE)

Immigration and Customs Enforcement. *See* United States Immigration and Customs Enforcement (ICE)

Inspector General. *See* United States Office of the Inspector General

Iran, 34

Jackson, Andrew, President, 336

Jefferson, Thomas, President, 41

Jinping, Xi, 30

Johnson, Lyndon, President, 46

Kelley, Brandon, 245–46

Kelly, John F., 144

Kennedy, John F., President, 46, 57

Kim Jong Un, 30

Klein, Frederico, 371n

Kushner, Jared, 32

Levitsky, Steven, 12, 34

LGBTQIA+, 99, 290

Liberty University, 293–94

Longi, Maria, 123–24, 208

Lopez, Ben, 3–6, 12, 266–67
Lorbel, Marci, 89

March for Our Lives, 98
March for Science, 64, 98, 105
Marsh, Steve, 129, 196–97
Massachusetts Institute of
    Technology (MIT) Institute for
    Policy Integrity, 326
Mattis, James, 76
McAleenan, Kevin, 164
McCafferty, Ralph, 51, 69, 76–77, 80,
    87–90, 95, 176–77, 207, 324–25
McCarthy, Joe, 57
McFarlane, Robert, 124
Mexico, 145
Milgram, Stanley, 14–15, 87
Miller, Steven, 335
Miller, Tim, 365n
MIT Institute for Policy Integrity.
    See Massachusetts Institute of
    Technology (MIT) Institute for
    Policy Integrity
Mnuchin, Steven, 163–64
Monier, Mel, 236
Mulvaney, Mick, 156, 163

National Institutes of Health
    (NIH), 68, 240
National Park Service
    (NPA), 337
National Science Foundation
    (NSF), 68, 206, 217, 255
National Security Council, 126, 175
Nazi Germany, 19–20
Nielsen, Kirstjen, 144–45, 164

NIH. See National Institutes of
    Health (NIH)
Nixon, Richard, 34
NPA. See National Park Service
    (NPA)
NSF. See National Science
    Foundation (NSF)
Nuremberg trials, 14

Oath of Office, 9, 24
Obama, Barack, President, 4, 43, 88,
    120, 123, 125, 143, 170, 218, 233, 245,
    248, 290
Office of Management and Budget.
    See United States Office of
    Management and Budget
    (OMB)
Office of Special Council. See
    United States Office of Special
    Council
Office of the Inspector General.
    See United States Office of the
    Inspector General
O'Leary, Rosemary, 242
Oliner, Pearl, 212–13, 387n, 389n
Oliner, Samuel, 212, 387n, 389n
OMB. See United States Office
    of Management and Budget
    (OMB)

Paris Accords, 112
Paris Climate Agreement, 34
Partnership for Public Service, 337
Patent and Trade Office. See United
    States Patent and Trade Office
    (USPTOJ)

Peace Corps, 43, 48

Pearce, Lisa, 249–52

Pelosi, Nancy, 176

Pence, Mike, Vice President, 123–24

Pendleton Act of 1883, 7

Perry, Rick, 150, 373n

Personnel Policy Organization, 335

Pew Research Center, 336

Pompeo, Mike, 130–31

Pratt, Nick, 168–70, 262, 268–69, 276

Presidential Management Fellows, 48, 335

Pressman, David, 126

Pride March, 99

Progressive Era, 336

Project 2025, 13, 392n

Pruitt, Scott, 4, 112, 116–18, 139, 154, 157, 178–79, 205, 233

Putin, Vladimir, 30

Reagan, Ronald, President, 56–57, 104, 125, 147, 323

Reich, Robert, 178

Richardson, Heather Cox, 34, 172–73

Robert, Kevin, 335

Rockman, Bert, 10

Schedule F, 334–35

Scott, James C., 236

Secret Service. See United States Secret Service

Senior Executive Service (SES), 17, 19–20, 26, 40, 52, 60, 65, 82–83, 86, 99–100, 102, 105–6, 111, 113, 116–18, 121, 130, 133, 138, 149, 157, 207, 219–20, 270, 288, 318

SES. See Senior Executive Service (SES)

Sherk, James, 332

Snyder, Timothy, 250, 288, 299, 329

Social Security Administration (SSA), 338

SSA. See Social Security Administration (SSA)

State Department. See United States Department of State (DOS)

Staub, Ervin, 281

Sullivan, Adele, 138–39, 146, 152, 154, 174–75, 177–79, 183, 224, 237, 331

Taylor, Bill, 129, 182, 260–61, 289, 303–18

Taylor, Miles, 335

Taylor, Shelley, 89

Third Reich, 312

Thompson, Jeffrey, 51, 233–34, 239–41, 265–66, 270, 280

Tillerson, Rex, 4, 116, 119, 153, 170–71

Treasury Department. See United States Department of the Treasury (USDT)

Tsang, Jo-Ann, 95

Turkey, 331

United Nations. Human Rights Council, 34

United Nations. Relief and Works Agency, 34

United Nations. Scientific and Educational Cultural Organization (UNESCO), 34

United States Agency for
International Development
(USAID), 22, 59, 123–24, 154–55,
158, 181

United States Bureau of Alcohol,
Tobacco, Firearms and
Explosives, 33

United States Census Bureau, 52, 73

United States Customs and Border
Protection (CBP), 33

United States Cybersecurity and
Infrastructure Security Agency,
164

United States Department of
Agriculture, 99–100

United States Department of
Commerce (DOC), 89,
120, 158

United States Department of
Defense, 31, 38–39, 51, 69,
71–74, 76, 87–88, 90, 100, 176,
206–7, 324

United States Department of
Energy (DOE), 88, 150, 156, 158,
161, 163, 190, 206, 235

United States Department of
Health and Human Services
(HHS), 22, 31, 46, 49, 53, 81, 101,
122, 132, 156, 158, 168, 181, 183–86,
219, 253, 257, 262, 268, 276, 332

United States Department of
Homeland Security, 20, 43, 59, 73,
75, 78, 80, 99–100, 122, 144, 160,
164–65, 175, 206, 335

United States Department
of Housing and Urban
Development, 132, 166, 181, 223,
257, 272, 327

United States Department of
Interior, 125, 206

United States Department of Justice
(DOJ), 22, 44, 82, 89, 100, 120,
206, 236, 254, 258, 267, 332

United States Department of Labor
(DOL), 68, 80, 89, 94, 98–99

United States Department of State
(DOS), 20, 22, 44, 48, 57, 66, 82,
89, 115, 119–20, 128–29, 134–35, 153,
156, 158, 162, 168, 170–71, 181–82,
199–200, 219, 221–22, 224, 252,
275, 332

United States Department of the
Treasury (USDT), 57, 88, 100,
118, 120, 127, 132, 156, 163, 167, 179,
181–82, 191, 206, 265, 277

United States Department of
Transportation, 31

United States Drug Enforcement
Administration (DEA), 33

United States Environmental
Protection Agency (EPA), 4,
22, 40, 45–46, 51–52, 58, 60–62,
82–83, 86, 89, 99–100, 102–6,
111–12, 116–18, 121, 132–33, 138–39,
142–43, 152, 154, 156–57, 165, 174,
181–83, 190, 203–6, 215–16, 219,
224, 226, 233–34, 236, 242, 249–51,
253, 257–59, 265, 270, 272, 273,
331–32

United States Federal Bureau
of Investigation (FBI), 9, 33,
126, 331

United States Federal Emergency
Management Agency (FEMA),
132, 181
United States Federal Home Loan
Mortgage Corporation (Freddie
Mac), 274
United States General Services
Administration (GSA), 52, 68,
118
United States Government
Accountability Office (GAO),
165
United States Immigration and
Customs Enforcement (ICE),
84, 120
United States Office of
Management and Budget
(OMB), 42, 57, 77, 96, 122, 163,
244, 335
United States Office of Special
Council, 374n
United States Office of the Inspector
General, 213, 220, 228, 270
United States Patent and Trade
Office (USPTOJ), 206
United States Secret Service, 33
USAID. *See* United States Agency
for International Development
(USAID)

USDT. *See* United States Department
of the Treasury (USDT)
USPTOJ. *See* United States Patent
and Trade Office (USPTOJ)

VA. *See* Veterans Affairs (VA)
Veterans Affairs (VA), 99–100, 338
Vindman, Alexander, Army
Lieutenant Colonel, 126
Vought, Russell, 335

Waldo, Dwight, 24–25, 54–56, 137,
324, 330
Waters, Lewis, 42, 77, 96–98, 244–45
*West Wing*, television program, 46
White Christian Nationalist
movement, 13
Whitman, Christina, 217–18
Williams, Andrew, 179–80, 277–78
Wolf, Chad F., 164–65
Women's March on the Capital,
64–65, 98–99, 102
Woodward, Bob, 32
World Health Organization
(WHO), 34

Zelenskyy, Volodymyr, 128–29
Ziblatt, Daniel, 12, 34
Zimbardo, Philip, 14, 70